International Papers in Political Economy

Series Editors
Philip Arestis
Department of Land Economy
University of Cambridge
Cambridge, UK

Malcolm Sawyer
University of Leeds
Leeds, UK

This series consists of an annual volume with a single theme. The objective of the IPPE is the publication of papers dealing with important topics within the broad framework of Political Economy.

The original series of *International Papers in Political Economy* started in 1993, until the new series began in 2005, and was published in the form of three issues a year with each issue containing a single extensive paper. Information on the old series and back copies can be obtained from the editors: Philip Arestis (pa267@cam.ac.uk) and Malcolm Sawyer (e-mail: mcs@lubs.leeds.ac.uk).

More information about this series at
http://www.palgrave.com/gp/series/14844

Philip Arestis · Malcolm Sawyer
Editors

Inequality

Trends, Causes, Consequences, Relevant Policies

palgrave
macmillan

Editors
Philip Arestis
Department of Land Economy
University of Cambridge
Cambridge, UK

Malcolm Sawyer
University of Leeds
Leeds, UK

International Papers in Political Economy
ISBN 978-3-030-08216-1 ISBN 978-3-319-91298-1 (eBook)
https://doi.org/10.1007/978-3-319-91298-1

This Palgrave Macmillan imprint is published by the registered company Springer Nature Switzerland AG
The registered company address is: Gewerbestrasse 11, 6330 Cham, Switzerland

Preface

This is the 15th volume of the series of *International Papers in Political Economy* (*IPPE*). This series consists of an annual volume with eight papers on a single theme. The objective of the *IPPE* is the publication of papers dealing with important topics within the broad framework of Political Economy.

The original series of *International Papers in Political Economy* started in 1993 until the new series began in 2005 and was published in the form of three issues a year with each issue containing a single extensive paper. Information on the old series and back copies can be obtained from the editors: Philip Arestis (e-mail: pa267@cam.ac.uk) and Malcolm Sawyer (e-mail: mcs@lubs.leeds.ac.uk).

The theme of this 15th volume of eight papers is *Inequality: Trends, Causes, Consequences, Relevant Policies*. The papers in this volume were initially presented at a one-day conference in Cambridge, UK (St Catharine's College), 22 March 2018. The conference was organised by the Department of Land Economy, University of Cambridge, under the aegis of the Cambridge Trust for New Thinking in Economics, entitled *Inequality: Trends, Causes, Consequences, Relevant Policies*. The Cambridge Trust for New Thinking in Economics fully supported and financed the conference. The papers were subsequently presented at the 15th International Conference, entitled *Developments in Economic Theory and Policy*, held at the University of the Basque Country UPV/EHU, Bilbao, Spain, 28–29 June 2018, which fully supported and funded the special sessions to which the papers included in this volume were presented. We are grateful to the organisers of the Bilbao conference and to the Cambridge Trust for all the help and funding provided.

Cambridge, UK
Leeds, UK

Philip Arestis
Malcolm Sawyer

Contents

Notes on Contributors

Michele Alacevich is Associate Professor of Economic History and the History of Economic Thought at the University of Bologna. He specializes in the history of twentieth-century development institutions and the history of social sciences, particularly the linkages between the history of ideas, economic and political history, and the history of economic thought. He is the author of *Inequality. A Short History* (Brookings Press and Agenda Publishing, 2018, with Anna Soci), *The Political Economy of the World Bank* (Stanford University Press, 2009), and *Economia Politica. Un'Introduzione Storica*, with Daniela Parisi, Il Mulino, 2009. His publications include articles in Past & Present, *Journal of Global History*, *History of Political Economy*, *Review of Political Economy*, *Rivista di Storia Economica*, and *Journal of the History of Economic Thought.* He is currently writing a book on Albert O. Hirschman for Polity Press. Before moving to Bologna University, he was at Loyola University (2014–2016), Associate Director for Research Activities at the Heyman Center for the Humanities, Columbia University (2011–2014), and a research scholar at Harvard University (2010–2011), at Columbia University (2009–2010), and at the World Bank (2006–2008). He holds a Ph.D. in Business History from the University of Milano (2006).

Philip Arestis is Professor and Senior Emeritus Fellow, and Director of Research, Cambridge Centre for Economics and Public Policy, Department of Land Economy, University of Cambridge, UK; Emeritus Fellow, Wolfson College; Professor of Economics, Department of Applied Economics V, University of the Basque Country, Spain; Distinguished Adjunct Professor of Economics, Department of Economics, University of Utah, US; Research Associate, Levy Economics Institute, New York, US; Visiting Professor, Leeds Business School, University of Leeds, UK (2003–2015); Professorial Research Associate, Department of Finance and Management Studies, School of Oriental and African Studies (SOAS), University of London, UK (2003–2010). He is a Fellow of the Forum, Macroeconomics and Macroeconomic Policies (FMM), the research network of the Macroeconomic Policy Institute (IMK) of Hans-Böckler Foundation, located in Germany. Professor Philip Arestis is holder of the British Hispanic Foundation 'Queen Victoria Eugenia' British Hispanic Chair of Doctoral Studies, and has been awarded 'homage' by the Brazilian Keynesian Association (AKB) for his contribution to the spread of Keynesianism in Brazil. He was Chief Academic Adviser to the UK Government Economic Service (GES) on Professional Developments in Economics (2005–2013). He held the title of Academician of the Academy of Social Sciences (AcSS) for contributions to Social Science, from September 2012 to July 2014, when he became a Fellow of the Academy of Social Sciences (FAcSS).

Professor Philip Arestis has recently received the following two awards: In January 2018 he was honoured through the Thomas Divine Award of the Association for Social Economics (ASE). This award is presented annually to an Association member who over a lifetime has made important contributions to social economics and the social economy. The award was given at the annual meeting of the ASSA, Philadelphia, USA, at their annual meeting of 4–6 January 2018. He was also honoured by Marquis Who's Who which gave him their official 2018 Albert Nelson Marquis Lifetime Achievement Award, for hard work and lifetime dedication to our profession. Professor Philip Arestis has published as sole author or editor, as well as co-author and co-editor, a number of books, contributed in the form of invited chapters to numerous books, produced research reports for research institutes, and has published widely in academic journals.

Eckhard Hein is Professor of Economics at the Berlin School of Economics and Law, the Co-Director of the Institute for International Political Economy Berlin (IPE), a Research Associate at the Levy Economics Institute at Bard College, a member of the coordination committee of the Forum for Macroeconomics and Macroeconomic Policies (FMM), and a managing co-editor of the *European Journal of Economics and Economic Policies: Intervention*. His research focuses on money, financial systems, distribution and growth, European economic policies and post-Keynesian macroeconomics. He has published widely in refereed academic journals, such as the *Cambridge Journal of Economics*, the *International Review of Applied Economics*, the *Journal of Post Keynesian Economics*, *Metroeconomica*, the *Review of Keynesian Economics* and the *Review of Political Economy*, among several others. His latest authored books are *The Macroeconomics of Finance-dominated Capitalism – and Its Crisis* (Edward Elgar, 2012), *Distribution and Growth After Keynes: A Post-Keynesian Guide* (Edward Elgar, 2014), and *The German Financial System and the Financial and Economic Crisis* (co-author, Springer, 2017).

Dimitra Kavarnou is a Senior Research Associate at Cambridge Real Estate Research Centre of the department of Land Economy, University of Cambridge. Prior to that, she was a Lecturer/Senior Lecturer in Real Estate, Economics and Finance in School of Architecture, Design and Built Environment in Nottingham Trent University, UK. She has finished her Ph.D. on Housing Economics in Real Estate & Planning department at Henley Business School, University of Reading, UK. During the same period, she participated to a number of research projects. Previously, she completed her MSc on Construction Project Management in Heriot—Watt University, in Edinburgh, Scotland UK. Before her MSc, she worked for a few years to the construction, shipping, and real estate sector and she is a graduate of BSc Business Administration—Management from University of Piraeus, Greece. Dimitra Kavarnou's research is on developing a research portfolio focusing on the dynamic interactions across urban and regional markets;

housing market dynamics; economic and econometric analysis; policy evaluation; impact assessment; housing and tourism, effects of tourism on real estate development and economics of inequality and sustainability.

Riccardo Pariboni is Postdoctoral Research Fellow at the Department of Economics of Roma Tre University in Rome, where he is lecturing and has lectured in: Economic Growth and Welfare Systems, Microeconomics of Development, Research Methods, Macroeconomics. Riccardo Pariboni received a Ph.D. in Economics in 2015, with a thesis on heterodox approaches to economic growth theory. During his Ph.D., he has been a visiting research student at Kingston University, London. His research focuses on causes and consequences of Inequality, Welfare Systems, Financial crisis and Economic Growth. He has published several scientific articles in international peer-reviewed Journals and book chapters on these topics. He has participated to numerous conferences in Europe throughout his academic path and has been one of the local co-organizer of the EAEPE 2017 Summer School, held at the Faculty of Economics of Roma Tre University. He is member of the European Association for Evolutionary Political Economy (EAEPE) and of the Italian Association for the History of Economics (STOREP).

Patricia Peinado is Assistant Professor of Economics at the University of the Basque Country. Her research interests are in the areas of social security, welfare state, public policy, feminist economics, and applied econometrics. She has estimated the effects that the reforms of the pay-as-you-go social security pension system in Spain may imply for the Spanish pensioners in general and for some vulnerable collectives in particular. Additionally, she has account for the gender effects of the reforms. Recently, she has estimated the relationship between labour market evolution and pensions in the light of the Great Recession. Her main publications have been in journals such as the *Journal of Pension Economics and Finance*, *Feminist Economics*, the *Journal of Panoeconomicus* and the *International Review of Applied Economics*. Additionally, she is highly concerned with the introduction of innovative techniques to teach Macroeconomics to undergraduates. Granted by the University of the Basque Country to take part in an innovative teaching program, she has recently published her Problem Based Learning (PBL) teaching material both, for students and lectures in *IKD-baliabideak*.

Malcolm Sawyer is now Emeritus Professor of Economics, Leeds University Business School, University of Leeds, UK. He has been the principal investigator for the European Union funded (8 million Euros) five-year research project Financialisation, Economy, Society and Sustainable Development, involving 15 partner institutions across Europe and more widely (www.fessud.eu). He was the managing editor of *International Review of Applied Economics* for over three decades, and has served on the editorial board of a range of journals and is editor of the series *New Directions in Modern Economics* published by Edward Elgar. He has published widely in the areas of post Keynesian and Kaleckian economics, fiscal and monetary policies, industrial economics and the UK and European economies. He is currently preparing a book on *The Power of Finance: Financialization and the Real Economy* (Agenda). He has authored 12 books, the most recent being *Can the Euro be Saved?* (Polity Press, 2017). He has edited over 30 books including the annual series *International Papers in Political Economy* (with Philip Arestis). He has published well over 100 papers in refereed journals and contributed chapters to over 100 books.

Felipe Serrano is Professor of Economics at the University of the Basque Country (UPV/EHU), in Bilbao, Spain. He was invited as a researcher at ISMEA in Paris. He is the head of the Department of Applied Economics V at the University of the Basque Country. His research interests are in the areas of social security, the welfare state, labour market, innovation, and economic policy. On different occasions, he has presented testimony before the Spanish Parliament on pension system reform. He is the author of a number of articles, books, and book chapters on those topics in edited books and in refereed journals such as *Economies et Societés*, *European Planning Studies*, the *Industrial and Labour Relations Review*, the *International Labour Review*, the *International Review of Applied Economics*, the *Journal of Economic Issues*, the *Journal of Pension Economics and Finance*, the *Journal of Post Keynesian Economics*, the *International Journal of Public Policy*.

Ahmad Seyf is currently teaching at the Department of Management and Human Resources at Regent's University, London. He has also taught at Staffordshire University and the University of Boston's London campus. His main research interests are International Business Economics, Globalisation and the Economic and Social History of the Middle East, and Economic Policies. He is a bilingual writer having written extensively on Iran, his country of birth. His recent publications include, 'Population and Agricultural Development in Iran, 1800–1906' in Middle Eastern Studies, 2009 and 'Iran and the Great Famine, 1870–1872' in Middle Eastern Studies, 2010. His published books include the following titles: *Iran's Contemporary Political Economy*, H&S Media, 2012; *The Economy of Iran Under Ahmadinejad*, H&S Media, 2012; *Crisis in Despotism in Iran*, Ameh Press, Tehran, 2014; *Capitalism and Democracy*, Mazmoon books, Tehran, 2016; *The Great Recession, an Iranian View*, Tehran, Mazmoon books (forthcoming); and *On the Negation of Neoliberalism*, Tehran, Hezareh-Sevvom (Forthcoming).

Nikodem Szumilo is a Fellow in Economic Geography at the London School of Economics and Political Science. In addition to inequality, his research focuses mainly applied regional, urban and real estate economics and finance. He is particularly focused on empirical research of social and environmental sustainability issues and their economic implications. His pioneering work on the financial value of sustainability in real estate has been recognized both nationally and internationally while his research on the economics of housing affordability continues to influence regional policies across the UK. He also received international awards for his work on ethics and financial risk which resulted in numerous presentations and workshops on real estate risk management and modelling. He is a member of the Cambridge Real Estate Research Centre, an affiliated lecturer at the Department of Land Economy at University of Cambridge and an honorary member of the Healthy Liveable Cities Research Group at RMIT's Centre for Urban Research. His applied economics work has been published in academic and professional magazines across the globe.

Pasquale Tridico is Professor at the Roma Tre University, Department of Economics, in Rome, Italy. He is director of the two-year master's degree in Labour market, industrial relations and welfare systems and director of the master's in Human development and food security. He lectures Labour economics and Economic policy, and is the Jean Monnet Chair of Economic growth and welfare systems. He is general secretary of the European Association for Evolutionary Political Economy (EAEPE). He was Marie Curie Fellow at Sussex University (2002–2003) and Fulbright Scholar at New York University (2010–2011). During his post-doctoral research (2005–2009), he was working in several Universities: Trinity College of Dublin (Ireland), Lancaster University (UK), Newcastle University (UK), and Warsaw University (Poland). Moreover, during 2009–2015, he was visiting professor for several semesters at the University of California in Los Angeles (USA), Wroclaw University of Economics (Poland), Paris 8 University (France), Technology University of Vienna (Austria), and Manchester Metropolitan University (UK). His research focuses on Inequality, Labour market, Welfare systems, Financialisation, Institutional economics and Varieties of capitalism. His latest book is: *Inequality in Financial Capitalism* (Routledge, 2017).

Robert H. Wade is professor of global political economy at the London School of Economics and Political Science. He was awarded the Leontief Prize in Economics in 2008, and the Best Book Award in Political Economy from the American Political Science Association. Brought up in New Zealand, he has done fieldwork in Pitcairn Island, central Italy, south India, South Korea, Taiwan, and inside the World Bank, where he worked as a staff economist. He has taught at Victoria University of Wellington, Sussex University, Princeton, MIT and Brown. His books include *Irrigation and Agricultural Politics in South Korea* (1982); *Village Republics: Economic Conditions of Collective Action in South India* (CUP, 1988); and *Governing the Market: Economic Theory and the Role of the State in East Asian Industrialization* (PUP, 1990). Recent papers include: "The American paradox: ideology of free markets and hidden practice of directional thrust", *Cambridge J. of Economics* (2017); "Global growth, inequality, and poverty: the globalization argument and the 'political' science of economics", in John Ravenhill (ed.), *Global Political Economy*, 2017; "Is Trump wrong on trade? A partial defence based on production and employment", *Real-world Economic Review* (2017).

List of Figures

List of Tables

Why Has Income Inequality Been Neglected in Economics and Public Policy?

Importance of Tackling Income Inequality and Relevant Economic Policies

Philip Arestis

1 Introduction

This contribution deals with inequality of income, which has increased over the last forty years or so. In fact, the increase in inequality started in the 1980s, after the 1945 to the 1970s reduction in inequality. Atkinson (2015) labels the change in the 1980s as the 'Inequality Turn'; Yates (2012) labels the subsequent period as the 'Great Inequality' era; and the former USA President Obama called increasing income inequality as the 'defining challenge of our time' (Dabla-Norris et al. 2015). Income inequality is evident in developed, emerging and developing countries (Dabla-Norris et al., op. cit.; see, also, Goldberg and Pavcnik 2007). An important and relevant observation is the substantial decline in wage shares across the world, with relevant statistics provided

P. Arestis (✉)
University of Cambridge, Cambridge, UK
e-mail: pa267@cam.ac.uk

P. Arestis
University of the Basque Country, Bilbao, Spain

P. Arestis and M. Sawyer (eds.), *Inequality*, International Papers in Political Economy,
https://doi.org/10.1007/978-3-319-91298-1_1

in *the Economist* (2015). It is reported therein that, in 2014, US real wages were 1.2% lower in relation to their 2009 level; in the UK, the median pay was 10% below its 2008 high; and in Germany, wages were 2.4% below their 2008 level. Distribution of income became more polarised in the OECD countries (OECD 2008, 2011), with the top-income groups increasing their shares substantially, especially the financial sector group (Arestis and Karakitsos 2013). This was particularly the case in the Anglo-Saxon countries, and especially so in the US (Atkinson et al. 2011). In fact, real wage growth has lagged behind productivity growth since the 1980s in the advanced economies and since the 1990s in developing and emerging economies (Stockhammer 2013). Dabla-Norris et al. (2015) also suggest that "average wages have risen at a slower pace than productivity growth amid large economic rents (for example, high profitability and large increase in executive compensation) accruing to the top end of the income distribution" (p. 13). That was the case over the period 2005–2012 in both of their samples of selected developed and emerging countries.

Inequality of wealth is also an important and relevant issue. An example of wealth inequality is the US; and as CBO (2016) states: "In 2013, families in the top 10 percent of the wealth distribution held 76 percent of all family wealth, families in the 51st to the 90th percentiles held 23 percent, and those in the bottom half of the distribution held 1 percent" (p. 1). In terms of the period 1989–2013, and the distribution of the US family wealth (defined as total assets minus total debt), the same study shows that it was more unequal in 2013 than in 1989. It is the case, though, that "personal distribution of wealth (both capital and land) is less available on an internationally comparable basis than in the case of income" (Atkinson 2015, p. 71). It is also the case that "the construction of wealth distribution statistics is much more problematic than that of income distribution. The availability of wealth surveys is much less than income surveys; reliance is often placed on estate duty and inheritance tax data, which have their own difficulties" (Sawyer 2015, p. 880). Alvaredo et al. (2017) stress that even now "available statistics on the distribution of wealth are highly imperfect" (p. 407). Davies et al. (2011) discuss relevant problems and provide results to show that "wealth is unambiguously more unequally distributed than income"; and also "that income inequality can be used to generate an imputation of wealth inequality when wealth distribution data are not available" (p. 242; see, also, Dabla-Norris et al. 2015). It is also suggested that although wealth inequality is greater than income inequality, once income inequality is curtailed, wealth inequality is also curtailed. Another difficulty with wealth is its measure of rich households in view of the globalised world and the offshore financial centres. As Alstadsæter et al. (2017) show, these centres "provide a variety of financial services to these individuals, many of which are legal and legitimate, but most of which make wealth harder to observe in traditional economic datasets, such as national accounts and tax records" (p. 1). In view of recent relevant data, Alstadsæter et al. (op. cit.) examine the implications for financial wealth inequality to conclude that "accounting for offshore assets increases the level and the rise of top wealth shares seen in tax data, but the magnitude of the effect varies across countries" (p. 18). Clearly, wealth inequality needs a separate contribution to be dealt with satisfactorily; we refer to it, nonetheless, in what follows as necessary.

A further relevant issue is gender inequality. Atkinson et al. (2014) provide evidence that women are seriously under-represented at the top 1% of gross income. Two examples are given to make the point: Canada where, in 2010, the relevant proportion of women was 21%; and in the UK, in 2011, the corresponding figure was 17%.[1] Gender inequality has worsened in view of neo-liberalism; this is so as a result of a number of changes in the labour market, which have disadvantaged women. Deregulation of the labour markets and the ensued flexibility have affected those in low-paid jobs. Given that women are over-represented in these jobs, they have suffered disproportionately. It is also the case that women have suffered a great deal more than men as a consequence of austerity policies because of their social positioning. They are likely to be more employed in the public sector, and it is the public sector that has experienced most austerity. In fact, there is evidence

[1]In the European Union (EU), the average gross hourly earnings of female employees are 16.3% below those of men. This 'gender pay gap' differs substantially among the EU countries. For example, in Italy and Luxembourg, it is at 5.5%, in Germany, at 22%, and Estonia at 26.9% (Eurostat, March 2017).

(Sands 2012), which suggests that in the UK, 70–80% of the effect of austerity has been experienced by women. Ponthieux and Mears (2015) review the relevant evidence in eight OECD countries, and conclude that "the gender wage gap has been decreasing more slowly since the late 1990s (except in the UK and Japan, where the narrowing has continued at the same pace) or stagnating, and even increasing in Italy" (p. 1008).[2] Where a decline in the gender-wage gap has occurred, it is entirely due to education and thereby better labour-market positioning (see Atkinson 2015, p. 40). Blau and Kahn (2017) provide evidence in the case of the US that suggests that gender pay gap fell from 1980 to 1989, continuing through 2010, but at a slower convergence; persistent gender pay gap still exists, which is larger at the top of the distribution and has decreased more slowly than at the middle and the bottom of the distribution. Over the period 1989–2010, improvement in women's education, experience and occupational representation, as well as elimination of the female shortfall in union representation, were the main causes of the reduction in the gender pay gap where it materialised. Goldin et al. (2017) examine the expanding gender inequality over the period 1995–2008, using the 2000 census, based on the Longitudinal Employer-Household Dynamics (LEHD) database, and conclude that the widening of gender inequality "is split between men's greater ability and preferences to move to higher paying firms and positions and their better facility to advance within firms" (p. 114). Women's greater family responsibilities enhance these factors significantly. This is probably the main reason that despite equal-pay laws, the pay-gap between men and women is no longer narrowing in rich countries especially.

It is thereby very important for an improved and enabling environment where increased labour force participation for women emerges. Lagarde (2017) reinforces this issue when she claims that gender equality matters for two reasons: "first of all, because women matter, full

[2]The members of the EU Parliament adopted, in March 2013, a proposal to enable progress on "equality between women and men in the European Union" (available at: http://www.europarl.europa.eu/sides/getDoc.do?pubRef=-//EP//TEXT+REPORT+A8-2015-0015+0+DOC+XML+V0//EN). This was part of a text asking the Commission and the EU members to set employment targets so that women can have the same opportunities as men.

stop. Second, there are large benefits for all of society, and this includes men, women, and children, to be had from raising women's participation in the economy - it can boost GDP growth, help economies diversify, and tackle income inequality ... At the IMF, we are incorporating gender-related considerations in the policy advice we provide to our member countries - so far, we have completed consultations along these lines with 22 countries, with more to come". It is also stated by Lagarde (op. cit.) that "despite progress made by most G7 countries in improving gender equality ... there is still a large unfinished agenda" (see, also, IMF 2017a). Clearly, gender inequality is also an area that needs a separate contribution to be dealt with satisfactorily.

We proceed in Sect. 2 with a discussion of the world state of inequality. In Sect. 3, we turn our attention to the importance of tackling inequality. Section 4 deals with inequality and economic growth, and Sect. 5 focuses on economic policies to tackle inequality. We summarise and conclude in Sect. 6.

2 World State of Inequality

The evidence produced by Atkinson et al. (2011) shows that the share of US total income going to top-income groups had risen dramatically prior to the GFC of 2007/2008. The top pre-tax decile income share reached almost 50% by 2007, the highest level on record. The share of an even wealthier group—the top 0.1%—more than quadrupled from 2.6 to 12.3% over the period 1976–2007. Also, and by the emergence of the GFC, Stiglitz (2013) reports that the top 0.1% of US households had an income that was 220 times larger than the average of the bottom 90%. Real wages in the US, where wages constitute the most important component of incomes, had fallen even behind productivity well before the onset of the Great Recession (GR). Tcherneva (2017) provides US data to suggest that the recovery of 2001–2007 produced no growth in the income of the bottom 90% of households. Indeed, and following the GFC and GR, the first years of the recovery, their income kept falling with all income benefits going to the wealthiest 10%. However, the average real income for the bottom 90% of households, and in 2014 and 2015, began to recover but still the growth in the economy delivered most of the benefits to the top 10%. Reeves (2017) notes that between 1979 and 2013, average income for the bottom 80% of US households rose by 42%; for the next 19%, it rose by 70% and for the top 1%, by 192%. Lensing and Markiewicz (2015) utilise a quantitative growth model to assess the welfare consequences of the increased income inequality from 1970 to 2013 in the US. Their results show that "the increase in income inequality since 1970 has delivered large welfare gains to the top income quintile of US households. For households, outside this exclusive group, the welfare losses have been substantial" (p. 22). Kuhn et al. (2017) also confirm the proposition that income and wealth inequality in the US, studied jointly over the period 1949–2013, follows 'increasing polarisation'. They also show that the US middle class was the main loser of the increasing income and wealth of the top 10%.

An important characteristic of the period 1983–2007, in terms of the declining wage and rising profit shares, was the increasing concentration of earnings at the top, especially in the financial sector. That was the case around the world, but especially so in the US (Arestis and Karakitsos 2013). Indeed, and as Galbraith (2012) also showed, countries with larger financial sectors had more inequality. In the US, the share of the financial sector to GDP almost doubled in size between 1981 and 2007, and more recently accounted for 8% of US GDP (Philippon 2008). Between 1981 and 2007, the US financial sector, as measured by the ratio of private credit to GDP, grew from 90 to 210%. Also, a sharp, nearly six-fold increase occurred in their profitability after 1982. Indeed, and over the same period, wages in the financial sector were higher than in other sectors, even after controlling for education (Philippon and Reshef 2009). Financial sector relative wages, and the ratio of the wage bill in the financial sector to its full-time-equivalent employment share, enjoyed a steep increase over the period from mid-1980s to 2006. Such inequality was one of the main causes of the GFC, as argued in Arestis and Karakitsos (2013) and Arestis (2016).[3]

[3]Goda et al. (2016) showed that the increase of income and wealth inequality was the cause of

It is the case, though, that despite inequality rising in the past four decades, its trend has not always been upwards. The historical record, as in Sawyer (1976), using a range of measures of inequality, as well as pre-tax and post-tax income, showed for 12 OECD countries (with comparable data) income inequality, and over the post World-War II period to mid-1970s, tended to decline or remain broadly constant. Atkinson (2015) suggests that there was a fall in inequality between 1914 and 1945, and after 1945 until the 1970s. That reduction in inequality was due to the two World Wars in view of the 'chaos' of the wars and occupations, and of the structural breaks imposed by the post-war settlements. In the case of the Second World War and afterwards, a greater sense of social solidarity and strengthening of trade unions were the main contributory factors to the lower inequality. In the 1970s, and in the US, inequality was similar to that of the late 1940s, as measured by the Gini coefficient, which ranges between 0 (complete equality) and 100 (complete inequality). Piketty (2014) also shows that between 1914 and the 1970s, income and wealth inequality in the US fell dramatically. After the 1970s, however, both income and wealth inequality rose back to the pre-1914 norms. In the past forty years or so, though, Piketty (op. cit.) shows that in the US, nearly 75% of the aggregate income growth went to the top of the distribution. And since 1980, "income inequality has exploded in the United States. The upper decile's share increased from 30 to 35% of national income in the 1970s to 40–45 in the 2000s—an increase of 15 points of national income" (p. 294). Piketty (2014) utilises the inequality $r>g$ (where r is return on capital and g rate of growth) to illustrate how inequality is compounded.

Atkinson (1997) suggests that 'unparalleled' rise in the UK inequality occurred in the 1980s: "the United Kingdom stands out for the sharpness of the rise in recorded income inequality in the 1980s" (p. 301).

the euro crisis of 2010. The high levels of income inequality produced high levels of debt and balance-of-payments imbalances, which caused the crisis. Their approach also demonstrated that both income and wealth inequality should be closely examined so that the close relationship between inequality and financial stability should be seriously considered.

Also, Turner (2010) suggested in the case of the UK: "there has been a sharp rise in income differential between many employees in the financial sector and average incomes across the whole of the economy". Hein and Mundt (2012) show that in the G20 developed economies, and since the early 1980s, a falling trend of the wage share clearly materialised. They also examine a group of emerging G20 countries, which experienced an overall falling trend of the wage share with the exception of India. In the European Union, and prior to the late 1970s, inequality declined in view of the expansion of the welfare state and social provision, along with progressive income taxation. However, and since the 1980s, the welfare state in the EU has failed to reduce inequality as a result of explicit policy decisions aimed at cutting back on benefits. Inequality has in fact increased between the highest and lowest incomes. Social Europe (2017) reports that between 2005 and 2015, the Gini coefficient in the EU rose from 30.6 to 31 and income disparity increased from 4.7 to 5.2 between the top and bottom 20% of income recipients. Social Europe (op. cit.) suggests that globalisation and migration, one of the manifestations of globalisation, put pressure on wages thereby becoming factors that led to inequality in the EU. Weakening of collective bargaining, the deterioration in working conditions, increased temporary working, and policies of internal wage devaluation were further sources of worsening prosperity for many people.

Actually, inequality between the OECD members is higher than within them. In Germany, for example, and according to the OECD (2008), income inequality over the years 2000–2005 grew faster than in any other OECD country.[4] Eurofound (2017) shows that prior to 2008, inequality amongst the EU countries had been reduced in view of the process of economic integration and income convergence. It accelerated by the creation of the euro, with inequality within countries remaining stable. After 2008, inequality has increased in view of the process of economic integration stalled due to the emergence of the

[4]Inequality in Germany is worse since the 1990 reunification. As reported in the Financial Times (18 August, 2017), household income inequality is close to that of the EU; wealth inequality is significantly less equal than the EU's—the bottom 40% of people in Germany have almost no assets at all, not even savings; it is the top 10% that have them.

GFC and the ensuing sovereign debt crisis, also because income inequality within the EU countries increased.[5] The main causes of that experience are thought to be unemployment and changes in the capacity of households and welfare states to cushion income effects.

Similar but less pronounced inequality shares are relevant in many other countries. In China, the top 1% income share gradually increased from 2.6% in 1986 to 5.9% in 2003. The financial intermediary shares to GDP in China rose from 1.6% in 1980 to 5.4% in 2008 (Greenspan 2010, p. 15). Alvaredo et al. (2017) compare the evolution of inequality in China, US and France over four decades, utilising data from WID. World (available at: www.wid.world). Inequality in China increased substantially after private enterprise was introduced. In 1978, the top 10% of Chinese earned just over a quarter of overall income before tax. That was significantly below the relevant proportions in the US and France. However, by 2015, the top 10% of Chinese earners were paid two-fifths of total income, above the relevant share in France, but still below the US. The bottom 50% income share in China was above the US and France in 1978, but by 2015, it was below that of France but still above that of the US. Alvaredo et al. (op. cit.) conclude that there has been a "rising top income and wealth share in nearly all countries in recent decades, but the magnitude varies substantially across countries; thereby suggesting different country-specific policies and institutions matter considerably" (p. 408).

Arestis and González Martínez (2016) summarise the Gini coefficients of the fifteen most unequal and fifteen least unequal countries around the world. The Gini coefficients reported in Arestis and González Martínez (op. cit.) clearly make the point of inequality and the urgency for relevant economic policies around the world to reduce inequality. It is the case that although inequality between countries over the last few decades has been reduced, inequality within many countries has been rising (the top 1% owns about half of the world's wealth), particularly in advanced countries. Income inequality has been

[5] The period the Eurofound (2017) examines is 2005–2014 (with the income variable referring to 2004–2013).

rising in most countries around the world since the early 1980s (see, also, OECD 2008). Milanovic (2011) shows that between the 1980s and 2010, "the United States and the United Kingdom - and indeed most advanced economies - have become much richer and much more unequal. In 2010, real per capita income in the United States was 65 percent above its 1980s level and in the United Kingdom, 77 percent higher. Over the same period, inequality in the United States increased from about 35 to 40 ….. and in the United Kingdom, from 30 to about 37 Gini points. These increases reflect significant adverse movements in income distributions. Overall, between the mid-1980s and the mid-2000s, inequality rose in 16 out of 20 rich OECD countries" (p. 8).

By contrast, inequality in Latin America was reduced in the 2000s, after a period of rising inequality in the 1970s and 1980s; the inequality reduction in Latin America "was achieved by a combination of changes in market incomes and expanded redistribution" (Atkinson 2015, p. 80). An interesting case in Latin America is the Brazilian experience, over the period 1996–2014, where the effect of the introduction of a minimum wage helped to produce a large decrease of inequality. This is empirically validated by Engbom and Moser (2017), who employ an equilibrium search model with heterogeneous firms and workers with their empirical results explaining 70% of the observed inequality decrease due to the rise in the minimum wage. The federal minimum wage in Brazil over the period 1996–2012 grew by 119% in real terms; labour productivity increased by 16.6% over the same period (Engbolt and Moser, op. cit., p. 6). Similar results are reported in Góes and Karpowicz (2017), for the period 2004–2014, in terms of regional inequality and inequality of outcomes, using the Gini coefficient, both between and within the 27 states. Their results are mainly due to labour income growth and redistributive policies, such as *Bolsa Família* (the social assistance programme to reduce poverty, introduced in 2004). It is also the case that other parts of Latin America have had similar experience (see, for example, Tsounta and Osueke 2014).[6]

[6]The UNDP (2017) report on income inequality in Sub-Saharan Africa shows inequality tending to decline in African countries.

The overall conclusion from this section's discussion is that rising inequality has played a serious role in creating the conditions for both chronic and acute economic instability. We turn our attention next to discuss the importance of tackling inequality.

3 Importance of Tackling Inequality

Our analysis so far clearly indicates that it is of vital importance to tackle inequality (see, also, Arestis and Sawyer 2011). Also Haldane (2017) suggests that "Until the crisis, it is difficult to identify a period in the past 50 years when inequality was close to the top of the public policy or academic agenda"; and it should have been. Keynes (1936) argued that the two outstanding faults of economic policy were the failure to secure full employment and to tackle the inequitable distribution of income. Reducing inequality enhances growth and with appropriate economic policies full employment could be achieved. Other studies have similar suggestions as in Kumhof and Rencière (2010): "Restoring equality by redistributing income from the rich to the poor would not only please the Robin Hoods of the world, but could also save the global economy from another major crisis" (p. 31; see, also, Berg and Ostry 2011; Stiglitz 2013, 2015; and OECD 2011). Such crisis, it is argued by Kumhof et al. (2015), could occur from high household debt and changes in income distribution. In both periods, 1920–1929 and 1983–2008, a large increase in the income of high-income households (5% of income distribution) along with a large increase in the household debt emerged and thereby higher leverage of low- to middle-income households (95% of income distribution) generated financial fragility, which eventually caused the Great Depression of 1929, the GFC of 2007 and the Great Recession of 2008 (see, also, Arestis 2016). This is shown by Kumhof et al. (2015) by presenting a theoretical framework and relevant US empirical support.[7] McCombie and

[7]A key assumption is that the top earners, whose income share increases, provide loans to bottom earners instead of increasing their consumption.

Spreafico (2015) summarise relevant empirical evidence to conclude that it "now strongly suggests that greater inequality is harmful for growth" (p. 20; see, also, Stiglitz 2015). Cynamon and Fazzari (2015, 2016) support the argument that rise in inequality in the personal distribution of income has been a barrier to growth and employment in the US. The massive consumer debt, though, for the bottom 95% unlike the top 5%, which had emerged prior to the GFC, mitigated the impact of inequality on aggregate demand but post-crisis inequality has held back output and employment. The slow and uneven recovery in the US since the GR is due to the existence of inadequate demand; the latter would be stronger if lower income groups received a higher share of income.

Dabla-Norris et al. (2015) provide evidence, utilising a sample of 159 developed, emerging and developing economies for the period 1980–2012, which suggests that there is an inverse relationship between the disposable income share of the top 20% and economic growth (a 1% increase in the disposable income of the top 20% is associated with a 0.08% decrease in GDP growth in the following five years). A similar increase in the disposable income of the bottom 20% produces a 0.38% higher income growth. This is also the case with the second and third quintiles (the middle class). The empirical results of Dabla-Norris et al. (op. cit.) are in line with the findings of the OECD (2014) study, which utilises a smaller sample of developed countries. The empirical evidence provided by Ostry (2015) suggests that more equality in the income distribution is robustly and positively associated with more and sustainable growth spells. Grigoli and Robles (2017) examine the possibility of non-linear income inequality in relation to economic development, and in the case of 77 countries. Under such a relationship, an 'inequality overhang' is identified whereby the relationship between inequality and economic development turns negative from positive. This, it is shown, occurs when the Gini coefficient reaches 27%, indicating that the inequality overhang occurs at low levels of income inequality. It is concluded that under such circumstances, the way to combat inequality is to improve access of households and business to banking services and promote participation of women in the labour force.

Policy-makers also refer to inequality. The Bank of England (2012) report shows that its 'unconventional' Quantitative Easing (QE) programme increased the value of the targeted assets by 26% with 40% of the gains having gone to the richest 5% of holders. The Bank of England (op. cit.) justifies it as follows: "By pushing up a range of asset prices, asset purchases have boosted the value of households' financial wealth held outside pension funds, but holdings are heavily skewed with the top 5% of households holding 40% of these assets".[8] The euro area has had similar results in view of the QE there, whereby the net wealth of the richest 20% increased by roughly 30% (ECB Annual Report, 2016). Similar results are relevant for the US economy, where the top 5% of wealthiest households own 82% of all individually held stocks and more than 90% of the individually held bonds (Hughes Hallett 2015). The Chair of the US Federal Reserve System made relevant comments. At the Federal Reserve Bank of Boston conference (October 2014), Yellen (2014) clearly admitted that "The extent of and continuing increase in inequality in the United States greatly concern me. The past several decades have seen the most sustained rise in inequality since the 19th century after more than 40 years of narrowing inequality following the Great Depression". Yellen (op. cit.) went on to suggest that "It is no secret that the past few decades of widening inequality can be summed up as significant income and wealth gains for those at the very top and stagnant living standards for the majority". The European Central Bank (ECB) President (Draqhi 2015) warned central banks of the dangers of aggressive monetary easing, including mass bond buying, which might lead to financial instability and thereby worsen income inequality. Draqui (op. cit.) suggests that distributional consequences may arise from "rising asset prices as a consequence of our purchases might benefit the wealthy disproportionately and thereby increase inequality". The IMF managing director and the governor of the Bank of England clearly stated at a conference in London ('Inclusive

[8]It is also the case that, in the UK, there have been massive property-price increases, essentially generated by the QE's liquidity increase. This has also benefitted the richest segment of the population, thereby adding to the top five percent real gains.

Capitalism', 27 May 2014) that rising inequality was a threat to economic growth and financial stability.

The IMF managing director (Lagarde 2014) made the point that "One of the leading economic stories of our time is increasing income inequality and the dark shadow it casts across the global economy" (p. 11). The IMF managing director went on to suggest that "The facts are familiar. Since 1980, the richest 1 percent increased their share of income in 24 out of 26 countries for which we have data. In the US, the share of income taken home by the top one percent more than doubled since the 1980s, returning to where it was on the eve of the Great Depression. In the UK, France, and Germany, the share of private capital in national income is now back to levels last seen almost a century ago" (p. 11). The Governor of the Bank of England (Carney 2014) clearly stated in his speech that "Bankers made enormous sums in the run-up to the crisis and were well compensated after it hit. In turn, taxpayers picked up the tab for their failure. That unjust sharing of risk and reward contributed directly to inequality but – more importantly – has had a corrosive effect on social fabric of which finance is part and on which it relies" (p. 36). The IMF managing director Lagarde (2015) summarises the relevant arguments when she suggests that growing income inequality has become a serious problem for economic growth and development; and that "if you want to see more *durable* growth, you need to generate more *equitable* growth". Also, a Bank of International Settlements study (Domanski et al. 2016) argues that unconventional monetary policy has contributed to rising wealth inequality in advanced economies since the GFC, essentially through increasing equity prices.

The inequality effects discussed above were greatly affected by a number of factors. Globalisation is one of them (IMF 2007). There is actually a great deal of evidence that inequality increased in developing countries as a result of globalisation in view of less skilled workers who are relatively abundant in these countries and are not better off in relation to higher skill workers or education levels (Goldberg and Pavcnik 2007). Not only is the increase in demand for educated workers being driven by globalisation but also by technological changes in terms of information and communication technologies, which have displaced low-skilled workers and created demand for those with better education. Another contributory factor to inequality is attempts at deregulation and liberalisation of finance in many countries around the world, especially so before the GFC. As a result, financial markets became bigger and more global. Of particular importance from this point of view, was the financial liberalisation framework in the US, another cause of the GFC (see Arestis and Karakitsos 2013; and Arestis 2016, for further details).

There were also significant fiscal costs to the relevant governments in view of the GFC and GR bailout payments to rescue their banking sectors, especially the 'too big to fail' banks. A relevant IMF (2009) report cites the fiscal costs in the case of a number of countries, most important of which are (the percentages cited are in terms of the relevant GDPs): Austria (8.9%), Canada (9.5%), Greece (5.4%), Ireland (5.4%), Netherlands (6.2%), Norway (15.8%), Sweden (5.2%), UK (18.9%), US (7.5%); in terms of advanced countries (5.8%) and emerging countries (0.3%). Clearly, emerging countries suffered significantly less than developed countries in view of the fact that most did not suffer from the GFC. The scaling back of redistributive tax- and transfer-policies has had significant redistributive effects, especially in the developed countries. An important implication of these fiscal costs is that cuts in welfare and national health system expenditures emerged, which had distributional effects from the bottom to the top whose salaries and bonuses were secured by the relevant fiscal costs. This redistribution was also helped by a sharp acceleration of the austerity policies, especially after the GFC, accompanied by labour market deregulation and thereby weakening the role of trade unions and pay norms, as well as privatisations in many countries, initiated in the late 1970s.

The reduced role of trade unions is highlighted by the OECD (2011) publication, which shows that in every OECD country, with the exception of Spain, trade union membership was lower in 2008 than in 1980. In the US, the overall trade union membership was reduced substantially from 1980 to 2017; it declined from 20.1% in 1983 (the first year for which comparable union data are available) to 11.9% in 2010. In 2014, the union membership rate was 11.1%, down 0.2 percentage point from 2013; in June 2016, it was 10.7%, which is half of what it was in the 1980s (US Bureau of Labour Statistics, 23 January, 2015 and 26 January, 2017). It is clear that the US case is an example where labour has no bargaining power. No wonder the labour GDP share is at a post-World War II low. This is a serious problem for an economy, which is 70% dependent on consumer spending. No wonder that over the period since the GFC and GR, the US economic 'recovery' has been unusually weak. Similar trends prevail in many other countries.[9] There is general agreement that such a decline in the role of trade unions and of collective bargaining coincides with widening of the pay distribution. The legal framework of trade unions is another important consideration. Atkinson (2015) provides a relevant example in the case of the UK: "a succession of laws enacted between 1980 and 1993 that reduced the autonomy of trade unions in the UK and the legitimacy of industrial action". This clearly implies that "The end result of the legislation is that unions are considerably weakened in their legal status and protection" (pp. 128–129).[10]

Atkinson (2015) summarises the contributory factors to inequality as follows; "globalisation, technological change (information and communications technology), growth of financial services; changing pay norms, reduced role of trade unions; scaling back of the redistributive tax-and-transfer policy" (p. 82). Atkinson (1997) refers to the demand for and supply of skilled and unskilled labour as a possible explanation of the earnings dispersion. When the relative number of skilled workers rises, then a rise in the demand for them emerges, thereby shifting the demand for labour. One explanation for this possibility is international trade liberalisation and increased competition from the countries where unskilled labour is abundant. Other relevant explanations emphasise technical change and the introduction of automation and information technology. Dabla-Norris et al. (2015) provide empirical evidence that supports the argument that less regulated labour markets, financial

[9]Gosling and Mashin (1995) provide evidence in the case of the UK that suggests the decline in unionisation accounted for 15–20% of earnings dispersion in the 1980s.

[10]Immigration could be another contributory factor, although the evidence suggests that it is a minor factor. Card (2009), for example, concludes that in the US, it only accounts for a small share (4–6%) of inequality.

deepening and technological progress explain income inequality over the last forty years. Financial openness played a reinforcing, but smaller, role, with improvements in health mitigated ½% of the 3% increase in the Gini index over the period of their investigation.

Stockhammer (2013), utilising panel estimations of the determinants of the wage share in 71 countries (28 developed and 43 developing and emerging countries) from 1970 to 2007, concludes that globalisation had negative effects; not just in developed but also in developing countries (see, also, Goldberg and Pavcnik 2007, on developing countries). It is also shown in Stockhammer (2013) that financialisation, welfare state retrenchment and decline in the bargaining power of trade unions over time had negative effects on the wage share. In addition, changes in technology had some effect on the wage share of the countries considered, but it was not one of the main drivers in income distribution. Stockhammer (op. cit.) also suggests that welfare state retrenchment, weakened bargaining power of labour and increased market power of firms in relation to labour are further factors that have contributed to the increased inequality. The empirical evidence provided suggests that financialisation, measured as foreign assets and liabilities relative to GDP, has been the main factor to the decline of the wage share, followed by globalisation and welfare state retrenchment.

Kristal and Cohen (2013) provide empirical evidence, based on 43 US private non-agricultural industries, which suggests that "the erosion of pay-setting institutions, mainly unionization and the real minimum wage, explains about 50 percent of rising wage inequality in US private industries between 1969 and 2007, while the spread of computer technology explains 12–14 percent between 1969 and 1997 and 21–24 percent between 1988 and 2007" (p. 37). It is also the case that "similar results showing a larger effect of de-unionization (vs. computerization) on inequality were found in Germany (King 2013), as well as in a study on 22 developed countries (OECD 2011)" (Kristal and Cohen 2013, p. 37). Furceri and Loungani (2013) suggest two further explanations of the increased inequality: capital account liberalisation and lower government budget deficits; 58 episodes of large-scale capital account reforms are considered in 17 advanced economies to conclude that "on average, capital account liberalization is followed by a significant and persistent increase in inequality. The Gini coefficient increases by about 1 percent a year after liberalization and by 2 percent after five years" (p. 26; see, also, Furceri and Loungani 2015).[11] It is also argued by Furceri and Loungani (2013) that "Over the past 30 years, there were 173 episodes of fiscal consolidation in our sample of 17 advanced economies. On average across these episodes, policy actions reduced the budget deficit by about 1 percent of GDP. There is clear evidence that the decline in budget deficits was followed by increases in inequality. The Gini coefficient increased by 2 percentage points two years following the fiscal consolidation and by nearly 1 percentage point after eight years" (pp. 26–27).

We proceed to discuss next how inequality affects economic growth.

4 Inequality and Economic Growth: Wage-Led or Profit-Led Demand

In discussing the significant changes in income inequality and how they affect economic growth, the distinction between 'wage-led' and 'profit-led' regimes is relevant. A wage-led regime is one where a shift in income towards wages results in higher growth, in view of the higher marginal propensity to consume out of wage income in relation to that out of profit income. A profit-led regime is one where a shift in income towards profits lowers income; this is so, since in a profit-led regime, redistribution of income to profits results in higher savings and reduction in aggregate demand. In this scenario, there are two demand effects in place: the domestic-demand effect, which captures the impact of changes in distribution on consumption and investment; and the open-economy effect, which accounts for the impact of the relevant changes on net exports. Rising wage shares are expected to have

[11] Lagarda et al. (2017) also examine empirically, in a panel of 141 countries from 1990 to 2013, the relationship between capital account liberalisation and inequality in the case of developing and emerging countries. Although they confirm this relationship, they suggest that it differs between booms, when there is a positive effect of capital account liberalisation on inequality, and busts, when inequality increases; thereby relevant policies are necessary.

a positive effect on consumption, but negative effect on investment (in view of falling profits as a result of higher wages, which are a cost factor) and net exports (in view of the sensitivity of net exports to unit labour cost).[12] Whether the first effect is larger than the sum of the other two is an empirical question. Still, it is the case that a higher wage share can have expansionary effects since wages are the main source of income for most households; higher wages feed into higher consumption; and since low-income households have a higher marginal propensity to consume than high-income households, low-income households spend a higher share of their income.

Redistribution of income to profits is thereby detrimental to growth. By contrast, "a wage-led strategy", as Lavoie and Stockhammer (2013) emphasise, "will generate a much more stable growth regime for the future" (pp. 13–14). This is, of course, particularly important in view of the 2007/2008 GFC and the subsequent GR, which weakened the power of labour to defend lower nominal and real wages (see, also, Hein and Mundt 2013). In large economic areas, like the euro one, where wage-led is in place, wage-led recovery policies, instead of wage moderation, can improve growth and employment. Indeed, a global wage-led recovery through a significant increase in wage share can lead to an increase in global growth. Such approach would also help to reduce the danger of another GFC by reducing inequality.

In addition, there are supply-side effects, which are also relevant. Changes in wage share affect productivity growth in view of improvement in labour relations, which enhance the propensity of workers to contribute to production. In this context, the Allen (2009) study is relevant, in that it shows that the British industrial revolution emerged in view of its comparatively high wages. Lavoie and Stockhammer (2013) conclude that changes in functional income distribution have

[12]Aggregate demand is: AD $= C + I + G + NX$, where C is consumption, I is investment, G is government expenditure and NX is net exports (exports minus imports). In the text, we refer to C, I and NX. Government expenditure is treated as an exogenous variable, so the relevant domestic components are consumption and investment and the external component is net exports.

supply-side effects in addition to demand-side effects.[13] The authors argue that the "summary variable for the supply side is labour productivity" (p. 26), and as such it is a wage-led partial productivity regime. Their empirical findings, which are based on data for the last thirty years, suggest that "aggregate demand and productivity in most G20 countries, would respond favourably to an increase in the wage share" (p. 7). Hein and Tarassow (2010) provide evidence in six OECD countries, over the period 1960–2007, to show that faster real wage growth leads to higher productivity growth. McCombie et al. (2002), reviewing 80 empirical studies, based on OECD countries, conclude that there is a causal link from growth of demand to productivity. Storm and Naastepad (2013) provide a review of the empirical evidence for the group of OECD countries, which suggests that in terms of the causal link from demand growth to productivity growth, a one percentage point change in demand growth is associated with a 0.46 percentage change in labour productivity growth. In terms of the relationship between real wage growth and productivity growth for the same group of countries, the relevant coefficient is 0.38, so that a one percentage change in real wage growth is associated with 0.38 percentage change in productivity growth.

Onaran and Galanis (2013) provide empirical evidence, in terms of wage-led and profit-led regimes, based on the examination of the effects of income distribution on growth in G20 countries; 16 large developed and developing countries, which comprise more than 80% of the global GDP. This is undertaken for the period 1960–2007 for developed countries and 1970–2007 for developing countries (in the case of China, the period is 1978–2007). The evidence provided by Onaran and Galanis (op. cit.) suggests that in most of the major advanced economies, there is a wage-led demand regime. Canada and Australia are two exceptions where a profit-led regime is confirmed. Their empirical evidence further suggests that a 1 percentage point simultaneous decline in the wage

[13] There is a difference between functional income distribution and personal income distribution. Functional income distribution refers to the division between groups of people (who own various kinds of resources, namely land, labour and capital), while personal income distribution refers to the division among individuals regardless of the groups to which they belong.

share of the 16 countries in their sample leads to a decline in global GDP by 0.36 percentage points. Also, if all wage-led countries were to return to their 1970s wage-share levels, global GDP would increase by 3.05 percentage points. When the external sector is included, aggregate demand remains wage-led in 16 of the developed G20, as well as in the euro area countries. Not only do these empirical findings hold true for the G20 developed economies, but also for most of the emerging market economies in this group, with the exception of South Africa.

Onaran and Galanis (2013) suggest that their empirical evidence implies three important conclusions: "First, domestic private demand (that is the sum of consumption and investment) is wage-led in all countries ..... Second, foreign trade forms only a small part of aggregate demand in large countries ..... Similarly, if countries, which have strong trade relations with each other ..... are considered as an aggregate economic area, the private demand regime is wage-led. Finally, the most novel finding is that even if there are some countries, which are profit-led, the global economy is wage-led. Thus, a simultaneous wage cut in a highly integrated global economy leaves most countries with only the negative domestic demand effects, and the global economy contracts. Furthermore, most profit-led countries contract when they decrease their wage-share, if a similar strategy is implemented also by their trading partners" (p. 87). Onaran and Obst (2015) examine empirically a simultaneous increase in the wage share in 15 countries of the EU, which leads to an increase in growth. They show that a 1% increase in the wage share would lead to a 0.30% increase in the GDP of the 15 European countries; 11 of these countries are wage-led and 4 are profit-led, when the 15 countries are examined in isolation. A further contribution is by Obst et al. (2017), who examine a demand-led growth model, including the government in an open economy context, in the case of the 15 West European states of the EU (EU15). The empirical results of the model suggest that a coordinated policy mix of progressive tax policy and pro-labour wage policy along with expansionary government expenditure leads to a significant rise in GDP (by 6.72%), and also to an improvement in the budget balance in all EU15 countries (by 0.69%).

Blecker (2015) argues that the time dimension of wage-led versus profit-led demand regimes is important and should be accounted for as in his study, where a distinction between short run and long run is the focus. In the short run, demand is likely to be profit-led and weakly wage-led; but in the long run, it is more strongly wage-led. The positive effects of higher profits or lower labour costs on investment and net exports are mainly short-run phenomena, while the positive effects of a wage-led long-run impact on consumption are stronger. Blecker (op. cit.) demonstrates that profits in the US are normally a leading variable for investment in expansions and recessions. In expansions, investment follows profits usually with no lags in terms of annual data, although they may in quarterly data; in downturns, longer lags are in place. Such relationships, which are justified formally by the accelerator theory of investment, disappear in the long term. It is also the case that net exports are affected in the short run if a rise in unit labour cost emerges, which makes domestic goods and services less competitive in relation to foreign ones, if the sum of the price elasticity of export and import demand exceeds unity in absolute terms. Consumption is the one part of aggregate demand, whose impact on income distribution is likely to be greater in the long run than in the short run. This is so in view of most households' attempt to maintain some degree of stability in their consumption behaviour with respect to income fluctuations in the short term. Household borrowing and debt are used in the short run, but this is constrained in the long run in view of debt accumulation. Wage income, therefore, influences workers' consumption a great deal more in the long run rather in the short run. Given that most consumers rely on labour income, it is concluded that the marginal propensity to consume is higher in the long run rather than in the short run out of wages. Capital income receivers have marginal propensities to consume, which not only are low but are pretty much the same in the short run and long run.

Blecker (2015) provides relevant correlations, utilising raw annual data for the US economy for the period 1948–2013, and also for sub-periods. Three measures of economic activity are utilised: GDP growth rate; manufacturing sector capacity utilisation rate; and capital accumulation (rate of non-residential private fixed assets). The relevant correlation coefficients provide support for the relevant hypothesis. Clearly, though, more sophisticated econometric techniques are necessary. Blecker (op. cit.) recognises this limitation and suggests that such techniques could better distinguish long-run versus short-run effects of income distribution on growth.

It is then clear that pro-labour distributional policies that promote wage policies, strengthening the welfare state and the power of the labour unions via improving the status of labour unions through changing union legislation to foster collective bargaining, and establishing sufficiently high minimum wages, are important economic policy ingredients. This, along with further economic policies, is discussed in the section that follows.

5 Economic Policies to Tackle Inequality

Relevant policies, and from the wage-led strategy point of view, include minimum wage policies, along with legislation that strengthens the status of labour unions and collective bargaining institutions. However, increasing the minimum wage may affect negatively the demand for labour.[14] It is the case, though, that "careful empirical research has found that moderate increases to the minimum wage have no effect on employment" (Bouchey 2015, p. 187). As stated above, Stockhammer (2013) strongly supports economic policies to reduce inequality. All in all, social institutions and the structure of the financial system are important ingredients of income distribution. Financial regulation, then, is a further important and relevant policy ingedient (see, for example, Arestis 2016).

In terms of fiscal policy, reform of taxes to make them fairer and more effective, especially so taxation on corporate profits, is very important. Indeed, Korinek and Kreamer (2013) advocate that redistributive policies "such as higher taxes on financial sector profits that are used to

[14]Clearly, though, this does not happen in a wage-led regime, where aggregate demand and employment rise.

strengthen the social safety net of the economy would constitute such a mechanism" (p. 6). Berg and Ostry (2011) also show that a redistributive tax system is associated with higher and durable economic growth. Raising the minimum wage and indexing it to inflation is another important tool to fight inequality (see, for example, *The Economist* 2014). A further example, and priority, is the removal of subsidies for the 'too-big-to-fail' financial institutions (see, also, *The Economist* 2012). Such a policy initiative would help to remove, to a large extent, one of the main contributory factors to the surge in income and wealth at the top of income distribution and to the financial sector in particular. A recovery led by domestic demand and increase in the wage share would help to reverse the major factor of inequality. Gains in competitiveness can and should be achieved through productivity increases rather than wage reductions and weak labour conditions. In this sense, strong trade unions, collective bargaining and high minimum wages are beneficial. All this would ensure that wage growth catches up with productivity growth, and hence consumption and income growth.

Muinelo-Gallo and Roca-Sagalés (2011) employ an endogenous growth model that incorporates fiscal policy and economic growth along with their effects on income inequality. Pooled-panel estimations are undertaken for 43 developed countries for the period 1972–2006 to conclude that increases in public investment expenditure reduce inequality without harming output, regardless of whether they are financed through direct or indirect taxes. Furceri and Li (2017), produce evidence in developing countries, by employing the Gini coefficients, which shows increases in public investment lower income inequality in the short and medium term—a 10% increase in public expenditure reduces the Gini coefficient by 0.2%, which is not really a significant effect if at all. We would suggest that such strategy should be complemented by coordinated fiscal and monetary policies, as argued in Arestis (2015) and further discussed below.

The International Labour Organisation (2008) study provides evidence to show that relevant policies can avoid income inequality, while achieving a high employment rate. This is the case for high, medium and low per-capita GDP countries. Examples provided by the International Labour Organisation (op. cit.) study among high per-capita GDP countries, where employment rates are high and income inequalities relatively low, are countries like Austria, Australia, the Nordics and Switzerland. These countries "are characterized by relatively strong, employment-oriented social protection, higher than average coverage of collective agreements and well-respected political rights" (p. 156). Examples among medium and low per-capita GDP are countries, like the Czech Republic and Uruguay, where relatively high employment is accompanied by limited income inequalities. It is suggested that these countries are also "associated with relatively developed social protection, stronger tripartite institutions than in other countries, and observance of political rights" (p. 6).

Bernanke (2015) suggests that the Fed monetary policy post GFC/GR may have produced inequality effects, but such effects "are almost certainly modest and transient". These effects are unlike the "deep structural changes in our economy that have taken place over many years, including globalisation, technological progress, demographic trends, and institutional changes in the labour market and elsewhere". Monetary policy is "neutral" or "nearly so in the longer term". In another speech (Bernanke (2017) states that "According to the World Bank, the United States has the highest Gini coefficient of the G7 industrial countries, relative to other U.S. demographic groups and working-class Europeans". No wonder, Bernanke (op. cit.) proposes further policies to tackle inequality, "such as fiscal policy (taxes and government spending programs) and policies aimed at improving workers' skills"; these policies are needed "to help ensure adequate demand and remedy the underlying source of trade imbalances".

More generally speaking, the state should be able to reduce inequality through progressive taxation and public expenditure policies.[15] These policies would tax the top more than the rest, and through the orientation of social expenditure towards the low-income households. By contrast, those programmes, which allow a country to give away resources

[15]There is the argument that fiscal policy is ineffective in view of the Ricardian Equivalence Theorem. As argued in Arestis (2011, 2012, and 2015) and Arestis and González Martinez (2015), such argument lacks convincing theoretical backing and empirical credence.

to the rich and well connected, increase inequality. A good example of the latter case is the enormous decrease in the progressivity of the income tax in the US and UK since 1980, which "probably explains much of the increase in the very highest earned income" (Pigetty 2014, pp. 495–496). As Godar et al. (2015) argue, progressive taxation not only corrects disparities in income and wealth distribution but also increases the fiscal space for expansion. In Germany, what is needed, therefore, Godar et al. (op. cit.) suggest, is to use the revenues from progressive taxation reforms to finance public investment projects, thereby enhancing aggregate domestic demand and also contributing to rebalancing within the Euro Area.

As discussed above, the IMF (2014) study suggests that there is growing evidence that high income inequality has increased in recent decades in developed, developing, and emerging countries; as such, it has been detrimental to macroeconomic stability and growth. It is thereby of paramount importance for governments to employ fiscal policy to influence income distribution. Fiscal policy, it is argued, is the primary tool for governments to affect income distribution and thereby inequality. This should be undertaken through both tax and spending policies. Another IMF (2015) study suggests that "Fiscal policy is a powerful and adaptable tool for achieving distributional objectives. Considering tax and spending programs together enhances the effectiveness of fiscal redistribution". Thereby, "improving both distributional outcomes and economic efficiency is possible" (p. 1). As for specific guidance on the use of fiscal policy for redistribution, this, it is suggested, is a country-specific problem (IMF 2014, 2015; see, also, Dabla-Norris et al. 2015). IMF (2017b) cites such an example in the case of Ireland's progressive tax-benefit system, which is one of the most effective means in the EU in redistributing income. Biswas et al. (2017) investigate how tax policies that reduce income inequality affect economic growth. This is undertaken by employing US state-based data and micro-level household tax returns over the period 1979–2008. Reducing income inequality between low- and median-income households enhances economic growth. But reducing income inequality through taxation between median and high-income households reduces economic growth. Supply side (business activity and female labour supply) and demand side (consumption demand) are the main mechanisms through which tax policies that reduce inequality affect economic growth.

Piketty (2014) argues for a progressive global tax on capital, "that is a tax on the net value of assets each person controls" (p. 516), which should be "a progressive annual tax on global wealth. The largest fortunes are to be taxed more heavily, and all types of assets are to be included: real estate, financial assets, and business assets – no exceptions" (p. 517). Such a proposition, it is argued, would offer the best option for keeping inequality under control, and such a tax is "by far less dangerous than the alternatives" (Piketty, op. cit., p. 516). Still, though, it is suggested that capital, income, and inheritance taxes play "useful and complementary" (p. 547) roles. It is also argued that a global tax on capital can impose effective regulation on the financial and banking system, which helps to avoid crises. Such tax would require international cooperation, and as such, Piketty (2014) admits, "it is a utopian idea", but "it is nevertheless useful" (p. 515). Still, and although implementing such a tax would be a serious challenge politically, Piketty (op. cit.) suggests that if the EU and the US supported such a tax, it would be a great beginning. It is further suggested that "Short of that, a regional or continental tax might be tried, in particular in Europe, starting with countries willing to accept such a tax" (p. 471; see, also, Piketty et al. 2014). It is further suggested that "Such a tax would also have another virtue: it would expose wealth to democratic scrutiny, which is a necessary condition for effective regulation of the banking system and international capital flows" (Piketty 2014, p. 471). Atkinson (2015) suggests in the context of global taxation that such a tax "under the auspices of OECD" (p. 201) could produce a 'World Tax Administration'.

Atkinson (2015) suggests that "One mechanism that reduced inequality in the post-war decades appears … to have been the rising share of wages in national income, a rise that was subsequently reversed" (p. 70). Also, and "At the same time, the distribution of capital income was becoming less unequal" (p. 71), which, however, did come to an end after the 1980s. Unemployment is another factor, which was significantly lower in the period after the Second World War until the late 1970s; subsequently, it increased substantially, especially in Europe.

And as Atkinson (op. cit.) suggests, "The government should adopt an explicit target for preventing and reducing unemployment and underpin this ambition by offering guaranteed public employment at the minimum wage to those who seek it" (p. 140). Atkinson (op. cit.) also suggests that "There should be a national pay policy, consisting of two elements: a statutory minimum wage set at a living wage, and a code of practice for pay above the minimum, agreed as part of a 'national conversation' involving the Social and Economic Council" (p. 148). It is also necessary, it is suggested, an unemployment target of 2% along with the government acting as 'an employer of last resort', thereby introducing guaranteed public employment; not forgetting of course that unemployment benefits should be higher than now. It is further proposed the introduction of a national pay and social policy, under the aegis of a Social and Economic Council involving trade unions, other social partners and non-governmental bodies; and establishing a substantially higher statutory minimum wage. 'Technological change' in a way that increases the 'employability of workers' (through funding of scientific research), a more secure legal framework for trade unions, more comprehensive taxation of inheritance and property tax, and expansion of universal benefits are further proposals. All these measures should produce a more equitable income distribution.

Furthermore, Atkinson (2015) suggests that "a more progressive structure for the personal income tax" (p. 290) is most appropriate to tackle inequality. It is also proposed that an 'Earned Income Discount' should be introduced, aiming at not raising the tax rate on low levels of earnings (and pensions) as a result of the implementation of the progressive tax structure. In addition, Atkinson (op. cit.) argues for renewal of 'social security for all' in view of the fact that "One reason for rising inequality in recent decades has been the scaling back of social protection at a time when needs are growing, not shrinking". It is indeed the case that in the past, and prior to that period, the welfare state had "played a major role in reducing inequality". The welfare state "is the primary vehicle by which our societies seek to ensure a minimum level of resources for all members" (p. 205). It is further suggested that radical reform of inheritance taxation is necessary, so that "receipts of inheritance and gifts inter vivos should be taxed under a progressive lifetime capital receipts tax" (p. 194). Proportional or progressive property taxation, a wealth tax, child benefits, which should be central to any policy action to reduce inequality, and a global taxation are all important ingredients. Atkinson (2015) suggests that economic policies to reduce inequality in the OECD and EU countries as a whole are indeed possible. Although Atkinson (op. cit.) recognises the difficulties of pursuing such a path, the suggested relevant proposals can be introduced on the basis of cooperation and coordination of economic policies of the group of countries concerned.

We would agree with Atkinson (2015) that it is of paramount importance to have in place proper distributional policies, especially fiscal policies along with wage policies, if a viable growth regime is to emerge and be sustained. However, we would go a step further and suggest that to reduce inequality significantly as Atkinson (2015) and, also, Arestis and Sawyer (2013) propose, proper coordination of monetary and fiscal policies along with financial stability, the main focus of monetary policy, would be the best way forward (see, also, Arestis 2012, 2015, 2016, 2017). Fiscal policy should be directed at reducing inequality through appropriate expenditure and progressive tax policies, which should be supported by monetary and financial stability policies. The latter should be concerned with reforms in an attempt to regulate and avoid the type of financial architecture that led to the GFC; for it is the case that such regulation had been neglected prior to the GFC. The regime of inflation targeting under the auspices of an independent central bank, and the neglect of proper regulation of the financial system, have not worked as efficiently as the proponents had expected, as many authors have demonstrated (see, for example, Angeriz and Arestis 2008; Angeriz et al. 2008; Stiglitz 2013, Chapter 9).

Most important, though, is that inflation targeting neglects distributional effects in view of its central assumption of the representative agent and its emphasis on inflation as the single target of economic policy, thereby neglecting unemployment. Such concerns clearly imply that prudential regulation and financial supervision are extremely important aspects. The role of monetary policy in promoting employment creation is another objective that needs to be properly implemented. Manipulation of the rate of interest by the Central Bank to keep the real interest rate below the productivity growth would have stimulating effects on aggregate demand (Hein and Mundt 2013). Such monetary policy should be implemented in coordination with fiscal policy and financial stability. Financial stability policies are necessary to avoid sharp and unsustainable increases in debt-to-income ratios among lower and middle-income households, thereby containing the leverage ratio and the risks of crises like the GFC. At the end of the day, crises can be avoided if economies are well managed and financial markets are sufficiently regulated. Another relevant suggestion is the introduction and implementation of a financial transaction tax, which should cover both spot and derivative assets. The purpose of such tax should be to curb speculation and raise substantial funds for public investment (see, for example, Arestis and Sawyer 2013; Seguino 2014). Such tax, though, requires international cooperation, which has not emerged yet. Also relevant proposals are the reconstruction of the international macroeconomic policy coordination, along with the suggestion of Keynes (1942) in terms of the creation of an 'international clearing union'; the latter contains a fixed but adjustable exchange rate system along with the 'bancor' as the international means of payment. Such proposals would help to coordinate action to tackle tax avoidance and tax evasion.

In terms of coordination of monetary with fiscal policy, Eggertsson (2006) suggests a concrete channel of fiscal expansion under coordination with monetary policy. Fiscal expansion enhances expectations about future inflation, and, provided the central bank collaborates with the fiscal authority, the real rate of interest is reduced, which stimulates spending. It is important, though, in this approach, for the monetary authority to trade off some inflation for lower unemployment. Under such possibility, a fiscal stimulus that increases inflationary pressures and a monetary authority that keeps constant the nominal interest rate produces a lower real interest rate, thereby giving rise to further increases in consumption and investment expenditures. Also, a lower real interest rate causes the real exchange rate to depreciate, which can play a role in stimulating aggregate demand.

The empirical evidence is very supportive in terms of coordinating fiscal and monetary policies. Eggertsson (2006), utilising a calibrated model not dissimilar in substance to the New Consensus

Macroeconomics, reaches the conclusion that under fiscal and monetary policy coordination, fiscal multipliers are higher than in the case of no coordination; they are, indeed, bigger than those found in the traditional Keynesian literature. Two types of fiscal multipliers are reported in Eggertsson (op. cit.): a real spending multiplier, where government consumption is raised but holding the budget balanced; and a deficit multiplier, where deficit spending increases. These fiscal multipliers are derived under two scenarios: when fiscal and monetary policies are coordinated; and when there is no policy coordination. The fiscal policy multiplier under coordination is 3.4 in the case of the real spending multiplier, and 3.8 under the deficit spending multiplier. When no policy coordination is present, i.e. when the central bank is 'goal independent', the real spending multiplier is unchanged, while the deficit spending multiplier is zero. Eggertsson (2006) explains this important difference in fiscal multipliers, when coordination is present in relation to those where coordination is absent, by the expectations channel as discussed above. It is also suggested by Eggertsson (op. cit.) that in the case of independent monetary and fiscal authorities, coordination of fiscal and monetary policy does not necessarily imply that the respective authorities need to lose their 'independence'. This is possible so long as both fiscal and monetary authorities have *a common objective*—for example, maximisation of social welfare (Eggertsson 2006). Under such arrangements, both authorities would have to agree on the variables to be included in the social welfare function and the nature of trade-offs between the objectives.[16]

In all the economic policies suggested above, pro-labour policies are vital. Such policies should include the following: tackling

[16]A recent contribution from the ECB (Corsetti et al. 2016) acknowledges the recent prolonged period of weak economic activity and very low inflation in the euro area, and suggests that monetary and fiscal policy 'together' are necessary to stabilise the level of economic activity and inflation, especially so when the central bank's policy rates stay close to the lower bound for a lengthy period. Under such circumstances, Corsetti et al. (op. cit.) suggest that "the multiplier effect of government spending on output at the lower bound can be sizable. For the multiplier to be sizable it is essential that monetary policy accommodates the fiscal stimulus" (p. 8). It is also suggested that "The necessary fiscal accommodation might be sizable, potentially falling outside the limits of the Stability and Growth Pact" (p. 15).

unemployment through employment-friendly growth; strengthening the welfare state, labour unions and labour market institutions, collective bargaining and trade unions, as well as improving union legislation. Increased unemployment benefits, higher minimum wages, and real wage growth in line with labour productivity are further policies that could help to reduce inequality. Only when wages grow with productivity growth, will consumption expenditure grow without raising debt levels to unsustainable levels that can trigger crises. Socioeconomic differences also cause inequalities, especially so in terms of access to education and training. Relevant policies are obviously needed for this purpose. Also measures to restrict financial speculation, including reining on excessive pay in the financial sector, and restructuring the financial sector to avoid financial crises. It is also important that fiscal and monetary policies are implemented to restore full employment alongside the policies for redistributive goals.[17]

6 Summary and Conclusions

We have discussed in this chapter the state of inequality in the world, the importance of tackling inequality, the relationship between inequality and economic growth, and economic policies to tackle inequality. We have concluded that such economic policies should be coordination of fiscal and monetary policies along with financial stability type of policies, without forgetting, of course, pro-labour distributional policies. A relevant question is whether it is likely that appropriate economic policies will be pursued to reduce inequality. Especially so since, and as Lagarde (2015) has suggested, "politicians, business leaders, topnotch economists, and even central bankers are talking about excessive

[17]An interesting and relevant question is the extent to which globalisation prevents policy-makers from pursuing the type of policies, discussed in the text, to reduce inequality. The argument is that such policies may reduce competitiveness in the globalised world markets. Atkinson (2015) examines this possibility to conclude that there may be relevant constraints, but this should be sorted out by policy-makers.

inequality of wealth and income. And these concerns can be heard across the political spectrum".

However, and unfortunately, tackling unequal distribution is an area where very little progress, if any, has taken place; and it is highly unlikely to materialise in view of the undue political influence of the top 1% influential group in the political system. Atkinson (2015) suggests that the influence of the upper class on government policy in their attempt to protect their wealth is an important factor on this score (see, also, Bonica et al. 2013). However, and as Atkinson (2015) notes, there are chances of a change in attitude on inequality for in the past significant reductions in inequality were achieved; and history can, and does, teach us a great deal. A final and important relevant consideration is that clearly "There has to be an appetite for action, and this requires political leadership. The inter-relation between inequality and politics is crucial. A major instrumental reason for concern about economic inequality is that concentrations of wealth and income convey political power and influence" (Atkinson, op. cit., p. 305). This clearly implies that "Any policy proposal to reduce inequality runs immediately into the issue that economic inequality is accompanied by political inequality, and the operation of the latter reduces the political possibility to address the former" (Sawyer 2015, p. 888).

References

Allen, R. (2009). *The British Industrial Revolution in Global Perspective.* Cambridge: Cambridge University Press.

Alstadsæter, A., Johannesen, N., & Zucman, G. (2017, September). *Who Owns the Wealth in Tax Havens? Macro Evidence and Implications for Global Inequality* (NBER Working Paper No. 23805). Washington, DC: National Bureau of Economics Research. Available at: http://www.nber.org/papers/w23805.

Alvaredo, F., Chancel, L., Piketty, T., Saez, E., & Zucman, G. (2017). Global Inequality Dynamics: New Findings from WID.World. *American Economic Review: Papers and Proceedings, 107*(5), 404–409.

Angeriz, A., & Arestis, P. (2008). Assessing Inflation Targeting Through Intervention Analysis. *Oxford Economic Papers, 60*(2), 293–317.
Angeriz, A., Arestis, P., & McCombie, J. (2008). *Does Central Bank Independence Affect Inflation Persistence and Volatility?* (CCEPP Working Paper). Cambridge Centre for Economic and Public Policy, Department of Land Economy, University of Cambridge.
Arestis, P. (2011). Keynesian Economics and the New Consensus in Macroeconomics. In E. Hein & E. Stockhammer (Eds.), *A Modern Guide to Keynesian Macroeconomics and Economic Policies*. Cheltenham: Edward Elgar.
Arestis, P. (2012). Fiscal Policy: A Strong Macroeconomic Role. *Review of Keynesian Economics, Inaugural Issue, 1*(1), 93–108.
Arestis, P. (2015). Coordination of Fiscal with Monetary and Financial Stability Policies Can Better Cure Unemployment. *Review of Keynesian Economics, 3*(2), 233–247.
Arestis, P. (2016). Main and Contributory Causes of the Recent Financial Crisis and Economic Policy Implications. In P. Arestis & M. Sawyer (Eds.), *Emerging Economies During and After the Great Recession*. Annual Edition of *International Papers in Political Economy*. Houndmills and Basingstoke: Palgrave Macmillan.
Arestis, P. (2017, forthcoming). Monetary Policy Since the Global Financial Crisis. In P. Arestis & M. C. Sawyer (Eds.), *Economic Policies Since the Global Financial Crisis*. Annual Edition of *International Papers in Political Economy*. Houndmills and Basingstoke: Palgrave Macmillan.
Arestis, P., & González Martinez, A. R. (2015). The Absence of Environmental Issues in the New Consensus Macroeconomics Is Only One of Numerous Criticisms. In P. Arestis & M. Sawyer (Eds.), *Finance and the Macroeconomics of Environmental Policies*. Houndmills and Basingstoke: Palgrave Macmillan.
Arestis, P., & González Martinez, A. R. (2016). Income Inequality: Implications and Relevant Economic Policies. *Panoeconomicus, 63*(1), 1–24.
Arestis, P., & Karakitsos, E. (2013). *Financial Stability in the Aftermath of the 'Great Recession'*. Houndmills and Basingstoke: Palgrave Macmillan.
Arestis, P., & Sawyer, M. (2011). Economic Theory and Policies: New Directions After Neoliberalism. In P. Arestis & M. Sawyer (Eds.), *New Economics as Mainstream Economics*. Annual Edition of International Papers in Political Economy. Houndmills and Basingstoke: Palgrave Macmillan.
Arestis, P., & Sawyer, M. (2013). The Potential of Financial Transactions Taxes. In P. Arestis & M. Sawyer (Eds.), *Economic Policies, Governance and the New*

Economics. Annual Edition of International Papers in Political Economy. Houndmills and Basingstoke: Palgrave Macmillan.

Atkinson, A. B. (1997). Bringing Income Distribution in from the Cold. *The Economic Journal, 107*(441), 297–321.

Atkinson, A. B. (2015). *Inequality: What Can Be Done?* Cambridge, MA: Harvard University Press.

Atkinson, A., Casarico, A., & Voitchovsky, S. (2014, July 10). *Top Incomes and the Glass Ceiling*. Available at: http://voxeu.org/article/gender-and-glass-ceiling.

Atkinson, A. B., Piketty, T., & Saez, E. (2011). Top Incomes in the Long Run of History. *Journal of Economic Literature, 49*(1), 3–71.

Bank of England. (2012, July 12). The Distributional Effects of Asset Purchases. *Bank of England Report*.

Bernanke, B. S. (2015). Monetary Policy and Inequality, Brookings, 01 June. Available at: https://www.brookings.edu/blog/ben-bernanke/2015/06/01/monetary-policy-and-inequality/.

Bernanke, B. (2017, June 26–28). *When Growth Is Not Enough*. ECB Forum on Central Banking (pp. 25–34). Sintra: Portugal.

Berg, A. G., & Ostry, J. D. (2011). *Inequality and Unsustainable Growth: Two Sides of the Same Coin?* (IMF Staff Discussion Note 11/08). Washington: International Monetary Fund. Available at: http://www.imf.org/external/pubs/ft/sdn/2011/sdn1108.pdf.

Biswas, S., Chadkraborty, I., & Hai, R. (2017). Income Inequality, Tax Policy, and Economic Growth. *The Economic Journal, 127*(601), 688–727.

Blau, F. D., & Khan, L. M. (2017). The Gender Wage Gap: Extent, Trends, and Explanations. *Journal of Economic Literature, 55*(3), 789–865.

Blecker, R. A. (2015). *Wage-Led and Profit-Led Demand Regimes: The Long and the Short of It*. Presented at the Research Network Macroeconomics and Macroeconomic Policies (FMM) Conference, Berlin, Germany, October 30–November 1, 2014, Revised February 2015. Available at: http://www.american.edu/cas/economics/research/upload/2015-05.pdf.

Bonica, A., McCarty, N., Poole, K. T., & Rosenthal, H. (2013). Why Hasn't Democracy Slowed Rising Inequality? *Journal of Economic Perspectives, 27*(3), 103–124.

Bouchey, H. (2015). Bringing Inequality Back In. *European Journal of Economics and Economic Policies: Intervention (EJEEP), 12*(2), 183–189.

Card, D. (2009). Immigration and Inequality. *American Economic Review, 99*(2), 1–19.

Carney, M. (2014). Inclusive Capitalism, Speech Given at the Conference on *Inclusive Capitalism*, London, 27 May. Available at: http://www.inc-cap.com/IC_ESSAY_Book_Introduction_Keynotes.pdf.

Congressional Budget Office (CBO). (2016, August). *Trends in Family Wealth, 1989 to 2013*. Congress of the United States CBO.

Corsetti, G., Dedola, L., Jarociński, M., Maćkowiak, B., & Schmidt, S. (2016, December). *Macroeconomic Stabilization, Monetary-Fiscal Interactions, and Europe's Monetary Union* (Discussion Paper No. 1988). Frankfurt, Germany: European Central Bank.

Cynamon, B. Z., & Fazzari, S. M. (2015). Rising Inequality and Stagnation in the US Economy. *European Journal of Economics and Economic Policies: Intervention (EJEEP), 12*(2), 170–182.

Cybamon, B. Z., & Fazzari, S. M. (2016). Inequality, the Great Recession and Slow Recovery. *Cambridge Journal of Economics, 40*(2), 373–399.

Dabla-Norris, E., Kochhar, K., Suphaphiphat, N., Ricka, F., & Tsounta, E. (2015). Causes and Consequences of Income Inequality: A Global Perspective. *IMF Staff Discussion Note, 15*(13), 1–39. Available at: https://www.imf.org/external/pubs/ft/sdn/2015/sdn1513.pdf.

Davies, J. B., Sandstorm, S., Shorrocks, A., & Wolf, E. N. (2011). The Level and Distribution of Global Household Wealth. *The Economic Journal, 121*(551), 223–254.

Domanski, D., Scatigna, M., & Zabai, A. (2016, March). Wealth Inequality and Monetary Policy. *BIS Quarterly Review,* 45–64. Basel, Switzerland: Bank of International Settlements.

Draqhi, M. (2015, May 14). *The ECB's Recent Monetary Policy Measures: Effectiveness and Challenges* (Camdessus Lecture, IMF). Washington, DC. Available at: https://www.ecb.europa.eu/press/key/date/2015/html/sp150514.en.html.

Eggertsson, G. B. (2006). *Fiscal Multipliers and Policy Coordination* (Federal Reserve Bank of New York Staff Reports, No. 241). New York: Federal Reserve Bank of New York.

Engbom, N., & Moser, C. (2017). *Earnings Inequality and the Minimum Wage: Evidence from Brazil* (CESifo Working Paper No. 6393). Germany: Center for Economic Studies. Munich.

Eurofound. (2017). *Income Inequalities and Employment Patterns in Europe Before and After the Great Recession*. Luxembourg: Publications Office of the European Union.

Furceri, D., & Li, B. G. (2017). *The Macroeconomic (and Distributional) Effects of Public Investment in Developing Countries* (IMF Working Paper No. 17/217). Washington, DC: International Monetary Fund.

Furceri, D., & Loungani, P. (2013). Who Let the Gini Out? *Finance and Development, 50*(4), 25–27.

Furceri, D., & Loungani, P. (2015). *Capital Account Liberalisation and Inequality* (IMF Working Paper No. 15/243). Washington, DC: International Monetary Fund.

Galbraith, J. K. (2012). *Inequality and Instability: A Study of the World Economy Just Before the Great Crisis*. Oxford: Oxford University Press.

Goda, T., Onaran, O., & Stockhammer, E. (2016). Income Inequality and Wealth Concentration in the Recent Crisis. *Development and Change, 48*(1), 3–27.

Godar, S., Paetz, C., & Truger, A. (2015). *The Scope for Progressive Tax Reform in the OECD Countries: A Macroeconomic Perspective with a Case Study for Germany* (IMK Macroeconomic Policy Institute Working Paper No. 150). Düsseldorf, Germany: Hans Böckler Stiftung.

Góes, C., & Karpowicz, I. (2017, September). *Inequality in Brazil: A Regional Perspective* (IMF Working Paper). Western Hemisphere Department. Washington, DC: International Monetary Fund.

Goldberg, P., & Pavcnik, N. (2007). Distributional Effects of Globalisation in Developing Countries. *Journal of Economic Literature, 45*(1), 39–82.

Goldin, C., Kerr Pekkala, S., Olivetti, Z., & Barth, E. (2017). The Expanding Gender Earnings Gap: Evidence from the LEHD-2000 Census. *American Economic Review: Papers and Proceedings, 107*(5), 110–114.

Gosling, A., & Machin, S. (1995). Trade Unions and the Dispersion of Earnings in UK Establishments 1980–90. *Oxford Bulletin of Economics and Statistics, 57*(2), 167–184.

Greenspan, A. (2010, Spring). *The Crisis*. Brookings Papers on Economic Activity. Available at: http://www.brookings.edu/~/media/Files/Programs/ES/BPEA/2010_spring_bpea_papers/spring2010_greenspan.pdf.

Grigoli, F., & Robles, A. (2017). *Inequality Overhang* (IMF Working Paper No. 17/76). Washington, DC: International Monetary Fund.

Haldane, A. (2017, March 20). *"Productivity Puzzles", Speech Given at the London School of Economics*. Available at: https://www.bankofengland.co.uk/speech/2017/productivity-puzzles.

Hein, E., & Mundt, M. (2012). *Financialisation and the Requirements and Potentials for Wage-Led Recovery—A Review Focusing on the G20* (Conditions of Work and Employment Series No. 37). Geneva: International Labour Organisation.

Hein, E., & Mundt, M. (2013). Financialisation, the Financial and Economic Crisis, and the Requirements and Potentials for Wage-Led Recovery. In M. Lavoie & E. Stockhammer (Eds.), *Wage-Led Growth: An Equitable Strategy for Economic Recovery*. Palgrave Macmillan and the International Labour Office: Houndmills and Basingstoke.

Hein, E., & Tarassow, A. (2010). Distribution, Aggregate Demand and Productivity Growth: Theory and Empirical Results for Six OECD Countries Based on a Post-Kaleckian Model. *Cambridge Journal of Economics, 34*(4), 727–754.

Hughes Hallett, A. (2015). *Quantitative Easing: Side Effects in the Financial Markets, in Inequality and in the Risk of Secular Stagnation*. European Parliament, Policy Department. Available at: http://www.europarl.europa.eu/committees/en/econ/monetary-dialogue.html.

IMF. (2007, April). *The Globalisation of Labour*. World Economic Outlook, Chapter 5. Washington, DC: International Monetary Fund.

IMF. (2009). *Fiscal Implications of the Global Economic and Financial Crisis* (IMF Staff Position Note, SPN/09/13, June). Washington, DC: International Monetary Fund.

IMF. (2014, January 23). *Fiscal Policy and Income Inequality* (IMF Policy Paper). Washington, DC: International Monetary Fund. Available at: http://www.imf.org/external/np/pp/eng/2014/012314.pdf.

IMF. (2015, September 25). *Harnessing the Power of Fiscal Policy to Mitigate Inequality* (IMF Survey Magazine: Policy, IMF Fiscal Affairs Department). Washington, DC: International Monetary Fund. Available at: http://www.imf.org/external/pubs/ft/survey/so/2015/pol092515a.htm.

IMF. (2017a). *Gender Budgeting in G7 Countries*. Washington, DC: International Monetary Fund. Available at: https://www.imf.org/en/Publications/Policy-Papers/Issues/2017/05/12/pp041917gender-budgeting-in-g7-countries.

IMF. (2017b, June 30). *Chart of the Week: Ireland's Fight against Income Inequality* (IMF Blog). Available at: https://blogs.imf.org/2017/06/30/chart-of-the-week-irelands-fight-against-income-inequality/.

ILO (International Labour Organisation; International Institute for Labour Studies). (2008). *Income Inequalities in the Age of Financial Globalisation* (World of Work Report 2008). Geneva, Switzerland.

Keynes, J. M. (1936). *The General Theory of Employment, Interest and Money*. London: Macmillan.

Keynes, J. M. (1942/1980). Proposals for an International Clearing Union. In D. Moggridge (Ed.), *The Collected Writings of John Maynard Keynes* (Vol. XXV, pp. 168–196). London: The Macmillan Press.

King, J. (2013, May). *Technological Change, Union Decline, and the Rise in German Wage Inequality, 1979–2012*. Paper presented at the RC28 Spring Meeting in Trento.

Korinek, A., & Kreamer, A. (2013, October). *The Redistributive Effects of Financial Deregulation* (NBER Working Paper No. 19572). Washington, DC: National Bureau of Economics Research.

Kristal, T., & Cohen, Y. (2013, June 19). *The Causes of Rising Wage Inequality: What Do Computerization and Fading Pay-Setting Institutions Do?* (Working Paper). Available at: http://ssrn.com/abstract=2424144 or http://dx.doi.org/10.2139/ssrn.2424144.

Kumhof, M., & Rencière, R. (2010). Leveraging Inequality. *Finance and Development, 47*(4), 28–31.

Kumhof, M., Rencière, R., & Winant, P. (2015). Inequality, Leverage, and Crises. *American Economic Review, 105*(3), 1217–1245.

Kuhn, M., Schularick, M., & Steins, U. I. (2017). *Income and Wealth Inequality in America, 1949–2013* (CESifo Working Paper No. 6608). Category 6: Fiscal Policy, Macroeconomics and Growth. Munich, Germany.

Lagarde, C. (2014, May 27). *Economic Inclusion and Financial Integrity*. Speech Given at the Conference on *Inclusive Capitalism*. London. Available at: http://www.inc-cap.com/IC_ESSAY_Book_Introduction_Keynotes.pdf.

Lagarde, C. (2015, June 17). *Lifting the Small Boats*. Address at Grandes Conferences Catholiques Brussels. Available at: http://www.imf.org/external/np/speeches/2015/061715.htm.

Lagarde, C. (2017, May 13). *Every Woman Counts: Gender Budgeting in G7 Countries* (IMF Blog). Available at: https://blogs.imf.org/2017/05/13/every-woman-counts-gender-budgeting-in-g7-countries/.

Lagarda, G., Linares, J., & Gallagher, K. P. (2017). *Capital Openness and Income Inequality: Smooth Sailing or Troubled Waters?* (GEGI Working Paper 010). Global Economic Governance Initiative, Boston University.

Lansing, K. J., & Markiewicz, A. (2015). *Top Incomes, Rising Inequality, and Welfare* (CESifo Working Paper No. 5517). Center for Economic Studies. Munich, Germany.

Lavoie, M., & Stockhammer, E. (2013). Wage-Led Growth: Concept, Theories and Policies. In M. Lavoie & E. Stockhammer (Eds.), *Wage-Led Growth: An Equitable Strategy for Economic Recovery*. Houndmills and Basingstoke: Palgrave Macmillan and the International Labour Office.

McCombie, J. S. L., Pugno, M., & Soro, B. (Eds.). (2002). *Productivity Growth and Economic Performance: Essays on Verdoorn's Law*. London: Macmillan.

McCombie, J. S. L., & Spreafico, M. R. M. (2015, April). *Income Inequality and Growth: Problems with the Orthodox Approach*. Paper presented at the session, Analyzing Growth and Inequality in the 21st Century, at the INET conference, Paris.

Milanovic, B. (2011). Income Inequality Has Risen over the Past Quarter-Century Instead of Falling as Expected. *Finance and Development, 48*(3), 6–11.

Muinelo-Gallo, L., & Roca-Sagalés, O. (2011). Economic Growth and Inequality: The Role of Fiscal Policies. *Australian Economic Papers, 50*(2–3), 74–97.

Obst, T., Onaran, O., & Nikolaidi, M. (2017). *The Effects of Income Distribution and Fiscal Policy on Growth, Investment and Budget Balance: the Case of Europe* (Greenwich Papers in Political Economy, No. GPERC 43). University of Greenwich, UK.

OECD. (2008). *Growing Unequal? Income Distribution and Poverty in OECD Countries*. Paris: OECD.

OECD. (2011). *Divided We Stand: Why Inequality Keeps Rising*. Paris: OECD.

OECD. (2014). *Rising Inequality: Youth and Poor Fall Further Behind*. Paris: OECD.

Onaran, O., & Galanis, G. (2013). Is Aggregate Demand Wage-Led or Profit-Led? A Global Model, Chapter 3. In M. Lavoie & E. Stockhammer (Eds.), *Wage-Led Growth: An Equitable Strategy for Economic Recovery* (pp. 71–99). Houndmills and Basingstoke: Palgrave Macmillan (Also, International Labour Organization: Geneva, Switzerland).

Onaran, O., & Obst, T. (2015). The Empirical Case for a Wage-Led Recovery. *Economic Policy Viewpoint, 7*(May).

Ostry, J. D. (2015). Inequality and the Duration of Growth. *European Journal of Economics and Economic Policies: Intervention (EJEEP), 12*(2), 147–157.

Philippon, T. (2008, November). *The Evolution of the US Financial Industry from 1860 to 2007* (Working Paper). New York: New York University.

Philippon, T., & Reshef, A. (2009). *Wages and Human Capital in the US Financial Industry: 1909–2006* (NBER Working Paper No. 14644). Washington, DC: National Bureau of Economics Research.

Piketty, T. (2014). *Capital in the Twenty-First Century* (A. Goldhammer, Trans.). Cambridge, MA: Harvard University Press.

Piketty, T., Saez, E., & Stantcheva, S. (2014). Optimal Taxation of Top Labor Incomes: A Tale of Three Elasticities. *American Economic Journal: Economic Policy, 6*(1), 230–271.

Ponthieux, S., & Meurs, D. (2015). Gender Inequality. In A. B. Atkinson & F. Bourguignon (Eds.), *Handbook of Income Distribution* (Vol. 2A). Amsterdam: Elsevier.

Reeves, R. (2017). *Dream Hoarders: How the American Upper Middle Class Is Leaving Everyone Else in the Dust. Why That Is a Problem, and What To Do About It.* Washington, DC: Brookings Institution Press.

Sands, D. (2012, March). *The Impact of Austerity on Women* (Fawcett Society Policy Briefing). Available at: https://www.fawcettsociety.org.uk/wp-content/uploads/2013/02/The-Impact-of-Austerity-on-Women-19th-March-2012.pdf.

Sawyer, M. (1976). *Income Distribution in OECD Countries.* Washington, DC: OECD.

Sawyer, M. (2015). Confronting Inequality: Review Article on Thomas Piketty on 'Capital in the 21st Century'. *International Review of Applied Economics, 29*(6), 878–889.

Seguino, S. (2014). Financialization, Distribution, and Inequality. In G. Sen & M. Durano (Eds.), *The Remaking of Social Contracts: Global Feminists in the 21st Century.* London: Zed Books.

Social Europe. (2017). *Inequality in Europe.* Social Europe Dossier. Published by Social Europe in Cooperation with Friedrich-Ebert-Stiftung and Hans Böckler Stiftung.

Stiglitz, J. (2013). *The Price of Inequality: How Today's Divided Society Endangers the Future.* New York: W. W. Norton.

Stiglitz, J. (2015). *The Great Divide: Unequal Societies and What We Can Do About Them.* London: Allen Lane.

Stockhammer, E. (2013). Why Have Wage-Shares Fallen? An Analysis of the Determinants of Functional Income Distribution, Chapter 2. In M. Lavoie & E. Stockhammer (Eds.), *Wage-Led Growth: An Equitable Strategy for Economic Recovery.* Houndmills and Basingstoke: Palgrave Macmillan (Also International Labour Organization Working Paper, in Conditions of Work and Employment Series, No. 35, 2013). Geneva, Switzerland.

Storm, S., & Naastepad, C. W. M. (2013). Wage-Led or Profit-Led Supply: Wages, Productivity and Investment, Chapter 4. In M. Lavoie & E. Stockhammer (Eds.), *Wage-Led Growth: An Equitable Strategy for Economic Recovery*. Houndmills and Basingstoke: Palgrave Macmillan (Also International Labour Organization Working Paper, in Conditions of Work and Employment Series, No. 36, 2012). Geneva, Switzerland.

Tcherneva, P. R. (2017). *Inequality Update: Who Gains When Income Grows?* (Policy Note 2017/1, April). Levy Economics Institute of Bard College.

The Economist. (2012, October 13). *Policy Prescription: A True Progressivism* (Special Report: World Economy).

The Economist. (2014, March 1). *Inequality v Growth*.

The Economist. (2015, May 2). *When What Comes Down Doesn't Go Up*.

Tsounta, E., & Osueke, A. J. (2014). *What is Behind Latin America's Declining Income Inequality* (IMF Working Paper No. 14/124, March). Washington, DC: International Monetary Fund.

Turner, A. (2010, March 17). *What Do Banks Do? What Should They Do and What Public Policies Are Needed to Ensure Best Results for the Real Economy?* Speech Given at the CASS Business School. Available at: http://www.fsa.gov.uk/pubs/speeches/at_17mar10.pdf.

United Nations Development Programme (UNDP). (2017, September). *Income Inequality Trends in Sub-Saharan Africa: Divergence, Determinants and Consequences*.

Yates, M. (2012). The Great Inequality. *Monthly Review, 63*(10), 1–18.

Yellen, J. L. (2014, October 17). *Perspectives on Inequality and Opportunity from the Survey of Consumer Finances*. Speech Given at the Conference on Economic Opportunity and Inequality, Federal Reserve Bank of Boston, Boston, MA. Available at: http://www.federalreserve.gov/newsevents/speech/yellen20141017a.htm.

Financialisation, Financial Crisis and Inequality

Malcolm Sawyer

1 Introduction

Financialisation involves the rising economic importance and the social and political power of finance and of the financial sector. Financialisation and the general expansion of the financial sector have been key features of capitalist economies for at least one and half centuries, though financialisation has proceeded with varying intensities and with some reversals. The specific ways in which financialisation has proceeded have varied across countries and over time. It is generally recognised that financialisation in the present era (broadly since the late 1970s) has been intertwined with globalisation (and indeed financialisation has been close to a global phenomenon, particularly in the first decade of the new millennium) and neo-liberalism. The period since circa 1980 has generally seen rising inequality in the Western

M. Sawyer (✉)
Leeds University Business School, University of Leeds, Leeds, UK
e-mail: malcolm_sawyer@btinternet.com

P. Arestis and M. Sawyer (eds.), *Inequality*, International Papers in Political Economy,
https://doi.org/10.1007/978-3-319-91298-1_2

industrialised economies[1] and the relationship between financialisation and inequality is the focus of this chapter. The rising economic and political power of finance and the financial sector would be anticipated to impact on the distribution of income, and a major purpose of this chapter is indeed to explore the variety of routes through which financialisation impacts on dimensions of income distribution.

The structure of this chapter is as follows. In the next Sect. 2, the nature and features of financialisation in the present era are outlined. Section 3 sets out some of the main trends in income distribution and inequality over the past three decades. Section 4 explores the links between the financial sector and inequality of income and earnings, and specifically the extent of inequality within the financial sector and the degree to which inequality in the financial sector contributes to overall inequality. In Sect. 5, the focus of attention is on the processes of financialisation and the distribution of income, and this is followed by remarks on stratification in the financial sector in Sect. 6. One dimension of financialisation is financial deepening and in Sect. 7, the ways in which financial deepening can impact on inequality and poverty are explored. Section 8 reviews the links between inequality and financial crisis and also remarks on the empirical findings between financialisation and debt expansion. Concluding remarks are offered in Sect. 9.

2 Financialisation in the Past Four Decades

Financialisation is viewed here in terms of a modification of a well-known quote from Epstein (2005). Financialisation is perceived in terms of the increasing role of financial motives, financial markets, financial actors and financial institutions in domestic and international economies, societies, the environment and changing relationships between the financial sector and the real non-financial sector. Financialisation, particularly in terms of the increasing role of financial

[1]See, UNDP (2017) for the inequality in African countries, which presents a rather different picture.

institutions and markets, has been an ongoing process throughout capitalism. Vercelli (2014) identifies two periods of intensive financialisation. The first financialisation is dated from the second half of the nineteenth century to the start of the Great Depression around 1929, with the expansion of the financial sector, a feature of the industrialising countries including those of Western Europe and North America. There was also an international dimension as international trade and lending grew. The second financialisation (also labelled neoliberal financialisation by Vercelli, op. cit.) comes in with the ending of the Bretton Woods fixed exchange rate system, with easing of exchange and capital control, and can be broadly dated from the mid-1970s onwards.

Fasianos et al. (2018), with specific reference to the USA during the twentieth century (plus the first decade of the 21st), identify "four distinct regimes, marked by structural breaks in the institutional setting of the economy, which affected the functioning of the financial sector" (p. 35). They identify a first period lasting from the beginning of the twentieth century until 1933, and the ensuing regulation of the financial sector, notably the Glass-Steagall Act. The second is the remaining years of the 1930s, and the third covers the years of the 'golden age of capitalist development' through to 1972. The fourth period encompasses 1974 to 2010 of 'financialized capitalism'. In the first period (1900–1933), the authors find for the USA that there was dominance of the financial sector with the income share of the financial sector 'moderate high'. There was shareholder orientation with moderate intensity of financial innovation. Household indebtedness was considered moderately high and income inequality high. Free capital mobility prevailed and there was inclination to financial crises. In the next two periods (1934–1940 and 1945–1973), the authors find that there was no financial sector dominance with the income share of the financial sector low. Financial regulation, low income inequality, absence of free capital mobility and low inclination to financial crises were other common features of the two periods. The authors considered that in the 1934–1940 period, intensity of financial innovation was moderate, switching to high in the 1945–1973 period. Household indebtedness moved from low in the earlier period to moderate in the later period. The final period (1974–2010) was judged rather similar to the first period. The differences, which indicate a more intense financialisation in the recent period, put the income share of the financial sector as high (rather than moderate high), and a high intensity of financial innovation and high household indebtedness.

The present era of financialisation since the end of the 1970s has displayed a range of significant features though the intensity of financialisation in some dimensions has slackened since the global financial crises of 2007–2009.[2,3]

A first feature is the rapid expansion of financial institutions and financial markets, a feature which has been shared with earlier periods of financialisation. However, starting with shares of output and of employment, there is a rather mixed picture. Of ten European countries[4] examined, 7 recorded decreases in value-added share over the period 1995–2007, whereas three recorded increases. In the post-crisis period of 2009–2014, four recorded decreases and six increases. Over the whole period 1995–2014, four recorded decreases and six increases in shares of value added of the financial sector. In terms of employment share, eight recorded declines over the period 1995–2007 and two increases. In the post-crisis period 2009–2014, all but one recorded declines, and over the full period 1995–2014, all recorded declines in employment share of the financial sector. The output share is considerably larger than the employment share (averages in the range 1 ½–2 ¼ times higher), implying substantial higher labour productivity in the financial sector.[5]

Bank deposits relative to GDP are a frequently used measure of the size of the banking system in empirical work on the effects of the

[2]The plural 'crises' is used to signify that there were a number of national financial crises (notably USA, UK, Iceland and Ireland) which interacted and which had contagion effects. The first signs of crisis came in August 2007, reached intensity in autumn 2008 and spilled over into 2009. The term global financial crisis is used, although as Jessop (2013) has argued, it is more appropriate to be called North Atlantic financial crisis.

[3]This listing is something of a reshuffle and elaboration of the listing in Ashman and Fine (2013) and other writings.

[4]Austria, Belgium, Finland, France, Germany, Italy, Netherlands, Spain, Sweden and UK.

[5]There are issues over the measurement of output (value added) in the financial sector: see, for example, Christophers (2011).

financial sector on economic performance. Bank loans are generally correlated with bank deposits as the major items on the asset and liability sides of the banks' balance sheet. When bank deposits are the major vehicle for savings, then cumulated household savings would also be correlated with bank deposits. The growth of the banking sector (as measured by bank deposits relative to GDP) for 12 countries is illustrated in Fig. 1a. In the countries reported on there, bank deposits (relative to GDP) had (using median) gone from 33% in 1960 to 67% in 1980, 106% in 2000, peaked in 2009 at 125%, later resuming rise to 131% in 2014. The statistics on bank deposits (relative to GDP) are often used in empirical work as a key measure of financial development or financial deepening to which reference is made below.

Stock market capitalisation (again relative to GDP) is a further statistic often used to measure financial development. The time path of stock market capitalisation is illustrated for the same countries in Fig. 1b, and the strong, if volatile, growth of stock market capitalisation is clearly illustrated. From a median of 22% in 1975 (when the data series begins and when many stock markets had slumped following the oil crisis), it rose to 46% in 2000, peaking in 2000 at 115%, and after a dip moving to 108% in 2007, and recording 89% in 2014.

These statistics on bank deposits and stock market capitalisation can illustrate that financial markets have tended to grow faster than financial institutions, and a shift from bank-based financial systems towards market-based ones.[6] The rise of bank deposits and stock market capitalisation also illustrate the rise in financial assets relative to GDP, and alongside a rise in financial liabilities (one dimension of which, household debt is discussed below).

During the present era of financialisation, there has been the expansion and proliferation of financial instruments including financial derivatives and securitisation (including asset-based securities, collateralised debt obligations CDOs). As Lindo (2018, p. 1) remarks, "the late 1980s marked the beginning of a new era in derivatives trading which has

[6]For overall discussion on and critique of bank-based vs. market-based financial systems, see Sawyer (2014).

(a)

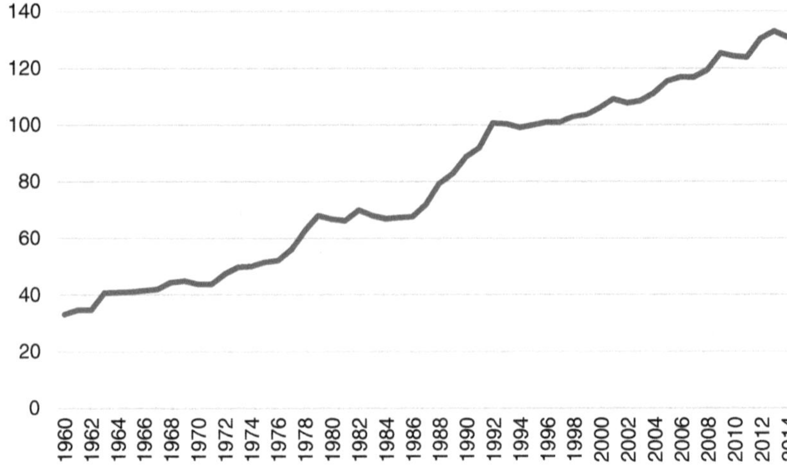

(b)

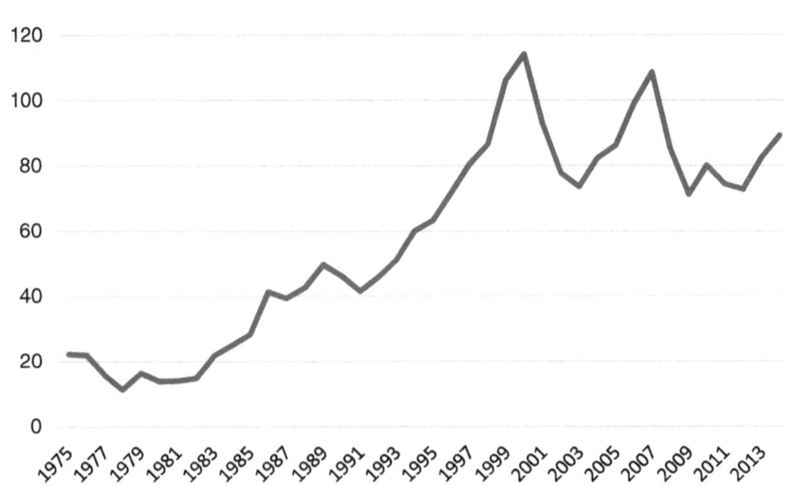

Fig. 1 Trends in size of financial institutions. **a** Bank deposits: GDP (%). Median of 12 countries. **b** Stock market capitalisation to GDP (%). Median of 12 countries (*Countries covered* Australia, Belgium, Canada, France, Germany, Italy, Japan, Netherlands, Spain, Sweden, UK, USA. *Source* Based on data from Financial Development and Structure Dataset, compiled by Aslı Demirgüç-Kunt, Martin Čihák, Erik Feyen, Thorsten Beck, Ross Levine, June 2016)

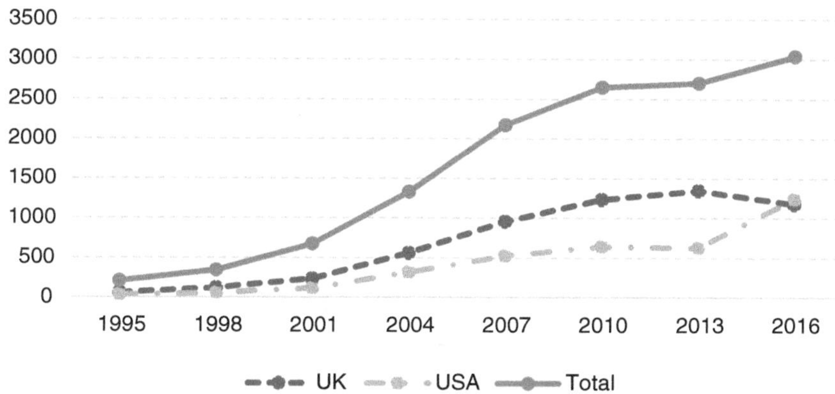

Fig. 2 Derivatives OTC $billion (*Source* Calculated from BIS data)

seen rapid growth in the volume and types of derivatives traded and the emergence, and use by market participants, of a vast literature of valuation and risk management models". Figure 2 illustrates the growth of the derivatives (OTC), and its concentration in the UK and USA. Following the financial crisis, derivatives markets continued to grow albeit at a slower pace. An over five-fold increase in the nine years to 2007 was followed by a 40% increase in the subsequent nine years.

The complexity of the financial instruments has meant that the risk evaluation of the financial instruments becomes virtually impossible. The development and growth of financial derivatives and securitisation (such as mortgage-backed securities) have been particularly significant in their consequences for risk and crisis. Kay (2015) argues that "volumes of trading in financial markets have reached absurd levels – levels that have impeded rather than enhanced the quality of intermediation and increased rather than diversified the amount of risk to which the global economy is exposed. The capital resources needed to reconcile these trading volumes with stability have not been available; nor will they ever be" (pp. 297–298). The complexity of financial products feeds into financial instability with resulting damage on the non-financial economy.

The financial assets of financial corporations other than banks (in trillions of dollars) over the period 2002–2015 are illustrated by category

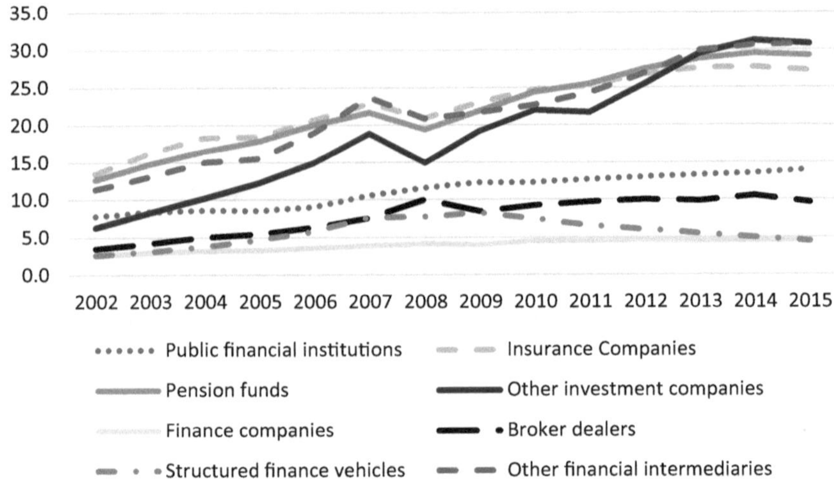

Fig. 3 Assets of financial corporations $trillions (*Source* Dataset accompanying Global Shadow Banking Monitoring Report 2016 from Financial Stability Board [available at http://www.fsb.org/2017/05/global-shadow-banking-monitoring-report-2016-monitoring-dataset/])

in Fig. 3, which serves to illustrate the rapid growth of the different forms of financial institutions and the extent to which growth continued after the global financial crises. The data refer to what is termed the 28-group,[7] which comprise the major financial centres. Banks refer to deposit-taking corporations and by way of comparison, their financial assets were $52 trillion in 2002, rising to $119.9 trillion in 2008 and then $129.6 trillion in 2015. Central bank financial assets rose substantially in the 2010s, reflecting quantitative easing from $4.5 trillion in 2002 to $13.2 trillion in 2008 and then $21.1 trillion in 2015.

The rise of household debt has often been seen as part of the processes of financialisation, and is part of the increased involvement of households with the financial sector. The significance of household debt for involvement in credit bubbles in periods when there is rapid

[7]Argentina, Australia, Belgium, Brazil, Canada, Cayman Islands, Chile, China, France, Germany, Hong Kong, India, Indonesia, Ireland, Italy, Japan, Korea, Mexico, the Netherlands, Russia, Saudi Arabia, Singapore, South Africa, Spain, Switzerland, Turkey, the UK and the US.

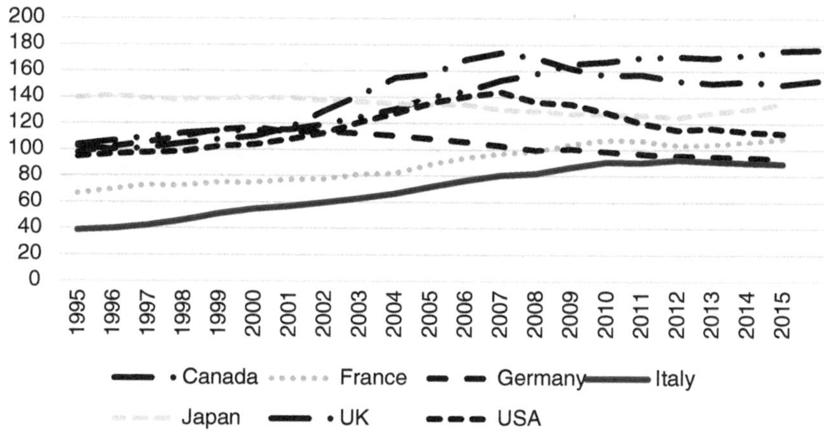

Fig. 4 Household debt as per cent of disposable income (*Source* Calculated from OECD Economic Outlook database)

expansion of household debt is discussed below. Household debt has also been viewed as a means by which households have responded to depressed incomes and rising inequality, which is also discussed below. Over the period 1995–2007, all of the countries in Fig. 4 except Japan showed an increase in household debt (relative to disposable income): the unweighted average increased by 50 percentage points which corresponded to a relative increase of over a half. In the period from 2007 to 2015, the debt ratio was rather flat: indeed, the unweighted average in 2015 was within 0.2 percentage points of the figure for 2007.

Financialisation has been related by many to the rise of rentier income. Rentier income is envisaged in terms of receipt of income and passivity. Rentier income can be viewed through the lens of the recipient—that is in terms of income received in a passive manner based on supply of funds. But rentier income can be viewed in terms of payments made by corporations and others to the supplier of funds. In a world where there were no financial intermediaries, then the payments made out by corporations would be equal to receipt of income by households. However, in a world where there are financial intermediaries, then much of the payment of rentier income goes in the first instance to financial institutions. In turn, financial institutions

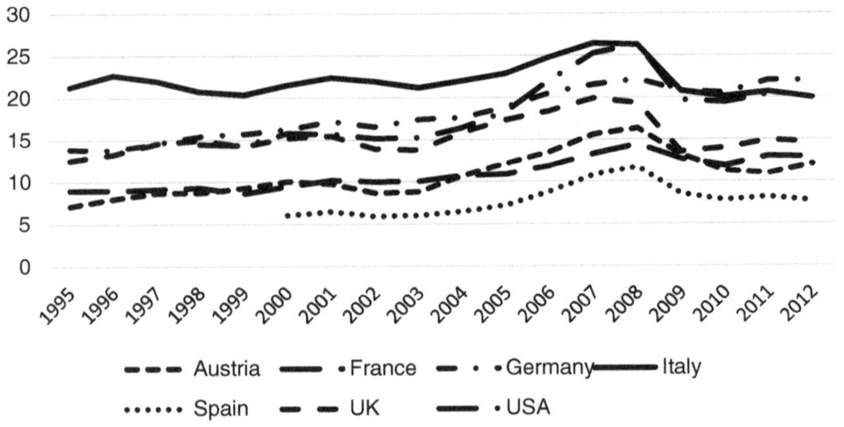

Fig. 5 Rentier income of households as % GDP (*Source* Calculated from data downloaded from http://stats.oecd.org/BrandedView.aspx?oecd_bv_id=na-data-en&doi=data-00820-en#, October 2017)

make charges for their services, and make rentier income payments to households. Further, households themselves are paying interest on past borrowing and those interest payments are at least indirectly received by other households, though again would in general pass through financial institutions. In Fig. 5, statistics are given for rentier income as received by households, which differs from rentier income as paid out by corporations. It is measured in current prices, and as such makes no allowance for inflation (so, interest payments are in nominal terms rather than real terms) nor does it incorporate capital gains. The general picture is one of rentier income rising up to the financial crisis with some declines thereafter arising from the low interest rate environment.

A remarkable feature of the era of financialisation since circa 1980 is that it has been a near global phenomenon, in that the financial sector has grown rapidly in many countries, although the liberalisation of the financial sector and its rapid growth generally started later. There has been what may be termed a globalised financialisation as financial flows between countries increased often fostered by relaxation and removal of exchange controls.

UNCTAD (2017) use IMF data on value of assets of financial institutions relative to GDP, values of cross-border assets and liabilities (relative to GDP), "financial concentration and power… approximated using a variable that measures the assets of the top five banks relative to GDP" (p. 96). The statistics mapped in their Figs. 5.1 and 5.2 show in their words "the dramatic acceleration of all indicators of financialization [for all countries] since the 1990s" (and their data extend back to 1975). Their data show that there is a substantially greater degree of financialisation in OECD countries than in developing and emerging economies. It is also argued that there was some deceleration of financialisation after the financial crises of 2007–2009 in OECD countries, which was not observed in developing countries.

The processes of international financialisation are argued by Bortz and Kaltenbrunner (2018) to involve more than simply an increase in cross-border capital flows. It also "entails distinct qualitative changes in the way economic agents are integrated into international capital markets" (Abstract). In a similar vein, Kaltenbrunner and Painceira (2018) argue that processes of financialisation in emerging economies are akin to those observed in industrialised capitalist economies and "are fundamentally shaped by their subordinated integration into a financialised and structured world economy" (p. 1).

The structure of the banking sector in particular has tended to change in the directions of becoming more concentrated (though some, such as the UK, were already highly concentrated), less regionalised as regional banking gave way to national banking and more internationalised. Detzer et al. (2013), drawing on ECB data, report unweighted average five-firm concentration ratio for the euroarea at 45.0% in 1997 rising to 57.0% in 2009. Relating to the period since 2003, ECB (2017) report "a gradual increase in market concentration" (p. 47).

Financial institutions have often been a mixture of privately owned mutual and cooperative-owned and state-owned. A feature of the present era of financialisation has often been some decline of mutual and cooperative ownership and particularly the role of state ownership.

The relationships between the financial sector and the non-financial sector evolve and change, with consequences for the ways in which financialisation operates. A reflection of such changes has been the view that one of the central features of financialisation is the pursuit of shareholder value by financial institutions, which have increasingly become owners of equity. The pursuit of shareholder value "is not a neutral concept, but an ideological construct that legitimates a far-reaching distribution of wealth and power amongst shareholders, managers and workers. Empirical phenomena interrogated in this body of work include executive compensation practices, corporate restructuring, shareholder activism and other investor behaviour, as well as the spread of the shareholder value ideology from the USA to other political economies" (Van der Zwan 2014, p. 102).

Increasing pursuit of shareholder value enhances the short-termism of management, and it is argued leads to "rising dividend payments; increasing interest rates and interest payments, ...; increasing top management salaries; increasing relevance of financial as compared to real investment and hence of the financial sector relative to the non-financial sector; hostile takeovers, mergers, and acquisitions; and liberalisation and globalisation of international finance and trade" (Hein 2015, pp. 924–925).

During this second period of financialisation, banking and financial crises became a common occurrence—424 crises were recorded by Laeven and Valencia (2013) in the period 1970–2011, of which 147 were banking crises, 211 currency crises and 66 were sovereign debt crises. Particularly large financial crises include Mexico/Latin America 1994 and the East Asian crisis 1997. "The existence of structural breaks incidence and onset of financial crisis variables indicate a markedly increased trend in financial crisis since the early 1980s" (Eichacker 2017, p. 58). Financial crises, particularly in the banking sector had major negative impacts on employment and output. The global financial crises of 2007/2009 had global effects—output in OECD countries declined by 3.6% in 2008–2009, unemployment rose by a third (6–8.1%) and sharp decline of international trade of over 11%.[8]

Van der Zwan (2014) lists as the third characteristic of financialisation the 'financialisation of the everyday'. This includes the increasing involvement of households in financial markets and financial decision-making through, for example, household debt and home

[8]Figures taken from OECD *Economic Outlook*, June 2013.

mortgages, private insurance and private pension plans and a range of other financial products. There has been the penetration of finance into a widening range of both economic and social reproduction—housing, pensions, health, etc. as a continuing feature of financialisation, leading to societal transformation. The trend away from social provision of pensions to private provision through funded schemes draws people into complex financial decisions and expands the scale of the financial sector.

These are general features of financialisation, but the growth of financial sectors has been pervasive across the world. The specific forms they take vary from country to country, and the timing of these developments similarly varies. The term 'variegated financialisation' can be used to signify the pervasive but differentiated forms of financialisation. Brown et al. (2017), and Ferreiro and Gómez (2016) provide evidence on the spread of the financial sector and the differences across countries leading into notions of variegated financialisation.

3 Trends in Income Distribution and Inequality

It has often been noted that the present era of financialisation, particularly in Western Europe and North America, has gone alongside rising levels of inequality of income and wealth. The trends have not been uniform, but, for many countries, inequality was higher in the mid-2000s than in 1980. It has also often been noted that (at least with reference to the USA) inequality (particularly relating to the share of the top 1%) had prior to the global financial crises risen to a level not seen since the late 1920s. It has then been argued that the high and rising level of inequality was viewed as a significant contributory factor in the generation of financial crisis, an argument which is examined below.

The trends for income inequality are here summarised to indicate that indeed inequality of income has been generally rising in industrialised countries. In Fig. 6, data are given on nine Western industrialised countries on inequality using the Gini coefficient as a measure of inequality. There is a general upward trend across the nine countries examined.

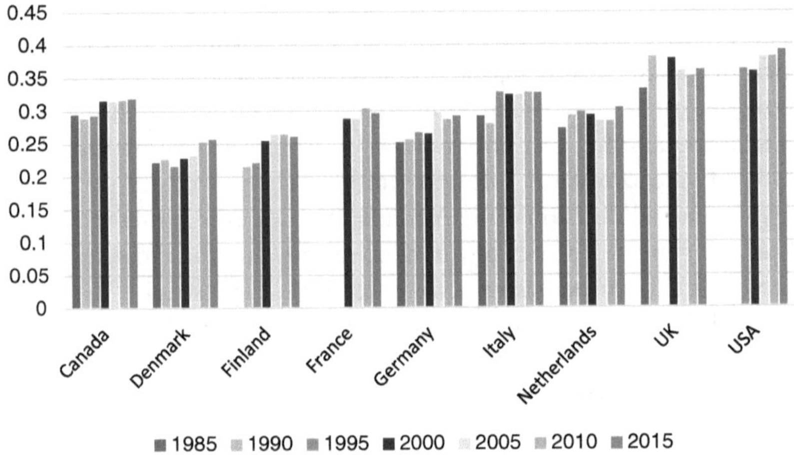

Fig. 6 Gini coefficient: post-tax, post-transfer income figures for Italy refer to 1984; 1991; 2014; for Denmark: 2013; for Germany 2014 (*Source* Calculated from WID Dataset World Wealth and Income Database: downloaded from http://wid.world/, February 2018)

The data source for Fig. 6 also provides measures of inequality based on the ratio of income share of the top decile to share of the bottom decile and the Palma ratio between the income of the top 10% and the income of the bottom 40% showing similar trends. The UK has a rather particular pattern, in that income inequality (on the measures examined) rose sharply during the 1980s under the Thatcher government and this is reflected in the figures here for 1985–1990.[9] After the early 1990s, income inequality in the UK has flattened out.

Figure 7 displays the share of the top 1% in incomes for six major countries since 1979. The general upward trend across all these countries is readily apparent with particularly sharp rises in the USA and in the UK until the global financial crises (and unlike the other measures

[9]In the data set used, figures for UK prior to 1985 were not reported. The UK Office for National Statistics does provide data: for example, the Gini coefficient for disposable income rose from 0.274 in 1979 to 0.368 in 1990, fluctuating thereafter with a recorded value of 0.322 in 2016/2017.

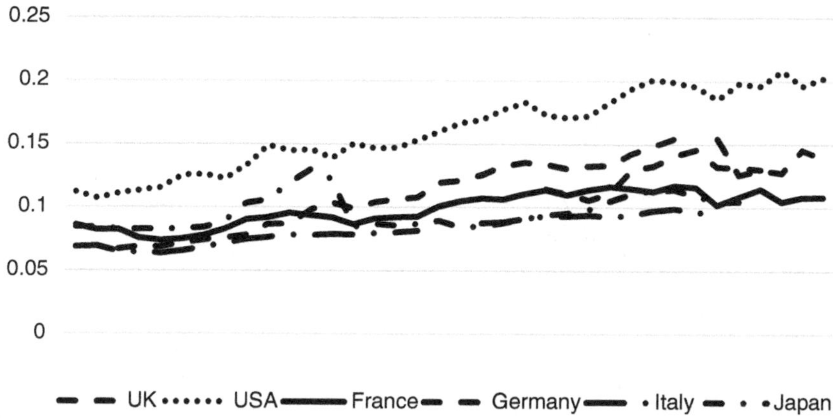

Fig. 7 Income share of top 1% (*Source* Calculated from WID Dataset World Wealth and Income. *Database* downloaded from http://wid.world/, February 2018)

of income inequality, the share of the top 1% rose throughout the 1980s, 1990s and into the 2000s).[10]

There have also been marked shifts in the distribution of income between labour and capital with a general downward trend in labour's share and corresponding rise in profits. For evidence on these trends in the distribution of income, Tridico and Pariboni (2018) in this volume cite a number of sources backing up the statement of generally falling share of labour and also produce their Fig. 2 in support.

4 The Financial Sector and Inequality of Income and Earnings

The financial sector has acquired the reputation of paying high incomes to bankers and for the financial sector having high levels of income equality within it, and for paying higher salaries than other sectors.

[10]The figures for Germany before 2001 are only available every three years, and those figures do not show up in this chart. In 1980, the share was 0.1072, and 0.1144 in 1989, virtually the same as the figure for 2001.

The enlargement of the financial sector can contribute directly to the overall level of the inequality of earnings and incomes through two routes. First, insofar as employment in the financial sector expands and the financial sector displays higher than average levels of inequality, then overall inequality of earnings will rise. Second, insofar as there is rising inequality of incomes within the financial sector, there could be a further contribution to higher inequality. In this section, how far those two routes of the financial sector contribute to inequality are examined.

The nature and source of high earnings in the financial sector are also highly significant, particularly in consideration of the efficiency of the financial sector. If there are higher and rising earnings, do they represent payment for enhanced productivity and effectiveness with links between wages, productivity and performance? Alternatively, do higher earnings in the financial sector reflect the power and ability of the top earners within the financial sector to extract economic rents, which would be rather in line with ideas on financialisation and the power of the financial sector?

We start by reviewing studies on inequality within the financial sector and the contribution of inequality within that sector to overall inequality.

Denk (2015, p. 6) reports that employees in the financial sector are heavily concentrated at the upper end of the overall earnings distribution. He finds the receipt of 'wage premia' by employees in financial institutions, which means that workers with similar observable characteristics including age, gender, education and experience are paid more in the financial sector than in other sectors, which can be seen as indication of rent extraction by financial sector workers. Two-thirds of the 'wage premia' in the financial sector are received by financial sector employees who are amongst the 10% of all workers with the highest earnings. Denk (2015) argues that it is these wage premia which account for most of the contribution of the financial sector to inequality of earnings. Some rough calculations undertaken by Denk (op. cit.) suggest that about half of the overall negative relationship between finance and income inequality can be explained by the concentration of financial sector employees at the upper end of the earnings distribution and sizeable wage premia for financial sector workers, particularly for top earners. Men employed in the financial sector are reported to earn on average a 22% higher income than women with the same profiles in terms of age, education and experience, which Denk (2015) reports as similar to that found in other sectors. However, in finance, the wage gap between men and women employed in finance increases with income and is higher than in other sectors at the top.

Bakija et al. (2012) examine patterns of income growth between 1979 and 2005 for top earners by occupation drawing on USA income tax returns. They report that executives, managers, supervisors, and financial professionals accounted for about 60% of the top 0.1% of income earners. Further, those groups account for 70% of the increase in the share of national income which went to the top 0.1% of the income distribution between 1979 and 2005. They identify that 13% of the top 1% of earners were in the financial sector and 18% in the top 0.1%. In their data, the share of the top 1% rises from 9.72% in 1979 (income including capital gains; 8.93% excluding capital gains) to 20.95% in 2005 (16.3% excluding capital gains). Income of financial professionals accounted for around 9% of the income of the top 1% in 1979 rising to 16% in 2005 (figures are little different whether or not capital gains included in income).

Philippon and Reshef (2012) find that wages in finance relative to nonfarm sector followed a U-shaped relationship between 1909 and 2006. In 2006, they report that average incomes in financial sector were 70% above those in the rest of the private sector. After adjustment for education, incomes were comparable in the financial sector and the rest of the private sector, but the premium in the financial sector averaged 50%. The differences were more pronounced at the top of the income distribution where the wages of top decile in finance grew to become 80% more than the wages of top decile of earners elsewhere. By 2005, executives in finance were earning 250% more than executives elsewhere, and it was found to be a 300% premium for workers in finance in the states of New York, New Jersey and Connecticut. They ascribed around half of the increase in the average premium to earnings risk, and one-fifth to changes in the size distribution of firm. They also argue that changes in financial regulation are important determinants of these changes in earnings in the financial sector. They further find that the financial sector accounted for between 15 and 25% of the rise in income inequality between after 1980.

Godechot (2012) reports that the share of the top 10% in wages in France rose from 26.45% ion 1996 to 27.74% in 2007; the corresponding figures are: for top 1%: 5.74–7.06%; top 0.1%: 1.20–2.01%; and top 0.01%: 0.27–0.65%. The financial sector's contribution to these rises in top income shares was 51% (top 10%), 47% (1%), 67% (0.1%) and 89% (top 0.01%).

Bell and Van Reenen (2014) note that the top 1% (by earnings) of workers increased their share of income from around 6% of total UK income in the late 1970s to 15% by the end of the 2000s. They further note that on this measure, the level of inequality had returned to the level of the inter-war years with the notable difference that while in the inter-war years, the high-income group was the rentier class based on the return on fixed capital, in the late 2000s, the high-income group is primarily high-wage workers. "In 2008, 28% of all top percentile earners in the UK were London bankers. But this dramatically understates their importance in the rise in overall wage inequality during the last decade. We estimate that somewhere between two-thirds and three-quarters of the overall increase in the share of wages taken by those in the top percentile have accrued to bankers" (Bell and Van Reenen 2014, p. F19). The term 'bankers' was used in Bell and Van Reenen (2014) to refer to the employees in the financial intermediation sector which also includes fund management and insurance businesses.

Philippon and Reshef (2013) find that wages in the financial sector are generally higher than in other sectors and have been rising in relative terms. There is an increasing trend over the period 1970–2005 of average wages in the financial sector relative to other sectors in USA, Netherlands, France, Germany, Denmark, Canada and Finland, and a mixed trend in Austria, Belgium, Japan, UK and Sweden. Throughout, the relative wage of workers in the financial sector is above 1 and as high as near 1.8. They argue that the increase in skill intensity cannot explain wages in the financial sector. For the relative wages of skilled workers in the financial sector, six countries are reported to have an increasing trend and five a mixed trend (and one, Canada, for which data are not available). With the exception of Finance in the first half of the period examined, the average wage of skilled workers in the financial sector is greater than average for other skilled workers.

Bivens and Mishel (2013, p. 66) calculate for the USA that the unadjusted ratio of financial sector pay (annual compensation per full-time employee) relative to pay of workers in the rest of the economy fluctuated below 1.1 between 1952 and 1982, and then gradually rose to reach 1.83 in 2007.

Tomaskovic-Devey and Lin (2011) report that just under a quarter of GDP and more than a quarter of profits accumulated in a definition of the financial sector broader than that used above. They report that in the American financial sector, employee compensation rose from being close to the average in 1980 to around 60% higher by 2008. They ascribe this shift as happening through decreases in market competition and regulation which provided the conditions of enhanced institutional market power to enable such a transfer of income.

Sum et al. (2008) consider growth of weekly earnings in the USA over the period 2002–2007. They report that typical full-time wage and salary workers had no increase in their weekly earnings over the period in spite of rising productivity and generally increasing employment opportunities. Non-supervisory workers' weekly earnings rose by $6, while earnings of all wage and salary earnings including that of manager and executives rose by over $60, which represented a gain of about 7% for this group of workers but a large portion (over one-third) of it was due to earnings gains of workers in the nation's investment banking and securities industries. The mean weekly earnings in investment banking and securities industries rose by $2408, a 54% increase. The weekly earnings (including bonuses) of wage and salary workers including manager and executive in the investment bank and securities industries in Manhattan ('Wall Street') rose by $8028, a 90% increase.

Kaplan and Rauh (2010) consider the degree to which inequality at the very top of the income distribution can be attributed to top executives of nonfinancial firms, financial service sector employees from investment banks, hedge funds, private equity (PE) funds, and mutual funds, lawyers and professional athletes and celebrities. Two measures of pay were considered—realised compensation which includes options exercised during the year, and ex ante compensation which uses estimated value of options granted during year. They study earnings of four groups: non-financial-firm top executives (Main Street), investment bankers, private equity and mutual funds investors (Wall Street), corporate lawyers, sports stars and celebrities. They calculate that these groups represent between 15 and 26.5% of the individuals who are in the top 0.1% of adjusted gross income. Their estimation is that Wall Street-related individuals form a higher proportion of the top gross income brackets than is the case for nonfinancial executives of public companies. They consider their assumption tends to understate position of Wall Street executives. In contrast to the representation of top public company executives in the top fractions of the income distribution, they find that the contributions of hedge fund managers, private equity investors, venture capitalist investors, and corporate lawyers have increased substantially over the past ten to twenty years, and likely by a greater amount than the top executives.

Lindley and McIntosh (2017) report that the wage premium in the UK finance sector is large (of the order of 40%) and increasing. They find that the largest returns within the financial sector are received by London-based male graduates in their 40s, and who are employed as dealers or brokers in the security broking sector. The premium is observable across different sub-sectors of finance and different occupations and different qualification levels. The wage premium is found across most other OECD countries. The wage premium "seems to be a pervasive feature of remuneration in the financial sector" (Lindley and McIntosh 2017, p. 589). They find that the UK financial wage premium has continued to rise after the 2007/2009 financial crisis. Lindley and McIntosh (2017) consider explanations of the financial sector wage premium including task-biased technical change with substitution of routine labour by capital equipment, skill intensity and cognitive abilities. They conclude that none of the possible explanations as to why finance sector workers are paid more than non-finance sector workers are robust. They "propose that the finance sector pay premium is, at least in part, due to the rent-sharing of that sector's profits" (p. 589), and argue that such a conclusion is supported by the prevalence of the pay premium across jobs at "all points of the occupation hierarchy, for workers of all skill types, and at all points of the wage distribution" (p. 589).

Bivens and Mishel (2013) discuss what may be termed economic rents—as the income received in excess of what would be needed to induce the person to supply labour to the specific activity or sector. They admit that the "evidence on rent-shifting behaviour should be viewed not as conclusive, but as highly suggestive" (p. 65). They point to the rise in the top incomes in the financial sector alongside its general expansion coinciding with regulatory changes in the direction of de-regulation and rising concentration in the financial sector. Further, "some potentially substantial share of the income for large financial institutions is based on implicit insurance against bankruptcy ... that large financial firms receive from the government ... with some financial firms seem to extract large rents largely by hiding financial risk, rather than managing it" (p. 65).

As Spreafico (2018) argues, the rapid rise in salaries of CEOs in general (and not just in the financial sector) in the past three decades cannot be explained on marginal productivity lines, as this rise in salaries is not matched by increases in the efficiency of firms or growth, and her argument can be extended to the salaries and bonuses of the top income receivers within the financial sector. Spreafico (2018) presents a full range of arguments against the links between wages and marginal productivity, which apply with full force in the financial sector.

Alvaredo et al. (2013) note the differences in the experiences of countries with regard to the share of the top 1% with marked rises in USA and UK and modest rises in other large industrialised economies. They argue that the explanation for the rising inequality in USA in particular cannot be explained by relying on forces common to industrialised economies such as impact of new technologies, globalisation, and demand and supply of skills. They advance the ideas that tax policy, changes in bargaining power and greater individualisation of pay, capital income and inherited wealth and the closer correlation between earned income and capital income help to explain the rise of the share of the top 1%.

Nau (2013) labels those households that receive some portion of their income from wealth as 'investors'. "This conceptualization differs from capitalists, a more commonly used term to indicate membership in a propertied class, in the following ways: (1) the universe of investments encompasses any sort of asset that can generate income; and (2) households can be investors and workers at the same time" (p. 441). In his empirical work, the focus is on the two decades of the 1990s and the 2000s in the USA. He argues that the importance of investment income has increased greatly in recent decades. Over the period 1992–2010, non-investment income among the top 1% was generally stagnant. He finds confirmation for the hypothesis that "elites have depended upon their investments to realize income growth, and that such windfalls were not shared with most other households" (p. 451). His Fig. 5 reports that by 2008, those with more than $2 million in financial investments accounted for over half of the income of the top 1%.

The work reviewed here refers to the financialisation era from circa 1980, though the evidence does not yet extend past the global financial crises. The dominant finding is that the financial sector itself tends to exhibit higher levels of inequality than other sectors, though it has to be noted that the number of countries covered is limited. The growth of the financial sector and the rising inequality within the financial sector have contributed markedly to the general rise in inequality. The financial sector is also seen to have higher earnings than the non-financial sector, with the earnings gap between financial and non-financial tending to widen. The evidence which has been brought forward here supports the view that the higher earnings in the financial sector reflect economic rents being gained by those in the financial sector rather than representing enhanced efficiency or productivity.

5 Financialisation and Income Distribution

In this section, there is a review of the research, which has examined the impacts of financialisation, viewed in a number of different dimensions, on income inequality and on the distribution of income between wages and profits. The research reviewed is econometric analysis, and it is only those dimensions of financialisation for which quantitative proxies are available which can be included. The quantitative proxies are in general rather simple measures such as ratio of bank deposits to GDP and many of them have been outlined above. The nature and dimensions of financialisation have been a much discussed one as noted above, and it is a term which is used in different ways by different authors. At best, the simple measures included in the econometric exercises which are labelled financialisation (or similar) reflect one or two dimensions of financialisation, and are limited to those dimensions for which a proxy is available.

Evans (2014) considers the trends in inequality in four countries. He concludes that the worsening of the distribution of income in Germany primarily arose from the labour market reforms introduced by the Social Democratic-Green coalition government in the early 2000s. There were a range of financial liberalisation measures introduced in Germany with diverse effects. In the USA, he finds that extensive liberalisation in the 1980s and the 1990s was closely associated with a major increase in inequality, arising from a combination of high incomes paid in the financial sector and the pressures coming from financial institutions on non-financial corporations to reduce wage costs and employment. However, in Brazil, government policies from 2003 onwards raised the minimum wage and pensions, and through new credit programmes, lower income groups acquired greater access to housing and consumer durables. Although incomes in Brazil remain highly unequal, inequality has declined. In India, there was a marked rise in inequality as the financial liberalisation of the early 1990s led to a reduction of credit programmes, particularly in rural areas, designed to counter inequality. There was an acceleration of economic growth but with the benefits accruing almost exclusively to middle- and upper-income sectors.

Davis and Kim (2015) in their sociological review of papers on financialisation focus on the impacts of the pursuit of shareholder value on corporate strategies and on earnings of top managements, and on the ways in which financialisation shapes the patters of inequality in society. They conclude that "financialization has shaped patterns of inequality, culture and social change in the broader society" (p. 203).

In Flaherty (2015), the measure of inequality is the income share of the top 1 per cent. He seeks to examine the impact of financialisation on inequality using a panel analysis of 14 OECD countries over the period 1990–2010. Market capitalisation, private sector credit (both as per cent of GDP) and the gross operating surplus of finance, insurance and real estate in gross operating surplus along with financial globalisation (external assets and liabilities as per cent of GDP) were the measures of financialisation used. The first and third of those variables are found to have a statistically significant effect in raising inequality. The extent of banking sector liberalisation, extent of banking sector supervision, and a financial reform index are used as measures of the regulatory environment. Flaherty (2015) finds that these measures are all associated with growth in the top income share. A range of control variables such as government consumption, union density, trade openness and economic globalisation were also included.

Zallewski and Whalen (2010) review the institutional routes through which financialisation can impact on inequality. They use an index of financial deepening, developed by IMF, which is based on three sub-indices that measure traditional banking activity, new financial intermediation and financial markets, as a measure of financialisation. Over the period 1995–2004, the financial index increased in 17 out of 18 industrial countries covered by an average of over 12%. They report a correlation coefficient across countries between the financial index and the Gini coefficient as a measure of income inequality of 0.184 in 1995 and 0.254 in 2004.

Tridico (2018) postulates that increases in inequality in OECD countries (which is measured in terms of personal distribution of income, using a range of measures including Gini coefficient, the Palma ratio) arise from radical changes in the main features of the socio-economic model in those countries. These changes involve a shift towards financialisation, which is measured in Tridico (2018) by market capitalisation of listed domestic companies as a percent of GDP which has a shortcoming of volatility reflecting the ups and downs of the stock market. Other institutional changes included in the study are pressures on labour through increased labour flexibility, the decline of trade union power and the reductions in social spending by government. The econometric results support the proposition that financialisation encouraged inequality.

Westcott and Murray (2017) focus on the ways in which the expansion of the financial sector and changes in financial institutions may impact on inequality. Increases in financial activities alongside rising asset prices suggest that financialisation made an important contribution to the increase of wealth for financial asset owners. Financial deepening and development of new types of financial institutions were seen as allowing those in possession of financial assets to increase their income and their wealth at a faster rate than those dependent on labour earnings.

Roberts and Kwon (2017) use a panel analysis of 17 OECD countries from 1980 to 2007. They find that growth in financial sectors and in financial sector employment is associated with higher income inequality, greater wage disparities and a greater concentration of income in the more affluent households. The size of those effects is found to be stronger in liberal market economy countries.

IILS (2008) focus on financial globalisation measured in their empirical work by the sum of foreign assets and liabilities, expressed as percent of GDP. It is argued that "the current dynamics of financial globalization have prevented a further convergence of wealth both across and within countries, with income inequality in low-income countries remaining unaffected by financial openness" (p. 44). It is found that financial globalisation depresses the share of wages in GDP even after allowing for the decline in wage share which can be attributed to trade openness (increasing elasticities of labour demand) and changes in labour market regulations and institutions. It is estimated that an increase in financial openness by 1 percentage point reduces the labour income share by 0.3 percentage points.

Darcillon (2015, p. 477) focuses on the impact of financialisation on workers' bargaining power and employment protection legislation in 16 OECD countries over the period 1970–2009. He argues that financialisation pushes labour markets in the decentralised bargaining direction and more flexible employment relations. Using panel data models, the results indicate "that financialization is clearly associated with a reduction in workers' bargaining power and in the strictness of employment protection" (p. 477). Financialisation is viewed in terms of a finance-led regime of accumulation and of the pursuit of shareholder value though it is measured by share of value added in finance and share of employment of finance.

Hein et al. (2017) view financialisation as potentially affecting wage and profits shares through three channels of the sectoral composition of the economy, the financial overhead costs and profit claims of the rentiers and the bargaining power of workers. They examine indicators for each of these channels for six OECD economies before and after the global financial crisis. They conclude that the relationship between financialisation and income distribution differs between those countries which they identify as 'debt-led private demand boom' (the US, the UK and Spain in their sample), the 'export-led mercantilist' countries (Germany and Sweden in their sample) and the 'domestic demand-led' economy of France. In their sample, all countries except the UK, saw a decline in the wage share in the period from the early 1990s until the crisis. However, the forces behind the general decline in the wage share differed. In the 'debt-led private demand' group, the sectoral shifts towards the financial sector with its higher profit share and the declines in the bargaining power of trade unions and workers were seen as the key forces. In the case of the USA, higher financial overheads and rentiers' claims on profits were factors contributing to the lower wage share. In the 'export led mercantalist' group, the changes in the sectoral composition of the economy did not help to explain the falling wage share. There was a general, though not universal, significance of the deterioration of workers' and trade unions' bargaining power for the falling wage share. These differences between the country groups have largely carried through to the post-crisis period.

Stockhammer (2015b) investigates the relative impacts of financialisation, globalisation, welfare state retrenchment and technological change on the functional income distribution. A dataset covering 28 advanced and 43 developing and emerging economies over the period 1970–2007 is used. Financialisation is measured in terms of financial globalisation, which is the logarithm of external assets plus external liabilities (relative to GDP). An index of financial reforms is also included. Stockhammer (2015b) finds that "financialization has had the largest contribution to the decline of the wage share" (p. 27) with globalisation also having a substantial effect.

Denk and Cournède (2015) use data from OECD countries over the past three decades and show that financial expansion has fuelled greater income inequality. They find that higher levels of credit intermediation and of stock market capitalisation are both related to a more unequal distribution of income. They use numerical simulations to indicate that expansion of the financial sector restrains the income growth of low- and middle-income households. The authors use three measures of financial size, all measured relative to GDP, which are the value added of the financial sector, credit by banks and other financial institutions to the non-financial private sector and stock market capitalisation. They find that, in general, more finance has been associated with higher income inequality, though no relationship was detected for the value added of the financial sector (which was indicated above to be often not growing relative to GDP).

Lin and Tomaskovic-Devey (2013) use cross-section time series American data at the industry level. They find a long-run relationship, which indicates that a higher ratio of financial income to profits is associated with a reduced labour share of income, increase in top executives' share of employee compensations and increase in the dispersion of earnings. After allowing for the effects of decline in unionisation, the effects of globalisation, technical change and capital investment, they find the effects of financialisation on inequality to be substantial. "Our counterfactual analysis suggests that financialization could account for more than half of the decline in labor's share of income, 9.6% of the growth in officers' share of compensation, and 10.2% of the growth in earnings dispersion between 1970 and 2008" (Lin and Tomaskovic-Devey 2013, p. 1284).

Alvarez (2015) investigates the connections between the financialisation of French corporations and the functional distribution of income in the non-financial sector. Firm-level data of 6980 French non-financial firms over the period 2004–2013 are utilised. Financialisation is measured in terms of the increasing dependence of earnings through financial channels. Increased dependence on financial profits and technological change are found to the most important determinants of functional income distribution, and more important than trade openness or labour market institutions.

Dünhaupt (2017) explores the relationship between financialisation and labour income share for data set of 13 countries over the period 1986–2007. Globalisation (trade openness, foreign direct investment, and prices of raw materials and semi-finished products), worker power (unemployment rate, union density and strike intensity) and government activity are also included in the regression analysis. Financialisation is viewed in terms of shareholder value orientation, which itself is proxied in terms of net interest and net dividend payments of non-financial corporation relative to the capital stock of the business sector. It is found that net dividend payments have a negative effect on wage share in all specifications. The net interest payment variable is not significant in some specifications, but in the absence of the dividend payments variable, it has a negative sign. The combined shareholder value variables with both dividends and net interest payment show a significant and negative effect on the labour share.

Das and Mohapatra (2003) present evidence of a strong statistical association between the event of liberalisation and income shares. Specifically, they find a positive coefficient between financial liberalisation and the top quintile's share of mean income, a negative coefficient between liberalisation and the income share of the middle-income groups, but no evidence of statistical association between liberalisation and the lowest income quintile is found.

Panico and Pinto (2018) and Panico et al. (2012) draw on Sraffian ideas to conduct a theoretical analysis of the links between income distribution and the size of the financial industry. They argue that the changes in financial regulations have permitted the sales of the financial sector to increase faster than the rest of the economy. The input and output compositions and income distribution vary. They conclude that "these changes have interacted with those originated by the alteration in the relations among managers, shareholders and workers and by the slow growth of the economy, generating further changes in the power relations among social groups, in the productive structure and in income distribution" (Panico and Pinto 2018, p. 56).

The studies, which have been reviewed in this section, have drawn on different dimensions of financialisation, and have used relatively simple proxies for the dimensions selected. The general conclusion from these contributions has been that financialisation, along with a range of other factors, such as trade union and collective bargaining power, does impact on the distribution of income, particularly the shares of income between labour and capital. The findings are in line with the expectations of the financialisation literature that financialisation raises the profits share and diminishes the labour share of income.

6 Stratification in the Financial Sector

Arestis et al. (2014) argue that the income distribution effects associated with financialisation, along the lines discussed in the previous section, have also gone alongside an occupational stratification process that has raised income of the managerial and financial occupations at the top of the income scale whilst leaving service occupations at the bottom of the US society. "The role of race norms seems to have been particularly strengthened by financialisation in the high-status managerial and financial occupations" (p. 1488). Further, the stratification of the USA labour market has been exacerbated by financialisation operating through the effect on social norms. In an earlier paper (Arestis et al. 2013), these authors had explored whether financialisation in the USA had created identity preference effects by linking managerial and financial occupations to high earnings, and in turn the high earnings of white men as the dominant demographic group in the work force. Their empirical results covering the period 1983–2009 confirmed that not only was there wage premium for those working in managerial and financial occupations, as the literature surveyed above had shown, but also that the wage premium received by financial occupations is not equally distributed among all gender and ethnic groups. Within each ethnic group, men took an increasing share of the finance wage premium at the expense of women.

7 Financial Deepening and Inequality

This section considers the effects of the expansion of financial institutions and their operations on inequality and poverty. Financial deepening is often used to describe the growth of the banking system and measured in simple terms by, e.g., ratio of bank deposits to GDP.

The growth of the banking system has implications for financial inclusion/exclusion. Financial development and deepening can take many forms and working through a variety of institutional arrangements, the relationships will vary over time and space. It is easy to point to features of the financial system and institutions, which are intended to aid the poor—micro-finance institutions, credit unions being notable examples. The literature does not yield any general conclusion on the effects of financial deepening on inequality, as much depends on the nature of the financial deepening, which financial institutions grow and the prevailing levels of financial deepening.

Demirguc-Kunt and Levine (2009) discuss the range of theories relating financial deepening and the evolution of inequality and poverty. They outline the various routes through which financial deepening can impact on inequality. They further argue that the theory on this matter is not unambiguous, and that while the theoretical analysis provides indications of a range of possible mechanisms linking inequality with the operation of the financial system, "many of the core questions about the nature of the relationship between inequality and finance are empirical" (p. 45). Although they find that the accumulating body of empirical evidence is far from conclusive, they do argue that the findings of "cross-country, firm-level, and industry-level studies, policy experiments, as well as general equilibrium model estimations all suggest that there is a strong beneficial effect of financial development on the poor and that poor households and smaller firms benefit more from this development compared with rich individuals and larger firms" (p. 46).

Kim and Lin (2011) argue that most theoretical studies point in the direction that financial deepening and development can be an instrument for improving the distribution of income. They conclude that whether or not that is the case depends on the stages of financial development in a country, with the benefits of financial deepening only occurring beyond a threshold level of financial development. Financial development tends to raise inequality below a critical value of financial development. Their policy implication is that a minimum level of financial development is needed in order for financial development to help reduce income inequality.

Beck et al. (2007) found that financial deepening helped the poor with the incomes of the poor growing faster than average per capita income. Their results indicate that around three-fifths of the effects of financial development on the poorest quintile come through aggregate growth and two-fifths through reduction in income inequality.

Greenwood and Jovanovic (1990) developed a theoretical model in which links between economic growth, financial development and the distribution of income were explored. In their model, which they viewed as consistent with casual observation, as income levels rise, the financial system becomes larger and economic growth becomes more rapid, and income inequality also rises. At a mature stage of development, with what they term a full developed financial structure a stable income distribution is found alongside a higher growth rate than initially.

Nikoloski (2013) uses a dynamic multivariate panel data analysis on 161 developed and developing countries over the period 1962–2006. Financial deepening is measured by the ratio of credit to the private sector by financial intermediaries to GDP and inequality is measured by the Gini coefficient. In the regression analysis of the relationship between inequality and the measure of financial deepening, a range of control variables are included, amongst them GDP per capita and its square, inflation rate, institutional development and government spending as per cent of GDP. Nikoloski (op. cit.) reports empirical evidence for an inverted U-shaped relationship between financial sector development and income inequality, and hence financial development is associated with higher inequality at lower levels of financial development, and with lower inequality at higher levels.

Jauch and Watzka (2016) investigate the link between financial development (measured by the ratio of credit to GDP) and inequality (measured by the Gini coefficient) using an unbalanced data set of up to 148 developed and developing countries over the period 1960–2008. Within countries, they find that financial development increases income inequality. They also report that more developed financial markets lead to higher income inequality. Control variables used include GDP per capita and its square, inflation rate, government expenditure and size of agricultural sector. A range of robustness checks are included. They conclude that there is the positive relationship between inequality and financial development which is highly significant but relatively small. With the Gini coefficient measured on a scale of 0–100, they report that an increase in the provision of credit by 10% would lead to an average increase in the Gini coefficient of 0.22.

As the literature has suggested, there are numerous routes through which financial developments and the growth of the financial sector can have influences on inequality. In econometric studies, financial deepening is typically measured by simple proxies which cannot reflect the complexities of the relationships between financial institutions and the public and the different forms of financial institutions. The empirical work, which has been reviewed here, presents a mixed picture of the relationships between financial deepening and inequality with some positive and some negative linkages.

8 Inequality and Financial Crisis

The sharp rise in inequality in the USA in the decade prior to the American sub-prime crisis has often been viewed as at least a contributory factor to the generation of that crisis. However, a banking and financial crisis also occurred in the UK where inequality had in general not risen in the previous decade except with regard to the share of the top 1%. Financial crises have generally been preceded by some combination of rapid credit expansion and rising asset prices. Credit expansion and rising asset prices both foster expansion of aggregate demand and of output and employment. Both are inherently unsustainable. The links of inequality with financial crisis would then run through credit expansion and rising asset prices. This section delves into the linkages between inequality, particularly rising inequality, and the occurrence of financial crisis. A route often suggested is that rising inequality pushes people who have lost out from rising inequality towards debt to maintain consumption levels, and the burst of debt accumulation proves unsustainable. This leads to an examination of inequality and household debt.

The general set of arguments has been summarised in Stockhammer (2015a) where he postulates four channels through which rising inequality contributed to the financial crisis of 2007/2009 with the crisis to be viewed as the interaction of the deregulation of the financial sector (a component of financialisation) with the effects of rising inequality.

The first of the channels identified is the demand depressing effects of rising inequality as income shifts from poorer income groups with high propensity to spend to richer income groups with lower propensity to spend. This, as a number of authors have argued, may well have slowed economic recovery. For the third channel, Stockhammer draws on the debt-led vs. export-led models, to suggest a channel in debt-led economies where "higher inequality has led to higher household debt as working-class families have tried to keep up with social consumption norms despite stagnating or falling real wages" (p. 936). This appears to particularly apply to the USA (often identified as a debt-led economy), whereas the UK which is also generally identified as debt-led experienced a credit boom with rising debt and house prices in the decade prior to the global financial crisis, but real wages had generally been rising (at least until 2005), and the sharp rise in inequality having occurred in the 1980s and flattened off since then. A further channel comes from "rising inequality [increasing] the propensity to speculate as richer households tend to hold riskier assets than other groups. The rise of hedge funds and subprime derivative in particular has been linked to rise of the super-rich" (p. 936). This appears to suggest that the overall degree of risk rises as the rich move into riskier assets, but no mechanisms are proposed by which overall risk would rise. However, we can point to the ways in which securitisation in effect raised risk.

The remaining channel (numbered two) is seen as financial liberalisation of the capital accounts allowed large current account imbalances.

In the context of the American financial sub-prime crisis of 2007/2009, many have argued for the role of rising inequality in the generation of the crisis. Rajan (2010) argued that the political response to rising inequality in the United States had been the expansion of lending to households, particularly low-income ones. The political response may have been planned or an unpremeditated reaction to constituent demands. There was the stimulating effect through aggregate demand, but with an unsustainable credit boom. Van Treeck and Sturn (2012) summarise the argument in terms of rising incomes in recent decades in the USA being confined to a relatively small group of households at the top of the income distribution. Increasing consumer expenditure of the lower and middle-income groups became mainly financed through rising debt rather than rising incomes. This was aided by government actions of deregulation of the financial sector which facilitated increased lending to households and through credit promotion policies. The debt-financed consumer-led demand expansion came to an end as the downturn in the US housing market, the sub-prime mortgage crisis took their toll and highlighted the over-indebtedness of American households. They conclude with specific reference to the USA that the changes in the functional distribution of income between wages and profits did not play an important part in explaining the increase in the consumer expenditure to output ratio and the decline in the savings ratio. However, they find substantial evidence that rising income inequality between households did make an important contribution to rising personal debt, falling household saving rate. Lower and middle-income households sought to keep up with the higher consumption levels of top-income households facilitated by readily available credit.

Van Treeck (2014) asks whether inequality caused the USA financial crisis (of August 2007). He concludes that "there is substantial evidence that the rising inter-household inequality in the United States has importantly contributed to the fall in the personal saving rate and the rise in personal debt (and a higher labour supply)" (p. 421). This may be seen as a 'demand-side' argument which van Treeck (op. cit.) relates to a 'relative income hypothesis' under which households seek to maintain consumption levels when their relative income declines through borrowing. In order for that to take place, there has to be a willingness of banks and financial institutions to lend.

Iacoviello (2008) approaches the issue through the construction of a theoretical model, which can mimic the time series behaviour of the distribution of earnings in the USA over the period 1963–2003. He claims to show that the model can replicate the trend and cyclical behaviour of household debt and the diverging patterns in consumption and wealth inequality over time. He argues that the prolonged rise in household debt during the 1980s and 1990s can be quantitatively explained only by the concurrent increase in income inequality.

Goda and Lysandrou (2014) focus on the toxic securities of collateral debt obligations (CDOs), which were central to the financial crises of 2007–2009. As discussed above, income inequality and stagnant incomes of most workers in the USA have been viewed as factors leading to rising household debt and sub-prime mortgages and then the financial crisis. They argue that low incomes can help explain the demand for mortgage loans; but it remains to be explained why financial institutions were prepared and able to meet the demand and why the mortgage loans were securitised and resecuritised into CDOs. They argue that wealth concentration amongst the world's richest individuals was a 'demand-pull factor' with a 'search for yield' as yields on bonds declined and CDOs appeared to offer high returns.

Considering the more general case of the links between inequality and financial crisis, drawing on 25 countries over 100 years, Atkinson and Morelli (2011) find 'no hard and fast pattern' as to whether or economic crises (in their Table A.1 the term systemic banking shocks is used) are preceded by rising inequality. They find 'more evidence that financial crises are followed by rising inequality'. Morelli and Atkinson (2015) extend the previous study by adding further data and investigating both the hypothesis that growth of inequality contributes to financial crisis and that the level of inequality does so. They find that the empirical evidence does not provide any convincing support for either of the hypotheses.

Bellettini and Delbono (2013) find that a large majority of banking crises in the last three decades took place in countries where income inequality before the crisis had been persistently higher than the average level in OECD countries. However, the banking crises did not appear to change the relative position of income inequality of the countries experiencing crisis as compared with average OECD levels. They finally conclude that "only in the 2000s relatively low income inequality seems associated to the lack of banking crises, whereas in the previous decades we do not detect any clear association" (Bellettini and Delbono, op. cit., p. 12).

UNCTAD (2017, p. 101) recognises that financial crises have multiple causes and rising inequality may not always be one of the causes, particularly in smaller countries which are vulnerable to changes in external conditions. In their Fig. 5.5, UNCTAD (2017) correlate changes in private debt and changes in inequality in developed countries and developing countries prior to financial crisis (using the Laeven and Valencia 2012, data on crises). This shows a generally positive correlation between debt and inequality prior to financial crisis. However, as they argue, the financial institutions and regulation have to provide the credit in the creation of credit bubbles leading to financial crisis. There is a general increase in the Palma ratio, with the income gap rising in 80% of cases in run-up to financial crisis, and also rising in 66% of cases after a financial crisis (UNCTAD 2017, p. 101).

Van Treeck and Sturn (2012) followed their study of the USA mentioned above by considering the cases of China and Germany. For China, they note that there is limited access to personal credit. A high level of savings by households is seen as stimulated by high income dispersion and a weak social safety net, and to that degree income inequality may push towards high savings rather than debt. Higher income inequality is viewed as contributing to higher intensity of status seeking, which appears to result in a higher personal propensity to save as households are precluded from the easy use of credit to support conspicuous consumption.

The authors note that domestic demand in Germany stopped growing in the first decade of the twenty-first century, and growth became heavily dependent on rising net exports. The stagnation of German unit nominal labour costs in the fixed exchange rate regime of the euro zone stimulated German exports. Further, the shift towards increased profit margins and lower labour income share weakened consumer expenditure. Rising income inequality and uncertainty of private households, which can be attributed in part to labour market and welfare state reforms, contributed to higher savings rather than to consumer borrowing.

Cardaci and Saraceno (2015) seek to analyse the impact of rising income inequality on the possibilities of a crisis in different institutional setting employing a macroeconomic model, and using agent-based modelling in a stock-flow consistent framework. They find that when inequality rises, low credit availability would mean a drop in aggregate demand, whereas relaxed credit constraints result in greater financial instability.

Bordo and Meissner (2012) use data from 14 advanced countries between 1920 and 2000 and their results do not indicate any general relationships between inequality and crisis. They note that the role of credit booms in increasing the risks of a banking crisis, but they did not find any evidence that a rise in the shares of the top income groups led to credit booms.

Michell (2015) views rising inequality and falling wage share as driven by globalisation, deregulation and financialisation, with a common theme being the weakening of the bargaining power of workers. He notes that there are two different and mutually reinforcing mechanisms for maintaining growth rates in the face of falling demand in response to a declining wage share, namely credit expansion to a household sector faced with stagnant or falling real income, and an increasing reliance on exports. The credit expansion will likely prove to be unsustainable and may lead into at least a slow-down in economic activity if not into a banking crisis. He argues that for the 2007/2009 financial crises, the proximate trigger was the non-performing mortgage debt, and the mortgage-backed securities collapse and the resulting contagion effects on those financial institutions which held the now toxic assets.

The effects on inequality on household debt have been examined by a number of authors. Klein (2015) investigates long-run relationships between income inequality and household debt in nine industrialised countries (Australia, Canada, France, UK, Italy, Japan, Norway, Sweden and United States). Two measures of household debt (private household credit and total bank loans) and four measures of inequality such as top 1% income share, inverted Pareto-Lorenz coefficient, the Gini coefficient and labour share of income are used. The results were robust across the four inequality measures, and it is reasonable to conclude that in developed economies there is a long-run relationship between income inequality and leverage. A 1% point increase in inequality is found to be associated with a 2–6% increase in household credit (varying across measures of inequality used).

Malinen (2016) finds a long-run steady-state relationship between income inequality and bank credit for a sample of eight countries (those in Klein's study less Italy), and for the period 1980–2009. Income inequality is found to have one-way Granger causality relationship with bank credit.

With particular reference to the US, Barba and Pivetti (2009) argue that rising household indebtedness should be seen mainly as a response to stagnating real wages and the cut back of the welfare state. As others have raised, they raise concerns over the sustainability of rising indebtedness, where debt has a stimulating effect in the short term, which cannot be sustained in the longer term.

Kim (2013) examines the relationship between output and household debt in the USA over the period 1951–2009 with a structural change in the fourth quarter of 1982 to allow for financial liberalisation measures at that time. He finds that in the pre-1982 period, household debt levels had no significant effects on output, though new borrowing did boost output. In the post-1982 period, household debt levels had negative effects on output while new borrowing continued to boost output. In a related study, Kim (2016) remarks that an additional economic stimulus comes in the short term from debt-financed household spending, but after a while, the accumulation of debt becomes excessive and unsustainable. The resulting crisis generates negative impacts on output in the long run. A system operating with high and often rising levels of household debt can become vulnerable to negative shocks, and the possibility of a severe economic down-turn.

The general conclusion which is to be drawn from the material reviewed above is that, under certain conditions, a rise in inequality may contribute to the generation of financial crisis. The key condition would be that the rise in inequality fosters an unsustainable rise in household debt, which, when the bubble of debt bursts, feeds into a financial crisis. That key condition clearly requires that people respond to declining income shares by borrowing to maintain consumption levels and that banks and other financial institutions are keen to extend loans. The situation in the USA in the early 2000s supported key condition being met. In other situations, that key condition has not held and inequality and financial crisis have not been correlated. As Bazillier and Hericourt (2017) conclude, "the links between inequalities and leverage are likely to be a mixture of direct and indirect causal relations, as well as coincidental factors" (p. 489). They also argue that "the effects of financial development and financial deregulation on income distribution are not necessarily identical and are conditioned strongly on the quality of institutions preventing rent-capturing behaviours" (p. 489).

9 Concluding Comments

The general conclusions which are drawn from this chapter in respect of financialisation and inequality in Western industrialised economies are four-fold. First, in a general sense, higher levels of inequality and declining labour share of income have accompanied financialisation in the present era from late 1970s onwards. Second, the financial sector itself tends to display high levels of inequality of earnings and income, and inequality in the financial sector has directly had an impact on overall inequality particularly in respect of the share of the top 1%. Third, there is evidence to support the view that financialisation has aided a shift in income distribution from wages to profits, but the difficulties of measuring financialisation in econometric exercises have been noted. Fourth, rising inequality looks to have been a contributory factor in the generation of the USA sub-prime crisis though other factors such as de-regulation, banks and financial institutions increased willingness to provide credit have to be involved. However, doubts have been raised as to whether that finding is of general application to financial crises in general.

References

Alvaredo, F., Atkinson, A. B., Piketty, T., & Saez, E. (2013). The Top 1 Percent in International and Historical Perspective. *Journal of Economic Perspectives, 27*(3), 3–20.

Alvarez, I. (2015). Financialization, Non-financial Corporations and Income Inequality: The Case of France. *Socio-Economic Review, 13*(3), 449–475. https://doi.org/10.1093/ser/mww00.

Arestis, P., Charles, A., & Fontana, G. (2013). Financialization, the Great Recession, and the Stratification of the US Labor Market. *Feminist Economics, 19*(3), 152–180. https://doi.org/10.1080/13545701.2013.795654.

Arestis, P., Charles, A., & Fontana, G. (2014). Identity Economics Meets Financialisation: Gender, Race and Occupational Stratification in the US Labour Market. *Cambridge Journal of Economics, 38*(6), 1471–1491.

Ashman, S., & Fine, B. (2013). Neo-liberalism, Varieties of Capitalism, and the Shifting Contours of Africa's Financial System. *Transformation: Critical Perspectives on Southern Africa, 81*(82), 144–178.

Atkinson, A. B., & Morelli, S. (2011). *Economic Crises and Inequality* (Human Development Research Paper, 2011/06).

Bakija, J., Cole, A., & Heim, B. T. (2012). *Jobs and Income Growth of Top Earners and the Causes of Changing Income Inequality: Evidence from US Tax Returns Data.* Williams College, US Department of Treasury and Indiana University.

Barba, A., & Pivetti, M. (2009). Rising Household Debt: Its Causes and Macroeconomic Implications—A Long Period Analysis. *Cambridge Journal of Economics, 33*(1), 113–137.

Bazillier, R., & Hericourt, J. (2017). The Circular Relationship Between Inequality, Leverage, and Financial Crises. *Journal of Economic Surveys, 31*(2), 463–496. https://doi.org/10.1111/joes.12150.

Beck, T., Levine, R., & Demirguc-Kunt, A. (2007). Finance, Inequality and the Poor. *Journal of Economic Growth, 12*(1), 27–49.

Bell, B., & Van Reenen, J. (2014). Bankers and Their Bonuses. *Economic Journal, 124,* F1–F21.

Bellettini, G., & Delbono, F. (2013). *Persistence of High Income Inequality and Banking Crises: 1980–2010* (CESifo Working Paper, No. 4293).

Bivens, J., & Mishel, L. (2013). The Pay of Corporate Executives and Financial Professionals as Evidence of Rents in Top 1 Percent Incomes. *Journal of Economic Perspectives, 27*(3), 57–78.

Bordo, M. D., & Meissner, C. M. (2012). Does Inequality Lead to a Financial Crisis? *Journal of International Money and Finance, 31,* 2147–2161.

Bortz, P. G., & Kaltenbrunner, A. (2018). The International Dimension of Financialization in Developing and Emerging Economies. *Development and Change, 49*(2), 375–393. https://doi.org/10.1111.dech.12371.

Brown, A., Spencer, D., & Veronese Passarella, M. (2017). The Extent and Variegation of Financialisation in Europe: A Preliminary Analysis. *Revista de Economia Mundial* [Journal of World Economy], *46*, 49–69.

Cardaci, A., & Saraceno, F. (2015). *Inequality, Financialisation and Economic Crises: An Agent Based Macro Model* (Working Paper 2015-21). Dipartimento di Economia, Universita degli di Milano.
Christophers, B. (2011). Making Finance Productive. *Economy and Society, 40*(1), 112–140.
Darcillon, T. (2015). How Does Finance Affect Labor Market Institutions? An Empirical Analysis in 16 OECD Countries. *Socio-Economic Review, 13*(3), 477–504. https://doi.org/10.1093/ser/mwu038.
Das, M., & Mohapatra, S. (2003). Income Inequality: The Aftermath of Stock Market Liberalization in Emerging Markets. *Journal of Empirical Finance, 10*(1), 217–248.
Davis, G., & Kim, S. (2015). Financialization of the Economy. *Annual Review of Sociology, 41,* 203–221.
Demirguc-Kunt, A., & Levine, R. (2009). *Finance and Inequality: Theory and Evidence* (NBER Working Paper No. 15275). Cambridge, MA. Available online http://www.nber.org/papers/w15275.
Denk, O. (2015). *Financial Sector Pay and Labour Income Inequality: Evidence from Europe* (OECD Economics Department Working Papers, No. 1225). Paris: OECD.
Denk, O., & Cournède, B. (2015). *Finance and Income Inequality in OECD Countries* (OECD Economics Department Working Papers, No. 1224). Paris: OECD. http://dx.doi.org/10.1787/5js04v5jm2hl-en.
Detzer, D., Dodig, N., Evans, T., Hein, E., & Herr, H. (2013). *The German Financial System* (FESSUD Studies in Financial Systems No. 3).
Dünhaupt, P. (2017). Determinants of Labour's Income Share in the Era of Financialisation. *Cambridge Journal of Economics, 41*(1), 283–306.
Eichacker, N. (2017). *Financial Underpinnings of Europe's Financial Crisis: Liberalization Integration and Asymmetric State Power*. Cheltenham: Edward Elgar.
Epstein, G. (2005). Introduction: Financialization and the World Economy. In G. Epstein (Ed.), *Financialization and the World Economy*. Cheltenham and Northampton: Edward Elgar.
European Central Bank (ECB). (2017, May). *Financial Integration in Europe*.
Evans, T. (2014). The Impact of Financial Liberalization on Income Inequality [Special Issue on The Challenge of Inequality]. *International Journal of Labour Research, 6*(1), 129–142.
Fasianos, A., Guevara, D., & Pierros, C. (2018, January). Have We Been Here Before? Phases of Financialization Within the Twentieth Century in

the US. *Review of Keynesian Economics, 6*(1), 34–61. https://doi.org/10.4337/roke.2018.01.03.

Ferreiro, J., & Gómez, C. (2016). Financialisation and Financial Balance Sheets of Economic Sectors in the Eurozone. In P. Arestis & M. Sawyer (Eds.), *Financial Liberalisation: Past, Present and Future.* Annual Edition of *International Papers in Political Economy.* Houndmills and Basingstoke: Palgrave Macmillan.

Flaherty, E. (2015). Top Incomes Under Finance-Driven Capitalism, 1990–2010: Power Resources and Regulatory Orders. *Socio-Economic Review, 13*(3), 417–447. https://doi.org/10.1093/ser/mwv011.

Goda, T., & Lysandrou, P. (2014). The Contribution of Wealth Concentration to the Subprime Crisis: A Quantitative Estimation. *Cambridge Journal of Economics, 38,* 301–327. https://doi.org/10.1093/cje/bet061.

Godechot, O. (2012). Is Finance Responsible for the Rise in Wage Inequality in France. *Socio-Economic Review, 109,* 447–470. https://doi.org/10.1093/ser/mws003.

Greenwood, J., & Jovanovic, B. (1990). Financial Development, Growth, and the Distribution of Income. *Journal of Political Economy, 98*(5), 1076–1107.

Hein, E. (2015). Finance-Dominated Capitalism and Redistribution of Income: A Kaleckian Perspective. *Cambridge Journal of Economics, 39*(3), 907–934.

Hein, E., Dünhaupt, P., Alfageme, A., & Kulesza, M. (2017). Financialisation and Distribution Before and After the Crisis: Patterns for Six OECD Countries. In P. Arestis & M. Sawyer (Eds.), *Economic Policies Since the Global Financial Crisis* (pp. 127–172). Houndsmill: Palgrave Macmillan.

Iacoviello, M. (2008). Household Debt and Income Inequality, 1963–2003. *Journal of Money Credit and Banking, 40*(5), 929–965.

International Institute for Labour Studies (IILS). (2008). *World of Work Report 2008: Income Inequalities in the Age of Financial Globalization.* Geneva: International Labour Organization.

Jauch, S., & Watzka, S. (2016). Financial Development and Income Inequality: A Panel Data Analysis. *Empirical Economics, 51*(1), 291–314.

Jessop, B. (2013). The North Atlantic Financial Crisis and Varieties of Capitalism: A Minsky and/or Marx Moment? And Perhaps Max Weber Too? In S. Fadda & P. Tridico (Eds.), *Financial Crisis, Labour Markets and Institutions* (pp. 40–59). London: Routledge.

Kaltenbrunner, A., & Painceira, J. P. (2018). Subordinated Financial Integration and Financialisation in Emerging Capitalist Economies: The Brazilian Experience. *New Political Economy, 23*(3), 290–313. https://doi.org/10.1080/13563467.2017.1349089.

Kaplan, S., & Rauh, J. (2010). Wall Street and Main Street: What Contributes to the Rise in the Highest Income? *Review of Financial Studies, 23*(3), 1004–1050.

Kay, J. (2015). *Other People's Money: Masters of the Universe or Servants of the People?* London: Profile Books.

Kim, Y. K. (2013). Household Debt, Financialisation, and Macroeconomic Performance in the United States, 1951–2009. *Journal of Post Keynesian Economics, 35,* 675–694.

Kim, Y. K. (2016). Macroeconomic Effects of Household Debt: An Empirical Analysis. *Review of Keynesian Economics, 4,* 127–150.

Kim, D. H., & Lin, S. C. (2011). Nonlinearity in the Financial Development-Income Inequality Nexus. *Journal of Comparative Economics, 39*(3), 310–325.

Klein, M. (2015). Inequality and Household Debt: A Panel Cointegration Analysis. *Empirica, 42,* 391–412.

Laeven, L., & Valencia, F. (2012). *Systemic Banking Crises Database: An Update* (IMF Working Papers, WP/12/163).

Laeven, L., & Valencia, F. (2013). Systemic Banking Crises Database. *IMF Economic Review, 61,* 225–270. https://doi.org/10.1057/imfer.2013.12.

Lin, K.-H., & Tomaskovic-Devey, D. (2013). Financialization and U.S. Income Inequality, 1970–2008. *American Journal of Sociology, 118*(5), 1284–1329.

Lindley, J., & McIntosh, S. (2017). Finance Sector Wage Growth and the Role of Human Capital. *Oxford Bulletin of Economics and Statistics, 79*(4), 570–691.

Lindo, D. (2018). Why Derivatives Need Models: The Political Economy of Derivative Valuation Models. *Cambridge Journal of Economics, 42*(4), 987–1008. https://doi.org/10.1093/cje/bex055.

Malinen, T. (2016). Does Income Inequality Contribute to Credit Cycles. *Journal of Economic Inequality, 14,* 309–325. https://doi.org/10.1007/s10888-016-9334-6.

Michell, J. (2015). Income Distribution and the Financial and Economic Crisis. In E. Hein, D. Detzer, & N. Dodig (Eds.), *The Demise of Finance-Dominated Capitalism Explaining the Financial and Economic Crises* (pp. 240–264). Cheltenham: Edward Elgar.

Morelli, S., & Atkinson, A. B. (2015). Inequality and Crises Revisited. *Economia Politica, 32*(1), 31–51.

Nau, M. (2013). Economic Elites, Investments, and Income Inequality. *Social Forces, 92,* 437–461.

Nikoloski, Z. (2013). Financial Sector Development and Inequality: Is There a Financial Kuznets Curve? *Journal of International Development, 25*(5), 897–911.

Panico, C., & Pinto, A. (2018). Income Inequality and the Financial Industry. *Metroeconomica, 69*(1), 39–59.

Panico, C., Pinto, A., & Puchet Anyul, M. (2012). Income Distribution and the Size of the Financial Sector: A Sraffian Analysis. *Cambridge Journal of Economics, 36*(6), 1455–1477.

Philippon, T., & Reshef, A. (2012). Wages and Human Capital in the U.S. Finance Industry: 1909–2006. *The Quarterly Journal of Economics, 127*(4), 1551–1609. org.wam.leeds.ac.uk. https://doi.org/10.1093/qje/qjs030.

Philippon, T., & Reshef, A. (2013). An International Look at the Growth of Modern Finance. *Journal of Economic Perspectives, 27*(2), 73–96.

Rajan, R. (2010). *Fault Lines*. Princeton, NJ: Princeton University Press.

Roberts, A., & Kwon, R. (2017). Finance, Inequality and the Varieties of Capitalism in Post-industrial Democracies. *Socio-Economic Review, 15*(3), 511–538. https://doi.org/10.1093/ser/mwx021.

Sawyer, M. (2014). *Bank-Based Versus Market-Based Financial Systems: A Critique of the Dichotomy* (FESSUD Working Papers, No. 19). Available at fessud.eu.

Spreafico, M. (2018). Is the Share of Income of the Top One Percent Due to the Marginal Product of Labour or Managerial Power? In P. Arestis (Ed.), *Alternative Approaches in Macroeconomics: Essays in Honour of John McCombie* (pp. 155–181). Houndsmill: Palgrave Macmillan.

Stockhammer, E. (2015a). Rising Inequality as a Root Cause of the Present Crisis. *Cambridge Journal of Economics, 39*, 935–958.

Stockhammer, E. (2015b). Determinants of the Wage Share: A Panel Analysis of Advanced and Developing Economies. *British Journal of Industrial Relations*. Advance access https://doi.org/10.1111/bjir.12165.

Sum, A., Tobar, P., McLaughlin, J., & Palma, S. (2008). The Great Divergence: Real-Wage Growth of all Workers Versus Finance Workers. *Challenge, 51*(3), 57–79.

Tomaskovic-Devey, D., & Lin, K.-H. (2011). Income Dynamics, Economic Rents, and the Financialization of the U.S. Economy. *American Sociological Review, 76*, 538–559.

Tridico, P. (2018, forthcoming). The Determinants of Income Inequality in OECD countries. *Cambridge Journal of Economics, 42*(4), 1009–1042. https://doi.org/10.1093/cje/bex069.

Tridico, P., & Pariboni, R. (2018). Theoretical and Empirical Analyses of the Rise of Income Inequality in Rich Countries. In P. Arestis & M. Sawyer (Eds.), *Inequality: Trends, Causes, Consequences, Relevant Policies*. Basingstoke: Palgrave Macmillan.

UNCTAD. (2017). *Trade and Development Report: Beyond Austerity Towards a Global New Deal*. Geneva: UNCTAD.

UNDP. (2017). *Income Inequality Trends in Sub-Saharan Africa: Divergence, Determinants, Consequences*. New York: UNDP.

Van der Zwan, N. (2014). State of the Art: Making Sense of Financialization. *Socio-Economic Review, 12*, 99–129.

Van Treeck, T. (2014). Did Inequality Cause the U.S. Financial Crisis? *Journal of Economic Surveys, 28*(3), 421–448.

Van Treeck, T., & Sturn, S. (2012). *Income Inequality as a Cause of the Great Recession? A Survey of Current Debates* (ILO Conditions of Work and Employment Series, No. 39).

Vercelli, A. (2014). Financialization in a Long-Run Perspective: An Evolutionary Approach. *International Journal of Political Economy, 42*(4), 19–46.

Westcott, M., & Murray, J. (2017). Financialisation and Inequality in Australia. *The Economic and Labour Relations Review, 28*(4), 519–537.

Zallewski, D., & Whalen, C. J. (2010). Financialization and Income Inequality: A Post Keynesian Institutionalist Analysis. *Journal of Economic Issues, 44*(3), 757–777.

Inequality and Growth: Marxian and Post-Keynesian/Kaleckian Perspectives on Distribution and Growth Regimes Before and After the Great Recession

Eckhard Hein

1 Introduction

The re-distribution of income from labour to capital, from workers to top-managers, and from low income households to the rich has been a main feature of finance-dominated capitalism since the early 1980s, which has led to the Great Financial Crisis and the Great Recession in 2007–9. The recovery from this crisis has been sluggish so far, and this has given rise to a renewed discussion about stagnation tendencies in capitalist economies (Summers 2014, 2015). Whereas in orthodox approaches, income distribution only has a restricted role to play, if at all, the interaction between distribution and growth is at the centre of Marxian and post-Keynesian/Kaleckian approaches

E. Hein (✉)
Institute for International Political Economy (IPE), Berlin School of Economics and Law, Berlin, Germany
e-mail: eckhard.hein@hwr-berlin.de

P. Arestis and M. Sawyer (eds.), *Inequality*, International Papers in Political Economy,
https://doi.org/10.1007/978-3-319-91298-1_3

when it comes to explaining medium- to long-run trends of economic growth—and stagnation. This contribution first provides Marxian and Kaleckian assessments of the distribution and growth regimes under finance-dominated capitalism, both before and after the recent crisis. Second, an interpretation of stagnation tendencies in a demand-led endogenous growth model with Kaleckian, Kaldorian and Marxian features is presented.

For this purpose, the contribution builds on the recent empirical literature on different demand and growth regimes under financialisation (Hein 2012), and on the research on the distributional effects of financialisation (Hein et al. 2017) in particular. Some stylised facts on distribution and growth regimes under financialisation before the crisis are provided in Sect. 2. In order to allow for a comparative assessment of the relationship between inequality and growth in these regimes from a Marxian and a Kaleckian perspective, the method of model closure, already used in Hein (2017a), is applied in Sect. 3. First, the two extreme growth regimes under financialisation before the crisis, the 'debt-led private demand boom' and the 'export-led mercantilist' regimes, are put forward in stylised Marxian and neo-Kaleckian models. Then the effects of a rising profit share, indicating rising inequality, are studied, holding behavioural equations constant. Finally, the changes in behavioural parameters for the two regimes in each approach are added, and the main features of the distribution and growth patterns observed before the crisis are generated. In Sect. 4, the analysis turns towards the crisis and post-crisis period. Empirically, the changes in distribution and growth regimes in this period are assessed, and these changes are interpreted in the context of the stylised neo-Kaleckian model from Sect. 3. Thereafter, this model is extended by Kaldorian and Marxian views on the determinants of technological progress and productivity growth in order to generate a demand-led endogenous growth model and to show how the effects of redistribution and current stagnation tendencies can be explained by this model. The final Sect. 5 summarises and concludes.

2 Stylised Facts: Distribution and Growth Regimes Under Financialisation Before the Crisis

From a macroeconomic perspective, finance-dominated capitalism or financialisation can be described by four characteristics, as elaborated in Hein (2012; 2014, Chapter 10), for example.

1. With regard to distribution, financialisation has been conducive to a rising gross profit share, including retained profits, dividends and interest payments, and thus a falling labour income share, on the one hand, and to increasing inequality of wages and top management salaries and thus of personal or household incomes, on the other hand. Hein (2015) has recently reviewed the evidence for a set of developed capitalist economies since the early 1980s and finds ample empirical support for falling labour income shares and increasing inequality in the personal/household distribution of market incomes with only a few exceptions, increasing inequality in the personal/household distribution of disposable income in most of the countries, an increase in the income share of the very top incomes not only in the USA and the UK, but also in several other countries for which data are available, with rising top management salaries as one of the major driving forces. Reviewing the empirical literature on the determinants of functional income distribution against the background of the Kaleckian theory of income distribution, it is argued that features of finance-dominated capitalism have contributed to the falling labour income share since the early 1980s through three main channels: the falling bargaining power of trade unions, rising profit claims imposed in particular by increasingly powerful rentiers and a change in the sectoral composition of the economy in favour of the financial corporate sector and at the expense of the non-financial corporate sector or the public sector with higher labour income shares. In Hein et al. (2017), the relative importance of these factors has been analysed for the six countries which are included in the current study, too.

2. Regarding investment in the capital stock, financialisation has meant increasing shareholder power vis-à-vis firms and workers, the demand for an increasing rate of return on equity held by rentiers, and an alignment of management with shareholder interests through short-run performance related pay schemes, such as bonuses, stock option programmes, and so on. On the one hand, this has imposed short-termism on management and has caused a decrease in management's animal spirits with respect to real investment in the capital stock and long-run growth of the firm, and increasing preference for financial investment, generating high profits in the short run. On the other hand, it has drained internal means of finance available for real investment purposes from non-financial corporations, through increasing dividend payments and share buybacks in order to boost stock prices and thus shareholder value. These 'preference' and 'internal means of finance' channels should each have negative partial effects on firms' real investment in capital stock. Econometric evidence for these two channels has been supplied by Stockhammer (2004), Van Treeck (2008), Orhangazi (2008), Onaran et al. (2011), Davis (2018), and Tori and Onaran (2016, 2017), confirming a depressing effect of increasing shareholder value orientation on investment in the capital stock, in particular for the USA but also for other economies, like the UK, France and other Western European countries.
3. Regarding consumption, financialisation has generated an increasing potential for wealth-based and debt-financed consumption in some countries, thus creating the potential to compensate for the depressing demand effects of financialisation, which have been imposed on the economy via re-distribution and the depressing impact of shareholder value orientation on real investment. Stock market and housing price booms have each increased notional wealth against which households were willing to borrow. Financial deregulation, changing financial norms, new financial instruments (credit card debt, home equity lending), deterioration of creditworthiness standards, triggered by securitisation of mortgage debt and 'originate and distribute' strategies of commercial banks, made credit increasingly available to low income, low wealth households, in particular. This potentially allowed for consumption to rise faster than median income and

thus to stabilise aggregate demand. But it also generated increasing debt-income ratios of private households. Several studies have shown that financial and housing wealth was a significant determinant of consumption, particularly in the USA, but also in countries like the UK, France, Italy, Japan and Canada (Boone and Girouard 2002; Ludvigson and Steindl 1999; Mehra 2001; Onaran et al. 2011). Furthermore, Barba and Pivetti (2009), Cynamon and Fazzari (2008), Guttmann and Plihon (2010), and van Treeck (2014) have presented extensive case studies on wealth-based and debt-financed consumption, with a focus on the USA. However, Kim (2013, 2016) in two recent studies on the USA has found that although new credit to households will boost aggregate demand and output in the short run, the effects of household debt variables on output and growth turn negative in the long run. This indicates contradictory effects of the flow of new credit and the stock of debt on consumption.
4. The liberalisation of international capital markets and capital accounts has allowed for rising and persistent current account imbalances at the global, but also at the regional levels, in particular within the Eurozone, as has been analysed by several authors, including Hein (2012, Chapter 6; 2014, Chapter 10), Stockhammer (2015), and UNCTAD (2009).

Under the conditions of the dominance of finance, income re-distribution at the expense of labour and low-income-households, and weak investment in the capital stock, different demand and growth regimes may emerge, as has been analysed by the authors mentioned in the previous paragraph, using different terminologies. Considering the growth contributions of the main demand aggregates (private consumption, public consumption, investment, net exports) and the sectoral financial balances of the main macroeconomic sectors (private household sector, financial and non-financial corporate sectors, government sector, external sector), in the current contribution three broad types of regimes will be distinguished: (a) a 'debt-led private demand boom' regime, (b) an 'export-led mercantilist' regime and (c) a 'domestic demand-led' regime.

The debt-led private demand boom regime is characterised by negative or close to zero financial balances of the private household sectors, which means that major parts of the private household sector have negative saving rates out of current income, are hence running current deficits, financed by increasing their stock of debt and/or reducing their stock of assets. These private household deficits are increased by corporate deficits and thus we have deficits of the private domestic sectors as a whole. The external sector has positive financial balances, which means that 'debt-led private demand boom' countries are usually running current account deficits. We have high growth contributions of private domestic demand, in particular private consumption, financed by credit to a considerable extent, and negative growth contributions of the balance of goods and services, driving the current account into deficit in the medium to long run.

The 'export-led mercantilist' regime is characterised by positive financial balances of the domestic sectors as a whole, and hence negative financial balances of the external sector, and thus, current account surpluses. The growth contributions of domestic demand are rather small or even negative in certain years, and growth is mainly driven by positive contributions of the balance of goods and services and hence rising net exports.

The 'domestic demand-led' regime is characterised by positive financial balances of the private household sector. Here, it is usually the government and, to a certain degree, the corporate sector, running deficits. The external sector is roughly balanced, with only slight deficits or surpluses. The 'domestic demand-led' countries are thus usually running balanced current accounts in the medium run, at least in the period before the crisis. We have positive growth contributions of domestic demand without credit-financed consumption, and slightly negative or positive growth contributions of the balance of goods and services on average over some medium run.

The demand and growth regimes can be distinguished by considering first the financial balances of the main macroeconomic sectors: the private sector, with the private household sector, the financial, and non-financial corporate sectors as sub-sectors, the government sector, and the external sector. Second, the growth contributions of the main demand aggregates are of interest. These are the growth contributions of private consumption, public consumption, as well as private and public investment, which sum up to the growth contribution of domestic demand, and then the growth contribution of the balance of goods and services, i.e. of net exports. On the one hand, this provides some information about the main drivers of growth, and, on the other hand, on how demand is financed. The sectoral financial balances of a country should sum up to zero, apart from statistical discrepancies, because a positive financial balance of one sector needs a respective negative financial balance of another sector. And the growth contributions of the demand aggregates should sum up to real GDP growth of the respective country.

In the pre-crisis period from 1999 until 2007, the USA, the UK and Spain were dominated by the 'debt-led private demand boom' regime. In this period, these countries faced rising inequality, i.e. falling wage shares in the USA and Spain, but a constant wage share in the UK, rising top income shares in all three countries and rising Gini coefficients for market and disposable household income in the USA and the UK, but constant household or personal income inequality measured by these indices in Spain (Table 1). In the pre-crisis period, these countries were characterised by negative financial balances of their domestic private sectors and negative or, in the UK, close to zero financial balances of the private household sectors, in particular (Table 2). The corporate sectors were in deficit, too. The external sectors were the surplus sectors, and the countries following the 'debt-led private demand boom' regime were thus characterised by current account deficits and negative net exports. As typical for this regime, we see high growth contributions of private domestic demand, and of private consumption demand in particular, financed by household deficits and thus rising credit to a

Table 1 Distribution trends for selected OECD countries before and after the financial and economic crisis 2007–9

			USA	UK	Spain	Germany	Sweden	France
Distribution trends	Adjusted wage share	Before	–	0	–	–	–	–
		After	–	–	–	0	0	+
	Top income share	Before	+	+	+	+	+	+
		After	+	–	–	?	0	0
	Gini coefficients	Before	+	+	0	+	+	0
		After	+	0	+	+	0	–

Notes + tendency to increase, – tendency to decrease, 0 no tendency, ? no data
Before: Early 1990s until the crisis 2007–9, After: after the crisis 2007–9
Source Hein et al. (2017)

Table 2 Key macroeconomic variables for selected OECD countries, average annual values per period

	USA		UK		Spain		Germany		Sweden		France	
	1999–2007	2008–2016	1999–2007	2008–2016	1999–2007	2008–2016	1999–2007	2008–2016	1999–2007	2008–2016	1999–2007	2008–2016
Financial balances of external sector as a share of nominal GDP, per cent	4.0	2.7	2.0	3.7	5.6	1.7	−2.4	−6.9	−6.4	−5.8	−0.7	2.3
Financial balances of public sector as share of nominal GDP, per cent	−3.0	−7.8	−1.7	−6.6	0.2	−7.5	−2.3	−0.8	1.1	−0.2	−2.5	−4.7
Financial balance of private sector as a share of nominal GDP, per cent	−0.9	5.2	−0.3	3.0	−5.8	5.8	4.7	7.7	5.3	6.0	3.2	2.4
– Financial balance of private household sector as a share of nominal GDP, per cent	−0.8	3.4	0.6	1.2	−1.0	1.8	5.0	5.1	2.4	6.6	3.4	3.6
– Financial balance of the corporate sector as a share of nominal GDP, per cent	−0.1	1.8	−0.8	1.8	−4.0	4.2	−0.3	2.5	2.8	−0.7	−0.2	−1.2
Real GDP growth, per cent	2.9	1.3	2.9	1.0	3.9	0.0	1.6	1.0	3.4	1.5	2.3	0.6
Growth contribution of domestic demand including stocks, percentage points	3.3	1.1	3.3	0.8	4.8	−1.2	0.8	1.0	2.7	1.7	2.6	0.8
– Growth contribution of private consumption, percentage points	2.3	1.1	2.3	0.5	2.2	−0.3	0.5	0.6	1.4	0.8	1.4	0.5
– Growth contribution of public consumption, percentage points	0.3	0.0	0.6	0.2	0.8	0.1	0.1	0.4	0.2	0.4	0.4	0.3
– Growth contribution of gross fixed capital formation, percentage points	0.7	0.1	0.5	0.0	1.7	−1.0	0.2	0.2	1.1	0.4	0.8	0.0
Growth contribution of the balance of goods and services, percentage points	−0.4	0.1	−0.3	0.0	−0.9	1.2	0.8	0.1	0.7	−0.2	−0.3	−0.2
Net exports of goods and services as a share of nominal GDP, per cent	−4.3	−3.3	−2.4	−2.2	−3.6	0.5	3.6	6.1	6.7	5.1	0.6	−1.9

Note Growth contributions of private consumption, public consumption and growth fixed capital formation may not sum up to growth contribution of domestic demand, because the latter also includes the change in inventories/stocks
Source European Commission (2017), own calculations

considerable degree. Private consumption contributed more than 55% to GDP growth in the case of Spain, and up to close to 80%, in the cases of the USA and the UK. The growth contributions of the balance of goods and services were negative and thus reduced GDP growth, most pronouncedly in Spain. The 'debt-led private demand boom' countries were thus the world demand engines before the crisis, mainly relying on increasing private debt, and household debt in particular.[1]

The 'export-led mercantilist' regime in the pre-crisis period dominated in Germany and Sweden. Here, we also see rising inequality, i.e. falling labour income shares, rising top income shares and increasing Gini coefficients for market and disposable incomes of households (Table 1). For the 'export-led mercantilist' countries, we observe positive financial balances of the domestic sectors as a whole, with significantly positive financial balances of the private sector, and a deficit of the public sector in Germany and a surplus in Sweden (Table 2). The private sector balance in Germany was composed of a significant surplus of private households and a small deficit in the corporate sector, whereas in Sweden both sub-sectors contributed to the private sector surplus. The external sector was in deficit in both countries, and considerably so in Sweden. These countries were thus running current account surpluses and positive balances of goods and services. In both countries, the growth contributions of domestic demand were rather small, and in Germany even negative in certain years. Private consumption only accounted for a bit more than 30% of GDP growth in the case of Germany and for 40% in the case of Sweden, each on average over the period. Growth was mainly driven by positive contributions of the balance of goods and services and hence rising net exports, which contributed about 50% in the case of Germany and 20% in the case of Sweden to GDP growth. These countries were thus free-riding on dynamic world demand generated by the 'debt-led private demand' boom countries in particular.[2]

Finally, we have in between the two extremes the 'domestic demand-led' regime, which in the pre-crisis period can be found in France.

[1]For more country specific information on these three debt-led private demand boom economies, before and after the crisis, see for example, Evans (2016) on the US, Lepper et al. (2016) on the UK and Ferreiro et al. (2016) on Spain.

[2]For more country specific information on these two export-led mercantilist economies, before and after the crisis, see for example, Detzer and Hein (2016) on Germany and Stenfors (2016) on Sweden.

Here, we also see rising inequality, as reflected in the falling labour income share and in rising top income shares, despite constant Gini coefficients for market and disposable income (Table 1). The French economy was characterised by positive financial balances of the private household sector and of the private sector as a whole (Table 2). Furthermore, we have slightly negative financial balances of the external sectors, and hence small current account and net export surpluses. Growth was exclusively driven by domestic demand, with relevant contributions by private consumption, however, without drawing on rising household credit, since private household financial balances remained considerably positive. Growth contributions of the balance of goods and services were slightly negative.[3]

The countries following the two extreme regimes before the crisis, the 'debt-led private demand boom' regime and the 'export-led mercantilist' regime, generated rising current account imbalances in the global economy, but also within the Eurozone (Hein 2013/14, 2017b). Apart from Germany and Sweden, mainly China and Japan, but also Argentina, Canada and Russia were among the surplus countries, and, apart from the USA, the UK and Spain, we had Italy, Turkey, South Africa and Australia among the deficit countries (IMF 2017). These global imbalances then led to the severity of the financial crisis and the Great Recession.

3 Distribution and Growth Before the Crisis: Stylised Facts and Regimes in Stylised Marxian and Kaleckian Models

Let us now present and compare the two extreme growth regimes before the crisis, the 'debt-led private demand boom' and the 'export-led mercantilist' regime, in a stylised Marxian and also in a stylised Kaleckian model of distribution and growth. For this purpose, the method of model closure is applied, as already presented in Hein (2017a) for a

[3]For more country specific information on the domestic demand-led economy of France, before and after the crisis, see, for example, Cournilleau and Creel (2016).

comparison of basic old neoclassical, new neoclassical, classical/Marxian and different versions of post-Keynesian growth theories. In what follows, the focus is on Marxian and Kaleckian models. In essence, we start with two equations for the basic model, and then further equations are added for each of the approaches in order to close the model. Each approach can then be described graphically in a two-quadrant system by the relationship between the rate of growth and the rate of profit, on the one hand, and by the relationship between the rate of profit and the rate of capacity utilisation, on the other. This presentation can then be used, first, to show the properties of the 'debt-led private demand boom' and the 'export-led mercantilist' regime from the two perspectives, and second, to discuss the effects of rising inequality and behavioural changes in the period leading to the Great Financial Crisis and the Great Recession.

3.1 The Basic Model

An open economy is assumed with a primitive government sector, which only appears as a deficit spending sector drawing on credit generated in the financial sector, so that taxation issues can be ignored. The private sector is composed of two classes, workers and capitalists, the latter including the financial capitalists or the rentiers. Capitalists own the means of production and receive profits, which are partly consumed and partly saved—buying assets issued by the corporate sector, and thus the capitalists themselves, or by the government, or depositing parts of the profits with the financial sector, which is also owned by the capitalists and not explicitly modelled here. Capitalists control the capital stock, hire labour, organise the production process and decide about investment and thus the expansion of the capital stock. For the latter, they draw on their own means of finance, issue stocks or corporate bonds or draw on credit endogenously generated and granted by the financial sector. By assumption, these transactions take place within the capitalist class and they are not modelled here. Workers offer labour power to capitalists and receive wages, which they partly use in order to purchase consumption goods and partly save. However, the propensity to save out of wages is much lower than the propensity to save out of profits.

In our model economy, a homogenous output (Y) is produced combining direct labour (L) and a non-depreciating capital stock (K) in the production process using a fixed coefficients production technology with a constant labour-output ratio ($a = L/Y$) and a constant capital-potential output ratio ($v = K/Y^p$). The homogeneous output can be used for consumption and investment purposes. For the sake of simplicity, overhead labour, depreciation of the capital stock, as well as raw materials and intermediate products are not considered. The rate of profit (r) relating the flow of profits (Π) to the nominal capital stock (pK) can be decomposed into the profit share (h), relating profits to nominal income (pY), the rate of capacity utilisation (u), relating actual output to potential output given by the capital stock (Y^p) and the inverse of the capital-potential output ratio ($1/v$), relating the capital stock to potential output:

$$r = \frac{\Pi}{pK} = \frac{\Pi}{pY}\frac{Y}{Y^p}\frac{Y^p}{K} = hu\frac{1}{v} \quad (1)$$

Our assumption regarding saving translates into the following domestic saving rate (σ), which relates the flow of total domestic saving (S) to the value of the capital stock:

$$\begin{aligned}\sigma &= \frac{S_\Pi + S_W + S_G}{pK} = \frac{s_\Pi \Pi + s_W W - D}{pK} = s_\Pi h\frac{u}{v} + s_W(1-h)\frac{u}{v} - d \\ &= [(s_\Pi - s_W)h + s_W]\frac{u}{v} - d, \quad 0 \le s_W < s_\Pi \le 1, \quad d \ge 0.\end{aligned} \quad (2)$$

Total saving is composed of saving out of profits (S_Π), saving out of wages (S_W) and government saving (S_G), which is zero or negative in our model, because we ignore taxation and only allow for government deficits ($D = -S_G \ge 0$). The saving rate is thus determined by the propensities to save out of profits (s_Π) and out of wages (s_W), by the components of the profit rate from Eq. (1), as well as by the government deficit rate (d), which is treated as a long-run exogenous policy variable. A rise in the profit share raises the saving rate, as well an increase in capacity utilisation, the functional propensities to save, and a reduction in the government deficit rate.

Next, the Marxian and Kaleckian closures of the model generating long-run distribution and growth equilibria for the 'debt-led private demand boom' and the 'export-led mercantilist' regimes are introduced. Then the cet. par. effects of changes in income shares for both regimes are examined, and finally, the replication of the stylised facts in the pre-crisis period is presented, taking into account rising inequality and further behavioural changes. The Marxian approach is discussed first, and then, we move to the Kaleckian approach.

3.2 Marxian Closure, Regime Generation and Effects of Distributional and Behavioural Changes Before the Crisis

Karl Marx (1867, 1885, 1894) in most of *Capital Vol. I – III* assumes that, in the long run, functional income distribution is determined by socio-institutional factors and power relationships determining a subsistence or conventional real wage rate. For a given production technology, the rate of profit then becomes a residual variable. With functional income distribution determined in this way, the rate of profit, together with capitalists' propensity to have and to accumulate thus determines the long-run equilibrium rates of capital accumulation and growth.[4] In this approach, in essence the validity of Say's law in Ricardo's version is assumed to hold in the long run[5]: Profits saved are completely used for investment and accumulation, so that no problems of effective demand for the economy as a whole arise in long-run growth. With positive saving out of wages, as well as the inflow of net foreign saving, we also have to assume that these are also channelled towards investment in the long run. For Marxians ignoring effective demand constraints in the long run does not mean that the growth path is characterised by full employment. On the contrary, unemployment is considered to be a persistent

[4]For a basic overview over Marxian theories of capital accumulation, see Shaikh (1978).

[5]Marx's theory also allows for another interpretation, in which aggregate demand, finance, credit and interest rates matter for the determination of long-run accumulation and growth, as for example Argitis (2001) and Hein (2006) have discussed.

feature of capitalism constraining distribution claims of workers and thus providing the conditions for positive profits, capital accumulation and growth. Furthermore from this perspective, capital accumulation feeds back on the rate of profit in the long run, and causes a tendency of the rate of profit to fall. The reason is a specific nature of technical progress causing a rising capital-potential output ratio, i.e. Marx's notion of a rising 'organic composition of capital', which he already explained in *Capital Vol. I*.

Adding an orthodox Marxian closure to our model, we have that productive capacities given by the capital stock are used at their normal or target rate (u_n) in the long-run growth equilibrium:

$$u = u_n \tag{3M}$$

Functional income distribution is determined by socio-institutional factors and distribution conflict. A subsistence or conventional real wage rate (w_s^r), for a given production technology and thus a given labour-output ratio, determines the profit share:

$$h = \frac{pY - wL}{pY} = 1 - w_s^r a \tag{4M}$$

with w representing the nominal wage rate. In the long run, the capital-potential output ratio may be rising with capital accumulation and growth, due to the Marxian type of technical change:

$$v = v(g), \quad \frac{\partial v}{\partial g} \geq 0 \tag{5M}$$

The net export rate (b) relates net exports (NX), as the difference between nominal exports (pX) and imports ($p_f eM$), to the nominal capital stock, with p_f representing the foreign price level and e the nominal exchange rate, each taken to be exogenous here. In this orthodox Marxian approach, net exports can be considered to be given by net capital flows, which are guided by the domestic (r) and the foreign rate of profit (r_f), as well as by a set of further institutional factors (z_i), as the openness and the degree of liberalisation of the capital account and the capital market of the respective country:

$$b = \frac{pX - p_f eM}{pK} = \frac{NX}{pK} = -\sigma_f = b\left[\left(r_f - r\right), z_i\right], \quad \frac{\partial b}{\partial\left(r_f - r\right)} > 0, \; \frac{\partial b}{\partial z_i} > 0 \quad \text{(6M)}$$

Institutional factors are treated as exogenous parameters, which remain constant whenever domestic profit rates change. Taken the foreign profit rate as given, net exports are thus negatively related to the domestic profit rate, because an increase in the domestic profit rate will reduce capital exports and increase capital imports.

Investment is given by domestic saving plus foreign saving (σ_f) flowing into the domestic economy associated with negative net exports ($\sigma_f = -b$), without explaining how income, profits and saving are generated in the first place. Each variable is normalised by the domestic capital stock, so that we have for the domestic rate of capital accumulation and growth (g):

$$g \equiv \sigma + \sigma_f \equiv \sigma - b \quad \text{(7M)}$$

Figure 2a presents the Marxian distribution and growth model for a 'debt-led private demand boom' economy and Fig. 2b for an 'export-led mercantilist' economy. On the left-hand side of both figures, we have the relationship between the rate of profit and the rate of capacity utilisation, as in Eq. (1). Since modern Marxians assume that, in the long run, productive capacities given by the capital stock are used at the normal rate, the long-run normal rate of profit (r^*) is then determined by the profit share and by the capital-potential output ratio. A rise in the profit share means a clockwise rotation of the profit rate function; and a rise in the capital-potential output ratio makes the function rotate counter-clockwise. On the right hand side of Fig. 2a, b, we have the relationship between the rate of profit, the domestic saving rate, the accumulation rate and the net export rate from Eqs. (2), (6M) and (7M). Figure 2a shows a 'debt-led private demand boom' economy with a current account deficit; the domestic saving rate is falling short of the domestic rate of capital accumulation and the difference is made up of negative net exports and hence the respective capital inflows, which are rising when the domestic profit rate is increasing, holding the foreign profit rate constant. Figure 2b shows an 'export-led mercantilist economy' with a current account surplus; the domestic saving rate exceeds the rate of capital accumulation and the difference is made up by positive net exports and hence the respective capital outflows which are falling with an increase in the domestic profit rate in isolation.

The causality in the Marxian approach runs from the left hand side of Fig. 1a, b to the right hand side. Distribution conflict determines the profit share and together with the technical conditions of production, indicated by the capital-potential output ratio, the profit rate. The latter, together with the propensities to save out of profits and wages and the government deficit rate, as well as the net export rate, determines equilibrium capital accumulation and growth. Under these conditions, any rise in the profit share or an increase in inequality in the personal or household distribution of income, raising the functional propensities to consume out of wages and out of profits and the differential between them, should cause a higher saving rate and a higher rate of capital accumulation in both the 'debt-led private demand boom' economies and the 'export-led mercantilist' economies. The same holds true for any fall in the government deficit rate.

The effect of a rise in the profit share without any behavioural change in a simple Marxian model is shown for both regimes in Fig. 2a, b. A higher profit share causes a clockwise rotation in the profit rate function in the left-hand side of these figures, which will then lead to higher equilibrium domestic saving and accumulation rates. Net export rates fall, if the rise in profit shares and rates takes place in isolation and capital imports thus rise, as assumed here. However, if profit shares and rates rise globally such that relative profit rates do not change by international comparison, net export rates should not be affected by redistribution.[6]

[6]Rising inequality in personal and household incomes, leading to higher average propensities to save out of wages and out of profits and to a higher differential between these two rates, should shift the saving rate curves in Fig. 3a, b rightwards and rotate them clockwise. Long-run equilibrium saving and accumulation rates thus rise. The effect on net exports depends on the development of domestic profit rates relative to foreign rates and on other institutional factors determining international capital movements.

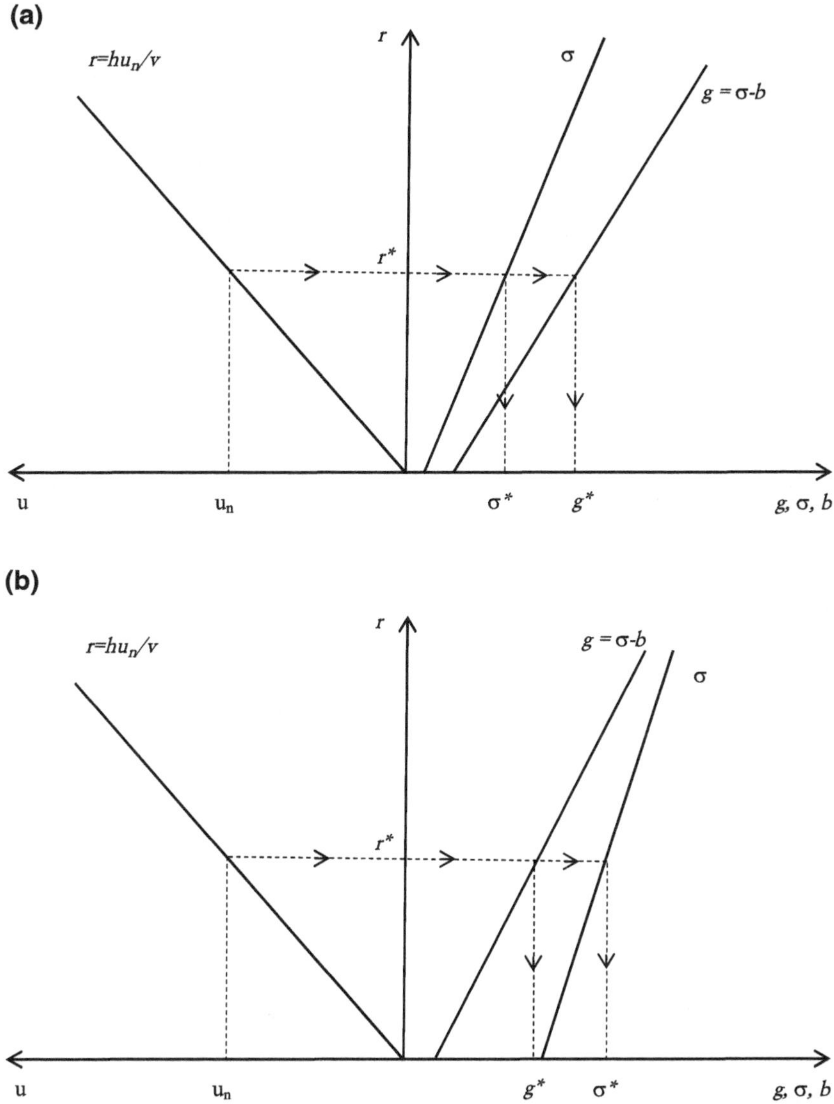

Fig. 1 A basic Marxian distribution and growth approach. **a** The 'debt-led private demand boom' regime. **b** The 'export-led mercantilist' regime

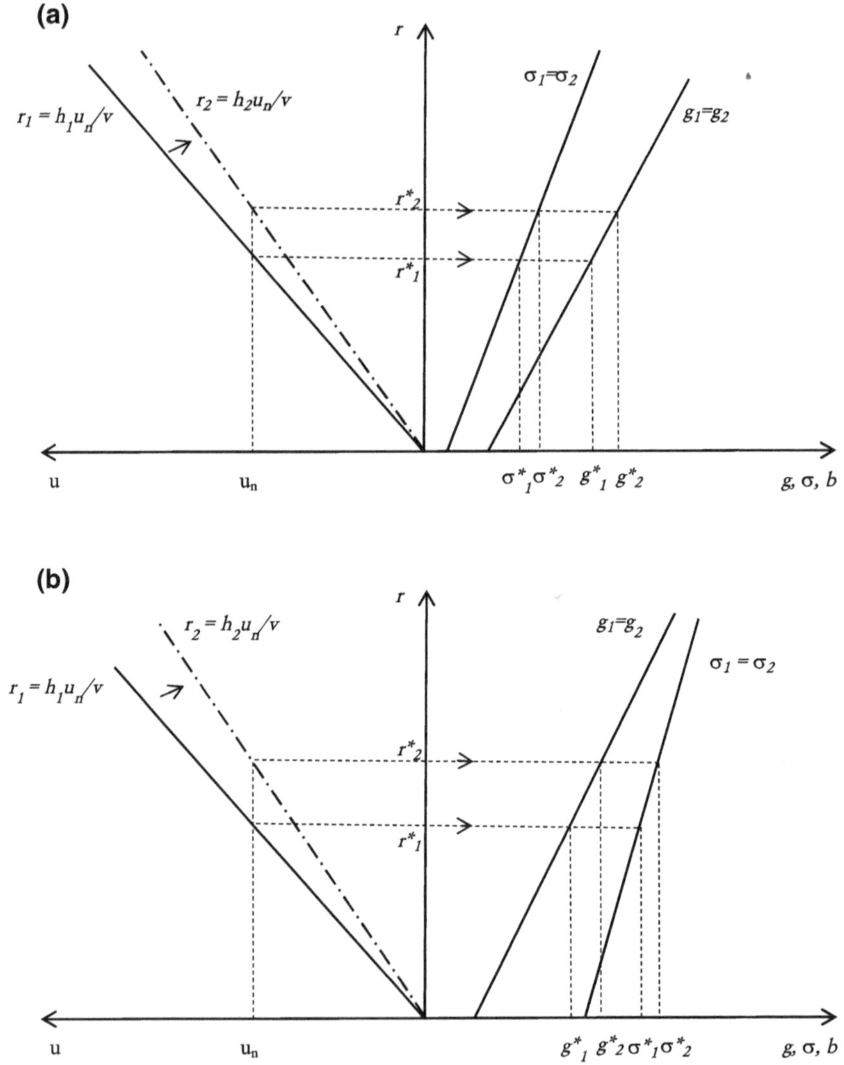

Fig. 2 A rising profit share in isolation in a basic Marxian approach. **a** The 'debt-led private demand boom' regime. **b** The 'export-led mercantilist' regime

However, the effects shown in Fig. 2a, b for an increase in the profit share are not consistent with the stylised facts summarised in Sect. 2 for the two regimes; they also contradict the stories several eminent Marxian authors have presented for the long-run period from the early 1980s until the Great Financial Crisis and the Great Recession. One of the leading proponents of the theory of 'the falling rate of profit due a rising organic composition of capital' (FRoP) and the resultant crisis of over-accumulation of capital, Shaikh (2011, 2016, Chapter 16), has put forward the following explanation. He argues that the long-run tendency of the normal or the maximum rate of profit to fall in the US non-financial business sector, due to Marxian technological progress causing a rising capital-potential output ratio in our model, was neutralised with respect to the rate of profit by redistribution at the expense of labour and thus by a rising profit share. This led to a constant trend for the total rate of profit, including interest and dividends, starting in the early 1980s, with remarkable cyclical fluctuations. A reduction in the interest rate (i) even allowed for an increase in the rate of profit of enterprise ($r_n = r - i$). Most importantly, low interest rates together with the liberalisation and deregulation of credit and financial markets provided the conditions for increasing debt-financed expenditures, and debt-financed household consumption in the face of stagnating real wages and a falling wage share in particular. The associated rise in household debt-income ratios then provided the grounds for the Great Financial Crisis and the Great Recession.[7]

A similar explanation of the developments leading to the 2007–9 crisis in the USA is presented by Kotz (2009, 2013), a proponent of the US Social-Structure-of-Accumulation (SSA) approach. According to this approach, previous deep crises in the developed capitalist economies, as the crisis of the mid 1970s in the USA in particular, indicating the end of the Golden Age and the 'regulated capitalist SSA', were caused by fall in the rate of profit due to a profit squeeze, i.e. a rise in

[7]"In the neoliberal era (1983–2007, EH), cheap finance became a way to expand employment through finance-related activities like real estate booms, export-led growth, foreign remittance growth, and so on. The crisis put an end to most of that" (Shaikh 2016, p. 739).

the wage share, and thus problems in the 'production of profits'. The 2007–9 crisis of the 'neoliberal SSA' in the USA, established in the early 1980s, however, is seen to be caused by problems in the 'realization of profits'. Real wage growth falling short of productivity growth since the early 1980s, and thus a fall in the wage share, together with rising inequality in household incomes caused potential demand problems triggering falling rates of utilisation in manufacturing. The deregulation of the financial sector facilitating stock market and housing price booms in the 1990s and early 2000s and rising debt-financed household consumption provided temporary solutions to these demand problems. However, because of rising household debt-income ratios, these solutions turned out to be unsustainable when stock market and housing prices stopped rising, which then triggered the Great Financial Crisis and the Great Recession.[8]

Finally, also prominent proponents of the Marxian monopoly capitalism school relating capitalist crises or stagnation to rising concentration of capital, rising profit shares and falling wage shares and thus to a lack of consumption demand, like Foster and Magdoff (2009) and Foster and McChesney (2012) have come up with a similar explanation for the 2007–9 US crisis as the proponents of the two other Marxian schools. In their view, credit-financed consumption demand has countered the tendency towards under-consumption and stagnation inherent in monopoly capitalism. The conditions were provided by the liberalisation of the financial sector and the increasingly speculative booms in the stock and housing markets.[9] The crisis was then triggered by financial instability associated with speculation and by over-indebtedness of private households in particular.

[8]"The structural crisis of the neoliberal SSA finally arrived, not due to a falling rate of profit, but due to the collapse of unsustainable trends that were essential features of the neoliberal SSA and of its ability to promote capital accumulation" (Kotz 2013, p. 345).

[9]"It was this underlying stagnation tendency (…) which was the reason the economy became so dependent on financialisation – or decades-long series of ever-larger speculative financial bubbles. In fact, a dangerous feedback loop between stagnation and financial bubbles has now emerged, reflecting the fact that stagnation and financialisation are increasingly interdependent phenomena: a problem which we refer to (…) as the stagnation-financialisation trap" (Foster and McChesney 2012, p. 4).

The three main strands of Marxian distribution, growth and crises theories have thus come up with similar explanations of the main trends leading to the crisis in the USA: demand problems related to the redistribution of income at the expense of labour and low income households have temporarily been compensated by the rise in credit-financed expenditures, and in credit-financed private consumption in particular. The liberalisation and deregulation of the financial sector, which facilitated the stock market and housing price booms, on the one hand, creating the conditions for wealth effects on consumption, and the deterioration of creditworthiness standards, on the other hand, have been a pre-condition for this. However, the associated over-indebtedness of private households and financial instabilities then triggered the financial and economic crisis. This explanation is fully consistent with the basics of the monopoly capitalism school. The principle mechanisms in the FRoP and SSA/profit-squeeze approaches, however, do not seem to be of any (SSA) or only little (FRoP) relevance for the explanation of the recent crises.

Let us now try to integrate this Marxian consensus view on distribution and growth before the crisis into our stylised Marxian model. The focus of the outlines presented here has been on the USA as a 'debt-led private demand boom' economy before the crisis, but also a Marxian view on the pre-crisis processes in an 'export-led mercantilist' economy as a kind of mirror image can be provided. Let us start with Fig. 3a, which shows the pre-crisis processes in a 'debt-led private demand boom' regime from a stylised Marxian perspective. According to the Marxian view, the economy is operating at a target or normal rate of capacity utilisation in the long run, and the rise in the profit share—overcompensating the rise in the capital-potential output ration in the FRoP approach—thus leads to a rise in the long-run normal rate of profit from r_1^* to r_2^*. However, this does not lead to rising capital accumulation, because the average propensities to save out of profits and out of wages have fallen due to rising debt-financed consumption. This is indicated by a leftwards shift and a counter-clockwise rotation of the domestic saving function. This overcompensates the effect of a rising profit share and normal profit rate on the equilibrium domestic saving rate, which, therefore, falls from σ_1^* to σ_2^*. The fall in the equilibrium

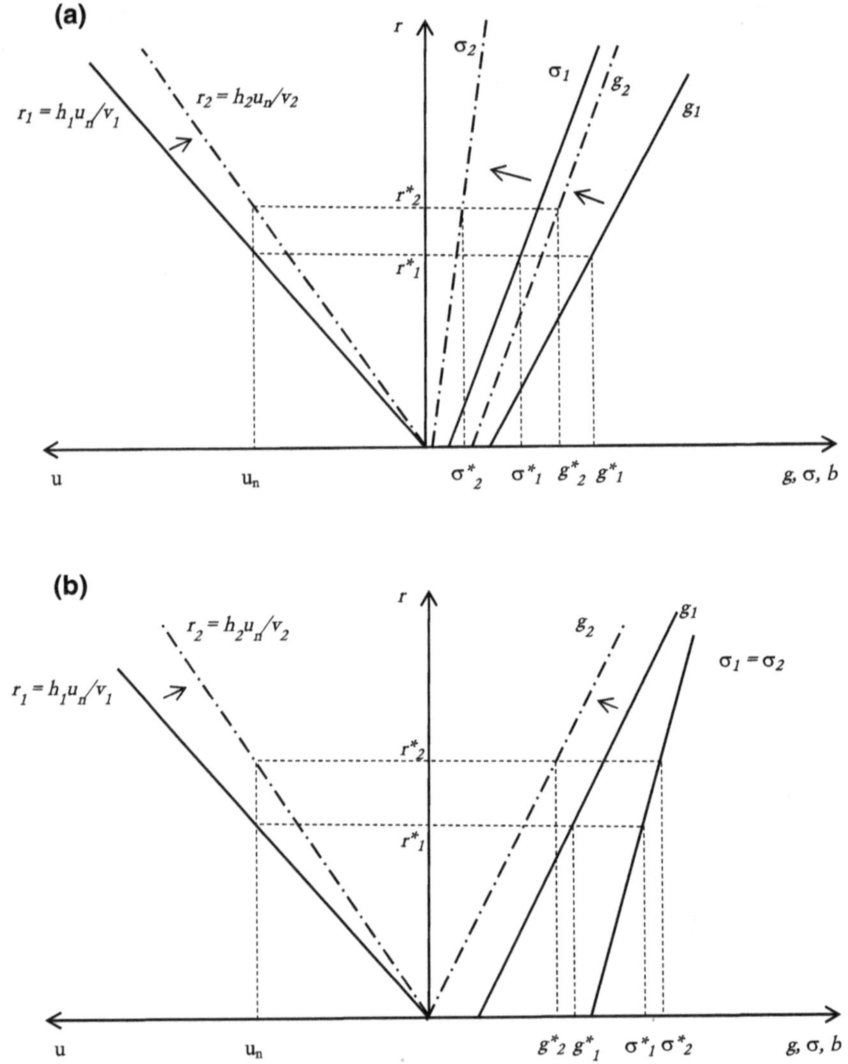

Fig. 3 Distributional and behavioural changes before the crises: a stylised Marxian approach. **a** The 'debt-led private demand boom' regime: rising profit share, rising rate of profit, falling average propensity to save due credit-financed consumption, and rising current account deficits/net capital imports. **b** The 'export-led mercantilist' regime: Rising profit share, rising rate of profit, rising average propensity to save, and rising current account surpluses/net capital exports

domestic saving rate is only partly compensated by an increase in the inflow of foreign saving triggered by a higher profit rate and an improvement of structural factors attracting foreign capital (financial market deregulation in particular) and associated with a rising current account deficits. Therefore, the equilibrium accumulation rate is falling as well, from g_1^* to g_2^*. The reason why this should happen, however, remains somewhat vague in this Marxian approach.

The pre-crisis processes associated with an increasing profit share and rising inequality in an 'export-led mercantilist' regime are shown in Fig. 3b. Since no compensating debt-financed consumption or rise in government deficits is at work in this regime, a rising profit share and a higher normal rate of profit is causing a higher equilibrium domestic saving rate, which thus increases from σ_1^* to σ_2^*. However, since capital is increasingly attracted by deregulated foreign capital markets promising higher rates of return (including speculative capital gains), capital outflows and current account surpluses are increasing, leading to a lower long-run equilibrium rate of domestic capital accumulation, which is falling from g_1^* to g_2^*. Again, it remains somewhat unclear in this Marxian approach why exactly domestic capital accumulation should shrink.

In the face of rising inequality and falling wage shares under the conditions of financialisation, the Marxian approach is thus able to generate 'profits without investment' constellations, i.e. rising normal rates of profits but falling rates of capital accumulation, for both the 'debt-led private demand boom' and the 'export-led mercantilist' economies, and thus to reproduce a stylised fact, which has been observed by several authors (Hein 2012; van Treeck 2009) for these two types of economies before the crises. The crucial condition is that the long-run increase in credit-financed expenditures, especially private consumption, in the 'debt-led private demand boom' economies, and thus a fall in the domestic saving rate here, more than absorbs the increase in long-run equilibrium domestic saving in the 'export-led mercantilist' economies triggered by rising inequality and a higher profit share, such that international capital re-allocation leads to a fall in capital accumulation in the 'export-led mercantilist' economies, too. Since domestic and foreign saving (and hence the current/capital account balance), and thus profitability in the long run drives investment in this Marxian approach, without explaining how rising profits and saving are realised in the first place, there is no independent role for the consideration of effective demand, and of investment independently of saving in particular. Therefore, this Marxian approach is unable to explicitly incorporate the effects of financialisation on business investment in the capital stock, which have been analysed in several studies referred to in Sect. 2 above, and to include these effects into the analysis of distributional effects in the different growth regimes under the conditions of rising financialisation before the crisis. Interestingly, neither Shaikh (2011; 2016, Chapter 16) nor Kotz (2009, 2013) provide any in-depth study of the changes in business investment behaviour in the neo-liberal or financialisation period. However, Foster and McChesney (2012, Chapter 2) from the Marxian monopoly capitalism school, which is closer to Kaleckian distribution and growth theory in principle, touch upon such an analysis and come up with observations and conclusions which are similar to those integrated into Kaleckian models of distribution and growth applied to the period of financialisation. Therefore, the following section turns towards the Kaleckian approach.

3.3 Kaleckian Closure, Regime Generation and Effects of Distributional and Behavioural Changes Before the Crisis

The stylised Marxian approach presented above suffers from the explicit consideration of the role of effective demand and of investment determination in long-run growth theory. Alternatively, we can now turn to the second generation of post-Keynesian distribution and growth models based on Michal Kalecki's (1954, 1971) and Josef Steindl's (1952) works. Here, the determination of income distribution by relative economic powers of capital and labour, mainly through firms' mark-up pricing on constant unit labour costs up to full capacity output in imperfectly competitive goods markets, is combined with the long-run independence of capital accumulation of firms from saving at the macroeconomic level, as a distinguishing feature of post-Keynesian distribution and growth models in general. Functional income distribution and hence the profit share are thus explained by relative economic powers of capital and labour, as in the Marxian approach. But then firms' investment decisions, together with net exports and government deficits, drive the system and saving adjusts through income and growth effects, with the rate of capacity utilisation as an accommodating variable beyond the short run.[10]

The effects of distributional changes on equilibrium capacity utilisation and growth in Kaleckian models depend on a variety of factors, as has been reviewed in Blecker (2002), Hein (2014, Chapter 6) and Lavoie (2014, Chapter 6.2). First, for a closed private economy the choice of the investment function, i.e. the relative importance of demand/utilisation and profitability indicators for investment decisions, has given rise to two variants of the model. The 'neo-Kaleckian' model, based on the works of Rowthorn (1981) and Dutt (1984), contains a strong accelerator effect of demand and no direct effect of profitability in the investment function. Without saving out of wages it generates uniquely expansionary effects of re-distribution in favour of the wage share on the rates of capacity utilisation, capital accumulation, growth and profit. Demand and growth are thus uniquely wage led and the 'paradox of costs' is valid, i.e. a fall in the profit share will trigger an increase in the profit rate. The 'post-Kaleckian' model, based on the works of Bhaduri and Marglin (1990) and Kurz (1990), however, also contains a direct profitability effect in the investment function. Therefore, its closed economy version without saving out of wages is able to generate wage- or profit-led regimes of demand and growth, depending on the relative weights of accelerator and profitability terms in the investment function and on the propensity to save from profits. Second, including international trade, the otherwise wage-led neo-Kaleckian model may also turn profit-led through a strong positive effect of the profit share on net exports, as has already been shown by

[10]The treatment of the rate of capacity utilisation as a long-run endogenous variable has been criticised, as reviewed by Hein (2014, Chapter 11) and Lavoie (2014, Chapter 6.5).

Blecker (1989). Third, including personal income distribution, wage inequality, relative income concerns and access to debt into the consumption function of the model, several recent contributions have shown that this might turn an otherwise wage-led demand and growth economy seemingly profit led, as recently reviewed by Hein and Prante (2018).

Adding a Kaleckian closure to our basic model, the rate of capacity utilisation is treated as a medium- to long-run endogenous variable. The profit share, and thus functional income distribution, is mainly determined by the mark-up (m) in firms' pricing in imperfectly competitive markets[11]:

$$h = h(\bar{m}), \quad \frac{\partial h}{\partial m} > 0 \tag{3K}$$

The mark-up itself is affected by several factors, such as the degree of competition in the goods market, the bargaining power of workers and also unit overhead costs, which are all treated as exogenously given. The capital-potential output ratio is also considered as an exogenous variable determined by technology, which does not systematically respond to distribution and activity variables in the model, different from the Marxian view:

$$v = \bar{v} \tag{4K}$$

With the profit share and the capital-potential output ratio as exogenously given variables, the rate of capacity utilisation becomes the variable adjusting the profit rate (Eq. 1) to its equilibrium value. As principle determinants in the investment function in Kaleckian models, we have firms' or managements' animal spirits (α), sometimes taken to represent the firms' assessment of the long-run growth trend of the economy. Furthermore, the (expected) rate of profit is of relevance, because it indicates internal means of finance required for attracting external investment finance, according to Kalecki's (1937) 'principle

[11]For the inclusions of the effects of costs of imported raw materials and intermediate products on the domestic profit share see Hein (2014, Chapter 7.3).

of increasing risk'. Also the dynamics of demand as a determinant of investment are reflected in the rate of profit through changes in capacity utilisation. Apart from animal spirits, we can thus include the three principle determinants of the profit rate from Eq. (1) into the Kaleckian accumulation function:

$$g = g(\alpha, h, u, v), \quad \frac{\partial g}{\partial \alpha} > 0, \frac{\partial g}{\partial h} \geq 0, \frac{\partial g}{\partial u} > 0, \frac{\partial g}{\partial v} = 0 \quad \text{(5K)}$$

Investment decisions will thus positively depend on the profit share and the rate of capacity utilisation, because each increase the (expected) rate of profit, cet. par.. Neo-Kaleckians, however, would insist that the partial effect of a change in the profit share is irrelevant for firms' decisions to invest, and hence that $\partial g/\partial h = 0$. In order to simplify the further exposition, but also for empirical reasons, this view is followed here.[12] Regarding exogenous changes in the capital-potential output ratio through technical change, the partial effects on investment decisions are not clear. On the one hand, a higher capital-potential output ratio means a lower rate of profit, which should dampen investment. On the other hand, however, a higher capital-potential output ratio means that a certain increase in demand requires a higher increase in the capital stock, which should boost investment. The sign of the sum of these two opposing effects is not clear ex ante, so that any direct effect of changes in the capital-potential output ratio on investment is disregard in what follows, and we treat the capital potential-output ratio as a constant, even in the face of technical change.[13]

The net export rate (b) is negatively affected by domestic capital accumulation and growth triggering rising imports, and positively affected by foreign accumulation and growth (g_f) generating rising exports.

[12]Most of the empirical estimations of the post-Kaleckian model find only little or no significant effects of profitability variables on investment. See Hein (2014, Chapter 7), Blecker (2016) and Stockhammer (2017) for recent reviews.

[13]Technical change is thus assumed to be 'Harrod-neutral', as in many post-Keynesian/Kaleckian distribution and growth models (Hein 2014, Chapter 8).

Also the real exchange rate ($e^r = ep_f/p$), given by the nominal exchange rate (e), the foreign price index (p_f) and the domestic price index (p), may have a positive effect on net exports, if exports and imports are price sensitive and the Marshall-Lerner conditions holds. It is assumed that the real exchange rate is positively related to the profit share[14]:

$$b = \frac{pX - p_f eM}{pK} = \frac{NX}{pK} = b\left[g, g_f, e^r(h)\right], \quad \frac{\partial b}{\partial g} < 0, \frac{\partial b}{\partial g_f} > 0, \frac{\partial b}{\partial e^r} \geq 0, \frac{\partial e^r}{\partial h} > 0 \tag{6K}$$

Finally, Eq. (7K) provides the goods market equilibrium condition:

$$g^* + b^* = \sigma^* \tag{7K}$$

Next, the two extreme regimes are presented, the 'debt-led private demand boom' regime and the 'export-led mercantilist' regime, in this stylised neo-Kaleckian distribution and growth model making use of Fig. 4a, b.[15] In the right hand quadrants we have the determination of the long-run goods market equilibrium from Eq. (7K), with the domestic saving rate from Eq. (2) and the accumulation rate from Eq. (5K) as positive functions of the rate of profit (or its components), and the net export rate from Eq. (6K) as a negative function of the domestic growth and accumulation rate, for a given profit share, real exchange rate and foreign growth rate. Note that the net export rate is negative for the 'debt-led private demand boom' regime in Fig. 4a and positive for the 'export-led mercantilist' regime in Fig. 4b. The goods market equilibrium then determines the equilibrium rate of capital accumulation, domestic saving rate (with the government deficit rate as an exogenous component), net export rate, as well as the equilibrium rate of capacity utilisation and, for a given profit share and capital-potential output ratio, also the equilibrium rate of profit in the left hand quadrant. A higher equilibrium accumulation and/or net export rate is thus associated with higher equilibrium rates of capacity utilisation and profit,

[14]See Hein (2014, Chapter 7.3) for a more detailed open economy Kaleckian distribution and growth model.

[15]More extensive and detailed elaborations on these regimes in Kaleckian stock-flow consistent models can be found in Hein (2014, Chapter 10) and in Detzer (2018), for example.

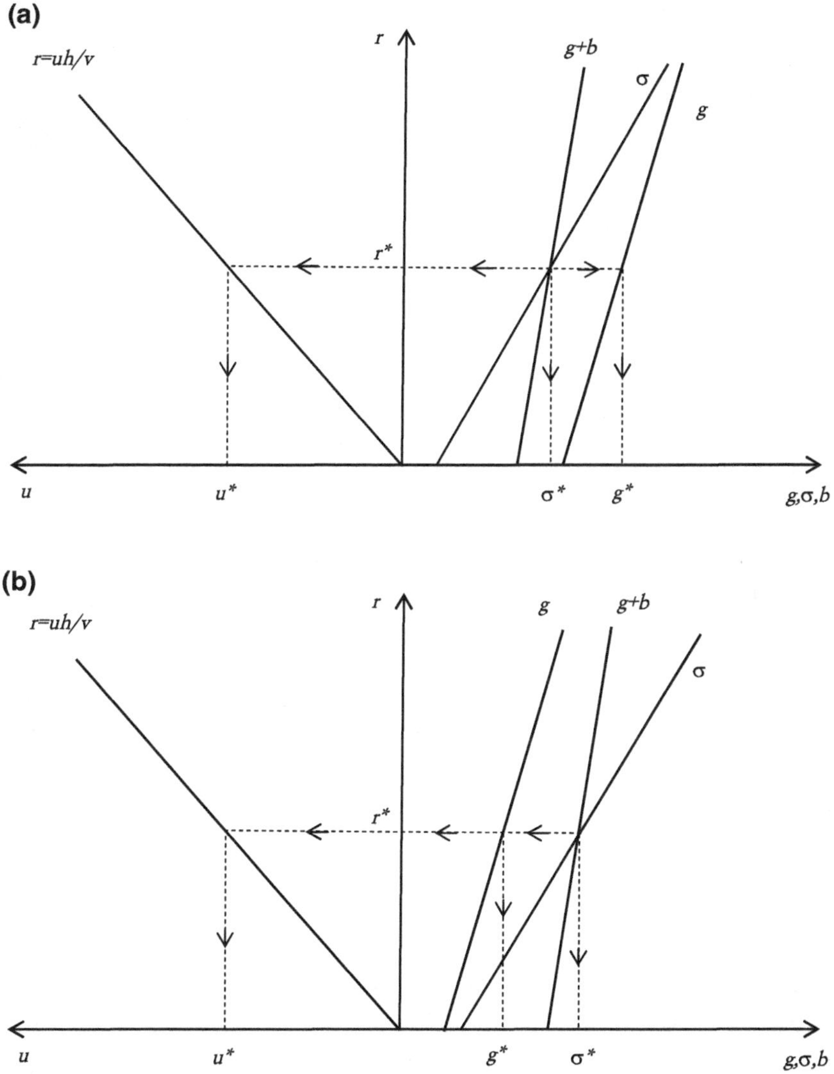

Fig. 4 A basic Kaleckian distribution and growth approach. **a** The 'debt-led private demand boom' regime. **b** The 'export-led mercantilist' regime

as are a lower domestic saving rate and thus a higher government deficit rate. In Fig. 4a, b this can be brought about by a rightward shift (higher animal spirits) or a clockwise rotation (higher utilisation rates triggering a higher responsiveness of the accumulation rate to a given rate of profit) of the accumulation function, by a rightward shift of the net export function (due to higher foreign growth or improved domestic price competitiveness), or by a leftward shift (rise in the government deficit rate, fall in the average propensity to save out of wages) or a counter-clockwise rotation (fall in the differential between the propensities to save out of profits and out of wages) of the saving function.

Any rise in the profit share will affect both the profit rate-curve in the left quadrant and potentially also the accumulation-curve in the right quadrant of the graphical presentation of the neo-Kaleckian model in Fig. 5a, b. On the one hand, a higher profit share causes a clockwise rotation of the *r*-curve, and, on the other hand, a higher profit share also affects the accumulation function and thus the *g*-curve. With a strong responsiveness of investment towards utilisation ($\partial g/\partial u$) and a very weak or even zero reaction towards the profit share ($\partial g/\partial h$), as assumed in the neo-Kaleckian model, a higher profit share and thus a lower rate of utilisation for every rate of profit, will trigger a counter-clockwise rotation of the accumulation function in the right hand side quadrants of Fig. 5a, b. Every rate of profit is now associated with a lower rate of utilisation, and firms' investment responds accordingly. Finally, if we again assume that the rise in the profit share takes place in a single country in isolation, net exports will slightly improve, so that the rotation of the ($g+ b$)-curve slightly deviates from the rotation of the *g*-curve. Taking these effects together, we can see that both the 'debt-led private demand boom' regime in Fig. 5a and the 'export-led mercantilist' regime in Fig. 5b are wage led: A rise in the profit share, cet. par., will lead to a fall in the equilibrium rates of capacity utilisation from u_1^* to u_2^*, profit from r_1^* to r_2^*, capital accumulation from g_1^* to g_2^*, and domestic saving from σ_1^* to σ_2^*. However, the equilibrium net export rates ($b^*=\sigma^*-g^*$) will rise in both regimes, assuming that the increase in the profit share and the concomitant improvement of price competitiveness raising exports and the fall in domestic capacity utilisation dampening imports take place in isolation. Obviously, if the rise

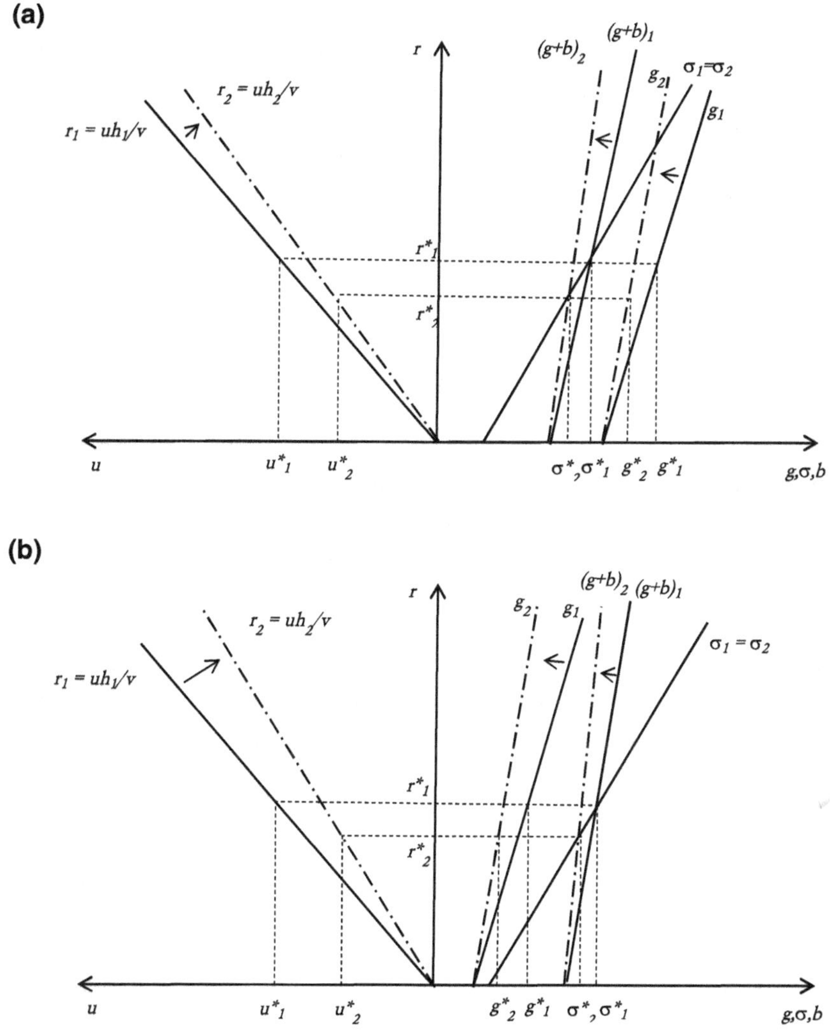

Fig. 5 A rising profit share in isolation in a basic neo-Kaleckian approach. **a** The 'debt-led private demand boom' regime. **b** The 'export-led mercantilist' regime

in the profit share takes place globally, thus in both regimes, neither will relative price competitiveness be improved nor will the respective export markets remain constant, so that an improvement of net exports cannot be taken for granted any more for individual countries and, of course, is impossible for all the countries taken together.[16]

In order to present the developments in the two regimes before the crisis in Fig. 6, further effects of financialisation and neoliberalism, as already outlined in Sect. 2 above, are taken into account.

Regarding investment in the capital stock, financialisation has meant increasing shareholder power vis-à-vis firms and workers. This has imposed short-termism on management and has caused a decrease in management's animal spirits with respect to real investment in the capital stock and long-run growth of the firm, and increasing preference for financial investment, generating high profits in the short run. On the other hand, paying out dividends and buying back shares in order to satisfy shareholders, has drained internal means of finance available for real investment purposes from non-financial corporations and thus required a higher total rate of profit to execute a certain rate of capital accumulation. The 'preference' and the 'internal means of finance' channel thus cause a leftwards shift and a counter-clockwise rotation of the accumulation function in both regimes, from g_1 to g_2, as can be seen in Fig. 6a, b.

Regarding the effects on consumption the two regimes have to be distinguished. In the 'debt-led private demand boom' regime we have increasing credit-financed consumption in particular. This has been due to relative income concerns ('keeping up with the Joneses'), the requirements to sustain necessary consumption in the face of falling wages, to considerable wealth effects on consumption associated with stock price and housing price booms, as well as to improved access to consumption credit due to financial innovations and liberalisation. A rising profit share and higher income inequality are thus associated with

[16]See Onaran and Galanis (2014) for supportive estimation results showing that globally simultaneous hikes in the profit share drastically reduce potentially positive effects on net exports and thus make overall wage-led results even more likely.

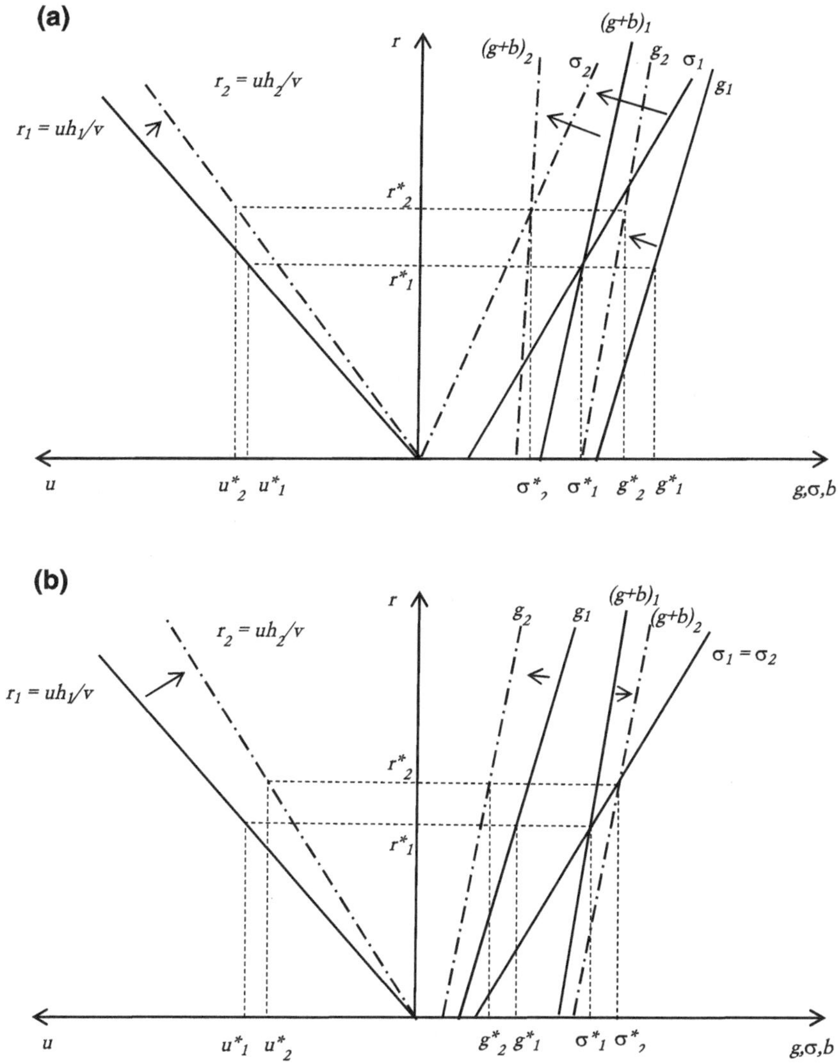

Fig. 6 Distributional and behavioural changes before the crisis: a stylised neo-Kaleckian approach. **a** The 'debt-led private demand boom' regime: rising profit share, falling average propensity to save due to relative income effects and credit-financed consumption, and rising current account deficits. **b** The 'export-led mercantilist' regime: rising profit share, rising average propensity to save due to higher profit share, and rising current account surpluses

lower propensities to save out of wages and out of profits, as well as with a lower differential between the two propensities. We thus observe a leftwards shift and a counter-clockwise rotation in the domestic saving function of Fig. 6a, assuming little change in the government deficit rate. In the 'export-led mercantilist' regime any expansionary effects on consumption have been absent for several, partly different reasons in different countries: a more developed welfare state providing basic consumption and public goods, absence of housing price booms, a less deregulated credit market etc. For the sake of simplicity, the domestic saving function in Fig. 6b has not been changed, ignoring potentially contractionary effects of rising inequality in personal and household incomes, leading to higher average propensities to save out of wages and out of profits and to a higher differential between these two rates, which would shift the saving rate curve rightwards and rotate it clockwise.

Regarding net exports and the current account balance, we can ignore the effects of re-distribution on relative price competitiveness, because profit shares and rates have improved globally in both types of regimes. Therefore, the net export function is mainly affected by relative demand dynamics and non-price competitiveness. In the 'debt-led private demand boom' economy, high domestic demand dynamics decrease net exports and increase current account deficits; the $(g+b)$-function in Fig. 6a thereby showing a more pronounced leftward shift than the accumulation function. In the 'export-led mercantilist' economies, low domestic demand dynamics due to regressive redistribution dampens imports and high foreign demand dynamics, particularly from the 'debt-led private demand boom' economies, raises exports, so that we have rising net exports and current account surpluses. In Fig. 6b, therefore, although the accumulation function is shifted leftwards, the $(g+b)$-function gets slightly shifted to the right.

As can be seen in Fig. 6, redistribution and changes in economic behaviour under the conditions of financialisation lead to the following changes in medium- to long-run equilibrium positions in the two regimes. We obtain that a higher profit share raises the equilibrium profit rates in both regimes from r_1^* to r_2^*. This is accompanied by a fall in equilibrium capital stock growth from g_1^* to g_2^*, which means that we have 'profits without investment' patterns in both cases. However, in the 'debt-led private demand boom' regime in Fig. 6a, this is accompanied by a rise in the equilibrium rate of capacity utilisation from u_1^* to u_2^*. Demand thus turns 'seemingly profit-led' here. Vigorous domestic demand dynamics in this regime also cause lower net exports and thus rising current account deficits. The 'export-led mercantilist' regime in Fig. 6b displays a fall in equilibrium capacity utilisation from u_1^* to u_2^*, but shows higher net exports and current account surpluses. This overall constellation has then given rise to unsustainable private debt dynamics in the 'debt-led private demand boom' economies, which in countries not being able to issue debt in their own currencies was coupled with unsustainable foreign debt dynamics. These unsustainable debt dynamics then triggered the crisis and led to the collapse of both pre-crisis regimes in course of the Great Financial Crisis and the Great Recession, as has been analysed in more detail in Hein (2012, Chapter 6), for example.

Summing up, the stylised neo-Kaleckian model presented in this section is easily able to reproduce the stylised facts, which have been observed by several authors (Hein 2012; van Treeck 2009) for the two extreme demand and growth regimes before the crises. Compared to the stylised Marxian approach, it provides a more convincing story due to the explicit consideration of demand dynamics and changes in investment determinants under the conditions of financialisation, in particular.

4 Distribution and Growth After the Crisis: Regime Changes and Stagnation Tendencies

As is well known, the Great Financial Crisis and the Great Recession started in the main 'debt-led private demand boom' economy, the USA, and were transmitted to the world economy through the international trade channel and the financial contagion channel. Initially, the 'export-led mercantilist' countries were hit particularly hard through these channels but then recovered at a relatively quick rate until 2011, whereas the other countries had some more problems (Dodig et al. 2016). The quick initial recovery of the 'export-led mercantilist' economies was driven by the ongoing dynamic development in countries such as China, India and other emerging market economies, which were hardly hit by the crisis. Overall, the recovery until recently, however, has been slow by historical comparisons, which has led Summers (2014, 2015) and others to rediscover the 'secular stagnation' hypothesis.[17] As can be seen comparing the values in Table 2, on average, in the crisis and post-crisis period GDP growth, and growth contributions of fixed investment in particular, have remained extremely weak compared to the pre-crisis period.

With the deep financial and economic crises some major changes in the demand and growth regimes took place, as can be seen looking at the average values for financial balances and GDP growth contributions in the period 2008–16 (Table 2). In the pre-crisis 'debt-led private demand boom' countries, the USA, the UK and Spain, the private sectors, i.e. the private households and partly the corporations, had to deleverage considerably. The financial balances of these sectors thus became positive, and the growth contributions of private consumption and investment shrank remarkably—in Spain they even became negative on average over the considered period. High public deficits stabilised the economy and allowed for low but positive growth in the USA and the UK, with the balances of goods and services slightly contributing to GDP growth in the USA. However, the current accounts remained considerably negative and thus the financial balance of the external sectors stayed positive. The USA and the UK hence moved from a 'debt-led private demand boom' regime towards a 'domestic demand-led' regime mainly stabilised by public sector deficits.

[17]See the contributions in Teulings and Baldwin (2014). For the presentation of post-Keynesian/Kaleckian critique of the current debate on 'secular stagnation' and for alternative interpretations of current stagnation tendencies, see Cynamon and Fazzari (2015, 2016), Hein (2016) and Palley (2016).

The willingness to continue to accept high current account deficits in these two countries has contributed to the stabilisation of global demand in the world economy.

Spain has been a different case. Initially in the crisis, high public-sector deficits allowed the private sector to generate financial surpluses and to deleverage. However, with the euro crisis since 2010 and the austerity policies implemented, public deficits have been reduced, public and private domestic demand have collapsed and real GDP growth has turned negative for a couple of years. Positive growth contributions only came from the balance of goods and services, the current account improved and has, on an annual basis, remained positive since 2013. Spain has thus moved from a 'debt-led private demand boom' economy towards an 'export-led mercantilist' economy. Both in the USA and the UK, as well as in Spain, the regime shifts have been associated with a further deterioration of income distribution (Table 1): labour income shares in all three countries have been falling further, Gini coefficients for the household distribution of income before and after taxes have been rising in the USA and Spain, and remained constant at very high levels in the UK, and only top income shares have been falling in the UK and Spain, but continued to rise in the USA. These developments have prevented a mass income- or wage-driven recovery in these countries, so that the options have been either drawing on government deficits (USA, UK) or on foreign sector deficits (Spain) as stabilisers of demand and growth. In terms of the stylised models discussed in Sect. 3, the constellation in the USA and the UK can still be described by the second equilibrium in Fig. 6a for the 'debt-led private demand boom' regime. The only difference is now that the low domestic saving rate is sustained by government deficits instead of private household deficits. The constellation for Spain, however, is moving towards the second equilibrium shown in Fig. 6b for the 'export-led mercantilist' regime.

In the 'export-led mercantilist' countries before the crisis, Germany and Sweden, the public sector initially accepted high financial deficits (Germany) or a strong reduction of surpluses leading to small deficits (Sweden) in the crisis and the years following in order to stabilise the private sector and the macro-economy. However, these deficits could be passively consolidated, because of the economic recovery, initially driven by net exports. The financial balances of the private sectors have remained positive, in particular for private households, and in Germany the corporations have remained in surplus, too, whereas in Sweden they have incurred a small deficit (Table 2). On average over the period 2008–16, the small economic growth has been driven by domestic demand, with significant contributions of private consumption. But the balances of goods and services have still contributed to growth in Germany. However, in Sweden, the growth contributions have even turned slightly negative. This shift towards domestic private demand as a main driver of growth has been made possible by halting the trend towards rising inequality (Table 1): labour income shares stopped falling, top income shares have not been rising any more, and in Sweden, Gini coefficients for pre- and post-tax household incomes have remained constant, whereas in Germany, however, they have continued to rise slightly. But these countries still show considerable current account and net export surpluses, and thus negative financial balances of the respective external sectors. In Germany, these surpluses have exceeded those before the crisis and have shown a rising tendency, whereas in Sweden, they have only slightly been lower than before the crisis. Germany has thus continued to follow the 'export-led mercantilist' regime after the crisis, and Sweden has only moderately deviated and become 'weakly export-led'. In terms of the stylised models discussed in Sect. 3, the regimes in both Germany and Sweden can thus still be described by the second equilibrium in Fig. 6b for the 'export-led mercantilist' regime.

The 'domestic demand-led' regime in France has not changed significantly in the crisis and the following years. Financial surpluses of private households have been mopped up by corporations, but even more so by the public sector (Table 2). Due to the stabilisation requirements in the crisis, public sector deficits have increased relative to the cycle before the crisis. The balance of the external sector, which had become positive already before the crisis has been rising, so that France on average over the second period has been running a current account and a net exports deficit. Public deficits in France have thus been helpful in stabilising global demand for goods and services, too. Growth in France has been driven by domestic demand, and mainly by private and public consumption. The former has been facilitated by a decline in inequality in the period after the crisis (Table 1). France is the only country in our data set, in which the labour income share has been slightly rising, the Gini coefficients for pre- and post-tax incomes of households have been falling and top income shares have at least remained constant in the period after the crisis.

From a global perspective, current account imbalances have been slightly reduced in and after the crisis, if compared to the years before the crises. However, they are still much more pronounced than in the early 2000s (IMF 2017). The high current account surpluses by the 'export-led mercantilist' countries, Germany, Spain and Sweden in our study, but also the Eurozone as a whole, China, Japan, Italy and Russia, have been matched by current account deficits of 'domestic demand-led' economies with high public sector deficits, in particular the USA, the UK and France in our study, and furthermore by emerging market and commodity producing countries like Argentina, Australia, Brazil, Canada, India, South Africa and Turkey.

The risks of such a global constellation are obvious. If ever more economies move towards an 'export-led mercantilist' strategy, the world economy will face an aggregation problem. It will become increasingly difficult to generate the related current account deficits in other regions of the world. Dominating tendencies towards demand stagnation are then the inescapable consequences. And to the degree that global demand stabilisation has to rely on public sector financial deficits in the mature 'domestic demand-led' economies, as well as on public and private sector deficits in emerging market economies, there are severe risks and dangers built up. First, high government deficits and debt in mature 'domestic demand-led' economies as stabilisers of national and global demand may be reversed for political reasons (debt ceilings, debt brakes), although there may be no risks of over-indebtedness of governments, if debt can be issued in the countries' own currency and is backed by the respective central bank. Second, capital inflows into emerging market economies may be unstable and face 'sudden stops' because of changes in expectations and/or over-indebtedness in foreign currency of these countries. And third, there are the risks of politically induced protection measures in order to reduce current account and net export deficits, which are considered to be too high.

Apart from these short- to medium-run problems of stability of such a global constellation, there arises a long-run stagnation problem associated with the still persisting 'profits without investment' patterns in the post-crisis regimes. Theoretically, these are shown in Fig. 6, which still explains the patterns in the major current 'domestic demand-led by government deficits' and the 'export-led mercantilist' regimes, as argued above. And empirically, the problem can be observed in Table 2 showing particular weak growth contributions of private investment accompanying high and in several countries even rising inequality. High and rising inequality—indicated by a high and rising profit share for the sake of simplicity—and depressed capital accumulation have re-enforcing depressing effects on productivity growth, thus contributing to long-run stagnation, as can be briefly shown, building on the neo-Kaleckian model presented in Sect. 3.

Starting with Rowthorn (1981), Dutt (1990, Chapter 5), Taylor (1991, Chapter 10) and Lavoie (1992, Chapter 6), several authors have introduced endogenous technological change and labour productivity growth into Kaleckian distribution and growth models, as reviewed and elaborated in Hein (2014, Chapter 8). Relying on Kaldor's (1957) technical progress function and/or on Kaldor's (1966) 'Verdoorn's Law', labour productivity growth is assumed to be positively affected by capital stock growth due to capital-embodied technological change, and/or demand growth due to dynamic returns to scale. Adding a Marxian component to the story, following Marx (1867) and integrating a wage-push variable into the productivity growth function of the model, it can be argued that a higher real wage rate or a higher wage share induces capitalists to speed up the implementation of labour augmenting technological progress in order to protect the profit share. Therefore, Eq. (8) is obtained for long-run productivity growth ($\hat{y}$), with z_i representing a set of further institutional factors determining productivity growth, like government technology policies, the education system, etc.:

$$\hat{y} = \hat{y}\left(g^{*}, h, z_i\right), \quad \frac{\partial \hat{y}}{\partial g^{*}} > 0, \frac{\partial \hat{y}}{\partial h} < 0, \frac{\partial \hat{y}}{\partial z_i} > 0 \tag{8}$$

Furthermore, we can assume that the goods market equilibrium rate of capital accumulation is positively affected by productivity growth, because of capital embodied technological change, in particular. Firms have to invest in new capital stock in order to benefit from technological inventions. Taking into account the exogenous parameters determining the goods market equilibrium rate of accumulation derived in Sect. 3, we arrive at the following equation for equilibrium capital accumulation:

$$\begin{aligned} g^{*} = g^{*}\left(\hat{y}, \alpha, h, s_W, s_\Pi, d, b\right), \frac{\partial g^{*}}{\partial \hat{y}} > 0, \frac{\partial g^{*}}{\partial h} < 0, \frac{\partial g^{*}}{\partial s_W} < 0, \\ \frac{\partial g^{*}}{\partial s_\Pi} < 0, \frac{\partial g^{*}}{\partial d} > 0, \frac{\partial g^{*}}{\partial b} > 0 \end{aligned} \tag{9}$$

Equations (8) and (9) describe a demand-determined endogenous growth model and Fig. 7 presents the long-run equilibrium values for capital accumulation (g_1^{**}) and productivity growth ($\hat{y}_1^{**}$), and thus the endogenous potential or 'natural' growth grate.[18] Any fall in the goods market equilibrium rate of capital accumulation—as the ones we have seen for both the 'debt-led private demand boom' and the 'export-led mercantilist' regimes before the crisis, which then have persisted in the post-crisis regimes—thus causes a leftward shift in the g^{*}-curve, and thus lower long-run equilibrium rates of capital accumulation and productivity

[18]For analytical treatments see Hein (2014, Chapter 8; 2017a).

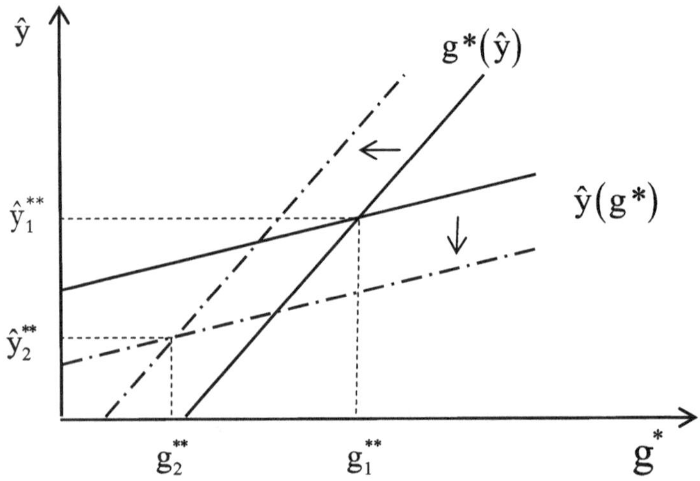

Fig. 7 A Kalecki-Kaldor-Marx endogenous growth model

growth, and hence potential growth emerge. Finally, Fig. 7 also shows the effect of a rise in the profit share on long-run potential growth. In this case, both curves get shifted and the long-run growth equilibrium falls from $g_1^{**}, \hat{y}_1^{**}$ to $g_2^{**}, \hat{y}_2^{**}$. Redistribution at the expense of wages is thus detrimental to long-run capital accumulation, productivity growth and thus to potential growth, although there may be short- to medium-run compensatory factors, which dampen or even overcompensate the effects on aggregate demand and the profit rate, i.e. rising deficit spending of private households, of the government or of the foreign sector. These, however, are difficult to sustain, as we have seen.

Summing up, post-crisis stagnation tendencies can be explained by those factors generating low capital stock growth, on the one hand, i.e. depressed animal spirits of management of non-financial corporations, high propensities to save out of the different types of income, low government deficit rates in particular in the 'export-led mercantilist' countries and high profit shares. On the other hand, high profit shares have a depressing effect on innovation activities of firms and on productivity growth; the latter being depressed by low capital accumulation, too.[19]

[19]For a more detailed discussion see Hein (2016, 2017a).

5 Summary and Conclusions

Addressing the issue of inequality and economic development, in this contribution, Marxian and Kaleckian assessments of the distribution and growth regimes under finance-dominated capitalism before the recent financial and economic crises have been provided. Based on this, an interpretation of regime shifts and stagnation tendencies after the crises in a demand-led endogenous productivity growth model with Kaleckian, Kaldorian and Marxian features have been presented.

First, the main macroeconomic features of financialisation have been recalled, and the main extreme growth regimes in the face of redistribution at the expense of the wage share and low income households, thus rising inequality, have been derived empirically, i.e. the 'debt-led private demand boom' and the 'export-led mercantilist' regimes. These regimes have been subsequently assessed in stylised Marxian and neo-Kaleckian distribution and growth models. Both models are able to generate these regimes, which contain and explain the 'profits without investment' phenomenon observed in empirical studies. However, it has been argued that the stylised neo-Kaleckian model is superior over the stylised Marxian model, because it explicitly takes into account the demand determinants of long-run growth, and thus in particular the effects of financialisation and re-distribution on investment. Finally, the changes in distribution and growth regimes in the crisis and post-crisis period have been assessed and interpreted in the context of the stylised neo-Kaleckian model. We have seen that, against the background of high and in some countries even rising inequality, the pre-crisis 'debt-led private demand boom' countries have either turned 'domestic demand-led' stabilised by government deficits or 'export-led mercantilist', with the pre-crisis 'export-led mercantilist' countries sticking to their regimes. This has meant that high inequality and global current account imbalances, as well as the related fragilities have been more or less maintained after the crisis, with government deficits in the current 'domestic demand-led' regimes assuming the role of the private household financial deficits in the pre-crisis 'debt-led private demand boom' regimes. Furthermore, since the 'profits without investment' phenomenon has been maintained in the post-crisis regimes, the neo-Kaleckian model has been extended by a productivity growth equation with Kaldorian and Marxian features, generating a demand-led endogenous growth model, and it has been shown how current stagnation tendencies can be explained by this model.

Summing up, in this contribution, in particular in the context of the neo-Kaleckian model, it has been shown that depressing effects of high and rising inequality on aggregate demand growth can temporarily be prevented by behavioural changes, i.e. higher deficit spending by private households, governments or external sectors. However, this may create financial fragility in the short to medium run, as well as depressed capital accumulation and potential growth in the long run.

Acknowledgements For helpful comments I would like to thank Philip Arestis, Daniel Detzer and Franz J. Prante. I am also indebted to Ryan Woodgate and Sophie Rotermund for research and editing assistance. Remaining errors are mine, of course.

References

Argitis, G. (2001). Intra-capitalists Conflict, Monetary Policy and Income Distribution. *Review of Political Economy, 13,* 453–470.

Barba, A., & Pivetti, M. (2009). Rising Household Debt: Its Causes and Macroeconomic Implications—A Long-Period Analysis. *Cambridge Journal of Economics, 33,* 113–137.

Bhaduri, A., & Marglin, S. (1990). Unemployment and the Real Wage: The Economic Basis for Contesting Political Ideologies. *Cambridge Journal of Economics, 14,* 375–93.

Blecker, R. A. (1989). International Competition, Income Distribution and Economic Growth. *Cambridge Journal of Economics, 13,* 395–412.

Blecker, R. A. (2002). Distribution, Demand and Growth in Neo-Kaleckian Macro-Models. In M. Setterfield (Ed.), *The Economics of Demand-Led Growth*. Cheltenham: Edward Elgar.

Blecker, R. A. (2016). Wage-Led Versus Profit-Led Demand Regimes: The Long and the Short of It. *Review of Keynesian Economics, 4,* 373–390.

Boone, L., & Girouard, N. (2002). The Stock Market, the Housing Market and Consumer Behaviour. *OECD Economic Studies, 35,* 175–200.

Cournilleau, G., & Creel, J. (2016). France, a Domestic Demand-Led Economy Under the Influence of External Shocks. In E. Hein, D. Detzer, & N. Dodig (Eds.), *Financialisation and the Financial and Economic Crises: Country Studies*. Cheltenham: Edward Elgar.

Cynamon, B., & Fazzari, S. M. (2008). Household Debt in the Consumer Age: Source of Growth—Risk of Collapse. *Capitalism and Society, 3*(2), 1–30.

Cynamon, B. Z., & Fazzari, S. M. (2015). Rising Inequality and Stagnation in the US Economy. *European Journal of Economics and Economic Policies: Intervention, 12*(2), 170–172.

Cynamon, B. Z., & Fazzari, S. M. (2016). Inequality, the Great Recession and Slow Recovery. *Cambridge Journal of Economics, 40,* 373–399.

Davis, L. (2018). Financialisation and the Nonfinancial Corporation: An Investigation of Firm Level Investment Behavior in the United States. *Metroeconomica, 69*(1), 270–3017.

Detzer, D. (2018). Inequality, Emulation and Debt: The Occurrence of Different Growth Regimes in the Age of Financialisation in a Stock/Flow Consistent Model. *Journal of Post Keynesian Economics, 41*(2), 284–315.

Detzer, D., & Hein, E. (2016). Financialisation and the Crises in the Export-Led Mercantilist German Economy. In E. Hein, D. Detzer, & N. Dodig (Eds.), *Financialisation and the Financial and Economic Crises: Country Studies*. Cheltenham: Edward Elgar.

Dodig, N., Hein, E., & Detzer, D. (2016). Financialisation and the Financial and Economic Crises: Theoretical Framework and Empirical Analysis for 15 Countries. In E. Hein, D. Detzer, & N. Dodig (Eds.), *Financialisation and the Financial and Economic Crises: Country Studies*. Cheltenham: Edward Elgar.

Dutt, A. K. (1984). Stagnation, Income Distribution and Monopoly Power. *Cambridge Journal of Economics, 8,* 25–40.

Dutt, A. K. (1990). *Growth, Distribution and Uneven Development.* Cambridge, UK: Cambridge University Press.

European Commission. (2017, April 7). *Annual Macroeconomic Database (AMECO)*. Available at: https://ec.europa.eu/info/business-economy-euro/indicators-statistics/economic-databases/macro-economic-database-ameco_en.

Evans, T. (2016). The Crisis of Finance-Led Capitalism in the United States. In E. Hein, D. Detzer, & N. Dodig (Eds.), *Financialisation and the Financial and Economic Crises: Country Studies*. Cheltenham: Edward Elgar.

Ferreiro, J., Galvez, C., & Gonzales, A. (2016). Financialisation and the Economic Crisis in Spain. In E. Hein, D. Detzer, & N. Dodig (Eds.), *Financialisation and the Financial and Economic Crises: Country Studies*. Cheltenham: Edward Elgar.

Foster, J. B., & Magdoff, F. (2009). *The Great Financial Crisis: Causes and Consequences*. New York: Monthly Review Press.

Foster, J. B., & McChesney, R. W. (2012). *The Endless Crisis: How Monopoly-Finance Capital Produces Stagnation and Upheaval from the USA to China*. New York: Monthly Review Press.

Guttmann, R., & Plihon, D. (2010). Consumer Debt and Financial Fragility. *International Review of Applied Economics, 24,* 269–283.

Hein, E. (2006). Money, Interest and Capital Accumulation in Karl Marx's Economics: A Monetary Interpretation and Some Similarities to Post-Keynesian Approaches. *European Journal of the History of Economic Thought, 13,* 113–140.

Hein, E. (2012). *The Macroeconomics of Finance-Dominated Capitalism—And Its Crisis*. Cheltenham: Edward Elgar.

Hein, E. (2013/14). The Crisis of Finance-Dominated Capitalism in the Euro Area, Deficiencies in the Economic Policy Architecture and Deflationary Stagnation Policies. *Journal of Post Keynesian Economics, 36*(2), 325–354.

Hein, E. (2014). *Distribution and Growth After Keynes: A Post-Keynesian Guide*. Cheltenham: Edward Elgar.

Hein, E. (2015). Finance-Dominated Capitalism and Re-distribution of Income—A Kaleckian Perspective. *Cambridge Journal of Economics, 39,* 907–934.

Hein, E. (2016). Secular Stagnation or Stagnation Policy? Steindl After Summers. *PSL Quarterly Review, 69*(276), 3–47.

Hein, E. (2017a). The Bhaduri/Marglin Post-Kaleckian Model in the History of Distribution and Growth Theories—An Assessment by Means of Model Closures. *Review of Keynesian Economics, 5*(2), 218–238.

Hein, E. (2017b). *Stagnation Policy in the Eurozone and Economic Policy Alternatives: A Steindlian/Neo-Kaleckian Perspective* (FMM Working Paper 5/2017). Forum Macroeconomics and Macroeconomic Policies.

Hein, E., Dünhaupt, P., Alfageme, A., & Kulesza, M. (2017). Financialisation and Distribution Before and After the Crisis: Patterns for Six OECD Countries. In P. Arestis & M. Sawyer (Eds.), *Economic Policies Since the Global Financial Crisis. International Papers in Political Economy*. Basingstoke: Palgrave Macmillan.

Hein, E., & Prante, F. J. (2018, forthcoming). Functional Distribution and Wage Inequality in Recent Kaleckian Growth Models. In H. Bougrine & L.-P. Rochon (Eds.), *Economic Growth and Macroeconomic Stabilization Policies in Post-Keynesian Economics, Essays in Honour of Marc Lavoie and Mario Seccareccia, Book Two*. Cheltenham: Edward Elgar.

International Monetary Fund (IMF). (2017, May 26). *World Economic Outlook Database*. Available at: https://www.imf.org/external/pubs/ft/weo/2017/01/weodata/index.aspx.

Kaldor, N. (1957). A Model of Economic Growth. *The Economic Journal, 67,* 591–624.

Kaldor, N. (1966). *Causes of the Slow Rate of Economic Growth in the United Kingdom*. Cambridge, UK: Cambridge University Press.

Kalecki, M. (1937). The Principle of Increasing Risk. *Economica, 4,* 440–447.

Kalecki, M. (1954). *Theory of Economic Dynamics*. London: George Allen and Unwin.

Kalecki, M. (1971). *Selected Essays on the Dynamics of the Capitalist Economy, 1933–70*. Cambridge, UK: Cambridge University Press.

Kim, Y. K. (2013). Household Debt, Financialisation, and Macroeconomic Performance in the United States, 1951–2009. *Journal of Post Keynesian Economics, 35,* 675–694.

Kim, Y. K. (2016). Macroeconomic Effects of Household Debt: An Empirical Analysis. *Review of Keynesian Economics, 4,* 127–150.

Kotz, D. M. (2009). The Financial and Economic Crisis of 2008: A Systemic Crisis of Neoliberal Capitalism. *Review of Radical Political Economics, 41,* 305–317.

Kotz, D. M. (2013). Social Structures of Accumulation, the Rate of Profit, and Economic Crises. In J. Wicks-Lim & R. Pollin (Eds.), *Capitalism on Trial: Explorations in the Tradition of Thomas E. Weisskopf.* Cheltenham, UK: Edward Elgar.

Kurz, H. D. (1990). Technical Change, Growth and Distribution: A Steady State Approach to Unsteady Growth. In H. D. Kurz (Ed.), *Capital, Distribution and Effective Demand: Studies in the Classical Approach to Economic Theory*. Cambridge: Polity Press.

Lavoie, M. (1992). *Foundations of Post-Keynesian Economic Analysis*. Aldershot, Brookfield: Edward Elgar.

Lavoie, M. (2014). *Post-Keynesian Economics: New Foundations*. Cheltenham: Edward Elgar.

Lepper, J., Shabani, M., Toporowski, J., & Tyson, J. (2016). Monetary Adjustment and Inflation of Financial Claims in the UK After 1980.

In E. Hein, D. Detzer, & N. Dodig (Eds.), *Financialisation and the Financial and Economic Crises: Country Studies*. Cheltenham: Edward Elgar.
Ludvigson, S., & Steindl, C. (1999, July). How Important is the Stock Market Effect on Consumption? *Federal Reserve Bank of New York Economic Policy Review, 5*(2), 29–51.
Marx, K. (1867/1967). *Das Kapital. Kritik der politischen Ökonomie, Erster Band: Der Produktionsprozeß des Kapitals* [Capital. A Critique of Political Economy, Volume 1: The Process of Capitalist Production], (4th ed. 1890, F. Engels, Ed.). New York: International Publisher.
Marx, K. (1885/1967). *Das Kapital. Kritik der politischen Ökonomie, Zweiter Band: Der Zirkulationsprozeß des Kapitals* [Capital. A Critique of Political Economy, Volume 2: The Process of Circulation of Capital], (2nd ed. 1893, F. Engels, Ed.). New York: International Publisher.
Marx, K. (1894/1967). *Das Kapital. Kritik der politischen Ökonomie, Dritter Band: Der Gesamtprozeß der kapitalistischen Produktion* [Capital. A Critique of Political Economy, Volume 3: The Process of Capitalist Production as A Whole], (F. Engels, Ed.). New York: International Publisher.
Mehra, Y. P. (2001). The Wealth Effect in Empirical Life-Cycle Aggregate Consumption Equations. *Federal Reserve Bank of Richmond Economic Quarterly, 87*(2), 45–68.
Onaran, Ö., & Galanis, G. (2014). Income Distribution and Growth: A Global Model. *Environment and Planning A, 46,* 2489–2513.
Onaran, Ö., Stockhammer, E., & Grafl, L. (2011). Financialisation, Income Distribution and Aggregate Demand in the USA. *Cambridge Journal of Economics, 35,* 637–661.
Orhangazi, Ö. (2008). Financialisation and Capital Accumulation in the Non-financial Corporate Sector: A Theoretical and Empirical Investigation on the US Economy: 1973–2003. *Cambridge Journal of Economics, 32,* 863–886.
Palley, T. I. (2016). Inequality, the Financial Crisis and Stagnation: Competing Stories and Why They Matter. *Real World Economics Review, 74,* 1–18.
Rowthorn, R. E. (1981). *Demand, Real Wages and Economic Growth* (pp. 1–39). Autumn: Thames Papers in Political Economy.
Shaikh, A. (1978). An Introduction to the History of Crisis Theories. In B. Steinberg (Ed.), *U.S. Capitalism in Crisis*. New York: URPE.
Shaikh, A. (2011). The First Great Depression of the 21st Century. *Socialist Register, 47,* 44–63.
Shaikh, A. (2016). *Capitalism: Competition, Conflict, Crises*. Oxford: Oxford University Press.

Steindl, J. (1952/1976). *Maturity and Stagnation in American Capitalism* (2nd ed.). Oxford: Blackwell; New York, London: Monthly Review Press.

Stenfors, A. (2016). Swedish Financialisation: 'Nordic Noir' or 'Safe Haven'? In E. Hein, D. Detzer, & N. Dodig (Eds.), *Financialisation and the Financial and Economic Crises: Country Studies*. Cheltenham: Edward Elgar.

Stockhammer, E. (2004). Financialisation and the Slowdown of Accumulation. *Cambridge Journal of Economics, 28,* 719–741.

Stockhammer, E. (2015). Rising Inequality as a Root Cause of the Present Crisis. *Cambridge Journal of Economics, 39,* 935–958.

Stockhammer, E. (2017). Wage-Led Versus Profit-Led Demand: What Have We Learned? A Kaleckian-Minskyan View. *Review of Keynesian Economics, 5,* 25–42.

Summers, L. A. (2014). U.S. Economic Prospects: Secular Stagnation, Hysteresis, and the Zero Lower Bound. *Business Economics, 49*(2), 65–73.

Summers, L. A. (2015). Demand Side Secular Stagnation. *American Economic Review: Papers and Proceedings, 105*(5), 60–65.

Taylor, L. (1991). *Income Distribution, Inflation, and Growth. Lectures on Structuralist Macroeconomic Theory*. Cambridge, MA and London: MIT Press.

Teulings, C., & Baldwin, R. (eds.) (2014). *Secular Stagnation: Facts, Causes and Cures (VoxEU.org eBook)*. London: Centre for Economic Policy Research (CEPR).

Tori, D., & Onaran, Ö. (2016). The Effects of Financialisation on Investment: Evidence from Firm-Level Data for the UK. *Post-Keynesian Economics Study Group* (Working Paper 1601).

Tori, D., & Onaran, Ö. (2017). *The Effects of Financialisation and Financial Development on Investment: Evidence from Firm-Level Data for Europe* (Greenwich Papers in Political Economy, No. 16089). Greenwich: University of Greenwich, Greenwich Political Economy Research Centre.

UNCTAD. (2009). *The Global Economic Crisis. Systemic Failures and Multilateral Remedies*. New York, Geneva: UNCTAD.

Van Treeck, T. (2008). Reconsidering the Investment-Profit Nexus in Finance-Led Economies: An ARDL-Based Approach. *Metroeconomica, 59,* 371–404.

van Treeck, T. (2009). The Political Economy Debate On 'Financialisation'—A Macroeconomic Perspective. *Review of International Political Economy, 16,* 907–944.

van Treeck, T. (2014). Did Inequality Cause the US Financial Crisis? *Journal of Economic Surveys, 28,* 421–448.

Theoretical and Empirical Analyses of the Rise of Income Inequality in Rich Countries

Pasquale Tridico and Riccardo Pariboni

1 Introduction

Since 1980, the establishment of a finance-led regime was introduced in the policy agenda of most advanced countries, and in particular under the Thatcher and Reagan administrations in the UK and the US. At first in the UK and the US and, later, in other advanced economies, a set of neoliberal policies boosting financialisation and globalisation were implemented. These policies included deregulation of the financial sector, liberalisation of trade, capital mobility, wage flexibility, privatisations, structural adjustments, retrenchment of welfare states, and the creation of a second pillar in the pension system (i.e. heavily encouraged private pension schemes).

According to Krippner (2005), financialisation can be identified as a political economy phenomenon where there is a growing dominance

P. Tridico (✉) · R. Pariboni
Department of Economics, Roma Tre University, Rome, Italy
e-mail: Tridico@uniroma3.it

R. Pariboni
e-mail: riccardo.pariboni@uniroma3.it

P. Arestis and M. Sawyer (eds.), *Inequality*, International Papers in Political Economy,
https://doi.org/10.1007/978-3-319-91298-1_4

of capital financial systems over bank-based financial systems. Epstein (2005, pp. 3–4) refers to financialisation as the increasing role of financial motives, financial markets, financial actors, and financial institutions in the operation of domestic and international economies. Hein (2017, p. 2), who uses interchangeably financialisation and finance-dominated capitalism (terminology which will also be used here), argues that it can be analysed from several perspectives: '*the deregulation of the financial sector and the rise of shadow banking, the ascendance of shareholder dominance at the firm level, the financialisation of everyday life, and the emergence of several macroeconomic regimes under the dominance of finance, among others*'.

The process of financialisation could be recognised, according to the Bank for International Settlements, in a daily volume of foreign exchange transactions of around 2 trillion dollars in 2006, just before the beginnings of the financial crash in the summer 2007. This amount is more or less equivalent to the GDP of France. In contrast, in 1989, this volume was about 500 billion dollars per day (BIS 2013).

A proxy that is used here for financialisation is 'Market capitalisation'—also known as capital market value—of listed domestic companies,[1] which refers to the rise of financial claims and incomes versus the real sector, and it amounts to the share price multiplied by the number of outstanding shares. Listed domestic companies are the domestically incorporated companies listed on the country's stock exchanges at the end of the year. These companies do not include investment companies, mutual funds, or other collective investment vehicles.

Figure 1 describes the increase of financialisation as proxied by stock market capitalisation in advanced countries since the 1970s. Financialisation increased, along with financial instability and fluctuations in the stock market. It is interesting to note the trend of the market capitalisation of listed companies before and after the crisis.

[1]According to the World Bank definition, "Listed domestic companies, including foreign companies which are exclusively listed, are those which have shares listed on an exchange at the end of the year. Investment funds, unit trusts, and companies whose only business goal is to hold shares of other listed companies, such as holding companies and investment companies, regardless of their legal status, are excluded. A company with several classes of shares is counted once. Only companies admitted to listing on the exchange are included." (https://data.worldbank.org/indicator/CM.MKT.LDOM.NO).

Fig. 1 Stock market capitalisation as a % of GDP, world, weighted average, 1975–2016 (*Source* The World Bank Database)

The data suggest that companies might have tried to protect themselves by opting to delist as the crisis began. Prior to that, the financial euphoria and manias, as Kindleberger (2005) argued, convinced many firms to be listed in the stock exchanges and to engage in speculative trading. Once the crisis of confidence, in 2007–2008, dampened the euphoria, average stock market capitalisation (as a % of GDP) decreased dramatically, and as Kindleberger (2005) predicted, panics substituted themselves for manias. Clearly, a 'reversed V' is visible in the figure below, with the average capitalisation in 2007, on the eve of the crisis, peaking around 115% of GDP, while the average in 2002 and in 2008 was 73 and 56%, respectively. In the mid-2010s, the trend is back to its increasing pattern, and in some countries market capitalisation goes well above 100% of GDP (such as 212% in Switzerland, around 150% in USA, 130% in Canada, 110% in Netherlands, 105%, in Australia etc.).

Throughout this chapter, we will show evidence according to which the financialisation of economies along with globalisation generated the main mechanism which allowed for the increase of income inequality. These processes have been taking place since at least 1980, when labour flexibility intensified, labour market institutions weakened as trade unions lost power, and public social spending started to retrench and did not compensate for the much vulnerabilities created by the globalisation process. In this context, wage share declined and functional income distribution worsened with an increase of profits, rents and financial compensation. A favourable tax policy towards the richest, payments of dividends and the structural change occurred in most advanced economies, i.e. a gradual abandonment of manufacturing in favour of services, also contributed to this result.

This chapter proceeds as follows: in Sect. 2, we investigate the main determinants of the fall in the wage share in advanced economies, namely financialisation, changes in the productive structures, globalisation, and the increase in labour flexibility. In Sect. 3, we discuss the impact of globalisation and financialisation on income inequality, while in Sect. 4, we try to establish a link between financialisation, the adoption of different welfare models and inequality. In Sect. 5, we deal with other possible factors that contribute to worsen income equality: the steady reduction in the degree of unionisation and the adoption of fiscal measures that tend to benefit the wealthier fractions of population. Section 6 deals with a possible interpretation of the slowdown of labour productivity, experienced by many advanced economies in recent years, according to which financialisation and unbalanced trends in income distribution represent a drag on the productivity dynamics. The last section concludes.

2 The Determinants of the Labour Share: Theory and Stylised Facts

In the last four decades, sluggish and stagnating wages have been a common feature in many advanced economies. This has been translated into a generalised decrease in the wage share,[2] an empirical regularity that

[2]Obviously not every country's wage share has displayed the same pattern. See, for example, the case of United Kingdom, which displayed a mildly increasing wage share in the 1990s, until the end of the 2000s.

has been confirmed and documented in the relevant literature (see, for example, Onaran and Galanis 2014; ILO and OECD 2015; ILO et al. 2015; Stockhammer 2015, 2017; Dünhaupt 2017).

As it has been widely discussed in the literature, these trends in income distribution have proven to be unsustainable and potentially explosive for the countries experiencing them. According to several authors (for example Barba and Pivetti 2009; Rajan 2010; Stockhammer 2015), household debt has acted as a substitute for stagnating wages in financing private consumption. However, this only postponed the demand generating problem ensuing from the compression of workers' purchasing power, as the burst of the debt-led growth bubble and pervasive financial instability proved at the onset of the Great Recession. The decrease in the wage share, moreover, poses a further threat by being potentially detrimental to the dynamics of labour productivity. This intuition dates back to Webb (1912) and has since been a key element of non-mainstream analyses of the determinants of labour productivity growth (see, for example, Sylos Labini 1999; Cassetti 2003; Naastepad 2006; Hein and Tarassow 2010; Tridico and Pariboni 2017a). To conclude this brief summary, it has to be recalled that, since Marglin and Bhaduri's contribution (Marglin and Bhaduri 1990), Post Keynesian economics has emphasised the causal effect of functional income distribution on growth with the introduction of the concepts of wage (or profit) led growth. Several empirical works have found that most advanced economies tend to be wage-led, with, in general, the exception of small open economies (see, for example, Hein and Vogel 2008; Hein and Tarassow 2010; Storm and Naastepad 2012; Onaran and Galanis 2014; Hartwig 2014, 2015; Onaran and Obst 2016). Independent of the merits of the wage versus profit-led growth literature,[3] Skott (2017) reminds us that a more equitable and balanced split of national income is a worthy outcome to be pursued, regardless of its impact on the dynamics of aggregate demand and GDP.

[3]See Pariboni (2016) and Skott (2017) for sceptical views on this stream of literature. The former, in particular, by criticizing the investment function adopted by Marglin and Bhaduri and their neglect of demand components other than induced consumption and investment, questions the validity of the Marglin and Bhaduri's taxonomy (wage-led versus profit-led).

2.1 Financialisation

In the introductory section, we have provided an overview on the multifaceted socio-economic phenomenon known as financialisation. As we have already maintained, financialisation has been one of the main forces behind the persisting decrease in the labour income share experienced by most advanced economies in the last decades. Its influence has been confirmed by several empirical studies (see, for example, Hein and Schoder 2011; Stockhammer 2013, 2017; Dünhaupt 2017) and finds its rationale in a growing body of theoretical literature. Argitis and Pitelis (2008) notice that financialisation has contributed to the increase in financial pay-out ratios, leading to distributional changes detrimental to non-shareholders. Indeed, Van der Zwan (2014, p. 108) makes clear that the shareholder value literature has acknowledged that financialisation is intrinsically a '*redistributive process.*' Shareholder value orientation is, however, only one of the main features of financialisation. For this reason, we believe it is reasonable to include, among the determinants of the wage share, both a variable related to the 'downsize and distribute' governance principle (see Lazonick and O'Sullivan 2000)—the share of income distributed by non-financial corporations in GDP[4]—and a more general variable—market capitalisation of listed domestic companies.[5] Financialisation is a complex social process and is likely to influence income distribution through several channels. Hein (2015, pp. 924–925), for example, provides a Kaleckian framework to single out seven stylised facts related to financialisation that have a direct impact on functional income distribution and include in the picture phenomena as different as the reduction of public intervention in the economy and the threats of hostile takeovers and mergers.

[4]We are referring here to the OECD variable 'Distributed income of corporations', for the sector 'Non-financial corporations'. 'Distributed income of corporations' is given by the sum of dividends and withdrawals from income of quasi-corporations, with the latter component being mostly negligible.

[5]Market capitalization is a variable with a trend similar to that of other possible proxies for financialisation, as dividend share, FDI and indexes of globalisation, as correlations between the variables show.

We also find particularly convincing the discussion of the effects of the financialisation of everyday life proposed by Van der Zwan (2014, p. 102). As the author argues, this circumstance tends to develop new subjectivities: workers slowly begin to perceive themselves as investors and owners of financial assets. The focus shifts on the individual dimension of responsibilities and the main purpose is self-fulfilment. As a consequence, class consciousness is undermined and the bargaining power of the worker class as a whole is under siege by individualism, in a context where '*the uneven distribution of financial power among social classes*' is functional to '*the structural inequalities that exist in an equity-based economy*' (Van der Zwan 2014, p. 103).[6]

Figure 2 shows trends of financialisation in a selected sub-sample of countries. Panel (a) includes Scandinavian, Mediterranean, and coordinated market economies (France and Germany), while panel (b) is focused on Anglo-Saxon countries. The general picture of Fig. 1 seems confirmed and 'reverse V' paths are broadly discernible; moreover, market capitalisation appears again on the rise, with the exceptions of Ireland, Spain, and of the countries for which we miss the data relative to the last few years. In Anglo-Saxon countries (Australia, Canada, United Kingdom and United States in our sample), however, the phenomenon takes place on a larger scale, confirming the received wisdom about the relevance of financial markets in the countries belonging to this socio-economic welfare model. Germany and Italy (and Ireland, an outlier within Anglo-Saxon countries) are on the other end of the spectrum, reaffirming the insights of Lapavitsas and Powell (2013): financialisation takes different shapes in different countries, due to institutional, historical, and political peculiarities.

2.2 Structural Change

According to Lapavitsas and Powell (2013, p. 362), '*financialisation represents a structural transformation of advanced economies resting on*

[6]"The role that financialisation played in lowering workers bargaining power" is recognised and admitted also by OECD (2012, p. 143).

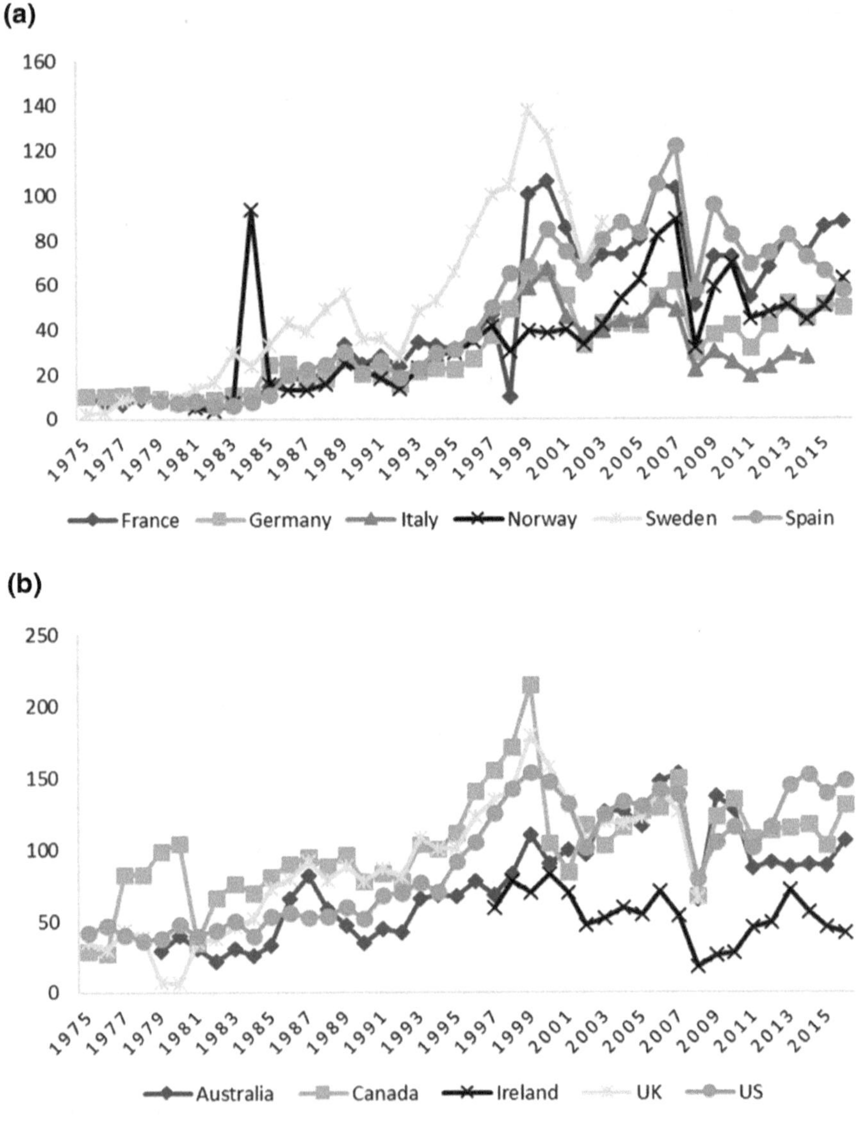

Fig. 2 Financialisation—Stock market capitalisation as a % of GDP, 1975–2016 (*Source* The World Bank Database)

altered relations among industrial enterprises, financial enterprises and workers.' We agree with the view that characterises financialisation as an element of a broader structural change that has been affecting advanced economies in the last 30–40 years. Indeed, in this time span, many advanced economies have experienced significant changes in their productive structures and in their industrial strategies. While the post-WWII period of expansion—labelled by some scholars as 'The Golden Age of Capitalism' (Marglin and Schor 1990)—was characterised by the manufacturing industry exerting a leading role, in more recent years, a massive shift in employment has been taking place in most Western countries. A steady decline in the share of workers in manufacturing and a transition towards the service sector are very well-known features of contemporary capitalism. The link between financialisation and de-industrialisation has been highlighted in Krippner (2005, p. 176), where the author considers both elements as fundamental keys to understand the transformation the United States was (and is) going through. Robert Boyer, in his prescient 2000 article (Boyer 2000), also identified the rising dominance of finance and the shift from manufacturing to services as elements of the emerging 'finance-led growth regime'.

Figure 3 synthetically conveys a picture of these trends, for a sample of selected countries, belonging to different institutional frameworks.[7]

France and Italy present the most clear-cut trends, with a sharp decrease in manufacturing employment mirrored by the rising contribution of finance and real estate activities to total economy's gross value added. These phenomena are less accentuated in Germany, a country that remains characterised by a stable and efficient manufacturing industry and by a relatively slower process of shift towards the financial business. The United Kingdom, in a sense, represents the other extreme of the spectrum, with the divarication between real and financial production already in place since the beginning of the 1980s and the faster process of deindustrialisation. Finally, Norway has experienced a similar

[7]See Lapavitsas and Powell (2013) for a comparative analysis of different forms of financialisation in different countries.

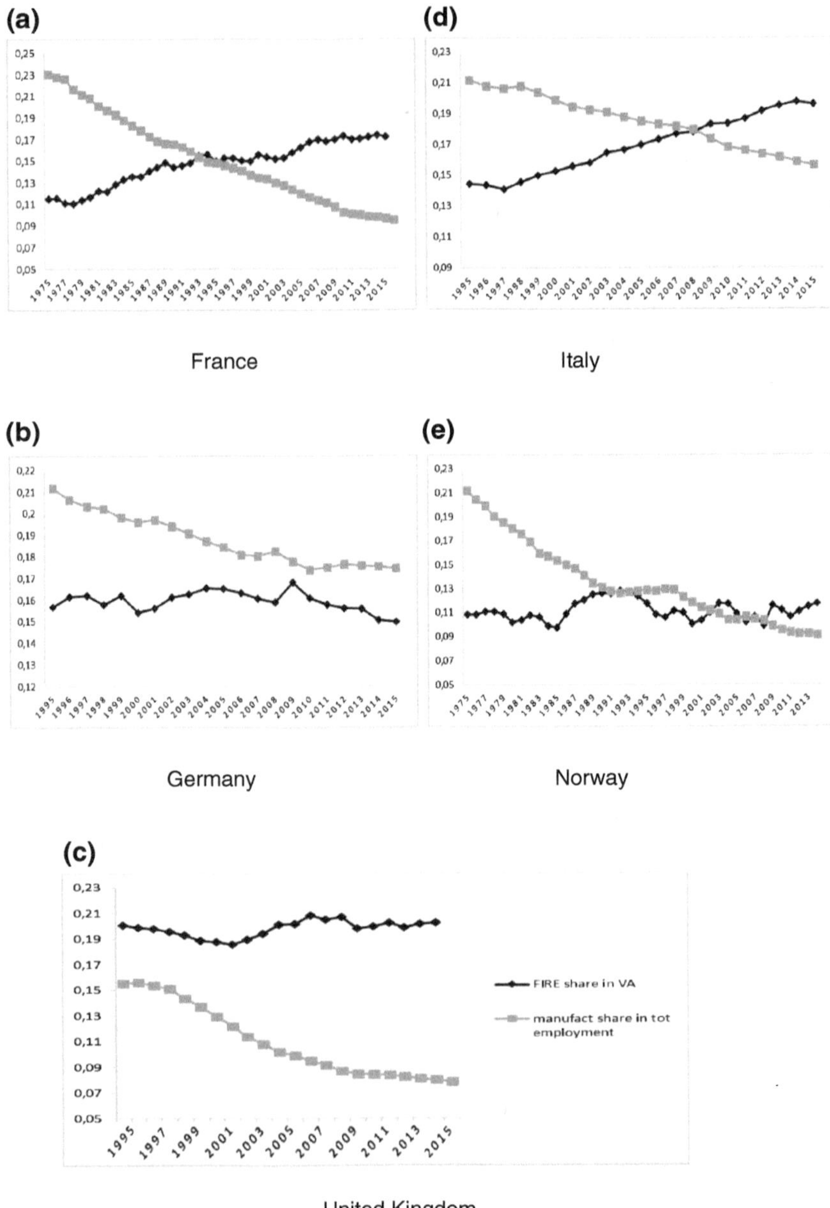

Fig. 3 Finance, insurance, and real estate (FIRE) activities share in gross value added (Following Krippner [2005], we treat finance and real estate as a single industry group, given the speculative aspects of real estate markets. We also

▶ decided not to report the employment share of FIRE activities in total employment, given that these industries are not employment-intensive [Krippner 2005, p. 175]. To stress the increasing relevance of finance, we opted for the share of value added produced in the related industries) (total activity): dark line; share of employment in manufacturing in total employment: light line (*Source* OECD)

decreasing pattern concerning the abandonment of manufacturing, but the shift towards services has interested mainly industries like 'community, social and personal services'.[8]

We include a variable for 'structural change'—namely, the share of employment in manufacturing in total employment—in our analysis, because we consider the drift away from manufacturing as a factor capable in itself to negatively affect the share of wages in income. Remunerations tend to be higher in manufacture than in most of the service industries,[9] as well as the degree of unionisation and the working-class coherence.[10] In a similar vein, Rodrik links the current weaknesses of the labour movement to the persistent trends of de-industrialisation across advanced and developing economies (Rodrik 2016) and warns against the perils that the abandonment of manufacturing poses for labour–capital relations and, more generally, for democracy (Rodrik 2013).

Even though it is outside the scope of this chapter, it is worth reminding that a process of ungoverned structural change, as described above, may also pose a threat to the dynamics of labour productivity.[11] Several service industries have a limited potential for productivity gains and are defined by labour–intensive production processes. Moreover, as pointed out by Wölfl (2005), service industries may suffer from specific

[8]This is the term used by the EU KLEMS Growth and Productivity Accounts to aggregate services industries like public administration, health, education etc.

[9]See Tridico and Pariboni (2017b) for some descriptive evidence.

[10]We refer with this term to "the unity and organisational ability of the working classes to assert their (economic) interests" (Stockhammer et al. 2016, p. 1805).

[11]This phenomenon goes by the name of *Baumol's disease* (see Baumol and Bowen 1965) in the related literature. A qualification and a reassessment of the *disease* has been advanced by Baumol himself. See, for example, Baumol et al. (1989) and Baumol (2002).

obstacles to innovation: for example the average small size of firms in this sector (and the related difficulties in gathering the necessary financing) leads to low investment, specifically in high-risk, high-tech capital assets (Wölfl 2005, p. 55). Also, investments in R&D and in workforce training tend to be underfunded and industries operating in the service sector often resort to non-firm specific technologies and knowledge, developed elsewhere (ibid.). Finally, we find persuasive the arguments that have been collectively labelled as the 'Manufacturing imperative' (Rodrik 2011), discussed and summarised in Cirillo and Guarascio (2015): an advanced manufacturing sector generates innovation spillovers in the service industries as well; manufactured capital goods, used by the service sector, embody most of the technical progress and knowledge generated in the economy moreover, being tradable, is an efficient vector to disseminate innovation.

2.3 Globalisation

Post-Keynesian and Critical Political Economy literatures tend to consider globalisation as an element of a more general and multi-dimensional process of Neoliberal restructuring. Globalisation and financialisation can be considered the two main pillars of this political project; the timing of the two principal waves of the former almost overlap with that of the latter and the two phenomena are complementary: '*financialization may thrive only to the extent that the spatial constraints of exchange are removed, while the process of globalization may be implemented to the extent that it is supported by internationalized finance*' (Vercelli 2013, p. 25). Onaran (2011), Stockhammer (2013, 2017) and Dünhaupt (2017), among other studies, find a significative negative effect of globalisation on the labour share in income. As Stockhammer (2017, p. 8) argues, globalisation exerts a downward pressure on the wage share mainly by altering the balance of powers between capital and labour: the looming threat of relocations can suffice to deter higher wage claims or to make wage cuts more palatable to workers. Capitalists can also exploit and take advantage of the expansion of the reserve army of labour, brought about by the inclusion in the global labour market of workers from developing countries.[12] Moreover, to keep production at home, governments can decide to implement selective tax reductions in favour of capital and embark on tax competition among themselves (Tridico 2017). Finally, although not an exhaustive list, in advanced economies globalisation is often associated with a decline in manufacture employment, which tends to be replaced by employment in low value-added service industries, with the consequences described in the previous sub-section.

3 Labour Flexibility and Labour Bargaining Power

The economic processes we have mentioned so far—financialisation, structural change, globalisation—have been associated with a stream of labour market reforms, i.e. an increase in labour flexibility and a reduction in employees' protections. We will investigate whether the flexibilisation of labour exerts a negative pressure on the wage share, as we expect. In this regard, our variable of interest is the EPL (Employment Protection Legislation) index: developed by the OECD, the index represents the level of protection offered by national legislation with respect to regular employment, temporary employment, and collective dismissal. In other words, the index offers a synthetic picture of the state of the regulations that allow employers to fire and hire workers at will (the index varies between 0 for very low protection and 6 for very high protection). Traditionally, European economies maintained higher levels of EPL in comparison to Anglo-Saxon economies (Nickell 1997). However, in the present period, labour flexibility has been increasing everywhere, although in Europe the policy agenda is moving towards a so called 'flexicurity', which would promote some types of jobs and income securities (i.e., employability) while accounting for the need for flexibility on the part of firms (Kok 2004; Boyer 2009; Tridico 2009).

[12]See Dünhaupt (2017, p. 290) and the literature reviewed there.

Typically, the case of Denmark represents a situation where a lower EPL is associated with income and job securities.

Our hypothesis is that a decrease in labour rigidity enhances capital's bargaining power: the precarious nature of job tenure makes workers reluctant to engage in workplace struggles.[13]

The institutional and structural changes that have occurred in the labour market over the last twenty years in Europe, and over the past 30 years in US, were critical to the financialisation process. These changes allowed for labour flexibility, wage moderation and, ultimately, inequality and profit soar. All this occurred with the demise of the Keynesian policies of public demand management.

The new, post-Fordist growth model requires a higher degree of labour flexibility because, with the massive shift from the industrial sector to the service sector, technology, and innovation bring about rapid structural changes which demand quick responses from firms. Therefore, labour should adjust to the firms' need. The financial sector in particular, because of its peculiarities, requires a very flexible workforce and fast adjustments, partially compensated by relatively higher remunerations. Shareholders want higher dividends because they invested their own capital in firms, taking on a higher level of risk. But, for shareholders to obtain higher dividends, wages have to be compressed and labour flexibility is instrumental to obtain this result.

As it has been shown elsewhere (Tridico 2012), there is a positive correlation between the level of market financialisation and the level of labour flexibility (EPL) and between EPL and Gini coefficient, so that countries with lower labour protections are also countries with higher inequality. In other words, when financialisation increases, one observes both increased flexibility and inequality.

A flexible labour market with compressed wages needs to be supplemented by available financing. Hence, to have developed financial tools to sustain consumption, which otherwise were compressed by low and

[13]In the literature, alternative measures of the institutional factors we proxy by means of EPL are also utilised; for example, Dünhaupt (2017) introduces 'labour's bargaining power'—proxied by several variables—among the determinants of the labour share; Stockhammer (2017) uses 'welfare state retrenchments'.

unstable wages. It is difficult to establish a causal relation, though: we cannot be certain whether financialisation required labour flexibility or if increased labour flexibility brought about hyper-financialisation. A simple correlation between these two complementary institutional forms of neoliberalism seems more likely.

The unemployment rate is used as a proxy for labour's bargaining power, as captured by a classic 'reserve army of labour' effect, as is often done in the literature (see, for example, Dünhaupt 2017; Stockhammer 2017).[14]

4 General Forces Driving Inequality: Globalisation and Financialisation

The link between globalisation and income distribution has been explored in detail in the literature calling on the Stolper and Samuelson theorem, according to which market integration might increase inequality and vulnerability because increased international trade raises the incomes of the owners of abundant factors and reduces the incomes of the owners of scarce factors (Stolper and Samuelson 1941). Since advanced industrial countries are more capital-intensive economies and abundant in skilled labour, trade is expected to be beneficial for skilled labour and detrimental to unskilled labour, thus increasing inequality of earnings. For labour-intensive economies, which are typically those of developing countries, trade is expected to increase regional disparities.

Globalisation and financialisation have taken place almost simultaneously in advanced economies. Globalisation, just like financialisation, is still a generic term which, in most definitions, is identified as a process of *intensification* of trade, capital mobility, finance, and labour mobility. Conversely, authors such as Hay and Wincott (2012) disagree with such a definition of globalisation and would rather define it as a process not only of *intensification* of those flows but also of *extensive increase*, on a global level, of trade, capital, labour mobility, and

[14]The downward pressure exerted on wages by unemployment is also reported in OECD (2014).

technological exchange (see, for example, Held et al. 1999). Because evidence of this second type of definition of globalisation is missing and because not all countries have taken part in the globalisation process (globalisation involves mostly OECD countries and some emerging economies), Hay and Wincott (2012) conclude that it would be more appropriate to speak about regionalisation rather than globalisation. For instance, trade, capital, and labour mobility increased particularly in the European Union (Europeanisation), among advanced and emerging economies (trans-regionalism), and between North American countries (with regional agreements such as NAFTA), etc. Hence, the interpretation of globalisation remains quite controversial and an on-going and evolutionary process.

Nonetheless, while it is true that globalisation and financialisation affect more advanced and increasingly more emerging economies—as for example BRIC countries—it is objectively impossible to deny the intensification of this process and the increase in the number of countries involved in the global economy over the last two decades.

It is possible to get a rough but straightforward picture of globalisation, as can be seen through the lenses of trade intensification, by looking at trends in world exports (and imports) as a percentage of GDP. With this in mind, it can be noticed that a first big wave of globalisation, identified purely according to the *intensive* definition, occurred after 1970 and may have been generated by a new international monetary system, the change in oil prices, and the birth of the European Monetary System. However, this first wave of globalisation was unstable and the process of intensification declined during the 1980s. Finally, the process of intensive globalisation, often accompanied by the extensive inclusion of more and more countries, steadily rejuvenated at the end of the 1980s when several institutional, geopolitical, and technological changes occurred.

Globalisation or, to be more precisely, trade openness (defined as imports and exports as a percentage of Gross Domestic Product) was and is supported by the mainstream neoclassical approach as being beneficial. Lewis (1980) and many other economists such as Lucas (1993) and Bhagwati (2004) believe trade is the engine of economic growth. However, the experience of globalisation so far has shown that the performance of open economies can vary dramatically (Rodrik 1999). Openness to and integration into the world economy should be accompanied by appropriate institutions, state strategies, and by an important welfare state that supports internal cohesion and maintains external competitive advantages. In fact, according to Rodrik (1999), the best-performing countries are the ones that are integrated in the world economy with institutions capable of supporting the impact of globalisation on the domestic market and social cohesion. Countries with poor social institutions, weak conflict management institutions (which means poor welfare states), and strong social cleavages suffer external shocks and do not perform well in the world economy.

The current financial and economic crisis, which started in the US in 2007, suggests Rodrik's argument still holds true: '*The world market is a source of disruption and upheaval as much as it is an opportunity for profit and economic growth. Without the complementary institutions at home—in the areas of governance, judiciary, civil liberties, social insurance, and education—one gets too much of the former and too little of the latter*' (Rodrik 1999, p. 96).

For Lucas (1993), international trade stimulates economic growth through a process of structural change and capital accumulation. According to Walsh and Whelan (2000), this is the case for Ireland, where a structural change had already taken place during the 1970s and would have created conditions that allowed the Irish economy to grow considerably in the 1990s and later in the 2000s.[15] Capital accumulation is determined by 'learning by doing' and 'learning by schooling' in a process of knowledge and innovation spillovers. A country that protects its goods made with intensive skilled work from international competition by raising tariffs on them will see a domestic increase in the price of those goods. Skilled workers' wages will increase and R&D will become more expensive. Consequently, investments in R&D will decrease and growth will be negatively affected. On the contrary, removing tariffs on those goods will cause a reduction in their price, a

[15]It is however argued that subsidies for inward foreign direct investment were the key factor in fostering Irish economic growth.

reduction in the cost of R&D, and thus an increase in investments in R&D with positive effects on growth (Lucas 1993).

This argument, however, does not take into consideration the inequality and uneven development caused by trade liberalisation and intensification via wage differentials. This issue had already been raised by Stolper and Samuelson, as we saw previously. Similarly, increased capital flows are expected to raise income inequality in advanced industrial economies because capital outflows from capital-rich countries to LDCs reduce domestic investment and lower the productive capability and demands for labour in these economies. Since, according to mainstream economics, a reduction in total capital in the production process would increase the marginal productivity of capital[16] and reduces the marginal effect of labour, capital outflows would increase the income of capital relative to labour, thus exacerbating income inequality. In particular, because foreign direct investment (FDI) outflows from advanced industrial economies tend to be concentrated in industries with low-skilled labour in the home country (Lee 1996), rapidly rising FDI outflows often reduce the demand for low-skilled labour and increase income gaps in industrialised countries. In fact, several studies find that FDI outflows are associated with expanded income inequality in industrialised countries (see, for example, Leamer 1996).

It is interesting to observe the expansion of Foreign Direct Investment, which experienced a strong increase in the 1990s due to the liberalisation of capital markets, followed by a collapse at the beginning of the 2000s due to the global uncertainty caused by the international events of September 11, 2001. A further and bigger increase in FDI flows can be

[16]It has to be recalled that non-mainstream economists tend to reject the very concept of marginal productivity of production factors and the theoretical legitimacy of aggregate production functions. See, for example, Garegnani (1970, 1976). Discussing Garegnani (1970), Petri notices that "income distribution can be seen as reflecting the 'marginal products' of an Aggregate Production Function only if the economy produces, to all relevant effects, a single good (that is if capital goods are produced with exactly the same physical input proportions as output), or at least if relative prices are unaffected by changes in distribution along the entire outward envelope of the w(r) curves" (Petri 2004, p. 334). He also adds that "the marginal product of capital – and hence the decreasing demand-for-capital schedule – is not determined without a full-employment-of-labour assumption" (ibid., p. 270). See, for example, Felipe and McCombie (2014) for a recent reassessment of the fundamental flaws of these aspects of Neoclassical theory.

observed immediately afterwards and up to the financial crash of 2007, reaching a peak in 2006–2007. Indeed, in these years, FDI reached their maximum level, around a one percentage point of GDP higher than the previous peak.[17] The current crisis, marked by financial instability and depression, caused a further squeeze in FDI, although it remains at a substantially higher level than at the beginning of the 1990s.

Globalisation poses several challenges to national economies and governments. One of the most important is its effect on inequality—both within and between countries—and its impact on welfare state sustainability.

The new macroeconomic consensus of the last two to three decades is strictly linked to, if not completely corresponding with, the Washington Consensus doctrine, which calls for the implementation of some institutional forms that better suit the globalisation process such as the financialisation of the economy and the introduction of labour flexibility in the economy (see Tridico 2012). Moreover, the new macroeconomic consensus removes by construction inequality from the picture, being grounded on the assumption of the representative agent. Acemoglu (2011) argues that the policies implemented over the last two decades in particular were more closely aligned with the preferences of a minority of high-income voters in USA. Instead of redistributive policies favouring low- and middle-income constituents, politicians implemented financial deregulation policies favouring a small group of influential high-income earners (many of whom worked in, or directly benefited from, the financial sector).

To sum up, inequality has increased in most advanced and emerging economies over the last two decades—an era of growing interconnectedness of the world economy—as many studies have already shown (Atkinson 1999; Galbraith 2012; Piketty 2014), a simple look at Gini coefficients across countries indicates that trend. As can be seen in Fig. 4, between 1985 and 2012 inequality has increased in all the countries in the sample, in

[17]In 2000, FDI (net inflows) as a percentage of GDP amounted to 4.35%. The share then steadily decreased until it reached a trough in 2003 (1.81%). The trend was, however, rapidly reversed: in 2007 Foreign Direct Investments were at their top, being equal to about 5.3% of the World GDP. In 2015–2016 the datum has stabilised around 3.05% of GDP.

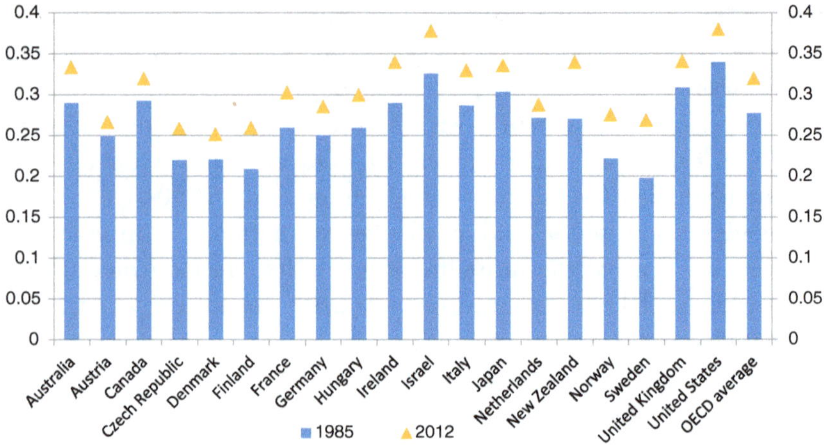

Fig. 4 Inequality—Gini coefficient (*Source* OECD. Stat database)

spite of these countries belonging to different welfare and socio-economic models. Austria and Netherlands, two small Continental Europe countries appear as those who experienced the smallest jump in inequality in the years under analysis. On the other extreme, and this might be considered not completely in line with standard received wisdom, Scandinavian countries as Finland, Norway, and Sweden stand out for the spike in the Gini coefficient, although they started from relatively lower levels.

5 Financialisation, Welfare Models, and Inequality

As has been shown elsewhere (Tridico 2018) empirical results suggest that what contributes to the increase or decrease of income inequality seems to be the nature of the socio-economic model that each country built during the decades after the Second World War. More specifically, what is most relevant is the set of policies that each country is currently able to implement in order to cope with the challenges of globalisation both in terms of income distribution and competitiveness (Rodrik 1999). These include in particular social protection against unemployment and low wages, welfare programs against poverty, health and education policies, social policy for housing, and so forth. In general, there seems to be a clear relationship between inequality and welfare expenditures in the sense that countries that spend more on welfare generally have a lower level of inequality (Tridico 2018).

After the Second World War, countries, especially those in Europe, invested increasing shares of their GDP in developing welfare states. This trend continued until the beginning of the 1990s. After that, and particularly after the peak reached in 1993, governments started to retrench welfare states and welfare expenditure was lower on the eve of the financial crisis in 2007 than in 1993 (OECD 2012).

According to the empirical evidence, which can be summarised in Fig. 5, Asian countries show the highest labour income shares, despite the huge decrease experienced in last decades. Furthermore, wage shares remain, on average, higher in Scandinavian and in Continental European countries, while they are lower in Anglo-Saxon, in Mediterranean and in Central and Eastern European countries. In our view, the most alarming

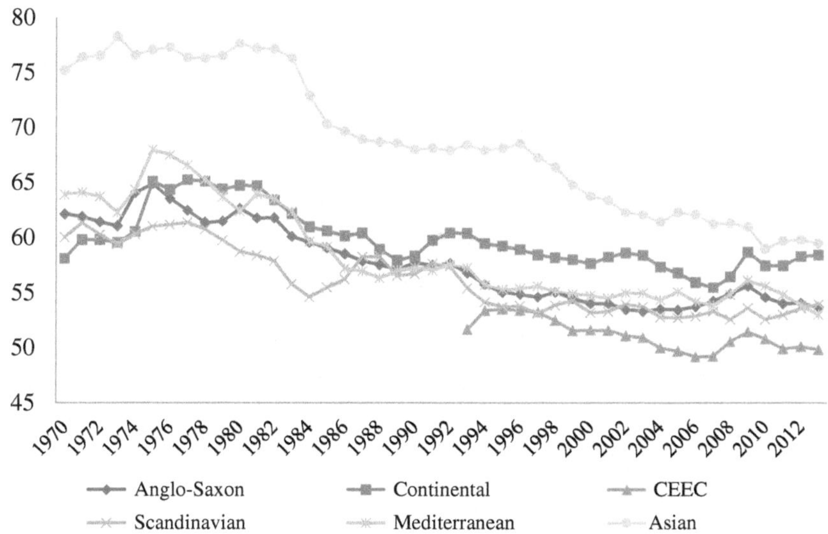

Fig. 5 Labour income shares by welfare model (1970/2013) (*Source* Our elaboration on data from ILO)

scenario refer to the Anglo-Saxon and the Mediterranean economies, which suffered the most from the restructuring process, occurred since the 1980s and progressively intensified. In this respect, it should be considered that globalisation has posed several challenges to national economies and governments. One of the most important issues is the pressure on labour relations and its impact on income inequality, both within and between countries, as well as its consequences on welfare state sustainability (Hay and Wincott 2012). In this context, the debate is very lively, and it has produced two main interpretations of the problem (see, for example, Tridico and Paternesi Meloni 2018).

The first one states that globalisation would press down the size of welfare states because social provision constitutes a cost for firms: since expanded welfare states lead to higher income taxes, social costs, and contributions, this would reduce prospective profits and increase companies' costs. These latter would be hence pushed to transfer capital abroad unless government retrenched welfare spending and reduced taxes: then, in order to maintain higher levels of investment and employment, the welfare state needs to be confined under the process of globalisation with bad consequences on income inequality. This interpretation is well known as the 'efficiency thesis', developed within the so-called 'neoliberal' paradigm: basically, it argues that globalisation has forced states to retrench social spending in order to achieve a market-friendly environment, to increasingly attract international capital and to foster external competitiveness (see Blackmon 2006; Castells 2004). Moreover, according to this view, welfare states can represent a cost for firms since due to capital mobility companies will de-localise to the lowest-cost location for production, putting pressure on governments to lower their welfare provision.

In contrast to this argument, a second approach emerged: the 'compensation thesis' maintains that since globalisation increases income inequality, welfare states should need to be expanded to mitigate vulnerability created by globalisation. In other words, increasing trade openness and capital mobility actually pressure governments to expand welfare support in order to compensate those who are damaged by the globalisation process (see Brady et al. 2005; Rodrik 1998): to put it simply, globalisation can produce net gains at the national level but within nations there can be winners and losers, then losers should be compensated by (partial) redistribution from the winners. In a way, following the 'compensation' argument, it can be also stated that welfare expansion would allow countries to further pursue globalisation. An extensive interpretation would then see welfare expansion not as a result but as a condition of globalisation: briefly, in order to continue (or to start) with the process of globalisation, policy makers must expand social safety nets.

Nonetheless, with respect to income inequality, it is widely recognised that the introduction of outsourcing practices and FDI outflows, globalisation has improved the bargaining position of capital relative to labour in higher-income countries. As Feenstra (1998) observes, the impact of globalisation on changing the bargaining position of labour and capital has far-reaching consequences—for instance, the decline in trade union power, particularly within export-oriented industries, may well account for a portion of increasing wage inequality in the United States and in other countries (Lavoie and Stockhammer 2013). Moreover, the decision (or just the possibility) of firms to relocate capital and production across countries has distributional effects since it can worsen the position of low-skilled workers in industrial countries by a combination of (1) growing globalisation; and (2) availability of new technologies. The first one, as well as exacerbating competition among workers, may increase the bargaining power of capital against labour, with the consequence that it is easier for capitalists to obtain tax reductions and welfare retrenchment, hence the states are willing to embark on tax competition among them in order to keep investment and production at home. The second one, according to the so-called *skill-biased technical change* argument, has a direct and negative impact on unskilled workers and their earnings—and consequently on real output in wage-led economies—in a context of lowering welfare support and social institutions.

As a consequence of these processes, during globalisation (and particularly during the 1990s and the 2000s) income inequality increased not only in emerging economies but also in advanced countries too.[18]

[18]See, for example, Atkinson (1999), Galbraith (2012) and Piketty (2014).

In this regard, Fig. 6 reports Gini coefficient across OECD countries, aggregated by welfare models.

As Fig. 6 shows, inequality is higher in Mediterranean and Anglo-Saxon countries. On the other hand, Scandinavian countries exhibit the lowest income inequality levels, despite a general, steady upward trend. Continental Europe and Central and Eastern European countries lay in between these two poles, while Asian countries display a pattern parallel (but at a slightly lower level) to that of Anglo-Saxon countries.

Financialisation (a process which involves a set of institutions and financial tools) and labour flexibility (a set of labour market policies that increase the ease with which businesses can fire and hire workers and cut wages) are two general categories of institutional arrangements that have gone hand in hand particularly during the last two decades, although not at the same pace everywhere. They have been introduced across the world by governments, in varying degrees, in order to take advantage of the globalisation process which most policy makers and governments believe will boost their national economy.

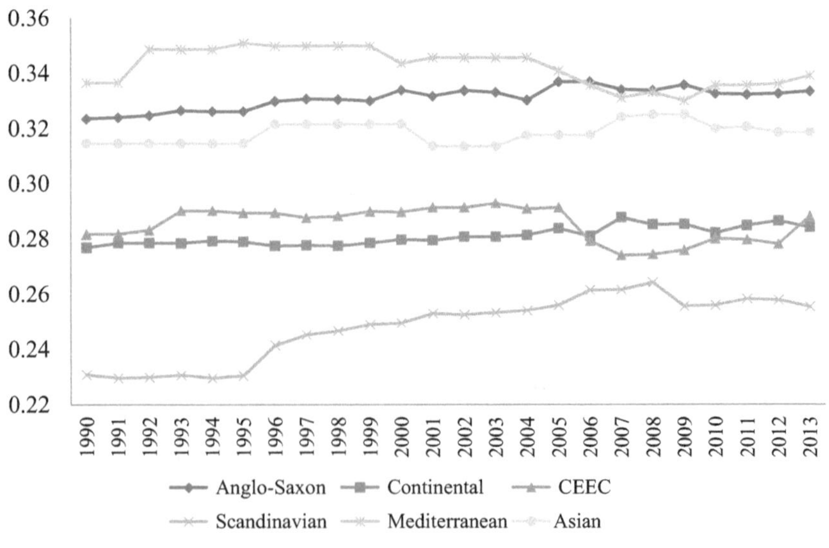

Fig. 6 Inequality (average Ginis) by welfare model (1990–2013) (*Source* Our elaboration on OCED)

Labour flexibility has increased almost everywhere in Europe and in advanced economies over the last 20 years. However, some countries, such as Austria, Belgium, France, and Germany have retained more rigid labour markets. Other economies, such as Denmark, Sweden, Finland, and the Netherlands, introduced higher levels of flexibility along with higher levels of security (OECD 2013). Countries such as the US, the UK, and Ireland increased (or maintained) their already very flexible labour markets. Finally, Mediterranean countries such as Italy, Spain, and Greece and most of the former communist economies in Europe combined very hybrid situations (of liberal and corporative elements) with an increased level of labour flexibility.

The political and economic roots of the financialisation process that brought about a new financial-led growth regime can be traced to the 1970s. After the fall of the Soviet Union, Alan Greenspan, who rose to oversee the US Federal Reserve by the end of the Reagan administration, believed that the world economy could expand greatly through the globalisation of the financial sector (Greenspan 2007). Many other economies followed the American example of a financial-led regime of accumulation, which used other institutional forms such as flexible labour and the nexus of compressed wages in order to increase firms' competitiveness (Tridico 2012). Shareholders sought higher dividends because they invested their own capital in firms, taking on a higher level of risk. Since the economic growth of advanced economies under financial capitalism has not been higher than under previous phases (the so-called Fordist period), as Fig. 7 shows, it follows that wages should be compressed in order for shareholders to obtain higher dividends. However, wages did not follow the increases in productivity and profits continued to soar (as was the case in most advanced countries and, in particular, in the US).

Figure 7 shows that the Fordist period (which is usually identified with the period before 1980) displays consistently higher GDP growth rates, in the countries under analysis and at the aggregate level. The decade 1981–1991 can be considered as a period of transition away from the previous accumulation regime and is characterised by the first traces of a growth slowdown, which fully manifests itself during the post-Fordist period, identified as the period from 1992 until today and marked by a steady acceleration in financialisation and globalisation.

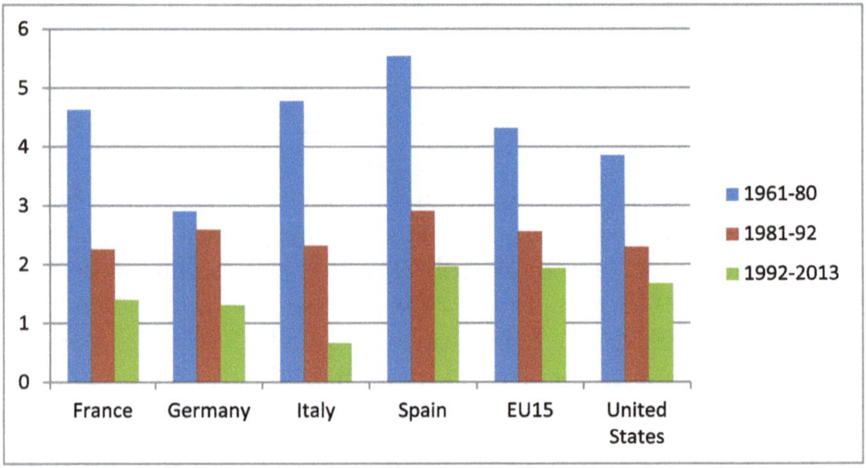

Fig. 7 Average GDP growth in the EU15 and the US (1961–2013) (*Source* The World Bank Database)

6 Other Determinants of Inequality: De-unionisation, Tax and Labour Market Institutions

As Lin and Tomaskovic-Devey (2013) argue, the increasing reliance by firms on earnings realised through financial channels generated surplus from production, strengthening owners' and elite workers' negotiating power relative to other workers. This resulted in the exclusion of most workers from revenue and, therefore, in the increase of inequality. Labour flexibility and wage contraction functioned to obtain this result (higher dividends for shareholders), at least in the short run.

The US promoted neo-liberalism as a main ideological paradigm for globalisation and financialisation through global, multi-, and bilateral measures under pressure from all the major international financial institutions, multinational corporations, and Wall Street institutions (Epstein 2005).

Importantly, within financial capitalism, the bargaining position of capital relative to labour in higher-income countries increased.

As Feenstra (1998, p. 46) observes, the impact of globalisation on changing the bargaining position of labour and capital has far-reaching consequences. The decline in union power, particularly within trade-oriented industries, may well account for a portion of the increased wage inequality in the United States and in other countries (Borjas and Ramey 1995; Gordon 2012). In this regard, a simple look at OECD data on trade union density shows a continuously decreasing trend for this variable, at the world level but also for most advanced economies.

Of particular interest seems to be the case of the USA where it is clear that throughout most of the twentieth century, the inverse relation existed between trade union membership and inequality. Gordon (2012) argues that between the New Deal—which granted, among other important things, workers' basic collective bargaining rights—and the end of 1960s, '*labor unions both sustained prosperity, and ensured that it was shared.*' Since the 1970s, and in particular during the Reagan administration, 'unions came under attack—in the workplace, in the courts, and in public policy. As a result, union membership has fallen and income inequality has worsened—reaching levels not seen since the 1920s.' Gordon (op. cit.) also shows evidence that the process of de-unionisation and the increase in inequality have moved hand in hand in the last 70 years: beginning from the 1950s, the degree of unionisation in the US slowly starts to decrease, with this diminution gaining momentum since the beginning of the 1980s. In the same time span, the share of income going to the top 10% displays a specular, opposite trend: it starts to increase in correspondence with the first signs of reduction in trade union density and then it accelerates its growth during the 1980s.

The decline in unionisation rates has contributed to the weakening of labour market institutions such as labour protection against firing and hiring, the level and duration of unemployment benefits with the introduction of constraints concerning eligibility, and the reduction in most cases of their length and amount, the minimum wage, etc. In Tridico (2017), a score of 9 indicators of labour market institutions is presented in correlation against the inequality index (Gini). This score is obtained through a factor analysis carried out in order to establish the most important elements which explain variation among the nine institutional indicators.[19] The evidence presented displays a clear correlation: the higher the score of the principal component (more protection in the labour market), the lower the Gini level, and vice versa.[20]

The OECD's Employment Protection Legislation (EPL) indicator is probably one of the most important labour market indicators, at least for our purposes in this paper, as far as it is able to capture labour market flexibility, which represents a crucial variable in our analysis and the evolution of which represents one of the most important changes in the labour market in the last two decades in many advanced economies. It measures the general level of worker protection in the labour market and, consequently, the level of labour flexibility (it varies between 0 for very low protection and 6 for very high protection). In essence, it shows the level of protection offered by national legislation with respect to regular employment, temporary employment, and collective dismissal; in other words, regulation that allows employers to fire and hire workers at will. Looking at the pattern of average EPL levels among OECD countries, a sharp and continuous decline can be observed, starting in 1990 and until 2013 (the last date for which OECD issues data on this index), pointing to a sustained increase in labour flexibility,

As already noted by Hall and Soskice (2001) and by Storm and Naastepad (2012), complementarities between labour flexibility and financialisation are strong in advanced economies. A flexible labour market with compressed wages needs to be supplemented by available financialisation, credit, and developed financial tools to sustain consumption, which otherwise would be compressed by low and unstable wages. Therefore, a large number of financial tools were invented to finance consumption, postpone payments, extend credit, and create extra-consumption. That being said, it is difficult to establish a causal relationship: we cannot be

---

[19]Active Policy 2012 (% of GDP), Passive Policy 2012 (% of GDP), Coverage (in % of workers) of trade Unions 2009–2011, Level of coordination bargaining wage, Length of unemployment subsidies (in months) 2011, Substitution rate for unemployment Subsidies (% 2009–2011), Minimum wage, hourly (US$ PPP), EPL and Trade Union density. All data from OECD online database.

[20]A similar result was obtained by Butcher et al. (2012) and by Autor et al. (2016) who found that minimum wages have little effect on employment, but do have impacts on wage inequality, in particular in the UK and in the US during the 1990s and 2000s.

certain whether financialisation requires labour flexibility or if increased labour flexibility brings about hyper-financialisation. A simple, but important, correlation between these two complementary institutional forms of neoliberalism seems more likely.

Labour flexibility allows for the reduction of firms' labour costs and, thus, wage savings at the expense of wage earners; that is, consumers. In such a situation, inequality increases and aggregate demand is restricted because consumption decreases.

It is very interesting to notice an inverse relationship between inequality and the EPL index (labour flexibility): the lower the EPL (higher labour flexibility), the higher the inequality. Continental and Scandinavian European countries have a higher EPL (lower labour flexibility) and lower inequality relative to Anglo-Saxon and Mediterranean countries, which generally show the opposite values of higher inequality and lower EPL (higher labour flexibility).[21]

As a result, one can see that high financialisation is typically associated with high Gini coefficients and high labour flexibility. More interesting are the parallel trends of these variables: when financialisation increases, both flexibility and inequality increases. In other words, as was argued elsewhere (Tridico 2012), the rise of inequality generated an increased demand for credit, which translated into a credit expansion provided for by accommodating monetary policies and financial deregulation. One should take particular notice of the particular path of Scandinavian countries (especially Sweden and Finland) which display a relatively high degree of financialisation, but yet, are able to limit inequality (which nevertheless is increasing) with their strong welfare states (along with other labour market institutions).

Last but not least, tax policy deserves further attention as far as increase in income inequality is concerned. Many economists in the recent years showed, empirically, a strong correlation between inequality and tax reduction, in particular for top income earners (Piketty 2014; Atkinson et al. 2011; Facundo et al. 2013). In fact, as extensively shown in Piketty (2014), the top marginal taxation, among advanced

[21]See Tridico (2018).

economies, decreased steadily since 1970 from 60 to 80%, and stabilised before 1990 around a rate of 40–50%. It can be noticed that this evolution has been very similar in countries such as, for example US, United Kingdom, Japan, Germany, and France and might have contributed, in that period, and immediately after, to the increase of inequality.

However, between 1990 up to today, top marginal rates on income earned was stable with little variation around 45% in most of advanced economies, and in the last part of this period, after 2007, slowly increased to 48%. Data on personal income tax show this pattern as discussed, for example, in Tridico (2018).

On the other hand, when looking at data on tax on dividends, both corporate income tax and personal income tax, between 2000–2017 in the 25 OECD countries under analysis, decreased steadily (the decrease of corporate income tax was more marked and it amounted to a diminution of almost 10 percentage points in the 17 years of the sample). This is consistent with our hypothesis of financialisation of the economy. Low taxes on dividends pushed economic agents to invest in the financial sectors and in particular on shares.

7 Inequality, Financialisation, and Economic Decline

We have discussed above the main determinants behind the rise in income inequality and the compression of the wage share, experienced by most advanced economies in the last decades. As we have argued, these phenomena prompted an intense debate on the macroeconomic consequences of inequality, particularly in connection with the specular diffusion of household debt which, according to several authors[22] has acted as a substitute for wages in financing private consumption. However, the ongoing worsening in income equality poses a further, perhaps less discussed threat. Storm and Naastepad (2015,

[22]See, for example, the already mentioned Barba and Pivetti (2009), Rajan (2010), Stockhammer (2015).

p. 973) rightfully identify as a main problem for the Eurozone '*the wide differentials in labour productivity and technological capabilities*' among its members. Similar supply-side aspects are often neglected or only marginally treated in the critical Keynesian literature, leaving the field open for the recipes proposed by the international institutions, according to which the simple remedy to lack of external competitiveness is internal devaluation and wage compression. Nonetheless, relying on a Classical-Kaldorian approach, it is possible to identify a weak GDP performance and a decline in the wage share as major explanatory factors of sluggish productivity. Moreover, drawing inspiration from recent Post-Keynesian literature, it can also be argued that the increases of income inequality and of the degree of financialisation of economies have hindered the dynamics of labour productivity.

A systemic picture can be drawn from the work of Paolo Sylos Labini (see, for example, Sylos Labini 1984, 1999), who stressed the connections among labour productivity, the dynamics of demand, the relative price of production inputs (capital and labour, in this case), and income distribution. It is possible to synthetically convey the main Sylos Labini's insights by means of the following productivity equation (Sylos Labini 1999, p. 259):

$$g^{\lambda} = g^{Y/L} = f(g^{Y},\ W/P_{\mathrm{ma}},\ 1-\Pi),\ \text{with}\ f'_{gY}, f'_{W/P_{\mathrm{ma}}}, f'_{1-\Pi} > 0 \quad (1)$$

The rate of growth of labour productivity λ—equal to the ratio between output (Y) and the level of employment (L)—is a positive function of output expansion, the relative cheapness of labour over capital (W is an index of the real wage, P_{ma} is the price index of machinery) and the wage share $(1-\Pi)$.

The first argument of the equation captures what the author calls the 'Smith effect' ('*the division of labour depends on the extent of the market; and the division of labour is at the origin of those* – Sylos Labini is referring here to labour productivity—*increases,*' Sylos Labini 1999, p. 258) and describes a mechanism similar to the already introduced Kaldor-Verdoorn effect. The second argument—the price of labour relative to the price of investment—is labelled as the 'Ricardo effect' and finds its rationale '*in the classical notion of induced, factor-biased technical change*' (Tronti 2010, p. 784).

Sylos Labini, however, focuses its attention on the productivity-enhancing role of the wage share: from the entrepreneur's perspective, the pressure exerted by the increasing cost of labour provides a stimulus to reorganise the production process in a more efficient way; moreover, it also incentives, by making the necessary investment relatively convenient, the adoption of technologically advanced equipment and machinery, which allow to raise production without having to increase the number of employees. As reported in Lavoie (2014), traces of this intuition date back to Webb (1912), a seminal contribution whose main purpose was to support a proposal for the establishment of a legal minimum wage. The basic idea is that, as long as wage compression is prevented, entrepreneurs have to find other ways to lower the production costs with respect to their competitors. Indeed, they are induced to hunt for productivity gains, to be generated by means of improvements in the productive process. Furthermore, the institution of a minimum wage is plausibly followed by an increase in the real wage, which can be troublesome and push out of the market firms which do not keep pace with technological innovations. As a consequence, the average productivity and efficiency of productive units which remain active are higher (Webb 1912, p. 984). As Webb vividly puts it, '*the enforcement of the Common Rule (i.e. a legal minimum wage) concentrates the pressure of competition on the brains of the employers and keeps them always on the stretch*' (Webb 1912, p. 983).

A similar line of reasoning is developed in Altman (1998), where the effect of higher wages on labour productivity is decomposed into several components: (a) the so-called x-inefficiencies are reduced. Low compensations and more in general a conflictual working environment are detrimental for the firm's work culture and negatively affect workers' effort. The improvement of workers' conditions, on the other hand, contributes to the establishment of more cooperative industrial relations and elicits employees' commitment; and (b) given that '*low wages can serve as a substitute for technological change*' (ibid., p. 101), firms which experience rising labour costs may be compelled to adopt already existing innovative techniques or to develop new ones.

The idea of a positive influence of the wage share on the economy's productivity has been picked up also by authors such Cassetti (2003) and Hein and Tarassow (2010), who include the Webb-Sylos Labini effect into a Kaleckian growth and distribution model. In these formalisations, as a response to an exogenous increase in workers' bargaining power, capitalists try to defend their income share by means of an improvement in productivity and the consequent reduction in labour unit costs. Post-Keynesian scholars have also substantiated convincingly the effects of income distribution on the productivity dynamics. Naastepad (2006) studies the Dutch case and concludes that '*a reduction in real wage growth is likely to slow down productivity growth*' (Naastepad 2006, p. 428): not only wage moderation inhibits induced technical change; if the economy's demand regime is wage-led, it harms labour productivity also indirectly, through the Kaldor-Verdoorn effect. Similar conclusions are presented in the empirical part of Hein and Tarassow (2010). The authors estimate the nature of the demand and productivity regimes of six OECD countries: a direct negative effect of the profit share on productivity growth is found for five out of the six countries in the sample, since at least the beginning of the 1980s. The indirect effect—operating through the impact of shifts in functional income distribution on GDP growth—is at work for the four countries that are found to be wage-led. Indeed, the analysis also confirms the prevalence of the Kaldor-Verdoorn effect for the whole period. Hartwig (2013) and Hartwig (2014) extend the Marglin-Bhaduri growth model (Bhaduri and Marglin 1990), to study the interaction between demand growth and productivity growth. The former analyses the case of Switzerland for the 1950–2010 period; the main result is that, despite the Swiss demand regime being profit led, the overall effect of real wage growth on productivity growth is (weakly) negative, and the productivity regime is wage-led. The latter (Hartwig 2014) performs a panel data analysis on OECD countries, concluding that, on average, 'real wage growth has a direct positive effect on productivity growth (the wage-induced technological progress) and an indirect positive effect that stems from real wage growth increasing demand growth (since the demand regime is wage-led), which in turn raises productivity growth through the Verdoorn channel' (Hartwig 2014, p. 429).

On the basis of the brief discussion above, it is possible to conclude that wage compression and a worsening in income distribution do not alone necessarily enhance the external competitiveness and dynamism of a country. On the contrary, they might create a drag on productivity and inhibit technical change. In this regard, the case of the Southern European countries described in Storm and Naastepad (2015) is paradigmatic: low wages countries tend to remain stuck in low-tech production segments, specialised in 'commodities and destination markets where demand growth is above average' (ibid., p. 968) and exposed to the competition of countries with a permanent advantage in terms of labour cheapness.

In this context, financialisation plays a prominent role as well. Financialisation is connected with both a re-distribution of income in favour of profit-recipients and labour productivity slowdown. This is an important point that finds empirical evidences and theoretical foundations. In his thorough overview, Hein (2015) singles out seven stylised facts connected to financialisation that, following a Kaleckian approach, impact directly functional income distribution: 'increasing shareholder value orientation and increasing short-termism of management; rising dividend payments; increasing interest rates and interest payments, in particular in the 1980s; increasing top management salaries; increasing relevance of financial as compared to real investment and hence of the financial sector relative to the non-financial sector; hostile takeovers, mergers and acquisitions; and liberalisation and globalisation of international finance and trade' (Hein 2015, pp. 924–925). Later on, the author also mentions the strong reduction of public intervention in the economy and the implementation of labour market deregulations, both occurred since the beginning of the 1980s. As also noticed by Hein, we can add that financialisation worsens income distribution—and in turn this affects labour productivity—also because of the following:

1. It favours the aggressive implementation of the principle 'downsize and distribute' so that corporations' managers have as the only objective to maximize and distribute dividends for the shareholders at the cost of squeezing production and cutting wages.

2. It favours an aggressive short terms strategy of corporations' managers interested mainly in the maximisation of bonuses and profits in the short term at the expenses of the wage bill.

We are interested here in assessing if and to what extent financialisation has affected the recent trends in productivity. This idea has been analytically investigated, within the framework of a Post-Kaleckian endogenous growth model, in Hein (2012). As the author maintains, financialisation might have, at first, a direct positive effect on productivity. However, also indirect effects are at work: financialisation might negatively affect demand growth and, through the functioning of the Kaldor-Verdoorn effect, also the dynamics of productivity. Moreover, financialisation is likely to weaken workers' bargaining power and reduce the wage share. Given that a wage-push component is included in the productivity equation, the overall effect can be plausibly expected to be negative. Indeed, there are several theoretical reasons to expect a negative relationship between financialisation and productivity growth. It seems possible, in particular, to identify a causal link that goes from the prominence attributed to shareholder value orientation—one of the main features of financialisation (see Lazonick and O'Sullivan 2000)—to a decline in aggregate investment. The spectacular increase in interest and dividend payments to rentiers not only implies a loss in firms' internal means of finance, but also makes the recourse to external sources to finance capital accumulation more expensive and complicated, as highlighted by the Kaleckian principle of increasing risk. Moreover, the implementation of remuneration schemes for managers based on the firm's short-term performance on the financial markets is supposed to cause a slowdown in investment in capital stock, replaced by financial operations as a major concern for management.[23]

[23]Orhangazi (2008) finds empirical evidence of a negative influence of financialisation on real investment, using data on US non-financial corporations for the 1973–2003 period. Similar results can be found in Onaran et al. (2011), regarding the US economy in 1960–2007. More recently, Tori and Onaran's analysis of the behaviour of physical investment in selected European countries show that "financialisation, depicted as the increasing orientation towards external financing, shareholder value orientation and the internal substitution of fixed investment by financial activity, had a fundamental role in suppressing investment in the NFCs (non-financial corporations)" (Tori and Onaran 2017, p. 35).

As a natural consequence of an unsatisfactory investment dynamics, productivity lags behind. This is one of the most relevant conclusions of Lazonick and O'Sullivan's (op. cit.) analysis, where it is noticed that US corporate managers—but the same holds true for most of the OECD countries—in recent years have faced the new challenges posed by international competitors mainly by downsizing firms and compressing labour costs. At the same time, they renounced attaining productivity gains through the reinvestment of profits and chose to pursue short-term profitability.

Financialisation diverts assets and resources towards speculative rather than productive investments with negative consequences on technological progress, which directly influences labour productivity. Labour flexibility influences negatively labour productivity because allows for size reduction and employment squeezing: it reduces income opportunities and the wage share, increases precarious jobs, and de-stabilises aggregate demand. At the same time, a flexible labour market with compressed and low wages needs to be supplemented by credit consumption and developed financial tools to sustain consumption, reinforcing a vicious circle.

Deregulation of labour markets, labour flexibility, capital mobility and global finance allow easily for labour pressure, cost compression, and wage stagnation. Consecutively, households are more and more pushed towards private indebtedness and credit consumption since their income constraints increase consistently in a period of wage stagnation. In this context, income inequality increases because labour, which is the most important production factor for income, is seen by the supply-side approach as a cost to be compressed rather than as a fundamental part of aggregate demand to be expanded.

The negative relation between labour productivity and labour flexibility can also be identified in the perspective of the models of the new consensus macroeconomics that describe, at margin, work effort to be positively correlated with wages, so that unstable jobs, flexibility, scarce incentives, and low paid jobs push workers to put little effort into their work. Moreover, this does not guarantee that firms and workers invest in training and education in order to improve the quality of human capital, with lower results in terms of productivity, ceteris paribus, by the economic system (Salop 1979; Shapiro and Stiglitz 1984). From a non-mainstream perspective, similar arguments can be found in the works of Vergeer and Kleinknecht. In Vergeer and Kleinknecht (2010), the authors perform a panel data analysis based on 19 OECD countries, for the period 1960–2004. Among their main results, flexible labour relations are found to damage labour productivity growth through multiple channels (p. 393) and to disincentive knowledge accumulation. Interestingly, Vergeer and Kleinknecht provide evidence that the labour productivity slowdown is not only due to the creation of precarious, deregulated, low-productivity jobs, but also the productivity of existing jobs is negatively affected. Vergeer and Kleinknecht (2014) perform a similar exercise for 20 OECD countries, in the same time span (1960–2004) of Vergeer and Kleinknecht (2010), substantially confirming the main findings presented there. Attention is drawn on the fact that easier hiring and firing procedures, leading to shorter job tenures, prevent the formation of firm-specific, 'tacit' knowledge, and hinder the functioning of the 'routinised' innovation model (Vergeer and Kleinknecht 2014, p. 383).

We have discussed so far mainly contributions belonging to non-mainstream schools of thought. Indeed, our section aims to enrich the Post-Keynesian literature concerned with the study of the endogenous dynamics of labour productivity. For a more orthodox account of similar issues, a useful reference is Cette et al. (2016), where the authors summarise some Neo-classical explanations for the pre-Great Recession decline in productivity. For what concerns Continental Europe, a main problem seems to be represented (not surprisingly) by structural rigidities in the labour and product markets, which prevented these countries from benefitting 'as much from reorganizations associated with ICT as the US and UK' (Cette et al. 2016, p. 7). Southern Europe, apparently, suffers from a further disease, represented by the fall in interest rates that followed the introduction of Euro. According to Cette and co-authors, and also to the literature mentioned in the article, low interest rates—and abundant credit—can affect negatively total factor productivity through three channels: (a) capital inflows tend to be misallocated towards low-productivity sectors like services or construction instead of manufacturing; (b) within a sector, low-productivity firms may get their investment project funded while the more efficient ones, for some reasons, may not; (c) low interest rates can damage the quality of a country's institutions. Within the mainstream, another recent, relevant contribution is Thimann (2015): competitiveness issues in the Eurozone are due to 'high labor costs relative to underlying productivity' (p. 142), with labour productivity problems not being addressed, given the lack of appropriate structural reforms (p. 155).

We will not discuss, in the remaining of the chapter, these ideas and we leave to future research a critical assessment of them.

As we have argued elsewhere (Tridico and Pariboni 2017a), an alternative take on the dynamics of labour productivity, based on the literature discussed in this section, can be summarised through an extended and modified Sylos Labini equation:

$$g^{\lambda} = g^{Y/L} = f(g^{Y}, 1 - \Pi, \text{Ineq}, \text{Fin}) \quad (2)$$

according to which the growth of labour productivity is thought to be a positive function of the rate of growth of the economy and of the wage share, while inequality and financialisation represent a drag on its dynamics.[24]

8 Concluding Remarks

The rise of income inequality and the related generalised compression of the share of income attributable to workers are probably THE economic facts of the last decades. In this chapter, we have attempted to provide a broad overview of these phenomena. We have identified, consistently with a vast body of mostly non-mainstream literature, financialisation, and globalisation as two of the main determinants of both wage share diminution and income equality worsening. In the introductory section, we have provided an overview on the multifaceted socio-economic phenomenon known as financialisation. As we have argued,

[24]See Tridico and Pariboni (2017a) for an empirical validation of this extended version of the Sylos Labini productivity equation.

financialisation's potentially disruptive effects on income distribution have been confirmed by several empirical studies and find their rationale in a growing body of theoretical literature: first of all, it has contributed to the increase in financial pay-out ratios, which lead to distributional changes detrimental to non-shareholders. Indeed, prominent scholars in the literature on shareholder value have acknowledged that financialisation is, by construction, a '*redistributive process.*' Multiple other channels can be and have been identified, but we believe it is useful to recall here the analysis on the effects of the financialisation of everyday life, as proposed by Van der Zwan (2014): new subjectivities are developed and workers begin to implicitly perceive themselves as investors and owners of financial assets. The individual dimension of responsibilities and the adoption of self-fulfilment as the main purpose of life undermine class consciousness. As a consequence, the bargaining power of the worker class as a whole is under siege by individualism and is harder and harder to defend and sustain a fair split of the social product. Globalisation, as well, exerts a pressure on wage recipients mainly by altering the balance of powers between labour and capital, which can benefit from the expansion of the global labour reserve army and use the threat of relocations to strengthen their bargaining position and obtain advantages from governments. We have also argued that globalisation and financialisation are not two separated, independent processes. Their timing is similar and tends to be complementary aspects of a broader political, economic, and social transformation, which has been synthetically labelled as Neoliberalism. The impact of financialisation, however, does not happen in a vacuum, but is mediated by the institutional framework, as we have discussed in the section devoted to the interaction with different welfare models. In fact, the choice of the socio-economic model, made by most countries in the decades after the Second World War, seems to contribute relevantly to the evolution over time of income inequality. The set of policies each country is able to implement in order to cope with the challenges of globalisation, both in terms of income distribution and competitiveness are of paramount importance: social protection against unemployment and low wages, welfare programs against poverty, health and education policies, social policy for housing, just to mention some of them, can alleviate the burden on the most vulnerable layers of a country's population. In general, there seems to be a clear relationship between inequality and welfare expenditures, meaning that countries spending more on welfare tend to have a lower level of inequality. The deregulation of the labour market and the stream of labour reforms aiming at increasing flexibility have also played a significant role with respect to both inequality and the shift of income in favour of the richer fractions of population, since the precarious nature of job tenure makes workers reluctant to engage in workplace struggles and capital's bargaining power is enhanced by a decrease in labour rigidity. Finally, the gradual abandonment of manufacturing and the structural change that has been taking place since the 1970s is likely to exert a downward pressure on wages as well, in connection with trends of de-unionisation and tax reforms that benefit the few. In this chapter, we have tried to build a bridge between different theoretical perspectives. The backbone of our argument could be considered somehow old-fashioned: the main force behind the distribution of the social product is the balance of bargaining power between social classes. Adopting this perspective, we have attempted to substantiate this claim by asking ourselves how financialisation and globalisation can alter the power equilibrium. We have then framed these questions in the context of alternative welfare socio-economic models and enriched the analysis with the explicit consideration of institutional features of these different models.

The phenomena briefly recalled here represent multiple aspects of an unsustainable and inequitable growth trajectory. The implications, however, go beyond the standard domain of heterodox economics. We started with Storm and Naastepad's (Storm and Naastepad 2015) who claim that differences in productivity and technological capabilities are of major importance to explain diverging economic performances across countries. We also agree with these authors that the mainstream received wisdom—according to which external competitiveness and labour productivity have to be enhanced through labour costs compression and labour flexibilisation—is extremely unconvincing. Hence, we sketched an alternative interpretative framework for the analysis of endogenous labour productivity: following a Classical-Kaldorian approach, we have argued that a weak GDP performance and a decrease in the wage share contribute to explain a decline in labour productivity growth. Drawing inspiration from recent Post-Keynesian literature, we have also identified financialisation and income inequality as factors with a negative influence on the evolution of labour productivity. Existing literature has extensively dealt with non-mainstream explanations of the labour productivity slowdown. With this contribution, we have attempted to provide a unified, systemic interpretation of multiple and complementary factors that are likely to represent a drag on the dynamics of productivity. In particular, we have tried to enrich and update the insights that can be derived from Sylos Labini's productivity function, complementing the traditional Kaldor-Verdoorn-Smith effect and cost-push effect with a consideration of the effects of financialisation and income inequality.

References

Acemoglu, D. (2011). *Thoughts on Inequality and the Financial Crisis*. Paper presented at the American Economic Association. Available at: http://economics.mit.edu/files/6348.

Altman, M. (1998). A High Wage Path to Economic Growth and Development. *Challenge, 41*(1), 91–104.

Argitis, G., & Pitelis, C. (2008). Global Finance and Systemic Instability. *Contributions to Political Economy, 27*, 1–11.

Atkinson, A. B. (1999). *The Economic Consequences of Rolling Back the Welfare State*. London and Cambridge, MA: MIT Press.

Atkinson, A. B., Piketty, T., & Saez, E. (2011). Top Incomes in the Long Run of History. *Journal of Economic Literature, 49*(1), 3–71.

Autor, D., Manning, A., & Smith, C. (2016). The Contribution of the Minimum Wage to U.S. Wage Inequality Over Three Decades: A Reassessment. *American Economic Journal: Applied Economics, 8*(1), 58–99.

Barba, A., & Pivetti, M. (2009). Rising Household Debt: Its Causes and Macroeconomic Implications—A Long Period Analysis. *Cambridge Journal of Economics, 33*(1), 113–137.

Baumol, W. J. (2002). Services as Leaders and the Leader of the Services. In J. Gadrey & F. Gallouj (Eds.), *Productivity, Innovation and Knowledge in Service* (pp. 147–163). Cheltenham: Edward Elgar.

Baumol, W. J., & Bowen, W. G. (1965). On the Performing Arts: The Anatomy of Their Economic Problems. *The American Economic Review, 55*(1/2), 495–502.
Baumol, W. J., Batey Blackman, S. A., & Wolff, E. N. (1989). *Productivity and American Leadership. The Long View*. London: MIT Press.
Bhaduri, A., & Marglin, S. (1990). Unemployment and the Real Wage: The Economic Basis for Contesting Political Ideologies. *Cambridge Journal of Economics, 14*(4), 375–393.
Bhagwati, J. (2004). *In Defense of Globalization*. Oxford: Oxford University Press.
BIS. (2013). *Triennial Central Bank Survey*. Bank for International Settlements, Monetary and Economic Department, Basel.
Blackmon, P. (2006). The State: Back in the Center of the Globalization Debate. *International Studies Review, 8*(1), 116–119.
Borjas, G. J., & Ramey, V. A. (1995). Foreign Competition, Market Power, and Wage Inequality. *The Quarterly Journal of Economics, 110*(4), 1075–1110.
Boyer, R. (2000). Is a Finance-Led Growth Regime a Viable Alternative to Fordism? A Preliminary Analysis. *Economy and Society, 29*(1), 111–145.
Boyer, R. (2009). Come conciliare la solidarietà sociale e l'efficienza economica nell'era della globalizzazione: un punto di vista regolazionista. *Argomenti, 25*(May/August), 5–31.
Brady, D., Beckfield, J., & Seeleib-Kaiser, M. (2005). Economic Globalization and the Welfare State in Affluent Democracies, 1975–2001. *American Sociological Review, 70*(6), 921–948.
Butcher, T., Dickens, R., & Manning, A. (2012). *Minimum Wages and Wage Inequality: Some Theory and an Application to the UK* (CEP Discussion Paper No. 1177).
Cassetti, M. (2003). Bargaining Power, Effective Demand and Technical Progress: A Kaleckian Model of Growth. *Cambridge Journal of Economics, 27*(3), 449–464.
Castells, M. (2004). Global Informational Capitalism. In A. G. McGrew & D. Held (Eds.), *The Global Transformations Reader: An Introduction to the Globalization Debate* (pp. 311–334). Cambridge: Polity Press.
Cette, G., Fernald, J., & Mojon, B. (2016). The Pre-great Recession Slowdown in Productivity. *European Economic Review, 88*(C), 3–20.
Cirillo, V., & Guarascio, D. (2015). Jobs and Competitiveness in a Polarised Europe. *Intereconomics, 50*(3), 156–160.

Dünhaupt, P. (2017). Determinants of Labour's Income Share in the Era of Financialisation. *Cambridge Journal of Economics, 41*(1), 283–306.
Epstein, G. (Ed.). (2005). *Financialization and the World Economy.* Cheltenham: Edward Elgar.
Facundo, A., Atkinson, A. B., Piketty, T., & Saez, E. (2013). The Top 1 Percent in International and Historical Perspective. *Journal of Economic Perspectives, 27*(3), 3–20.
Feenstra, R. C. (1998). Integration of Trade and Disintegration of Production in the Global Economy. *Journal of Economic Perspectives, 12*(4), 31–50.
Felipe, J., & McCombie, J. S. L. (2014). The Aggregate Production Function: 'Not Even Wrong'. *Review of Political Economy, 26*(1), 60–84.
Galbraith, J. K. (2012). *Inequality and Instability.* Oxford: Oxford University Press.
Garegnani, P. (1970). Heterogeneous Capital, the Production Function and the Theory of Distribution. *The Review of Economic Studies, 37*(3), 407–436.
Garegnani, P. (1976). The Neoclassical Production Function: Comment. *The American Economic Review, 66*(3), 424–427.
Gordon, C. (2012, June). *Union Decline and Rising Inequality in Two Charts.* Economic Policy Institute. Available at: www.epi.org/blog/union-decline-rising-inequality-charts.
Greenspan, A. (2007). *The Age of Turbulence: Adventures in a New World.* New York: The Penguin Press.
Hall, P. A., & Soskice, D. (2001). *Varieties of Capitalism: The Institutional Foundations of Comparative Advantage.* Oxford: Oxford University Press.
Hartwig, J. (2013). Distribution and Growth in Demand and Productivity in Switzerland (1950–2010). *Applied Economics Letters, 20*(10), 938–944.
Hartwig, J. (2014). Testing the Bhaduri–Marglin Model with OECD Panel Data. *International Review of Applied Economics, 28*(4), 419–435.
Hartwig, J. (2015). Structural Change, Aggregate Demand and Employment Dynamics in the OECD, 1970–2010. *Structural Change and Economic Dynamics, 34*(3), 36–45.
Hay, C., & Wincott, D. (2012). *The Political Economy of European Welfare Capitalism.* New York: Palgrave Macmillan.
Hein, E. (2012). Financialization, Distribution, Capital Accumulation, and Productivity Growth in a Post-Kaleckian Model. *Journal of Post Keynesian Economics, 34*(3), 475–496.

Hein, E. (2015). Finance-Dominated Capitalism and Redistribution of Income: A Kaleckian Perspective. *Cambridge Journal of Economics, 39*(3), 907–934.
Hein, E. (2017). *Financialisation and Tendencies Towards Stagnation: The Role of Macroeconomic Regime Changes in the Course of and After the Financial and Economic Crisis 2007–9* (Working Paper 90/2017). IPE-Berlin.
Hein, E., & Schoder, C. (2011). Interest Rates, Distribution and Capital Accumulation—A Post-Kaleckian Perspective on the US and Germany. *International Review of Applied Economics, 25*(6), 693–723.
Hein, E., & Tarassow, A. (2010). Distribution, Aggregate Demand and Productivity Growth: Theory and Empirical Results for Six OECD Countries Based on a Post-Kaleckian Model. *Cambridge Journal of Economics, 34*(4), 727–754.
Hein, E., & Vogel, L. (2008). Distribution and Growth Reconsidered—Empirical Results for Six OECD Countries. *Cambridge Journal of Economics, 32*(3), 479–511.
Held, D., McGrew, A., Goldblatt, D., & Perraton, J. (1999). *Global Transformations: Politics, Economics and Culture*. Cambridge: Polity.
ILO, IMF, OECD, & World Bank. (2015, September). *Income Inequality and Labour Income Share in G20 Countries: Trends, Impacts and Causes*. Report prepared for the G20 Labour and Employment Ministers Meeting and Joint Meeting with the G20 Finance Ministers, Ankara.
ILO, & OECD. (2015, February). *The Labour Share in G20 Economies*. Report prepared for the G20 Employment Working Group, Antalya.
Kindleberger, C. P. (2005). *Manias, Panics, and Crashes: A History of Financial Crises*. New York: Wiley.
Kok, W. (2004). *Kok Report: Facing the Challenge. The Lisbon Strategy for Employment and Growth*. Report from the High Level Group, chaired by Wim Kok. Available at: http://www.umic.pt/images/stories/publicacoes200801/kok_report_en.pdf.
Krippner, G. R. (2005). The Financialization of the American Economy. *Socio-Economic Review, 3*(2), 173–208.
Lapavitsas, C., & Powell, J. (2013). Financialisation Varied: A Comparative Analysis of Advanced Economies. *Cambridge Journal of Regions, Economy and Society, 6*(3), 359–379.
Lavoie, M. (2014). *Post-Keynesian Economics. New Foundations*. Cheltenham: Elgar.
Lavoie, M., & Stockhammer, E. (2013). *Wage-Led Growth: An Equitable Strategy for Economic Recovery*. Basingstoke: Palgrave Macmillan.

Lazonick, W., & O'Sullivan, M. (2000). Maximizing Shareholder Value: A New Ideology for Corporate Governance. *Economy and Society, 29*(1), 13–35.

Leamer, E. (1996). Wage Inequality from International Competition and Technological Changes: Theory and Country Experience. *American Economic Review, 86*(2), 309–314.

Lee, E. (1996). Globalization and Employment: Is Anxiety Justified? *International Labour Review, 135*(5), 485–497.

Lewis, A. (1980). The Slowing Down of the Engine of Growth: Nobel Lecture. *American Economic Review, 70*(4), 555–564.

Lin, K.-H., & Tomaskovic-Devey, D. (2013). Financialization and US Income Inequality, 1970–2008. *American Journal of Sociology, 118*(5), 1284–1329.

Lucas, R. (1993). Making a Miracle. *Econometrica, 61*(2), 251–257.

Marglin, S. A., & Bhaduri, A. (1990). Profit Squeeze and Keynesian Theory. In S. A. Marglin & J. B. Schor (Eds.), *The Golden Age of Capitalism: Reinterpreting the Postwar Experience* (pp. 153–186). Oxford: Clarendon.

Marglin, S. A., & Schor, J. B. (Eds.). (1990). *The Golden Age of Capitalism. Rethinking the Postwar Experience.* Oxford: Clarendon.

Naastepad, C. W. M. (2006). Technology, Demand and Distribution: A Cumulative Growth Model with an Application to the Dutch Productivity Growth Slowdown. *Cambridge Journal of Economics, 30*(3), 403–434.

Nickell, S. (1997). Unemployment and Labor Market Rigidities: Europe Versus North America. *Journal of Economic Perspectives, 11*(3), 55–74.

OECD. (2012). Labour Losing to Capital: What Explains the Declining Labour Share? *OECD Employment Outlook, 2012,* 109–161.

OECD. (2013). Protecting Jobs, Enhancing Flexibility: A New Look at the Employment Protection Legislation. In O. E. C. D. Employment (Ed.), *Outlook*. Paris: OECD.

OECD. (2014). *OECD Employment Outlook 2014.*

Onaran, O. (2011). Globalisation, Macroeconomic Performance and Distribution. In E. Hein & E. Stockhammer (Eds.), *A Modern Guide to Keynesian Macroeconomics and Economic Policies* (pp. 240–266). Cheltenham: Edward Elgar.

Onaran, Ö., & Galanis, G. (2014). Income Distribution and Growth: A Global Model. *Environment and Planning A, 46*(10), 2489–2513.

Onaran, Ö., & Obst, T. (2016). Wage-Led Growth in the EU15 Member-States: The Effects of Income Distribution on Growth, Investment, Trade Balance and Inflation. *Cambridge Journal of Economics, 40*(6), 1517–1551.

Onaran, Ö., Stockhammer, E., & Grafl, L. (2011). Financialisation, Income Distribution and Aggregate Demand in the USA. *Cambridge Journal of Economics, 35*(4), 637–661.

Orhangazi, Ö. (2008). Financialisation and Capital Accumulation in the Non-financial Corporate Sector: A Theoretical and Empirical Investigation on the US Economy: 1973–2003. *Cambridge Journal of Economics, 32*(6), 863–886.

Pariboni, R. (2016). Autonomous Demand and the Marglin-Bhaduri Model: A Critical Note. *Review of Keynesian Economics, 4*(4), 409–428.

Petri, F. (2004). *General Equilibrium, Capital and Macroeconomics*. Cheltenham: Edward Elgar.

Piketty, T. (2014). *Capital in the Twenty-First Century*. Cambridge, MA: Belknap Press.

Rajan, R. (2010). *Fault Lines: How Hidden Fractures Still Threaten the World Economy*. Princeton: Princeton University Press.

Rodrik, D. (1998). Why Do More Open Economies Have Bigger Governments? *Journal of Political Economy, 106*(5), 997–1032.

Rodrik, D. (1999). *Making Openness Work*. Baltimore: John Hopkins University Press.

Rodrik, D. (2011). The Manufacturing Imperative. *Project Syndicate*. Available at: https://www.project-syndicate.org/commentary/the-manufacturing-imperative?barrier=accessreg.

Rodrik, D. (2013). The Perils of Premature Deindustrialization. *Project Syndicate*. Available at: http://staging.memofin.fr/uploads/library/pdf/The%20Perils%20of%20Premature%20Deindustrialization%20by%20Dani%20Rodrik%20-%20Project%20Syndicate.pdf.

Rodrik, D. (2016). Premature Deindustrialization. *Journal of Economic Growth, 21*(1), 1–33.

Salop, S. C. (1979). Monopolistic Competition with Outside Goods. *The Bell Journal of Economics, 10*(1), 141–156.

Shapiro, C., & Stiglitz, J. E. (1984). Equilibrium Unemployment as a Worker Discipline Device. *The American Economic Review, 74*(3), 433–444.

Skott, P. (2017). Weaknesses of "Wage-Led Growth". *Review of Keynesian Economics, 5*(3), 336–359.

Stockhammer, E. (2013). *Why the Wage Share Has Fallen? A Panel Analysis of the Determinants of Functional Income Distribution* (ILO Conditions of Work and Employment Series No. 35).

Stockhammer, E. (2015). Rising Inequality as a Cause of the Present Crisis. *Cambridge Journal of Economics, 39*(3), 935–958.

Stockhammer, E. (2017). Determinants of the Wage Share: A Panel Analysis of Advanced and Developing Economies. *British Journal of Industrial Relations, 55*(1), 3–33.

Stockhammer, E., Durand, C., & List, L. (2016). European Growth Models and Working Class Restructuring: An International Post-Keynesian Political Economy Perspective. *Environment and Planning A, 48*(9), 1804–1828.

Stolper, W. F., & Samuelson, P. A. (1941). Protection and Real Wages. *Review of Economic Studies, 9*(1), 58–73.

Storm, S., & Naastepad, C. W. M. (2012). *Macroeconomics Beyond the NAIRU.* Cambridge, MA: Harvard University Press.

Storm, S., & Naastepad, C. W. M. (2015). Europe's Hunger Games: Income Distribution, Cost Competitiveness and Crisis. *Cambridge Journal of Economics, 39*(3), 959–986.

Sylos Labini, P. (1984). *The Forces of Economic Growth and Decline.* Cambridge: MIT Press.

Sylos Labini, P. (1999). The Employment Issues: Investment, Flexibility and the Competition of Developing Countries. *BNL Quarterly Review, 52*(10), 257–280.

Thimann, C. (2015). The Microeconomic Dimensions of the Eurozone Crisis and Why European Politics Cannot Solve Them. *Journal of Economic Perspectives, 29*(3), 141–164.

Tori, D., & Onaran, O. (2017). *The Effects of Financialisation and Financial Development on Investment: Evidence from Firm-Level Data in Europe.* SSRN Electronic Journal.

Tridico, P. (2009). Flessibilità e istituzioni nel mercato del lavoro: dagli economisti classici agli economisti istituzionalisti. *Lavoro & Economia, 1*(January/May), 113–139.

Tridico, P. (2012). Financial Crisis and Global Imbalances: Its Labour Market Origins and the Aftermath. *Cambridge Journal of Economics, 36*(1), 17–42.

Tridico, P. (2017). *Inequality in Financial Capitalism.* London: Routledge.

Tridico, P. (2018). The Determinants of Income Inequality in OECD Countries. *Cambridge Journal of Economics, 42*(4), 1009–1042.

Tridico, P., & Pariboni, R. (2017a). Inequality, Financialization and Economic Decline. *Journal of Post Keynesian Economics.* https://doi.org/10.1080/01603477.2017.1338966.

Tridico, P., & Pariboni, R. (2017b). *Structural Change, Aggregate Demand and the Decline of Labour Productivity: A Comparative Perspective* (Working Paper 221). Dipartimento di Economia Roma Tre.

Tridico, P., & Paternesi Meloni, W. (2018). Economic Growth, Welfare Models and Inequality in the Context of Globalisation. *The Economic and Labour Relations Review*. https://doi.org/10.1177/1035304618758941.

Tronti, L. (2010). The Italian Productivity Slow-Down: The Role of the Bargaining Model. *International Journal of Manpower, 31*(7), 770–792.

Van der Zwan, N. (2014). Making Sense of Financialization. *Socio-Economic Review, 12*(1), 99–129.

Vercelli, A. (2013). Financialization in a Long-Run Perspective. An Evolutionary Approach. *International Journal of Political Economy, 42*(4), 19–46.

Vergeer, R., & Kleinknecht, A. (2010). The Impact of Labor Market Deregulation on Productivity: A Panel Data Analysis of 19 OECD Countries (1960–2004). *Journal of Post Keynesian Economics, 33*(2), 371–408.

Vergeer, R., & Kleinknecht, A. (2014). Do Labour Market Reforms Reduce Labour Productivity Growth? A Panel Data Analysis of 20 OECD Countries (1960–2004). *International Labour Review, 153*(3), 365–393.

Walsh, P., & Whelan, C. (2000). The Importance of Structural Change in Industry for Growth. *Journal of the Statistical and Social Inquiry Society of Ireland, 29*, 1–32.

Webb, S. (1912). The Economic Theory of a Legal Minimum Wage. *Journal of Political Economy, 20*(10), 973–998.

Wölfl, A. (2005). *The Service Economy in OECD Countries* (OECD Science, Technology and Industry Working Papers 2005/03).

Can Tax Reforms Reduce Inequality?

Ahmad Seyf

1 Introduction

Discussions about inequality, especially economic inequality[1] seems to be everywhere. With few exceptions, inequality has been rising in the past four decades almost everywhere. At the same time, it is true that significant progress has been made on various aspects of social inequality, race, gender for instance in the last 100 years. But it is equally true that much of that progress in economic inequality stalled in the last 40 years or so. In more recent times, while we may have increased our knowledge about inequality, considerable less research has been

[1]We define economic inequality as the difference between levels of income, assets, wealth and capital and living standards, including inequalities in employment.

A. Seyf (✉)
Member, Cambridge Centre for Economic and Public Policy,
Cambridge, UK

P. Arestis and M. Sawyer (eds.), *Inequality*, International Papers in Political Economy,
https://doi.org/10.1007/978-3-319-91298-1_5

produced to inform policy makers about intervention to reduce it. Areas that require special attention are the following:

- The research community knows far too little about inequality of opportunity relative to what is known about inequality of outcomes.
- The research of the last few decades has been much more successful at documenting the patterns, trends, and (to some extent) causes of social inequality than it has been at examining its consequences or identifying effective strategies for reducing it.
- Last but not least, the problem of inequality has been framed in both research and in public debate as a problem of poverty. In other words, research often asks 'why are the poor poor?' or 'what are the consequences of poverty?' rather than 'why education and health outcomes, and the distribution of political power are so unequal?' and further, 'what are the consequences of inequality for society?' (Carter and Reardon 2014, p. 2)

It should be pointed out from the outset, that there is nothing natural about this growing inequality. More focused attention should be given to unpacking the combination of economic, political, social and cultural influences that shape individuals and communities' life chances and welfare. In this contribution, however, we focus on tax reforms to reduce inequality.

The structure of the chapter is as follows: Sect. 2 offers a relevant literature review, giving an outline of the evolution of inequality in the last four decades. Section 3 discusses the impact of tax reform on inequality. Section 4 assesses the re-distributional impacts of taxes and transfers in a sample of 24 emerging countries. The impact of different components is de-constructed too, and examined separately. Section 5 assesses the distributional impact of taxes and transfers in a sample of 17 developed economies. Section 6 brings these findings together and offers some policy recommendations and the chapter ends with a summary and conclusions.

2 Literature Review

The coexistence of deep and persistent inequalities in conjunction with increasing prosperity is a paradox of our time. This paradox has called into question the way our global economy is being managed. It is true that mainly owing to a reduction in poverty in China and India, global levels of economic inequality have declined but inequality within countries, including in China (Piketty et al. 2017) and India (Chancel and Piketty 2017) has increased in the past four decades and has even accelerated since the Global Financial Crisis (GFC) of 2008 and the subsequent Great Recession (GR). In addition, the persistent inequalities have many dimensions. Over and above inequalities in wealth and income, inequalities in health and education, and access to welfare services, and especially gender and racial inequalities are present too. It used to be argued that some inequalities may be pro-growth, but more recent academic research (OECD 2015a), has shown that not only do deep social inequalities endanger social cohesion, but also undermine sustainable growth. Examining the rising trend of inequality in the OECD countries, Keeley (2015) pointed out a number of factors. Two factors that could be mentioned are technological change and changes in pay norms and in taxation. Growth of part-time employment is another factor as it demonstrates the shifting of social patterns. Other factor according to Keeley (op. cit.) is income shift from labour to capital. Keeley (2015) went on to add that in the 1980s, the richest 10% of the population in the OECD countries earned 7 times more than the poorest 10%. In 2015, they then earned nearly ten times more.

The situation regarding wealth is much worse. The richest 10% controlled 50% of all total household wealth and the top 1% held 18% compared to only 3% for the poorest 40% (Keeley 2015, p. 3). There is a broad agreement on the problems caused by rising inequality; nonetheless, the economic cost of rising inequality is often overlooked. Keeley (op. cit., p. 3) points out that the rise in inequality observed between 1985 and 2005 in 19 OECD countries 'knocked 4.7 percentage points off cumulative growth between 1990 and 2010.' OECD (2014, p. 2) offers a higher estimate, confirming that there is a negative and statistically significant impact on growth and the average rise in Gini coefficient over the previous two decades dragged growth by 0.35% per year for 25 years 'a cumulated loss in GDP at the end of the period of 8.5 percent.'

However, what seems to be happening is worrying. In 2013, about a third of total employment in OECD countries was in 'non-standard' jobs. These are jobs meeting certain conditions; these are temporary, and permanently part time and mostly self-employed.

To make matters worse, 40% of employed youth have 'non-standard jobs and 50% of temporary workers are under 30 years old (ibid., p. 4).

Until recently, the most well established view on linkages between growth and income distribution was the Kuznets hypothesis (Barro 2008). This approach postulated that growth would first lead to an increase, and then to a decrease in income inequality. Further development of this approach led to a situation in the middle of the twentieth century, which gave rise to the idea that 'a rising tide lifts all boats': that is to say, economic growth would bring increasing wealth and higher living standards to all sections of society. In the 1950s and 1960s, there was some evidence behind that claim and it looked as if that was the case. Ignoring the role played by trade unions and the welfare state, there are still some who consider the distribution of productivity gains during the 1950s and 1960s to be a free market phenomenon that can be repeated.

We reject this assertion, and argue instead that the welfare gains of the 1950s and 1960s relied on market outcomes strongly moderated by institutional factors. In view of the role that institutions play in economic progress, we argue that institutions and norms affect the distribution of created values as well as their aggregate size. Our argument leads to an explanation of earnings levels and inequality in which skill-biased technical change, globalisation and related factors function within an institutional framework, including anti-trade union measures, which have been set up in the past four decades. In our narrative, the recent impacts of technology and trade have been amplified by the collapse of the institutions of the post-war years, a collapse that arose because economic forces led to a shift in the political environment over the 1970s and 1980s. If our interpretation is correct, no rebalancing of the labour force can restore a more equal distribution of productivity gains without government intervention to reverse many of the destructive changes that had taken place in the past four decades.

In more recent decades, in the ensuing economic and political debate, this 'rising tide hypothesis' evolved into a much more specific idea, that policies favouring the richer classes, would be benefiting everyone. To put it differently, resources allocated to the rich would be utilised in a way that the benefits would inevitably 'trickle down' to the rest. Even now ten years after the GFC, discussions and debates favouring further tax cuts to the rich relies heavily on this assumption.

Alves da Silva (2017, p. 1) using data for Brazil and relying implicitly on the notion of 'trickle down' claims that 'higher growth leads to lower income inequality, consequently pursuing growth enhancing policies should be translated not only in higher growth but also in better income distribution.' Similarly, Barro (2008, p. 8) updating an earlier study concludes that 'international data show that the Kuznets curve is a clear empirical phenomenon. Income inequality first rises but subsequently decline with per capital GDP.'

After four decades of the dominance of the 'trickle down' economics, we now know if anything is trickling; it is actually trickling up and serious measures are needed to stop this trend. Hacker and Pierson (2010, pp. 21–25) examine the changes in households' real earnings between 1979 and 2006 in the US. The average household income rose by more than 50% during this period, from $47,900 in 1979 to $71,900 in 2006. But the average income of the poorest 20% rose from $14,900 to $16,500, a 10% rise over the 27 years. The second poorest 20%, enjoyed a rise of 18%, but the income of the richest 1% rose from $337,100 in 1979 to more than $1.2 million in 2006, an increase of nearly 260%. They then went on to estimate what would have happened had the income of all households increased by the same percentage as the average household income, and concluded that 'the entire bottom 90 percent saw their income rise more slowly than average household income between 1979 and 2006' (ibid., p. 25). The gap between the average income of the 20% poorest households and the income of the top 1% that stood at $322,200 in 1979 went up to $1,183,500 in 2006, nearly a fourfold increase. Other researchers studying the income distribution in the US came to the same conclusion. Papadimitriou et al. (2014, p. 5), writing on the US, confirm this trend and point out that between 1980 and 2012 the real income of the top 1% increased by more than $2 trillion and close to $5 trillion in 2012 dollars. By contrast, the average income for the bottom 90% while increasing in the first three decades after World War II 'has stagnated since then. In fact, the real average income of the bottom 90 percent of the distribution was lower in 2012 compared to 40 years earlier' (ibid., p. 5). Tcherneva (2014, p. 1) also confirms this trend by indicating that from 2009 through 2013 while the US economy was recovering from one of the biggest economic downturn in recent memory, 116% of the income growth went to the top 10%, 95% to the top 1% and 21% to the remaining 9%, while the average income of the bottom 90% fell during this growth period. Jacobson and Occhino (2012, p. 2) stated that income inequality was declining up to the late 1970s, not only in the USA but also in a number of other industrialised economies too, but the trend has since reversed. Between 1967 and 1980, the average real income of the bottom 20% of household grew by 1.34% annually, faster than the 1.09% of the top 20% and the 0.67% of the top 5%. After 1980, it was different. The real income of the bottom 20% grew by only 0.05%, while it grew by 1.24% for the top 20% and by 1.67% for the top 5%. Taking a longer view of the changes in income distribution in the US, Fig. 1 shows that in contrast to Kuznets' hypothesis and claim by Barro (2008, p. 8), the share of the top 10% of the richest decile increased by 20% between 1970 and 2015.

In the UK, there has been a similar trend. In 1978, someone in the richest decile of the population had an income three times that of his/her contemporary at the poorest decile of the distribution. But in 2010, this ratio went up to five to one. In 1978, 7.1 million people had incomes below 60% of the median income, and by 2009–2010, that figure stood at 13.5 million, a rise of more than 90% (Mirrlees et al. 2010, pp. 8–9). This development should not be surprising, as it is also known that those who were among the 5% of the poorest population, have seen their income rise by 30% between 1979 and 2010, whereas the income of those at the top 5% richest in the distribution, increased by 100% during the same period (ibid., p. 9). Writing on China, Li Shi

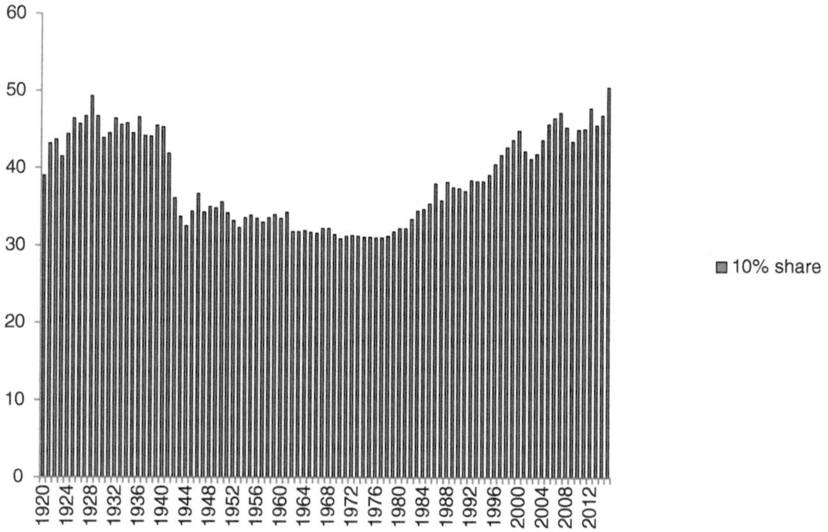

Fig. 1 US, top 10% national income share, 1920–2015 (*Source* Data extracted from Gordon [2017])

(2016, p. 84) pointed out that during the past three decades, China's economic growth has been among the fastest in the world. At the same time, China experienced one of the fastest increases in income and wealth inequality too. Between 1985 and 2014, the economy grew at about 10% on average per year, and the Gini coefficient for disposable income has also increased from 0.38 to 0.47 during the same period.

Fredrikson (2012, p. 2) examining the situation in the EU concluded that inequality has risen quite substantially since the mid-1980s and the main driver of this development was the sharp rise in the share of the top 10% of the population. For the period between the mid-1980s and 2008, the average annual income rise for the poorest 10% was 0.87%, whereas the top 10% enjoyed an annual average rise of 2.23%, more than 2.5 times (ibid., p. 10). Alvaredo et al (2017, p. 20) studied the development of inequality in the Middle East and found that the share of the total income going to the top 10% income earners is about 61%, as compared to 36% in Western Europe and 47% in the USA. Taking the income share of the top 1%, a similar picture emerges in the Middle

East. The top percentile income share is about 27% in the Middle East vs. 12% in Western Europe, 20% in the USA, 28% in Brazil, 18% in South Africa, 14% in China and 21% in India (ibid., p. 22).

With this development in place, we should be mindful of the fact that the global economy is undergoing major transformations with serious implications for public policy making. Not only is there continued technological change, but productivity growth has also slowed down. In addition to the growing divide, these transformations create new demand for public policies to facilitate these developments. While tax and welfare policies, especially progressive direct taxes, play a mitigating role in reducing inequality, other components of public policies should be implemented to foster sustainable and inclusive growth. However, as we discuss in the next section, there is no unique pattern of impact and it is this diversity that makes the role of taxation and welfare spending rather complex. What is true in all cases, however, is that progressive taxes and transfers would reduce inequality. Several studies have shown that enhancing the scale of the intervention would improve the redistributive impact of taxes and transfers (Prasad 2008; Jellema et al. 2017; Cabrera et al. 2014; IMF 2014b; Baanante 2013). But the IMF (2017b, p. 23) while accepting that more resources may be needed, argues that in view of a high degree of uncertainty surrounding the global economic outlook as well as high levels of public debt, taxes and transfers have 'the difficult task of achieving more and better in a more constrained environment' (ibid., p. ix).

However, finding additional resources is easier said than done. In the developing and emerging economies, it cannot be done, and in the rich economies, austerity would ensure that it would not happen either. In developing economies, given their low income level; the tax base is relatively weak. Furthermore, the problems created by tax evasion and tax avoidance are relatively more serious for them than in the case of high income economies. Furthermore, there is a serious inadequacy of institutional efficiency in tax collection, in addition to the existence of a large informal sector, which does not pay income taxes. In the high income economies, and in the EU, for instance, the so-called 'financial consolidation' requires a cut rather than an increase in these programs. As an indication of the general tendency, between 2010 and

2016, social spending as a percentage of GDP declined in 14 out of 23 OECD countries. In the US, social spending as percentage of GDP remained the same; Ireland suffered the greatest decline while Finland enjoyed the highest rise in social spending.[2]

This said, however, better targeting could be achieved by changing the composition of taxes, i.e. introducing progressive direct taxes and either reducing or redirecting the indirect taxes on items that are usually consumed by the richer deciles. If the trends in taxation in the last two decades are anything to go by, capture of politics by the rich and super-rich has changed the tax composition in favour of the rich and has also reduced the progressivity of direct taxation. It is almost universally true that the generosity of social programme favouring the poorer households has reduced; while at the same time, the state is more generous towards the rich. First of all, this generosity manifested itself in substantially reduced tax rates for the rich. In addition, governments' drifts in closing loopholes enabled the rich and big corporations to engineer lower profit figures, hence, pay even less tax. In a way, we face a double whammy, not only the effective rates of tax are lower, but also the base at which this lower rate is applied is allowed to shrink. This engineering requires artful schemes from the 'experts'. It is here that tax havens play a crucial role. Related to the issue of the weakening of the revenue base of the state, another factor that needs to be examined is what IMF (2014a, p. 101) calls the 'implicit subsidies for banks.' According to the IMF (2014a, p. 102), one of the most troubling legacies of the GFC, 2007–2008 is the widely held view that some banks are 'too big to fail' and further, this is based on the belief that the failure of systemically important banks would have such a negative impact on the financial system and the economy as a whole that whatever it takes to prevent such a failure should be undertaken. Estimates of the implicit subsidies are made and the numbers are simply astonishing. The implicit subsidies to banks which are seen to be globally too big to fail

[2]OECD (2017), "Social Expenditure: Aggregated data", OECD Social Expenditure Statistics (database). Available at: http://dx.doi.org/10.1787/data-00166-en (Accessed on 24 November 2017).

in 2011–2012 'represent around $15–$70 billion in the United States, $25–$110 billion in Japan, $20–$110 billion in the United Kingdom, and up to $90–$300 billion in the euro area' (IMF 2014a, p. 104). It is to be noted here that this concept is directly linked with the level of market concentration in banking, and further, and as the IMF (2014a, p. 104) claims, in most capitalist economies, governments and central banks 'often encouraged consolidation in the banking industry in an attempt to fight the financial crisis' (ibid., p. 104). Putting these two together, what governments and central banks have done, has effectively increased the amount of implicit subsidies that these banks receive. In the next section, we examine the impact of taxes and welfare payments on inequality.

3 Role of Taxes in Inequality

It is true that to a large extent; the rise in inequalities is policy-driven, that is, most of the major drivers identified in the literature point to a certain extent to a policy failure. In this context, we mention in passing the erosion of labour institutions (Acemoglu et al. 2001; Brennan 2016; Jaumotte and Buitron 2015), the decline in fiscal progressivity (IMF 2017a), skill-biased technical change (Kang 2015), trade and financial liberalisation (Danhaupt 2013; Denk and Cournede 2015), and the increasing political power of the wealthy (Hacker and Pierson 2010). In this section, we examine the role that taxes and transfers play in bringing down inequality and would also examine how the impact of these measures could be improved.

As a starting point, the last four decades could be outlined in the following manner.

- Historically speaking, the advanced capitalist economies grew at slower rates than in the 'golden age' though faster than pre-World War II.
- Within countries inequality increased everywhere in the industrialised countries.

- Under the pretext of encouraging saving and investment, hence economic growth, the top tax rates on income and wealth have declined.

Clearly, in terms of higher and more sustained economic growth, there has been no pay-off and there is no evidence in support of this claim.

It is most likely that in contrast to the promises, the skewed income distribution did not increase the size of the GDP much. This brings us to pose the question:

Would there be any negative trade-off if policies were implemented designed to reverse this trend? We would look into this in more detail, but would argue that if the income growth for the bottom 90% were boosted, there would be a better chance to revive and sustain economic growth. If the pattern of growth is shifted so that the benefits of growth accrue disproportionately to low income and poor households, this will be the most sustainable route to reduce inequality and promote growth. First, if the income of the poor is adjusted upwards, there will be less demand for redistributive efforts from the government. Furthermore, since the poor households have higher marginal propensity to consume, domestic aggregate demand would be boosted and further, it is more likely that this extra income will be spent on goods and services, produced domestically which, in turn would improve job creation in the economy. Specific policies that could be used here are adjusting minimum wages and increasing investments in training schemes and make these services accessible to a larger segment of the population. Enhancing the skill level would in turn improve productivity and improves growth prospect.

Looking at the evolution of marginal rate of tax for top earners, the IMF (2017a, p. ix) concludes that 'optimal tax theory suggests significantly higher marginal tax rates on top income earners than current rates, which have been on a declining trend.' Other researchers advocated similar view points (Hungerford 2012). Hungerford (op. cit., p. 16) provides statistical evidence showing that the persistent decline in the marginal rate of tax for top earners had no positive impact on saving, investment or growth, but increased inequality. Looking at the USA, he argues that throughout the late 1940s and 1950s, the top marginal tax rate was typically above 90%, whereas by 2012, this rate was down to 35%. The top capital gains tax was 25% in the 1950s and 1960s; went up to 35% in the 1970s. Likewise, by 2012, this rate was also reduced to 15%. On the other hand, the real GDP growth rate averaged 4.2% and real per capita GDP increased annually by 2.4% in the 1950s. In the 2000s, however, the average real GDP growth rate was only 1.7% and real per capita GDP increased annually by less than 1%. The share of 0.1% rose from 4.2% in 1945 to 12.3%, nearly 3 fold increases in 2007. On the other hand, the average tax rate paid by the top 0.1% fell from 50% in 1945 to about 25% in 2009 (ibid., p. 16).

In the UK, the pattern of changes in the income distribution was different, and the rise in inequality was concentrated in the period 1979 to 1992, and then levelled off. Other measures of inequality, however, such as the share of the top 1% has increased. In 2010–2011, the top 1% of income tax payers were expected to pay nearly 28% of all the income tax revenue received by the government more than double the 11% they contributed by the richest 1% in the late 1970s. Nonetheless, Mirrlees et al. (2010, p. 10) argues that 'this extraordinary level of, and increase in, the contribution of the richest is not down to a more progressive income tax structure—quite the reverse, as higher rates of income tax are much reduced. Rather, it is down to the very high level of income enjoyed by the richest relative to those received by everyone else.' Examining the evolution of inequality in India, an economy with an impressive growth rate in the last few years, Chancel and Piketty (2017, p. 1) observe 'the share of national income accruing to the top 1% income earners is now at its highest level since the creation of the Indian Income tax in 1922.' The top 1% of earners had less than 21% of total income in the late 1930s, and this share went down to 6% in the early 1980s, rising again to 22% now. As we have already alluded to another high growth economy, namely China, experienced sharp rise in inequality too, despite enjoying a very high growth rate for a few decades (Zhou and Song 2016).

It can be concluded from the evidence offered, that non-inclusive growth strategy needs to be re-examined and replaced. We would argue the case for a strategy that while leading to a reduction in inequality would also increase growth. There are two ways that this could be done.

We can first identify policies that would promote growth and then examine their distributional effect. Alternatively, we can identify policies that best address inequality and then evaluate their impact on growth. To get this mix right, i.e. promoting growth and equity at the same time is essential for the success of any programme. Ignoring growth and focusing on redistribution based on transfers and taxes, may be effective but will not be financially sustainable. Accepting the view that growing inequality reduces growth (OECD 2014; Ostry et al. 2014; Berg and Ostry 2011), the fact of the matter not only is the situation of the very poorest decile of the population that contributes to reducing growth, but also that of a much broader group of working and lower middle class households. On the other hand, relying solely on growth and overlooking equity, could only make the situation worse as it has done in the last four decades. An effective and efficient strategy should meet three conditions:

- It should be countercyclical, i.e. relies on automatic stabilizer and is symmetric too, expand in bad times and tighten in good times.
- It must be growth friendly, using tax and expenditure to support the stock of physical capital, and the labour force. It should address the productivity growth slowdown as the most reliable strategy to improve financial sustainability of these measures.
- The package of policies should promote inclusion. One way of doing this is by promoting 'equality of opportunity', i.e. through investment in human capital and offering greater protection against risk of losing their jobs. It is broadly true that policies to reduce inequality of opportunity would improve income distribution while at the same time boost productivity. It is to be noted here that inequality of outcome and that of opportunities are highly inter-dependent. Overlooking the inequality of opportunities, systemic patterns of discrimination and exclusion would prevent the poorer households to access economic and other resources, effectively enhancing the existing growing divide. While trying to reduce inequality of opportunities is important, it is not enough on its own. It follows from this that an effective policy to tackle inequality should address both. There is no 'one-size fits all' policy package for different countries, as

the overall conditions giving rise to this growing inequality is country specific.

An inclusive growth should focus on the creation of productive employment to ensure that the benefits of growth are shared by the largest possible segment of the population. In the absence of other assets, labour income is the main source of income for the bulk of the population and employment is a very important channel through which income generated from economic growth could be distributed. Let us also add here that the quality of these jobs should be an issue too. We share the view expressed by the UN (2013, p. 230) that 'if countries are to reduce inequality sustainably, the economy needs to create a sufficient number of jobs to secure employment for the majority of the population (quantity); the employment generated needs to provide sufficient income, security and stability to workers (quality); and it needs to be accessible to all groups within a population (equal access).'

Some of the policies briefly discussed above would take time to produce their positive results, such as greater investment in education. However, the problems associated with the existing levels of inequality are alarmingly acute and require serious efforts for short term fixing too. We would argue that it is here that the use of taxes and transfers, especially progressive taxes, is more urgently required to tackle this growing malaise.

Taxes could play two main functions: mobilise revenue to ensure macro stability and to promote redistribution and reduce inequality. To achieve these objectives, it should be efficient, i.e. less costly to be implemented, and further, the negative effects of the tax system on welfare must be minimised. Last but not least, transparency is essential, i.e. no taxes by 'stealth'. Broadly speaking, taxes tend to disrupt the signalling function of a market economy. An employer pays more for an hour of labour than what the employee receives. Likewise, VAT means a retailer receives less for a product she sells than her customer pays for it. In the case of developing countries, there are additional problems that should be addressed. Most of these economies suffer from weak administration and also have a large informal sector. Historically, there is a fragile social contract between citizens and the state. Furthermore, political institutions enjoy low credibility and there is a very strong tie with the economic elite. Following these points, it should be stressed that in these countries, redistribution is most effective via public expenditure rather than the revenue side, i.e. taxation. However, a well-designed policy mix could be effective too. Sabaini et al. (2016, pp. 206–207) point out that there was 'a shift in political preferences towards left parties' and shows that from the early 2000s to 2016, income inequality decreased in Latin America by five Gini points. Inter alia, taxation played an important role, thanks to the growing emphasis placed by governments on tax progressivity. In the 1980s and 1990s, economic efficiency was more important than equity to policy makers. For that purpose, trade taxes were reduced and replaced by VAT and other consumption taxes; both tend to be regressive of course. The maximum marginal rate of taxes was reduced too and in extreme cases, such as Uruguay in 1974 and Paraguay in 1992, personal income tax was abolished. This misguided mix of policies led to a sharp rise in inequality. However, the direction of tax policy has changed during the 1990s. A summary of what was subsequently undertaken is given below:

- Taxation reverted to its original role of providing resources for development and reducing inequality.
- The state eliminated or reduced a long list of exemptions, deductions and tax holiday.
- A dual tax system of personal income tax was introduced including a progressive tax schedule for labour- based income and a flat tax rate for capital income.
- Interestingly, this taxation shift started in Uruguay in 2007, Peru and some others followed from 2009.

Two further measures were introduced:

- Simplified taxation regimes for the small business sector.
- Some governments in the region introduced tax on financial transactions.

As a result of these reforms, the average tax revenue to GDP ratio gradually increased, reaching 21% of the GDP in 2016 from a very low rate of 13% in the 1990s (Sabaini et al., pp. 206–207).

Different countries use a mix of measures to achieve their stated objectives. Looking at the OECD, for instance countries can be grouped according to their inequality patterns and mix of policies implemented to tackle inequality. Overall, we can identify several social welfare models in the OECD.

The Nordic countries and the Netherlands are characterised by below-average disposable income inequality thanks to little dispersion in wages, relatively lower level of unemployment but except in Sweden, a higher than OECD average part time jobs. They use universal cash transfers and progressive income taxation. These countries use extensive fiscal interventions in labour markets and allow relatively strong labour unions. One of the main aims of these policies is to promote employment, which has a positive impact on inequality. The second model includes Ireland, Japan, New Zealand, the UK and the USA as well as Australia. These countries have a higher than average wage dispersion, weaker unions and a relatively high incidence of low paid employment. The use of cash transfers is less than other OECD countries, and in Australia and New Zealand these transfers are targeted to low income groups whereas in the US and Japan, most of the cash transfers are on old-age pensions. One of the main drivers of rising inequality in these countries is relatively very high part-time employment. It should be pointed out that in the OECD countries, the average involuntary part-time employment as a proportion of part time employment increased from less than 11% in 2000 to 17.4% in 2015. In some countries, it was much higher, for instance, in France, it was 40% and in Italy and Spain, it was higher than 63% in 2015 (OECD 2016, p. 228). In addition, OECD (2015b, p. 20) reports that most of the increase in part-time has been involuntary and 'reflects s shortage of opportunities for full-time employment.' Except in Ireland, their overall employment rate is above the average for the OECD and that in turn have a mitigating impact on inequality. The size of cash transfers is not very big, but these are more targeted and taxes are more progressive than the average among OECD members. Inequality in these countries is higher than the OECD average. In Japan, there is an additional problem of above average part time employment (20.6% vs. 17.4% OECD average, OECD 2016, p. 228).

In the third model, consisting of Austria, Germany, France, Hungary, Luxembourg, social policy is heavily insurance-based and this would lower the progressivity of these measures; hence, their impact on inequality. Cash transfers targeted primarily at old- age pensions, and, except in Germany, the role of personal income tax is not very significant.

The final social welfare model includes Chile, Greece, Italy, Portugal, and Spain, Turkey with relatively higher inequality than others in the OECD. Two drivers could be identified: these countries suffer from wide wage dispersion and low employment rate. Like others, cash transfers are used, but their sizes are relatively small, and mostly insurance-based, and hence, have little re-distributional impact. In Chile and Turkey, the welfare system is less developed and furthermore, the levels of transfers and taxes in these countries rely more heavily on consumption taxes for their revenue, which is below the OECD average. The size of tax system is smaller but more progressive and yet, both inequality and poverty in these countries are higher than the OECD average (OECD 2012; Hoeller et al. 2012).

4 The Distributional Impact of Taxes and Transfer in the Emerging Economies

In this section, we turn to examine the distributional impact of taxes and transfers in a sample of 24 emerging economies. The impact of different components is de-constructed too, and examined separately. In the case of income, it is useful to consider various concepts of income before we proceed. Researchers at Commitment to Equity (hereafter, CEQ) have come up with a summary of these different concepts (Fig. 2).[3]

[3]The data used are from national household surveys; the unit is 'representative households'.

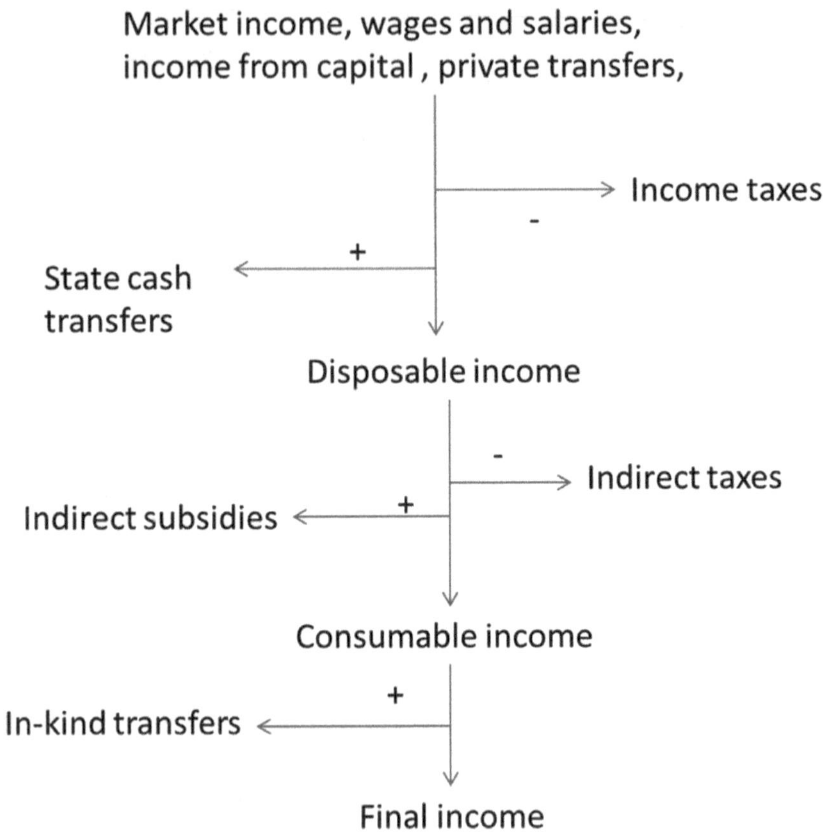

Fig. 2 Basic income concepts (*Source* Adapted from Lustig [2015, p. 9])

These researchers have also developed technical capabilities enabling the examination of the distributional impact of each of fiscal components (Lustig 2017). Without doubt, it is a major progress in our endeavour to examine some economic issues that produce serious social outcomes; henceforth, this attempt enables policy makers to reduce the negative impacts. There is no doubt that progressive taxes reduce inequality, not homogenously, but surely these measures are effective everywhere they have been implemented. In this context, using different concepts of income enables one to compare incomes before taxes and transfers with income after taxes and transfers. One can also assess the impact of transfers in kind, such as education and health care services offered by the state. In a major study by Inchauste and Lustig (2017), on the distributional impact of taxes and transfers on income distribution, evidence is offered as to the impact of fiscal measures on income distribution in eight low and middle income economies. At the same time, CEQ produced several studies, using the same concepts of income and the same analytical approach to study the distributional impacts of these measures in another 16 countries. Overall, I have compiled data on the impact of fiscal measures in 24 countries for further examination.

There are several reasons as to why I have chosen these countries for further examination. First, the list is comprehensive; countries from Asia, Africa, Europe, Latin America and the Middle East are present. Second, as the same concepts of income are used, using the same technique to measure inequality, and hence, our results are comparable without creating any problem of incompatibility.

In the 24 studies, the Gini coefficient, a common measure of income inequality, has been calculated for each of these income concepts. Hence comparing the Gini coefficient for market income, with Gini coefficient for disposable income captures the impact of direct taxation on income distribution. Similarly, other Gini coefficients inform us about the impact of other fiscal measures that the state may have undertaken. As a starting point, comparing Gini coefficients for market income with Gini coefficient for final income confirms the view that progressive taxes and transfers have positive impact on inequality and reduces it (Fig. 3).

Examining details of each individual study would go beyond the scope of this chapter, but a number of general conclusions emerge.

- Given the results obtained in these studies, it is clear that the inequality in market income is the highest amongst income types.
- Progressive taxes and transfers definitely reduce inequality as can be seen above, but the scale of the decline is different in different countries.

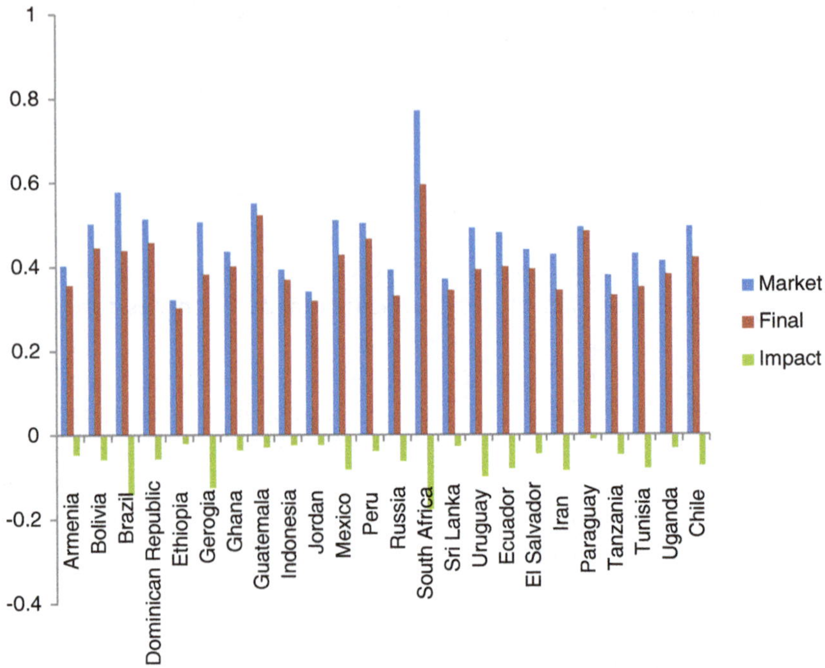

Fig. 3 The distributional impact of fiscal policy (*Source* Based on statistics given in: Alam et al. (2017; Jordan), Higgins et al. (2013; Paraguay), Jellema et al. (2017; Indonesia), Cancho and Bondareako (2017; Georgia), Inchauste et al. (2017; South Africa), Paz-Arauco et al. (2012; Bolivia), Cabrera et al. (2014; Guatemala), Arunatilake et al. (2017; Sri Lanka), Baanante (2013; Peru), Enami et al. (2016; Iran), Ruble et al. (2013; Brazil), Younger and Khachetryan (2017; Armenia), Pinto et al. (2015; Ecuador), Beneke et al. (2017; El Salvador), Haas et al. (2017; Uganda), Myamba et al. (2016; Tanzania), Martinez-Aguilar et al. (2017, Chile), for the remaining countries, Inchauste and Lustig 2017)

In the above example, the fall in Gini coefficient in Brazil, South Africa, Georgia is the highest in this sample. The impact in Jordan, Indonesia and Paraguay is minimal. In Georgia, despite the fact that indirect taxes make a bigger contribution to government revenues from taxation, Chancho and Bondarenko (2017) show that the social spending is reasonably targeted to the bottom of the distribution, and 'while indirect taxes reduced the income of the poor, social spending raised their income considerably' (p. 129). Furthermore, 'the income of the bottom

60 percent increased moving from market income to final income, with the largest increase experienced by the poorest 20 percent' (ibid., p. 129). By contrast, in the case of Jordan, one possible reason for the weak impact of taxes and transfers may be the extensive use of indirect taxation without sufficient mitigating social spending. Alam et al. (2017, p. 6) point out that for Jordan revenues from indirect taxation account for more than two thirds of government revenues from taxes. It seems that Paraguay suffers from the same problem since its government relies heavily on value added tax to the extent that while income taxes raised about 11% of government revenue, nearly 34% of it is raised via VAT (Higgins et al. 2013, p. 6). The conduct of taxes and transfers in Paraguay is so inadequate that Higgins et al. (ibid.) examining the situation in this country compare it with seven other Latin American economies and conclude that, based on market income, Paraguay has one of the lowest inequalities before government intervention. However, the final income Gini coefficient for Paraguay is the second highest among Latin American economies in this sample, which is interpreted as the failure of these measures. The use of direct taxes and transfers reduce it by less than one percent, but extensive use of indirect taxes reverses this progress. Another possible contributing factor to the relative failure in Paraguay is that the revenue base of the government is rather weak. Indonesia likewise raised more revenue from indirect taxes than direct taxes and Jellema et al. (2017, p. 33) point out that while these measures reduce both poverty and inequality, 'however, the magnitudes are modest' as we have witnessed in the data presented earlier. In South Africa, possibly the most unequal society in Africa, the government is using its fiscal instruments to significantly reduce market income inequality and poverty through a progressive tax system and highly progressive social spending programme. It looks as if the state gets its 'targeting' right, the rich bear the brunt of taxes, and the government redirects these resources to the poorest in society to raise their income (Inchauste et al. 2017, p. 23). It is further revealed by Inchauste et al. (op. cit.) that only the top three deciles of the income distribution pay more in taxes than they receive in transfers; hence, a serious decline in the Gini coefficient emerges as we have already reported.

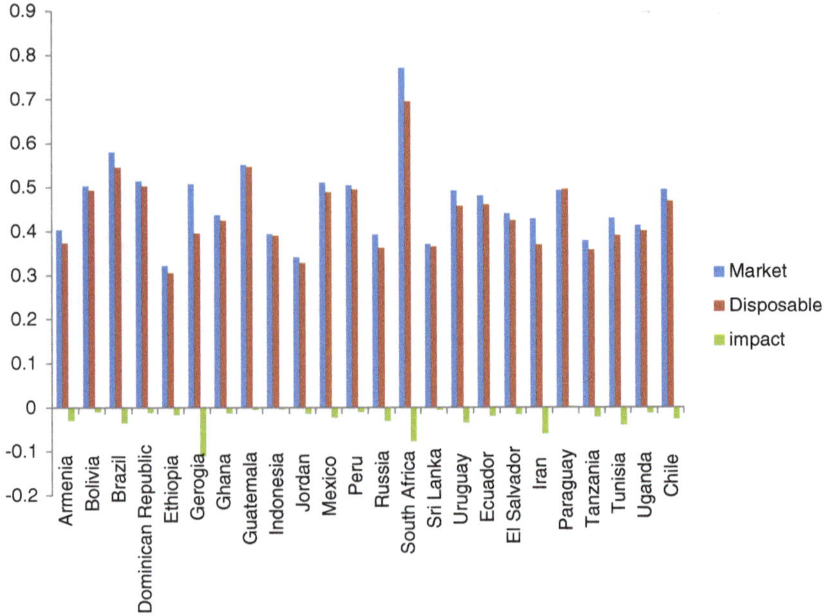

Fig. 4 The distributional impact of income tax and direct cash transfers (*Source* as for Fig. 3)

4.1 The Distributional Impact of Direct Taxation and Transfers

Comparing the Gini coefficients for market income and disposable income enables us to assess the impact of direct taxes and direct cash transfers on inequality in these countries. As can be seen in Fig. 4, these measures have reduced the Gini coefficient in all, except one, countries in our sample.

In Paraguay, the Gini coefficient has actually increased slightly indicating more inequality following the intervention by the government in these areas. In Bolivia, Indonesia, Peru and Sri Lanka, the impact was minimal. Georgia experienced the highest decline in its Gini coefficient, 22 percentage points followed by Iran where the decline was 14%. Looking at the underlining factors causing these impacts, a number of interesting points emerge. In Paraguay, it seems as if the government failed in its targeting and as Higgins et al. (2013, p. 16) point out 'a significant number of the near poor pay enough direct taxes to make them poor … direct transfers reduce poverty slightly, but their impact is overshadowed by the poverty increasing impact of direct and indirect taxes.' In the case of Bolivia, Paz Arauco et al. (2012, p. 3) make two points. One, the targeting is misplaced and there appears to be significant leakages to the non-poor, and second, the size of the transfers was relatively small. Direct transfers account for 2% of GDP.

Cobrera et al. (2014, p. 8) assessing the situation in Guatemala show that taxes and transfers achieve almost nothing in terms of reducing inequality and poverty overall because tax revenues are not only low but also severely regressive. Extensive use of consumption taxes offset the benefits of cash transfers and more than 60% of government revenues are raised by indirect taxation and the share of direct taxation is less than 27%. Direct taxes are somewhat progressive but 'they are painstakingly low' (ibid., p. 3). They add (ibid., p. 3) that 'in contrast, consumption taxes are outright regressive and increase inequality after direct and consumption taxes and direct transfers is the same as market income inequality.' In their view, the share of direct taxes should increase, but at the same time, 'Guatemala is a textbook case of the power of elites to block pro-poor tax reforms' (ibid., p. 24). Jellema et al. (2017, p. 21) writing on Indonesia, point out that 'approximately two-fifth of poor individuals are impoverished by fiscal policy;' and further, this outcome 'indicates that a progressive, poverty-reducing fiscal system like Indonesia's does not necessarily produce net positive transfers for all poor households.' Jellema et al. (op. cit., p. 34) stress the fact that direct transfers are equalising and more effectively target the poor than in-kind transfers or subsidies but the problem seems to be that direct transfers are very small in magnitude, less than half a percentage point of GDP, hence its impact is minor as the size of the transfers is so small that it does not cover all those who my need them.

In the case of Sri Lanka and the failure of its fiscal measures to reduce inequality, both the size and their progressivity seem to be the culprit. In Sri Lanka, most of government revenues are raised via indirect taxes (Arunatilake et al. 2017, p. 269). Furthermore, there appears to be additional problems. The government sustained fiscal deficits of 7–8%

of GDP annually during 2002–2012, leading to significant accumulation of public debt. Arunatilake et al. (2017, p. 268) refer to 'limited fiscal space' given the low revenue, hence, leading to 'limited impacts'. To see how limited this fiscal space is, let us recall that with revenue equal to 10.7% of GDP in 2014 'Sri Lanka now has one of the lowest tax-revenue–to-GDP ratios in the world' (ibid., p. 268). Most of the revenues are collected via indirect taxes; in fact, two and a half times more than what is collected via direct taxation. Total tax collection in 2009 amounted to 12.8% of GDP of which 7.2% were indirect taxes and the 2.9%, direct taxes (ibid., pp. 269–270).

On Peru, Baanante (2013) points out that the extent of inequality reduction by fiscal measures in Peru is rather small. The main reason for this is relatively small scale of this spending. Social spending in Peru is below the Latin American average, as is its tax revenue; however, revenue raised via indirect taxes is above the average for Latin America. Regarding the use of taxes and transfers in Georgia, policy makers appear to come up with a number of interesting ideas to enhance their redistributive impact. For instance, income from the primary supply of agricultural products produced domestically, and up to $83,350, is exempt from income tax. There are also tax exemptions for a single mother or for a person with a disability. In addition, Georgia spends 6.1% of GDP on direct transfers and social assistance programmes, which is one of the highest among the middle income economies. Georgia's non-contributory public pension scheme provides a flat universal pension to all elderly people (Cancho and Bondarenko 2017, pp. 119–121). In the case of Iran, it raises more revenues from direct taxes than from indirect taxes and its total social spending is about 14% of GDP. Enami et al. (2016, p. 9) show that Iran has several transfer programmes, and broadly speaking, fiscal measures reduced Gini coefficient by nearly 20% (ibid., p. 18) and the main role here is played by direct transfers. The main cash transfer was universal when it was first introduced. The top 20% of population was subsequently excluded and Enami et al. (2016) argue that if the exclusion was extended to the top 40%, and were combined with a moderate increase in the cash transfers to the bottom deciles, 'the additional reduction in poverty and inequality would be considerable' (p. 31). For Brazil, Ruble et al. (2013, p. 7) point out that primary spending is close to OECD average, but taxes on consumption are the main source of government revenues, representing 12.9% while direct taxes are only 8.2% of the GDP.

4.2 The Distributional Impact of Indirect Taxation and Indirect Subsidies

Moving from disposable income to consumable income, the impact of indirect taxes and indirect subsidies can be examined.

As can be seen in Fig. 5, the distributional impact of these two measures is rather limited and in half of the countries in our sample; there was an increase in their Gini coefficients for disposable income. The highest rise was in Georgia, where the Gini coefficient increases by 0.016 point or more than 4%. The highest fall was in Tanzania where there was more than 3% decline. Broadly speaking, the Gini coefficient for disposable income was higher than the Gini coefficients for consumable income in Armenia, Bolivia, Brazil, Georgia, Guatemala, Indonesia, Russia, South Africa, Uruguay, Iran, Paraguay. In Georgia, Cancho and Bondarenko (2017) confirm that while direct taxes are progressive, the burden of indirect taxation is more evenly distributed with the poor losing a higher percentage of income. Indirect taxes represent 55% of government revenues from taxes whereas the share of progressive and well-targeted income tax is only 29% (ibid., p. 8). Furthermore, 'Georgia's excise taxes are more regressive than the VAT. Excises are the only taxes the government can levy under the Economic Liberty Act without a referendum….overall the net fiscal system is more un-equalising with the current system of indirect taxes than with direct taxes' (ibid., p. 31). Writing on Brazil, Higgins and Pereira (2013) believe that a large proportion of direct transfer beneficiaries are non-poor, and further, indirect taxes paid by the poor often surpass the benefits they receive; hence, there is relatively low impact on inequality in relation to total spending. It should be noted, though, that inequality has fallen in Brazil in every year since 2001, but still there is a very high level of inequality. Factors reducing inequality in Brazil are as follows:

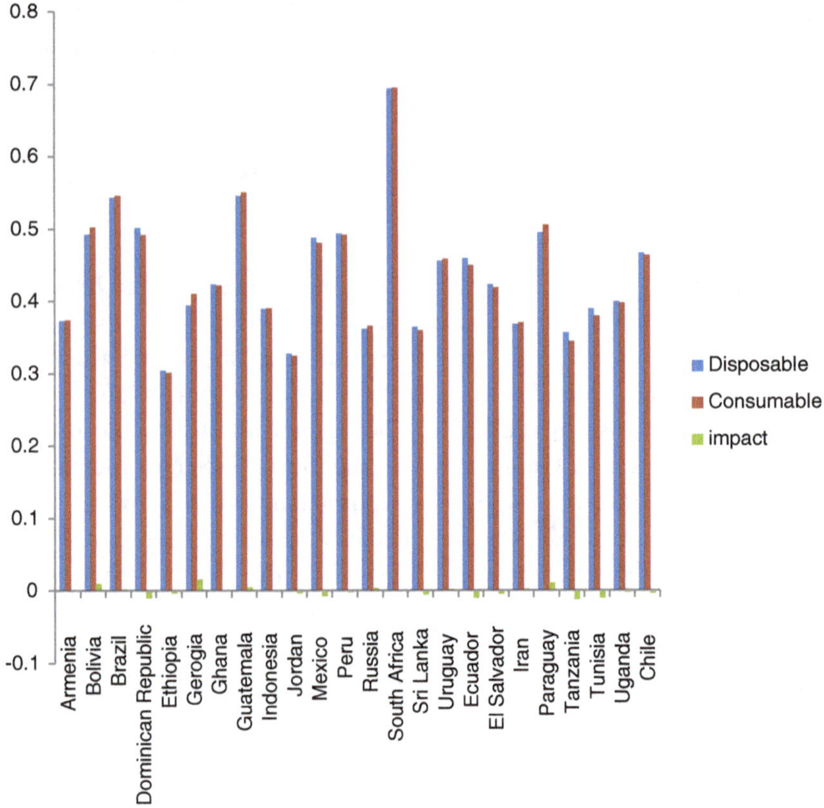

Fig. 5 The distributional impact of indirect taxes and indirect subsidies (*Source* as for Fig. 3)

- increased public cash transfers;
- more equal distribution of educational attainment resulting from easier and expanded access to education in the 1990s;
- social spending becomes larger and more progressive (Cornia 2015; Tsounta and Osueke 2014). That said, direct transfers are poorly targeted, 74% of total direct transfer benefits the non-poor (Higgins and Pereira, op. cit., p. 11). Higgins and Pereira (2013, p. 13) summarise the situation rather nicely, in terms of direct transfers, Brazil has relatively high spending, poor targeting, and low effectiveness and add that, 'in many cases, the benefits of transfer programmes are

offset by indirect taxes.' Lustig (2015, p. 29) also points out that in Brazil 'it is the consequence of consumption taxes- including taxes on basic foodstuffs- that wipe out the benefits from direct transfers such as Bolas Familia for a considerable number of the market income poor.'

In the case of Bolivia, the situation is more complex. Paz Arauco et al. (2012, p. 2) testify that despite the fact that social spending was expanded between 2007 and 2009, from 11.9 to 15.1% of GDP, its distributional impact was limited. While 'personal income in Bolivia is not taxable, there are four indirect taxes applied to consumption, accounting for 41 percent of total tax revenue in 2009' (ibid., p. 5). It looks as if indirect taxes have a major role in reducing the distributional impact of fiscal measures in Bolivia. When the impact of indirect taxes and subsidies is assessed, Paz Arauco et al. (2012, p. 11) conclude that 'only people from the two poorest deciles receive more than what they contribute.' As indicated earlier, the size of the package does not seem to be the main culprit. It is worrying to learn that 'the largest cash transfers in terms of GDP, shows a distribution biased towards the three richest deciles' (ibid., p. 15).

Given poor targeting, there are 'significant leakages to the non-poor population and the small size of the transfers, 62 percent of benefits distributed through direct transfers are received by the non-poor' (ibid., p. 15). By contrast, Myamba et al. (2016, p. 8), examining the situation in Tanzania believe that cash transfer programmes have an excellent targeting mechanism. However, there is widespread agreement that tax evasion through informality is an important problem in this country. Interestingly enough, results show that indirect taxes, VAT, import duties and excises reduce inequality in Tanzania, albeit by a smaller amount (ibid., p. 15); but at the same time, it is also true that 'government causes significant increases in poverty with the indirect taxes that it levies (p. 16).' Myamba et al. (2016, p. 29) conclude that about half of this redistribution comes from very progressive direct taxation. The rest comes from unusually progressive indirect taxation and progressive in-kind transfers in health and education.

4.3 The Distributional Impact of in-Kind Transfers

Comparing the Gini coefficients for consumable income with the Gini coefficients for final income would capture the impact of in-kind transfers. Examining the impact of in-kind transfers, we learn that in 23 out of 24 countries in our sample, these transfers reduced inequality. It was only in Ethiopia that there was no change. The highest fall in the Gini coefficient happened in Brazil; the Gini coefficient declined there by 0.11 points, followed by 0.1 declines in South Africa and between 0.05 to 0.07 points in Ecuador, Mexico and Uruguay. In countries such as Sri Lanka, Armenia and Jordan, the fall in inequality was not as pronounced. Before discussing some of the underlying factors causing such a drastic fall, let us point out that it should not be surprising to see that in-kind transfers have such a strong downward influence on inequality. By and large, while the scale may still be inadequate, governments spend more on education and health than they do on direct transfers or indirect subsidies in these countries (Fig. 6).

Given the serious redistribution impact of in-kind transfers, the result in Jordan is slightly puzzling. The government spends more than 3% of GDP on education and primary and secondary schooling are free and compulsory. Alam et al. (2017, p. 10) claim that Jordan has one of the most modern health care infrastructure in the Middle Ease and like education it absorbs more than 3% of GDP. One possible explanation for weak impact may be that public health insurance covers only about 40% of the population. Writing on Armenia, Younger and Khachatryan (2017, p. 4) argue that fiscal interventions are all very well targeted but the scale is seriously inadequate. In the case of Brazil, it should not be surprising to see that in-kind transfers have such a drastic impact on inequality. All the measures taken together, except in-kind transfers, reduced the Gini coefficient by 0.035 points but following the in-kind transfers, the Gini coefficient fell by another 0.075 points, more than twice the impact of all other measures combined.

There is always room for improvement, but Brazil spends about 11% of GDP on education and health, and as Higgins and Pereira (2013, p. 5) point out education is free at all levels and health is also free publicly,

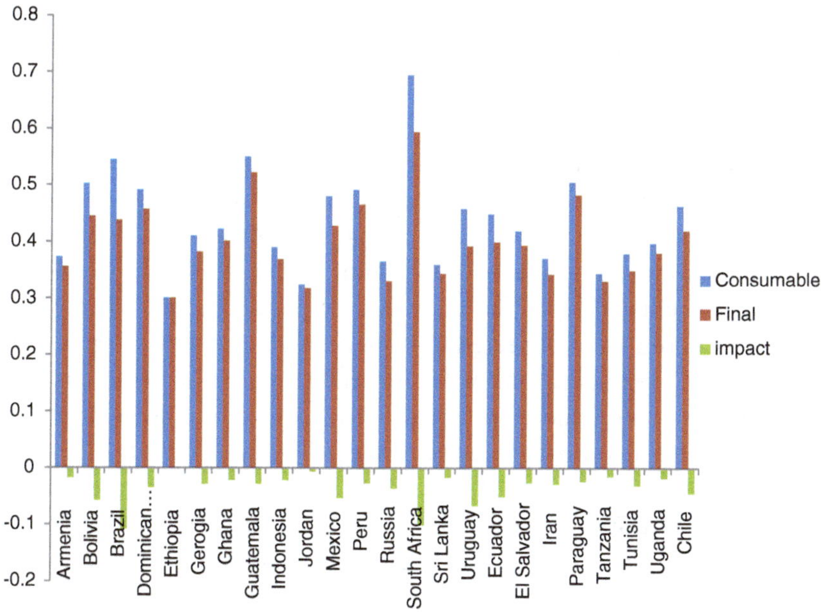

Fig. 6 The distributional impact of in-kind transfers (*Source* as for Fig. 3)

providing day care facilities for poor households. Likewise, health care is also free for all types of care and a system created by the 1988 Constitution 'guarantees access to health care to every citizen at public health facilities.' Regarding South Africa, Inchauste et al. (2017, p. 4) show that spending on primary and secondary education is very well targeted to the poor and the same is true about spending on health. In-kind transfers absorb 12.6% of country's GDP, 7 percentages of which is spent on education (ibid., pp. 7–9). Schooling is compulsory for all children aged 7–15 years. While there is a fee to be paid, 'schools in poorer neighbourhoods are designated "no fee" schools, which receive a slightly higher state subsidy to compensate for the absence of school fees.' It is further reported that in 2011, 78% of students attended no-fee schools (ibid., p. 10). The health care system is divided into public care (serving more than 89% of the population) and private care which is rather expensive and mainly used by the rich and well-off inhabitants. Primary health care is available free to everyone, but hospital services are offered at a heavily subsidised rate.

There are widespread exemptions for a whole variety of people, those with low income, pregnant women and those who are on social benefits. It is true that South Africa starts at a very high level of inequality, but the use of taxes, both direct and indirect as well as cash transfers, lowers Gini coefficient by 0.076; whereas, the impact of in-kind transfers reduces Gini coefficient by 0.098 point, nearly a 30% larger impact. Spending on education in South Africa, with the exception of higher education, is pro-poor reflected in a very high enrolment rates, over 97% for 7–15 year-olds and 83% for 16–18 year olds (ibid., p. 19). Spending on adult education is also pro-poor, about 50% of all the spending on adult training centres benefits households with income of less than $4 a day (ibid., p. 19). Health spending is not as pro-poor as spending on education, but public spending on health is relatively well targeted. It may not be because the poorer households have a higher utilisation rates, but because the rich and the high income households choose not to use the public health care system. For the financial year 2010/2011, South Africa spent more than 4% of GDP on public health, which serves about 83%, nearly 42 million of the South African population. The remaining 17% or 8.3 million people mostly use private health insurance (ibid., p. 20). One issue of concern is the total private sector health related spending, which is slightly more than what is spent by the state on public health, i.e. 4.3% versus 4.1% of GDP. So in effect, the average per person expenditure on health in the private health care is more than five times what is being spent for public health services.

To sum up our discussion so far, there is no doubt that taxes and transfers, especially when progressive, would reduce income inequality. However, despite all these measures, in thirteen countries in our sample the Gini coefficient for final income is more than 0.3 but less than 0.4, and for eleven countries the Gini coefficient is more than 0.4.

There is no doubt that there would always be room for improvement in the use of taxes and transfers, but, this relatively poor result is affected by three factors:

- relatively high inequality in market income;
- relatively inadequate size of social spending in most of these economies; and
- in view of the regressive nature of indirect taxation, the sources of finance for these programmes should change. IMF (2014b, p. 18) offers two interesting observations. One, in the advanced economies, not only do they raise more revenue than the emerging economies, more than 30% of GDP on average compared with 15–20%, but also more importantly, most of the revenues are raised via direct taxation. By contrast, as we indicated earlier, the bulk of the revenues in our sample are raised through regressive indirect taxation.

On the relative size of social spending and its impact on inequality, a note of caution is in order. Looking at the impact of fiscal measures on the Gini coefficients for final income, a mixed picture emerges. In our sample, no such a direct link could be observed. The lowest expenditure was in Indonesia, less than 5% of GDP and the highest, more than 25% of GDP concurred with the situation in Brazil.

In our sample, two countries spend anything similar to the average social spending in Europe. Thirteen countries spend less than 10% of GDP, and in the case of another 7 countries, the social spending is more than 10 but less than 15%. While we agree that the size of social budget is an important factor enhancing the re-distributional impact of fiscal measures, judging by our data, no robust relationship between the two could be established.

In our sample, in terms of GDP, Brazil spends more than others on social issues, but the fall in Brazil's Gini coefficient is only second highest. On the other hand, Paraguay spends more than 12 other countries in this sample on social issues, but the impact of these measures on inequality is almost negligible. In short, while the scale of intervention is important, equally significant is how well these measures are targeted, transfers to the poor, and taxes to the rich.

5 The Distributional Impact of Taxes and Transfers in the Developed Economies

In this section, we turn to examining the distributional impact of taxes and transfers in a sample of 17 developed countries. In advanced economies, taxes and transfers reduce inequality quite substantially, whereas in emerging economies the scope is rather limited. First, progressive direct taxes and transfers can reduce disposable income inequality as compared with the inequality that the market transactions generate. Second, when examining consumption taxes, it can affect consumable income inequality. Finally, through in-kind transfers; such as education and health, which can reduce the inequality of 'final income'; that is, consumable income adjusted for in-kind transfers. The impact of in-kind transfers such as those for education and health is likely to be long-term, and will affect market income inequality over time by changing the distribution of human capital. These types of transfers are most likely to be effective across generations by promoting social mobility. To a large extent, the effectiveness of these measures depends on both the magnitude of taxes and transfers and their progressivity. In follows from this that to enhance their effectiveness, taxes and transfers should be progressive. Looking at different types of income, and how to tax them, it looks as if in the last four decades, we have had our priority wrong. For instance, capital income, which is more concentrated than labour income, is taxed more lightly than labour income. If this anomaly is corrected and more revenue is thus generated, it would be easier to maintain the progressivity of income tax system.

In our examination of the role of taxes and transfers in advanced economies, in addition to IMF (2017b), we have four further pieces of research (Jesuit and Mahler 2017; Caminada et al. 2017; Guillaud et al. 2017; Figari and Paulus 2015) that have provided evidence for our discussion in this section. Jesuit and Mahler (2017) took a sample of 20 developed economies and the sample size for Caminada et al. (2017) was 47. Both of these studies consider pension as transfers, whereas Guillaud et al. (2017) who utilised a sample of 22 OECD member countries looked at pensions as part of market income in their analysis.

Figari and Paulus (2015) looked at three countries, but utilised an extended income concept that in addition to looking at indirect taxation also includes in-kind transfers. There will be some over-lapping of evidence but their findings are different too. On top of these five, we have access to the 'Leiden LIS Budget Incidence Fiscal Redistribution Dataset on Income Inequality'[4] where detailed evidence is provided and will be utilised.

Three different concepts of income are used here, with the exception of those derived from Figari and Paulus (2015): Primary income, which covers labour and capital income; plus any private transfers. Examining this concept further would inform on income inequality before social transfers and taxation. Gross income is primary income plus any social security transfers and here we measure the re-distributional effect of social transfers. Lastly, we examine the inequality in disposable income, that is, we subtract income taxes and any social security contributions. Looking at the evolution of disposable income informs us about income inequality after social transfers and taxes. It would be ideal if we could examine the impact of indirect taxes and in-kind transfers too, but, lack of data made this task impossible. In these studies, as indicated earlier, only Figari and Paulus (2015) use an extended concept of income but only report on three countries, of which only one is included in our country sample, the UK.

Let us first see how has inequality changed in these countries when transfers and taxes are taken into consideration (Fig. 7).[5]

A number of general points could be made:

- There is a substantial decrease in inequality as measured by the Gini coefficient, as between that for primary income and disposable income in all countries, with the exception of South Korea.

[4]This dataset is available at: https://www.universiteitleiden.nl/binaries/content/assets/rechtsgeleerdheid/fiscaal-en-economische-vakken/economie/llbifr-dataset-on-income-inequality---november-2017.pdf.

[5]For eleven of the countries in this list, the year is 2013. Six of the 17 countries differ as follows: for France and Canada, it is 2010, Sweden, 2005, Italy, 2014, Japan, 2008, and South Korea, 2012.

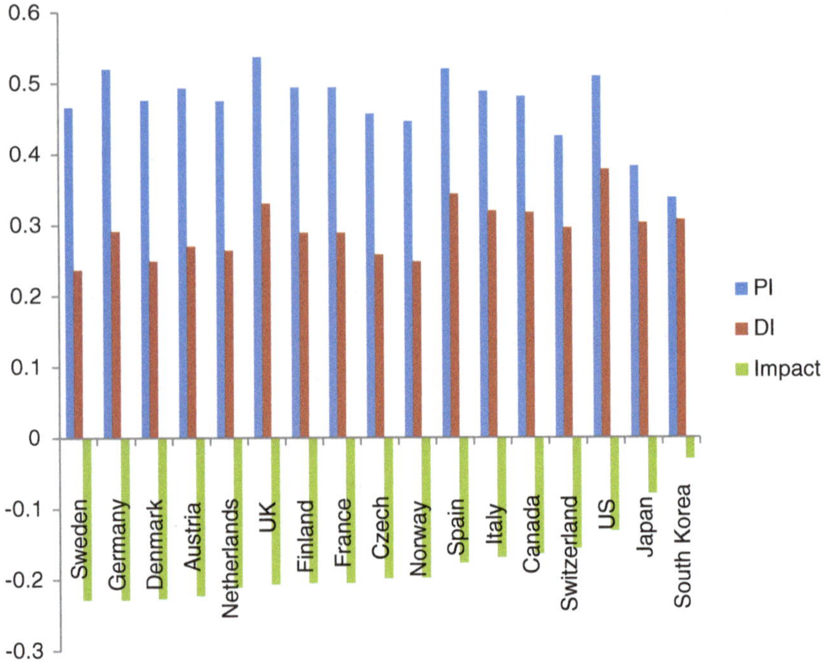

Fig. 7 Gini coefficients for Primary income (PI) and Disposable income (DI) (*Source* LIS dataset on income inequality, available at: https://www.universiteitleiden.nl/binaries/content/assets/rechtsgeleerdheid/fiscaal-en-economische-vakken/economie/llbifr-dataset-on-income-inequality—november-2017.pdf)

In South Korea, and to some extent in Japan, there is a fall in inequality of income when the Gini coefficients for primary and disposable incomes are compared, but compared with others, the scale of the decrease is not significant.

- In all countries, transfers, especially pensions, are by far the main driver of decline in inequality, with the exception of Japan and Sweden.
- In terms of percentage decline in Gini coefficient, the highest fall was in Sweden (49%) and the lowest happened in South Korea where it fell by just 9%. Excluding South Korea, the average decline in inequality was a little over 39% in these countries.

Caminada et al. (2017, p. 4) have stressed the fact that with the exception of the USA, in the mid-2000s, the average distributional effect of public cash transfers was twice as large as what was achieved by taxation. This said, however, they also show that while inequality in market income has been sharply moderated, it was not compensated in full, though, meaning that inequality in disposable income increased too, but not by the same scale. In their findings, the average Gini coefficient for market income was 0.483 but post-government's intervention this average went down to 0.347, a Gini reduction of 0.136 points or 28% (ibid., p. 5). They have also shown that out of this decline, 23% fall is linked with transfers and 5% is caused by taxes (ibid., p. 22). We have selected 17 countries from their sample, and for the selected countries, all advanced economies, the results were slightly different. The average Gini coefficient for market income was 0.47 and went down to 0.291 when we included the impact of taxes and transfers, a fall of 0.179 points or more than 38%. It is not surprising that the distributional impact of these measures is stronger in this smaller sample. Jesuit and Mahler (2017, p. 13) study is similar, covering more or less the same countries, 14 out of 17 of our selected countries are included in their sample here.

Once again, the driver for most of the decline in inequality is the pensions which on average reduce the Gini coefficient by 0.091 points which is more than twice the impact of other transfer programs combined. In Belgium and the Netherlands, the impact was more pronounced than others, and reduced the Gini coefficient by 0.115 points. At the other end, the impact of pensions in reducing inequality was lowest in the US, Canada and Japan (ibid., p. 13). Jesuit and Mahler (op. cit., p. 21) note that during the period 1970–2010, the Gini coefficient for market income increased significantly in these countries; in fact it increased by 0.110 points, but when they examined the changes in the Gini coefficient for disposable income, which captures the impact of taxes and transfers, the average went up by only 0.018 points, still an increase but a very modest one. Among this group of countries, the highest increase was in the UK where the Gini coefficient increased by 0.190 points and the next in line in terms of increase was Germany followed by the USA (ibid., p. 23). Their results seem to confirm that redistribution resulting from taxes did not change much and remained flat in the previous four decades.

In addition to pensions, the impact of child benefits, unemployment compensation and housing benefits on Gini coefficient is also examined. While every one of these programs made a positive contribution to the decline in inequality, but their impacts were minor, and unemployment benefits, for instance, reduced the Gini coefficient by 0.011 points on average for these countries. This brings us to raise the issue that it might be the right time to reform our tax systems to enhance the distributional impact.

Figari and Paulus (2015, p. 361) using an extended concept of income found lower levels of inequality, with their estimate for the Gini coefficient for the UK being reported at 0.26, whereas other studies give us a figure of 0.33, which is more than 25% higher. Furthermore, by looking at main drivers for lowering inequality, in the UK, they found that the main driver was means tested benefits and not the public pensions as claimed by others (ibid., p. 363).

In discussing the use of tax and transfer policies to reduce inequality, we often come up face to face with the claim that this could harm growth by reducing market efficiency. Accepting the so-called 'trade off' between equity and efficiency overlooks policies that could enhance both. As we have shown earlier in this chapter, government spending on education and health would surely reduce inequality and these kind of productive expenditure would be pro-growth too.

In most of the economies of our sample, the tax code is less progressive than it may appear as those sources of income which tend to be received by the rich such as capital gains and dividends are taxed at a preferred rate. The incomes of lower- and middle-income taxpayers predominantly come from wages, which when all the other deductions included, generally incur a higher rate of taxation than capital gains and dividends. Not only is this treatment not fair, but also in practice, it invites manipulation of how income is reported to the tax authorities and how business owners choose to pay themselves and their workers.

So tax reform should, as much as possible, narrow the differences between the ways different income types are treated and if it fails to give preferential treatment to income from work, at least, it should treat labour income in the same way that it treats income from capital. Whatever the claim, the fact of the matter is that in the past four decades wealth and income trickled up and were transferred from the poor and middle classes to the wealthy. Given the current state of the global economy, there is simply no good reason to continue maintaining this mechanism, and drastic measures to change it are essential. Incomes and wealth have risen at the top, but wages have grown too slowly for the working and middle class. To mention in passing, this pattern would lead to a sluggish growth of aggregate demand and that in turn, would generate all kinds of problems for the management of the macro economy everywhere. We must ensure that whatever reforms we undertake, the poor, the working class and the middle class would not have their share of taxes increase. At the same time and perhaps more important, we should make sure that the wealthy would not have their share of taxes decreases either. It is important that tax reform raises more revenues so that the size of social spending could increase.

Revenue-raising reforms must strengthen the tax system in both the short run and the long term. In most of the countries that we have chosen in our sample, the tax system chronically underfunds public investments the people at large collectively support and want; and does so in a way that pushes low-income families further into poverty while allowing big corporations and the wealthy to avoid paying their fair share of taxes. An effective and efficient tax reform should raise revenue in the short run so that pressing needs could be financed, while simultaneously creating a sustainable long term revenue base to meet those future needs that are likely to be more urgent. It is absolutely essential that tax reform would not create greater problems for inequality and poverty than what they are already. It is not easy but could be done if sufficient political will is at the right place. Each of these goals can be achieved by trying to close unwarranted loopholes for capital gains and offshore corporate profits, while preserving and expanding valuable low-income tax credits and pro-investment tax allowances.

6 Policies to Tackle Growing Inequality

Let us begin with a simple statement that the present economic and social inequalities are unsustainable. In recent decades, income inequality has increased in nearly all countries and Alvaredo et al. (2018, p. 8) warns 'It is our belief, however, that if rising inequality is not properly monitored and addressed, it can lead to various sorts of political, economic, and social catastrophes'.

Short of offering structural changes in the working of capitalism, the use of progressive taxes and transfers is an effective mechanism that can help reduce income inequality through various channels. The extent of fiscal redistribution depends on both the magnitude of taxes and transfers and their progressivity. If we implement progressive direct taxes and transfers, these measures reduce disposable income inequality, that is, inequality of income after taxes and transfers. Indirect taxation; consumption taxes which, is increasingly popular with policy makers as a source of raising revenue but with negative impact on equity, would lower inequality in consumable income. There are two ways that the impact of consumption taxes could improve. First, policy makers exclude items that are usually consumed by lower deciles in the income distribution and taxes are targeted towards items consumed by the rich and wealthy. Second, the revenue raised via consumption taxes would be allocated to welfare programs benefiting the lower deciles in the distribution. Finally, via in-kind transfer spending, the distribution of final income would be affected. It should be noted that greater spending on education and health also influence market income inequality over time by improving the distribution of human capital and consequently promotes social mobility too.

As indicated in this contribution, worsening inequality is not 'as act of God or nature' and depends on policy decisions and changes that have been made in the last four decades; concerning trade unions, banks, wages and our tax system. If sufficiently strong political will is in the right place, this trend could be reversed. In relation to taxes, as a major source of revenue, IMF (2017a, p. ix) seems to be in favour of some kind of wealth tax and increase in the marginal tax rate for top income earners. While we share the view that the top rate of tax should increase and the declining trend of recent years should be reversed, we argue that given the level of financial secrecy and secret jurisdiction, we share Zucman's observation 'it is not possible to tax wealth if we cannot measure it' (2015, p. 99). We would further argue that the IMF as a powerful global organisation should use its influence for a global financial register so that such a tax could be applied.

Moving from the tax side to the spending side, an important debate here is the choice between universal and means tested transfers to achieve distributional objectives. In view of financial constraints, some researchers argue in favour of better targeting, i.e. more means-tested measures, while others, points out the weaker redistribution impact of means-tested transfers. It goes without saying that greater use of means-testing could potentially stretch the administrative ability of the welfare system and may lead to mis-allocation of resources. Looking at the transfers' side of taxes and transfers, one measure; the Universal Basic Income (UBI) is discussed in many circles. A number of factors could be mentioned in its favour.

- It could address poverty and inequality more efficiently than means-tested transfers.
- It could be used to mitigate the decline in income and uncertainty generated by technological change, and automation in particular.
- It is also suggested that the UBI may be used as leverage for pursuing essential but unpopular structural reforms, such as subsidies removals.
- On the negative side, however, the opponents argue that there would be unacceptable level of leakage of benefits to higher income groups.

Our main concern about the UBI, is the uncertainty about its source of finance. There are two ways that this could be financed. First, trying to raise revenue by raising taxes, or by reducing other social expenditure and allocating what become available to UBI. In both cases, the final outcome is not very clear. The fiscal cost of UBI will depend at what level it would be set. The IMF (2017a, pp. 52–53) offers a brief empirical assessment of UBI in 8 countries, the level of UBI is set at 25% of the country net median market income and some interesting results are produced. On average, it would cost about 6.5% of GDP in the advance economies and 3.8% of GDP in the selected emerging economies. In the case of all countries in this small sample, there is a fall in Gini coefficients as well as in the poverty rate. Our counterfactual argument here would be if the health or education expenditure in the UK increases by 6.5% of the GDP—the cost of UBI—how would the

Gini coefficient be affected by this? In relation to France and the US, the situation is the same, except that in the USA the Gini coefficient falls by 0.02 points (ibid., p. 53).

We would argue that given the fact that having a job is no longer a protection against poverty, and further, there is continued growth of non-standard work, taxes and transfers should promote good-quality jobs. While in-work benefits continue, every measure should be taken, including in-work training to improve the productivity, hence, pay and conditions of workers.

7 Summary and Conclusions

This chapter highlighted the distributional impact of taxes and transfers by taking two samples, 24 emerging economies and 17 developed countries for this purpose. It is clear that the use of these measures would reduce income inequality, far greater in the developed countries than in the emerging economies. One of the factors contributing to a bigger impact is the relative size of these programs. In the case of emerging countries, education and health expenditure had the bigger impact on reducing inequality while in the developed economies, pensions played that role. A number of structural factors contributing to this growing divide have been mentioned but this chapter has focused on discussing taxes and transfers and their impact on inequality. Given the risk associated with growing inequality, the use of progressive taxes and transfers is strongly recommended but to enhance the effectiveness of these measures the prevailing international tax system must be overhauled too.

References

Acemoglu, D., Aghion, P., & Violante, G. L. (2001). *Deunionizaion, Technical Change and Inequality* (Carnegie-Rochester Conference Series on Public Policy 55, pp. 229–264).

Alam, S. A., Inchauste, G., & Serajuddin, U. (2017). *The Distributional Impact of Fiscal Policy in Jordan* (Working Paper Series). CEQ Institute, Commitment to Equity, Tulane University.

Alvaredo, F., Assouada, F., & Piketty, T. (2017). *Measuring Inequality in the Middle East, 1990–2016—The World's Most Unequal Region?* (Wid-World Working Paper, 2017/15).

Alvaredo, F., Saez, E., Zucman, G. F., Chancel, L., & Piketty, T. (2018). World Inequality Report, World Inequality LAB.

Alves da Silva, M. E. (2017). *Does Inequality Benefit Growth! New Evidence Using a Panel Var Approach*. Available at: https://www.anpec.org.br/encontro/2017/submissao/files_I/i6-8f4b9258b8349e15c8d628ccb4efdbc0.pdf.

Arunatilake, N., Inchauste, G., & Lustig, N. (2017). The Incidence of Taxes and Spending in Sri Lanka. In Inchauste and Lustig (Eds.), *The Distributional Impact of Taxes and Transfers*. Washington, DC: World Bank.

Baanante, M. J. (2013). *The Incidence of Social Spending and Taxes in Peru* (Working Paper Series). CEQ Institute, Commitment to Equity, Tulane University.

Barro, R. J. (2008). *Inequality and Growth Revisited.* Asian Development Bank. Available at: https://www.adb.org/sites/default/files/publication/28468/wp11-inequality-growth-revisited.pdf.

Beneke, M., Lustig, N., & Oliva, J. A. (2017). *The Impact of Taxes and Social Spending on Inequality and Poverty in El Salvador* (Working Paper Series). CEQ Institute, Commitment to Equity, Tulane University.

Berg, A. G., & Ostry, J. D. (2011). *Inequality and Unsustainable Growth: Two Sides of the Same Coin?* (IMF Staff Discussion Note, SDN/11/08).

Brennan, J. (2016). *Rising Corporate Concentration, Declining Trade Union Power, and the Growing Income Gap: American Prosperity in Historical Perspective.* Available at: http://www.levyinstitute.org/pubs/e_pamphlet_1.pdf.

Cabrera, M., Lustig, N., & Moran, H. (2014). *Fiscal Policy, Inequality and the Ethnic Divide in Guatemala* (Working Paper Series). CEQ Institute, Commitment to Equity, Tulane University.

Caminada, K., Wang, J., Goudswaard, K., & Wang, C. (2017). *Income Inequality and Fiscal Redistribution in 45 LIS Countries, 1967–2014* (LIS Working Paper Series, No. 724).

Cancho, C., & Bondarenko, E. (2017). *The Distributional Impact of Fiscal Policy in Georgia* (Working Paper Series). CEQ Institute, Commitment to Equity, Tulane University.

Carter, P. L., & Reardon, S. F. (2014). *Inequality Matters.* Available at: https://ed.stanford.edu/sites/default/files/inequalitymatters.pdf.

Chancel, L., & Piketty, T. (2017). *Indian Income Inequality, 1922–2014—From British Raj to Billionaire Raj* (Wid-World Working Paper, 2017/11).

Cornia, G. A. (2015). *Income Inequality in Latin America: Recent Decline and Prospects for Its Further Reduction* (WIDER Working Paper, No. 2015/020).

Denk, O., & Cournède, B. (2015). *Finance and Income Inequality in OECD Countries* (OECD Economics Department Working Papers, No. 1224). Paris: OECD Publishing. Available at: http://dx.doi.org/10.1787/5js04v5jm2hl-en.

Dunhaupt, P. (2013). *The Effect of Financialisation on Labour's Share of Income* (Working Paper, No. 17/2013). Berlin: Institute for International Political Economy.

Enami, A., Lustig, N., & Taqdiri, A. (2016). *Fiscal Policy, Inequality and Poverty in Iran, Assessing the Impact and Effectiveness of Taxes and Transfers* (Working Paper Series). CEQ Institute, Commitment to Equity, Tulane University.

Figari, F., & Paulus, A. (2015). The Distributional Effects of Taxes and Transfers Under Alternative Income Concepts: The Importance of Three "I"s. *Public Finance Review, 43,* 347–372.

Fredriksen, K. B. (2012). *Income Inequality in the European Union* (OECD Economics Department Working Papers, No. 952). OECD Publishing. Available at: http://dx.doi.org/10.1787/5k9bdt47q5zt-en.

Gordon, C. (2017). *Growing Apart, a Political History of American Inequality.* Available at: http://scalar.usc.edu/works/growing-apart-a-political-history-of-american-inequality/index.

Guillaud, E., Olckers, M., & Zemmour, M. (2017). *Four Levers of Redistribution: The Impact of Tax and Transfer System on Inequality Reduction.* Available at: http://www.lisdatacenter.org/wp-content/uploads/s32.pdf.

Haas, A., Jellema, J., Lustig, N., & Wolf, S. (2017). *The Impact of Taxes, Transfers and Subsidies on Inequality and Poverty in Uganda* (Working Paper Series). CEQ Institute, Commitment to Equity, Tulane University.

Hacker, J. S., & Pierson, P. (2010). *Winner-Take-All Politics; How Washington Made the Rich Richer—And Turned its Back on the Middle Class.* New York: Simon & Schuster.

Higgins, S., Lustig, N., Ramirez, J., & Swanson, W. (2013). *Social Spending, Taxes and Income Redistribution in Paraguay* (Working Paper Series). CEQ Institute, Commitment to Equity, Tulane University.

Higgins, S., & Pereira, C. (2013). *The Effects of Brazil's High Taxation and Social Spending on the Distribution of Household Income* (Working Paper Series). CEQ Institute, Commitment to Equity, Tulane University.

Hoeller, P., Joumard, I., Pisu, M., & Bloch, D. (2012). *Less Income Inequality and More Growth—Are They Compatible? Part 1, Mapping Income Inequality Across the OECD* (OECD Economics Department Working Papers, No. 924). OECD Publishing. Available at: http://dx.doi.org/10.1787/5k9h297wxbnr-en.

Hungerford, T. L. (2012). *Taxes and the Economy: An Economic Analysis of the Top Tax Rates Since 1945*. Available at: http://graphics8.nytimes.com/news/business/0915taxesandeconomy.pdf.

IMF. (2014a). *Global Financial Stability Report, Moving from Liquidity to Growth Driven Markets*. Washington, DC.

IMF. (2014b). *Fiscal Policy and Income Inequality*. Available at: https://www.imf.org/external/np/pp/eng/2014/012314.pdf.

IMF. (2017a). *Fiscal Monitor: Tackling Inequality*. Washington, DC.

IMF. (2017b). *Fiscal Monitor: Achieving More with Less*. Washington, DC.

Inchauste, G., & Lustig, N. (Eds.). (2017). *The Distributional Impact of Taxes and Transfers*. Washington, DC: World Bank.

Inchauste, G., Lustig, N., Maboshe, M., Purfield, C., & Woolard, I. (2017). *The Distributional Impact of Fiscal Policy in South Africa* (Working Paper Series). CEQ Institute, Commitment to Equity, Tulane University.

Jacobson, M., & Occhino F. (2012). *Behind the Decline in Labour's Share of Income* (Economic Trends, pp. 5–7). Federal Reserve Bank of Cleveland.

Jaumotte, F., & Buitron, C. O. (2015). *Inequality and Labour Market Institutions* (IMF Staff Discussion Note, SDN/14/14).

Jellema, J., Wai-Poi, M., & Afkar, R. (2017). *The Distributional Impact of Fiscal Policy in Indonesia* (Working Paper Series). CEQ Institute, Commitment to Equity, Tulane University.

Jesuit, D. K., & Mahler, V. A. (2017). *Fiscal Redistribution in Comparative Perspective: Recent Evidence from the Luxembourg Income Study (LIS) Datacenter* (LIS Working Paper Series, No. 717).

Kang, J. W. (2015). *Interrelation Between Growth and Inequality* (WP No. 447). Asian Development Bank.

Keeley, B. (2015). *Income Inequality: The Gap Between Rich and Poor*. OECD, Insights. Paris: OECD Publishing.

Lustig, N. (2015). *Fiscal Redistribution in Middle Income Countries: Brazil, Chile, Colombia, Indonesia, Mexico, Peru and South Africa*. Available at: https://www.cgdev.org/sites/default/files/Lustig_FiscalRedistMidIncomeCountries_wp410.pdf.

Lustig, N. (Ed.). (2017). *CEQ Handbook: Estimating the Impact of Fiscal Policy on Inequality and Poverty*. Available at: http://www.commitmentoequity.org/publications-ceq-handbook/.

Martinez-Aguilar, S., Fuchs, A., Ortiz-Juarez, E., & DelCarmen, G. (2017). *The Impact of Fiscal Policy on Inequality and Poverty in Chile* (Working Paper Series). CEQ Institute, Commitment to Equity, Tulane University.

Mirrlees, J., et al. (Eds.). (2010). *Dimensions of Tax Design: The Mirrlees Review*. Oxford, UK: Oxford University Press for the Institute for Fiscal Studies.

Myamba, F., Younger, S. D., & Mdadila, K. (2016). *Fiscal Incidence in Tanzania* (Working Paper Series). CEQ Institute, Commitment to Equity, Tulane University.

OECD. (2012, January). *Income Inequality and Growth: The Role of Taxes and Transfers* (OECD Department Policy Notes, No. 9).

OECD. (2014). *Focus on Inequality and Growth—December 2014*. Available at: www.oecd.org/social/inequality-and-poverty.htm.

OECD. (2015a). *In It Together: Why Less Inequality Benefits All* (OECD Social, Employment and Migration Working Papers, No. 171) Paris: OECD Publishing. Available at: http://dx.doi.org/10.1787/5jrrwdt037mv-en.

OECD. (2015b). *OECD Employment Outlook 2015*. Available at: http://ifuturo.org/documentacion/Employment%20outlook%202015.pdf.

OECD. (2016). *OECD Employment Outlook 2016*. Available at: http://www.oecd-ilibrary.org/employment/oecd-employment-outlook-2016_empl_outlook-2016-en.

Ostry, J. D., Berg, A., & Tsangarides, C. G. (2014). *Redistribution, Inequality and Growth*. IMF Staff Discussion Note. Available at: https://www.imf.org/external/pubs/ft/sdn/2014/sdn1402.pdf.

Papadimitriou, D. R., Nikiforos, M., Zezza, G., & Hannsgen, G. (2014). *Is Rising Inequality a Hindrance to the US Economic Recovery*. Strategic Analysis, Levy Institute.

Paz-Arauco, V., Molina, G. G., Pozo, W. J., & Aguilar, E. Y. (2012). *Explaining Low Redistributive Impact in Bolivia* (Working Paper Series). CEQ Institute, Commitment to Equity, Tulane University.

Piketty, T., Yang, L., & Zucman, G. (2017). *Capital Accumulation, Private Property and Rising Inequality in China, 1978–2015* (Wid-World Working Paper Series No. 2017/6).

Pinto, F. P. L., Pinto, M. C. L., Pinto, M. A. L., & Saa, R. (2015). *Social Spending, Taxes and Income Redistribution in Ecuador* (Working Paper Series). CEQ Institute, Commitment to Equity, Tulane University.

Prasad, N. (2008). *Policies for Redistribution: The Use of Taxes and Social Transfers* (International Institute of Labour Studies, DP/194/2008).

Ruble, W., Higgins, S., Lustig, N., & Smeeding, T. (2013). *Comparing the Incidence of Taxes and Social Spending in Brazil and the United States* (Working Paper Series). CEQ Institute, Commitment to Equity, Tulane University.

Sabaini, J. C. G., Martorano, B., & Moran, D. (2016). *"Taxation and Inequality: Lessons from Latin America", in ISSC, IDS and UNESCO (2016).* World Social Science Report 2016, Challenging Inequalities: Pathways to a Just World. Paris: UNESCO Publishing.

Shi, L. (2016). *"Recent Changes in Income Inequality in China", in ISSC, IDS and UNESCO (2016).* World Social Science Report 2016, Challenging Inequalities: Pathways to a Just World. Paris: UNESCO Publishing.

Tcherneva, P. R. (2014). *Growth for Whom?* Levy Institute. Available at: http://www.levyinstitute.org/pubs/op_47.pdf.

Tsounta, E., & Osueke, A. (2014). *What Is Behind Latin America's Declining Income Inequality?* Available at: https://www.imf.org/external/pubs/ft/wp/2014/wp14124.pdf.

United Nations. (2013). *Humanity Divided: Confronting Inequality in Developing Countries.* New York: United Nations.

Younger, S. D., & Khachatryan, A. (2017). *Fiscal Incidence in Armenia* (Working Paper Series). CEQ Institute, Commitment to Equity, Tulane University.

Zhou, Y., & Song, L. (2016). *Income Inequality in China: Causes and Policy Responses.* Available at: https://openresearch-repository.anu.edu.au/bitstream/1885/107259/2/01_Zhou_Income_Inequaity_2016.pdf.

Zucman, G. (2015). *The Hidden Wealth of Nations: The Scourge of Tax Haven.* Chicago: Chicago Press.

Gender Inequality in the Labour Market and the Great Recession

Patricia Peinado and Felipe Serrano

1 Gender Equality: A Fundamental Human Right

Gender equality is a fundamental human right. According to the definition given by the United Nations (UN 2018), "Human rights are rights inherent to all human beings, whatever our nationality, place of residence, sex, national or ethnic origin, colour, religion, language, or any other status. We are all equally entitled to our human rights without discrimination", moreover, it continues "These rights are all interrelated, interdependent and indivisible". What is more, the argument is raised that beyond being a fundamental human right, gender equality is "a necessary foundation for a peaceful, prosperous and sustainable world" and consequently, the provision of females "with equal access to

P. Peinado (✉) · F. Serrano
University of the Basque Country, Bilbao, Spain
e-mail: patricia.peinado@ehu.es

F. Serrano
e-mail: felipe.serrano@ehu.es

P. Arestis and M. Sawyer (eds.), *Inequality*, International Papers in Political Economy,
https://doi.org/10.1007/978-3-319-91298-1_6

education, health care, decent work, and representation in political and economic decision-making processes will fuel sustainable economies and benefit societies and humanity at large".

The 10th of December was declared the "Day of Human Rights" as Human Rights were recognised by the UN in the Universal Declaration of Human Rights during its 183rd plenary meeting held in Paris on 10 December 1944. Additionally, during UN's Beijing Platform for Action of the year 1995, the concept of 'Gender Mainstreaming' was adopted. In 1997, it was defined by the UN Economic and Social Council (ECOSOC) as "the process of assessing the implications for women and men of any planned action"; which includes all levels and areas of legislation and policies or programmes. The concept of gender mainstreaming makes "the concerns and experiences of women as well as of men an integral part of the design, implementation, monitoring and evaluation of policies and programmes in all political, economic and societal spheres" being the last aim "to achieve gender equality." However, in the year 2018, far from having eradicated the existence of inequalities between women and men, we still find gender equality as a major challenge included in all the main political agendas and statues of different governments, organisations, associations and institutions in general. The UN have recently included among the 17 goals defined to reach sustainable development, a specific gender equality goal (number five),[1] recognising that "While the world has achieved progress towards gender equality and women's empowerment under the Millennium Development Goals (including equal access to primary education between girls and boys), women and girls continue to suffer discrimination and violence in every part of the world" (ILO 2018).

In the European Union (EU) gender equality is not only "a fundamental right" and "a common value", but also a strategic objective considered "a necessary condition" paramount to achieve "the objectives of growth, employment and social cohesion" (EIGE 2018). Empirical

[1]The United Nations (UN) specifically defines, "Goal 5: Achieve gender equality and empower all women and girls".

evidence supports these arguments. According to the latest report on the impacts on GDP of gender equality by 2050, improving gender equality would increase GDP per capita in the EU from 6.1 to 9.6%[2] (EIGE 2017). As a consequence, among the EU's institutions responsible for designing the policies and strategies to address gender mainstreaming and reach gender equality, the European Commission (EC 2006, 2010, 2015) has recently designed three different strategies to achieve gender equality: (i) The Roadmap for Gender Equality between Women and Men 2006–2010; (ii) The 2010–2015 strategy for equality between women and men; and (iii) The Strategic Engagement for Gender Equality 2016–2019; highlighting that "Over the last 60 years, changes and persistent policy efforts have established a trend towards gender equality" (EC 2017, p. 7). However, as this latest report on gender equality published by the EC concludes, "Over the last years, the gaps in pay, employment and working hours have been plateauing". What is more, as it is stated, at the rate of change registered, "it will take more than a century to close the overall gender gap in earnings". Moreover, they add, "in the 21st century, the disproportionate weight of care responsibilities on women will continue to shrink their economic independence and have a lifelong effect on their career, earnings and pensions" (EC 2017, p. 53).

It may be concluded, in the light of the arguments above, understanding the causes and consequences of gender inequalities is an issue that could only be understood from an holistic perspective; that is to say, all the dimensions of the phenomena need to be considered. In this chapter, we focus our attention on the labour market dimension of gender differences. More precisely, we focus on the study of gender differences in employment, unemployment and wages during the years prior and posterior to the Great Recession (GR) in the EU.

---

[2]See Agénor and Canuto (2015) for an assessment on the long-run positive impact of gender equality on Brazil's economic growth and Elborgh-Woytek et al. (2013) for its overall impact.

2 Gender Differences in the Labour Market: Literature Review and Own Contribution

2.1 Literature Review

Gender differences in the labour market have been widely studied during the last decades (Blau and Kahn 1992, 1995, 1996a, b, 2001, 2013, 2017; Edin and Richardson 2002; Kidd and Shannon 1996; Kunze 2017a; Olivetti and Petrongolo 2008; Ngai and Petrongolo 2017). Empirical evidence shows the existence and persistence of differences in labour market outcomes that left females in a disadvantageous position compared to male counterparts: (i) rates of employment are generally lower among women compared to men; (ii) rates of unemployment have generally proven to be higher for females than for males; while, (iii) females tend to show lower earnings than males.

All these research outcomes on gender differences in the labour market may be classified in two different groups. On the one hand, the research conducted to analyse country-level (within country) gender differences as recently identified by Ngai and Petrongolo (2017) or Blau and Kahn (2017). On the other hand, there is a series of studies performed to understand gender international differences; that is to say, research focused on the causes of the existence of different labour market outcomes across countries (Kunze 2017a; Olivetti and Petrongolo 2008; Blau and Kahn 1992, 1995, 1996a, b, 2001, 2013, 2017).

Whether within a given country or across different countries, empirical evidence sheds light on the possible causes of the existence of these differences; especially regarding the paramount 'gender pay gap' (GPG). According to Blau and Kahn (2017), we can classify these factors in three different groups. In the first group we find the set of factors traditionally used to explain gender differences in the labour market. These are (i) the labour force participation of women, which shows a rapid increase after the World War II mainly linked to the increase in returns to female labour force (Goldin et al. 2006; Juhn and Murphy 1997; Blau and Kahn 2007); (ii) the problem of females' selection bias; as observed it is the wages of those women who certainly participate in the labour market (Heckman 1979); (iii) the increasing levels of education among women, who have overtaken men in education (Blau et al. 2014) although no clear explanation has been demonstrated yet for this fact (Blau and Kahn 2017); (iv) the work experience and number of hours worked, which explain a higher proportion of gender differences in the past than in the present time, although still important[3]; (v) the gender differences in formal training and turnover related to the hypothesis that women tend to receive less training at work[4] than men due to females' higher probability of quitting a job for family responsibilities; (vi) the gender division of labour and motherhood as non-market job is said to negatively affect females' labour performance; (vii) the occupational segregation, which has diminished but still explains "one-third of the gender gap in 2010" (Blau and Kahn 2017, p. 827); and, finally, (viii) the deeply debated and illegal labour market discrimination,[5] where Becker (1971) was one of the first to provide an (neo-classical) economic analysis.

A second group of factors to explain labour market differences between females and males are (i) the social norms; (ii) the psychological attributes (Mueller and Plug 2006) and (iii) some non-cognitive skills. A good example of these is the lower willingness of women to negotiate (Babcock and Laschever 2003) or the lower female tendency for competition (Bertrand 2011). Similarly, women's risk aversion tends to be higher (Croson and Gneezy 2009). All these personal features are said to ultimately negatively affect the wages of females as well as their representation in high-level jobs, leading to an increase in gender differences.

Finally, a third group of factors, starting with the contribution by Juhn et al. (1991), addresses the explanation of labour market

[3]In the study by Blau and Kahn (2017), it is demonstrated that while gender differences in experience accounted for 24% of the gender gap in the 1980s, it only counted for 16% by 2010.

[4]Notice that less work training eventually implies a reduction of females' relative human capital.

[5]Since 1970 a total amount of 13 pieces of legislation to ensure equal treatment at work have been adopted. In 2000, the new EU legislation laws on equal rights between genders were adopted to prohibit gender discrimination because of racial and ethnic origin, religion and belief, disability, sexual orientation or age (EC 2018)

differences among males and females from the demand and supply forces of the world-economy and the labour-market institutions. Empirical evidence shows that countries with stronger union density tend to show a more compressed wage structure linked to the existence of higher minimum wages that mainly affect women thus narrowing the 'gender pay gap' (Blau and Kahn 1996a); although there is also evidence that highly centralised unions lower relative employment among females by lowering employment and raising unemployment (Bertola et al. 2007).

As pointed above, all these factors may help to explain both, country level gender differences and differences across countries. Some of the factors explaining country-level differences, such as differences in human capital or gender discrimination exerted by employers, may also be extrapolated to explain gender differences across countries. There is evidence of the existence of a positive correlation between country's size of 'gender pay gap' and the related skill regards. Moreover, 'gender pay gap' tends to be higher in countries showing larger sectoral differences (Blau and Kahn 1992, 1995, 1996a, b). However, international differences in the 'gender pay gap' are only understood in the light of the third group of factors; that is to say, when the factors influencing overall wage structure are included. Among these factors, there is some evidence showing the importance of labour market supply and demand forces[6] (Blau and Kahn 2001, 2013, 2017). However, relative wage inequality[7] and non-egalitarian institutional wage-setting[8] are considered the major causes of its existence (Kidd and Shannon 1996; Edin and Richardson 2002; Blau and Kahn 2001). A very enlightening contribution in this respect is the research by Blau and Kahn (2001), where they provide evidence that "rather than to changes over time within

[6]"More compressed male wage structures and lower female net supply are associated with a lower 'gender pay gap'" (Blau and Kahn 2001, p. 138).

[7]In the pair-wise comparison between the US and other advance economies, performed by Blau and Kahn (1992, 1995, 1996b), it is found that the higher wage inequality existing in the US is the main reason for the 'gender pay gap' to be relatively higher. This may be called "the paradox of American women with relatively higher qualifications" (Blau and Kahn 2001).

[8]Using microdata for 22 countries, Blau and Kahn (2001) find strong evidence of the importance of institutional setting to explain the existence of the 'gender pay gap'.

countries" (Blau and Kahn 2001, p. 131) it is the "long-run differences across countries" (Blau and Kahn 2001, p. 131) that can mainly explain differences in the 'gender pay gap'; this is by pointing to the institutional setting as the major cross-country existing difference. Moreover, in order to test their hypothesis they include a series of labour market institutions and settings[9] as explanatory variables of the international differences in the 'gender pay gap'; showing strong evidence that the extent of collective bargaining as well as agreements providing higher wage floors, work towards the objective of wage equality between females and males.

Some researchers have studied the general effects of the 'great recession'[10] on labour market outcomes. There is a series of country-level studies such as the performed by Coulter (2016) for the UK, in which he attributes macroeconomic policies "more supportive of growth than in previous recessions" as well as the "several decades of innovation in labour market policy" Coulter (2016, p. 197) the better performance of the UK economy compared to other European continental countries or the US. However, he also explains that this performance is linked to part-time and insecure job creation together with a fall in real wages and a loss of productivity. A study by Garibaldi and Taddei (2013), for the case of Italy, argues that, as a consequence of the two-tier labour market reforms implemented there is a dual labour market in Italy formed by a group of workers in permanent jobs or insiders and a group of workers temporary jobs in which young generations are specially concentrated and, consequently, burdened. Rinne and Zimmermann (2012) conclude that the German 'miracle' observed during the 'great recession' is a consequence of the combination of a set of variables, from labour market reforms to the crisis mainly affecting export-led companies or automatic stabilisers. They highlight the role of "short-time work and long-term shortages of skilled workers" (Rinne and Zimmermann, op. cit., p. 1) as key factors for the surprisingly

[9]These are: (i) collective bargaining coverage; (ii) minimum wage laws; (iii) unemployment insurance systems; (iv) job protection; and (v) parental leave entitlements (Blau and Kahn 2001).

[10]By 'great recession', we refer to the years 2008–2013.

good performance of the German economy. Additionally, some authors have focused on comparing the outcomes for the different countries in the EU. This is the case of the EC (2017), Dreger et al. (2014) or Boll et al. (2016) for the EU as a whole or the research by Bentolila et al. (2012) in which French and Spanish labour markets are compared. In this last research, authors estimate that if only the Spanish labour market had followed the same labour market protectionism as done by France, 45% of the increase in unemployment during the GR would have been avoided.

However, among the studies on the effects of the GR on labour market outcomes in the EU, some literature has focused specific attention on the effects on gender differences. Following the same classification used before, we can distinguish between: (i) country-level studies; and, (ii) international studies. Within the first group, Addabbo et al. (2015) perform a study in which they analyse the effects of the GR on labour force participation in Italy and Spain. Concretely, they address the important issue of whether responses to the GR have been mainly dominated by the added-worker effect (AWE) or by the discouraged worker effect (DWE), finding that AWE is dominant in the case of Spanish females while DWE drives Italy's females' patrol of decision. De la Rica and Rebollo-Sanz (2015) use the Continuous Survey of Labour Careers in Spain to show the unemployment ins and outs during the GR. According to their findings unemployment during the GR remained almost constant for females; however, they estimate a 1.5% increase in unemployment for males; that is to say, unemployment ins are found to be greater for men. On the other side, they find that while the probability of exiting unemployment decreases 15 percentage points (pp) for males it only decreases 8 pp for females. Piazzalunga and Di Tomasso (2015) show that austerity policies are the major cause explaining the increase in the Italian gender gap. Concretely, according to the estimates of the authors, wage freezing accounts for 100% of the increase in the gender gap registered during the crisis.

Among the international studies at the EU level, Brunet and Jeffers (2017) show that gender gaps have decreased during the GR. However, they work on the hypothesis that this reduction is not always linked to a real improvement of females' labour market situation. In fact, they point to males' worsening as the major cause for the reduction in the gaps. In the same direction, but pointing at differences among regions and education levels, Jaba et al. (2015) provide evidence of the reduction in the 'gender employment gap' (GEG) in the EU. According to their estimates, both, education and GDP are factors that significantly explain the evolution of the GEG in the EU15 during the period 2003–2012. Baussola and Mussida (2017) perform an analysis to compare unemployment differentials in Italy, Spain, France and the UK. They find that a significant 'gender unemployment gap' (GUG) in Italy and the UK. According to the authors Italy's behaviour is supported by worsening conditions in males during the crisis while, in the case of the UK, it is higher male unemployment rates that explain the finding. Boll et al. (2016) estimates both, the size and factors explaining the existence of the EU 'gender pay gap' (GPG). They find that more frequent part-time jobs among females as well as job segregation are the key drivers of gender differences in earnings in the European context.

As may be concluded, these last type of international studies, which are usually performed for the periods preceding the GR in comparison to the outcomes during the GR, give estimates of the magnitude and possible explanations for the causes behind the existence of gender differences in the labour market for both, the EU in general and in the specific countries of each study in particular. However, we notice that none of these studies gives a detailed description of the endogenous variables most frequently used to measure labour market gender differences. We refer to the variables describing the evolution of (i) employment, (ii) unemployment and (iii) earnings. Moreover, research is focused on the comparison of the outcomes prior to the GR to those found during the GR but very little is concluded for the last years of first signs of recovery, that is to say 2014, 2015 and 2016.[11] The aim of the present chapter is to fill these gaps.

[11]We start at the beginning of the twenty-first century and finish the last year for which data are available (2016).

2.2 Our Contribution on Evolution of Gender Differences

Concretely, our contribution adds an insight to the existing literature on the evolution of gender differences on employment, unemployment and earnings in two ways. First, in addition to comparing the outcomes before and after the GR, we extend the analysis to the last years 2014–2016 of first signs of recovery. Second, we address the comparison among the different countries in our study looking at their outcomes along the period analysed and separately, at the different sub-periods comprising the years prior to the GR, the years of deepest GR and the first years of recovery. Notice that it is beyond the scope of this chapter to address the causes of the existence of gender disparities that are very clearly and proficiently identified in the literature.[12] Our aim is less pretentious, although we still consider the interest of researchers and policy makers aiming to understand the evolution of labour market gender differences before, during and after the GR. In order to reach our aim, we describe the gender dimension of, first, the evolution of the rate of employment; second, the evolution of the rate of unemployment and finally, the evolution of earnings.

The study is performed in two steps. In a first step we look at the evolution of these three dimensions of the labour market for the EU as a whole as well as for a set of countries that we consider especially representative in the EU; these are: France, Germany, Italy, Spain and the United Kingdom (UK). In a second step, we describe the evolution of each variable separately for females and males and that of the corresponding gender gaps in employment, unemployment and earnings. In this manner, we are able to (i) assess the general impact of the GR on labour market outcomes; (ii) compare the overall impact to that for each specific country separately for females and males; and (iii) assess the effect on gender differences. In order to perform the analysis, we use data from the Labour Force Survey (LFS) and the Structure of Earnings

[12]See Sect. 2.1 for a review of the literature.

Survey (SES). Concretely, we compute the 'gender employment gap' (GEG) and the 'gender unemployment gap' (GUG) for the period (2002–2016) from the LFS and use the data on 'gender pay gap' (GPG) available for the period (2006–2015) from SES.

The rest of the chapter is arranged as follows. In Sect. 3 data from LFS is used to describe the evolution of the rate of employment and unemployment as well as to compute and describe the gender employment and unemployment gaps. In Sect. 4 we describe the evolution of the 'gender pay gap'. In all cases, the analysis starts giving a general overview of the evolution for the EU and the countries included; subsequently we look into the gender dimension of the phenomena. Further discussion and main conclusions are provided in Sects. 5 and 6.

3 Towards the Objective of Gender Equality: Employment and Unemployment

The objective of this section is to understand the evolution of labour market gender[13] differences in employment and unemployment from 2001 to 2016. We divide the period analysed into three[14] different sub-periods: (i) The *Pre-Great Recession* period, which comprises the years prior to the burst of the GR from 2001 to 2008 (both included); (ii) The *Great-Recession* period, which starts in 2009 and finishes in the year 2013; and (iii) The *post-Great Recession* period of first signs of recovery, which is observed from 2014 onwards (2014–2016 in our data).

[13]The difference between sex and gender is an issue under debate. However, now, there is arrangement on using the differences in sexes to split statistical data and, as a consequence in the present paper we follow this general agreement. We perform the analysis using data for men and women although we use the term 'gender' as a synonym of 'sex' throughout this chapter. Similarly, we use indistinctly the term women and female as well as men and male.

[14]We have established these three periods according to the evolution of GDP in the euro area. In the years 2009–2014 the GDP at constant prices was below the GDP in 2008. We consider that the financial crisis ended the year when the GDP shows values similar to those prior to the crisis.

Table 1 Rate of growth of the rate of employment (%)

	Pre GR	GR	Post GR
	2001–2007	2008–2013	2014–2016
All			
EU	0.69	−0.49	1.33
Germany	0.96	0.95	0.54
Spain	1.59	−3.18	2.78
France	0.40	−0.28	0.31
Italy	0.97	−1.08	1.01
UK	0.02	−0.27	1.40
Females			
EU	1.17	−0.03	1.45
Germany	1.37	1.42	0.86
Spain	3.67	−1.91	2.59
France	1.01	0.03	0.55
Italy	2.02	−0.29	1.14
UK	0.15	0.03	1.50
Males			
EU	0.36	−0.92	1.19
Germany	0.63	0.58	0.17
Spain	0.17	−4.14	3.06
France	−0.10	−0.55	0.10
Italy	0.33	−1.59	0.92
UK	−0.11	−0.51	1.27

Averages for the periods
Source Authors' own estimates from Labour Force Survey (LFS)

We address the analysis by looking at two different dimensions of the labour market. We describe the evolution of the rates of employment and the rates of unemployment. Although paramount in labour market, we have decided not to describe the participation rate for two main reasons. First, it would not provide significant information, given its relationship with employment and unemployment. Second, because it would imply a longer analysis, which would prevent us from performing the rest of the analysis in detail.

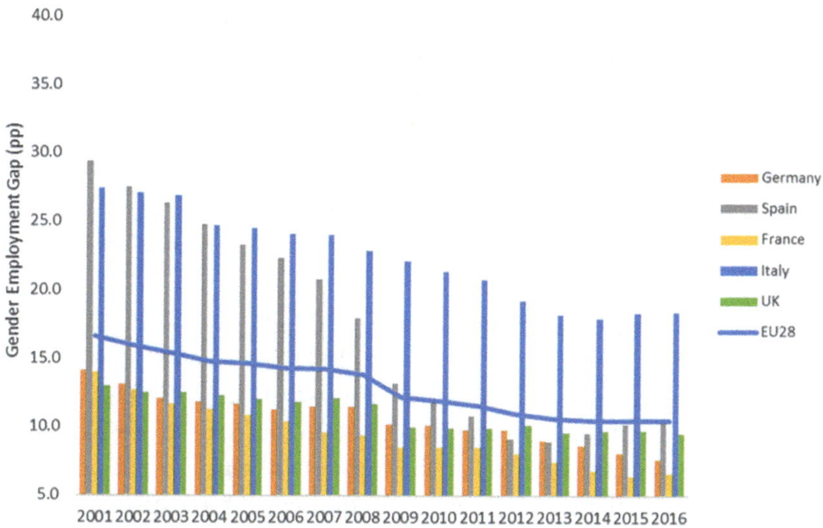

Fig. 1 Evolution of the 'gender employment gap' (GEG) in the EU and a selected group of countries. Period (2001–2016) (*Source* Authors' elaboration from LFS)

3.1 Gender Differences in Employment: The 'Gender Employment Gap' (GEG)

Table 1 shows the average rate of growth of the rate of employment[15] in the EU as well as in the countries included in our analysis (France, Germany, Italy, Spain and the UK) for each sub-period analysed both, for the whole population and distinguishing by gender (females and males). Figure 1 shows, the evolution of the 'gender employment gap' (GEG) in the EU and the countries in our study, as stated above.

---

[15]The rate of employment is defined as the number of people with a job contract divided by the number of people at the age of work. It is convenient to specify that there is not a common agreement for all the countries in the EU to define this rate. As an example, in Spain, it is considered that the age for a person to legally be able to work is 16, being working age population between 16 and 64 years old (both included). In the case of the EU, working age adults comprises the individuals between 15 and 64 years old (both included). Accordingly, we use the individuals of this range of age in our study, as provided by The Eurostat, defining the rate of employment as the number of people with a job contract in a certain area divided by the number of people who, in that area, are 15 or more years old and younger than 65.

The GEG is defined as the difference between the rate of employment for males and females as in expression 1.

$$\mathrm{GEG}_{tr} = e^{m}_{tr} - e^{f}_{tr} \qquad (1)$$

where e^{m}_{tr} represents the rate of employment for males of region r in year t and e^{f}_{tr} is the value of the rate of employment for females in region r in year t.

The rate of employment in the EU is 62.6% at the beginning of the period considered; that is to say, in 2001. As may be drawn from Table 1, during the whole sub-period prior to GR (2002–2008) there is a positive and almost constant increase in the rate of employment, which reaches a peak (65.7%) in the last year of the sub-period, 2008. The average annual rate of growth of employment is equal to 0.69% in this period. After the onset of the GR the positive trend changes. The average annual rate of growth of employment turns negative for the period 2008–2013 (−0.49%). The first year of the crisis the rate of employment falls 1.3 pp driving the rate of employment to a value equal to 64.5%. From this stage on, the rate of employment in the EU plateaus around the 64% level (between 64.1 and 64.2 to be exact). The year 2013 shows the first signs of recovery in terms of employment. There is a trough at 64.1% level followed by a rapid increase in the employment rate, being its value equal to 64.9, 65.7 and 66.7% in the years 2014, 2015 and 2016, respectively. The average rate of growth of employment for this post GR period is equal to 1.33%.

In light of the cross-country evolution of the rates of employment we can conclude the existence of non-uniform patrol of business cycle employment elasticities; that is to say, the response of employment to changes in the business cycle seems to be different across countries. The Spanish labour market is the one that most intensely seems to react to these variations. In the years previous to the GR, when housing bubble reached the maximum intensity, the average rate of growth of the rate of employment was equal to 1.59%. This value, being higher than 0.69%, registered for the EU as a whole. Moreover, the rate is highest among all the countries studied. As a result, the rate of employment increases from 57.8% in 2001 to 64.5% in the year 2008. During the years of the GR, however, employment destruction is also greater, in comparison to the rest of countries in our study. Between the years 2008 and 2013, the average rate of growth of the rate of employment is equal to −3.2% (negative and highest among the countries in our study). The lowest value for the rate of employment is registered in 2013 (54.8%). The recovery of the economic cycle from 2013 onwards accelerates the creation of employment. Accordingly, the average rate of growth of the variable that occupies our attention again yields positive (2.8%).

The most singular performance is displayed by the German economy. After a period of stagnation at the beginning of the century, there is a persistent increase in the rate of employment for all the years considered. As may be drawn from Table 1, the average rate of growth of the rates of employment was positive for the three periods considered. What is more, it was even lower (0.54%) for the years of recovery than for the central years of the crisis (0.95%). As a result, the rate of employment grew from a value slightly higher than 65% in 2001 to a value equal to almost 75% in 2016.

The rate of employment in France plateaus at around 64% value for the whole period (2001–2016). The French labor market shows the lowest sensitivity to changes in the economic cycle. During the years of economic growth at the beginning of the period analysed; that is to say, before the burst of the GR, the rate of employment increased at an average rate equal to 0.40%, somewhat higher than that shown during the last years of recovery (0.31). During the years of the crisis, the growth rate was practically identical to that of the UK (0.27%). The evolution of the rate of employment in the UK, on the other hand, presents some singularities, especially in view of the outcomes for the rest of countries studied. During the years of economic growth prior to the GR, the rate of employment plateaued at around 72%. The average rate of growth of the rate of employment for that period was equal to 0.02%. Later, during the years of the crisis the rate of employment decreased somewhat, although not significantly; it has shown signs of recovery again during the recent years, when the rate of employment has reached a value equal to 73.5%.

The analysis of the evolution of the rate of employment allows concluding the existence of a similar pattern between the Italian and the Spanish labour markets. In both countries employment had similar intensities during the GR. In addition, these two countries had the lowest employment levels among the countries selected. The value registered by the rate of employment in Italy at the beginning of the period (year 2001) was equal to 55.5%, being 2.3 pp higher for Spain (rate of employment equal to 57.8%). At the end of the period, the value of the respective rates was equal to 57.2 and 59.5%; keeping Italy the initial distance relatively to Spain in 2.3 pp. Moreover, these two countries also had the lowest rates of employment relatively to the average registered for the EU.

The evolution of the rate of employment, however, is not identical for females and males. At the beginning of the period (2001) the value of the rate of employment for men was equal to 70.9% while, at the end of the whole period (2016) the value was equal to 71.9%, which implies an average increase for the whole period analysed equal to 1.4%. As shown in the estimates of Table 1, prior to the GR, the rate of employment for men had an average increase equal to 0.36%; during the GR, the rate diminished at an average rate equal to −0.91% and, during the years of first recovery the value registered an average increase of 1.19%.

The rate of employment for females at the beginning of the period (2001) was equal to 54.3%, while the value at the end of the period was equal to 61.4%. This evolution implies an average growth of women's rate of employment equal to 13.7%. The pattern of increase, however, is not constant. The years prior to the GR, female rate of employment increased at an average rate equal to 1.17%; the years of the GR implied a stagnation of that evolution, being the average rate of growth even negative and equal to −0.03%. Finally, the first years of recovery showed a very optimistic scenario, with the average rate of growth equalled to 1.45% (see column three in Table 1).

Especially helpful in understanding the evolution of differences in employment between genders is the 'gender employment gap' (GEG) presented in Fig. 1. As it is observed, at the beginning of the period gender differences in employment in the EU amounted to 16.6

percentage points (pp). The GEG was positive for the whole period; it reached a value equal to 10.5 in the last year (2016). In light of these two values, we get the implication that by 2016, 36.7% of the gender differences in the rate of employment existing in 2001 disappeared. This finding leads us to reach a second conclusion: the existence of convergence between the rates of employment for women and men during the period analysed. However, this apparently positive result in the path for raising the challenge of gender equality is also an indication of the long way ahead; since two-thirds of the GEG existing at the beginning of the 2000's has not been closed yet (as revealed by the difference in more than 10 pp between the rates of employment of men and women in the year 2016).

The improvement in the GEG in the EU during the years of crisis is driven by the asymmetric behaviour of the rates of employment registered for each gender. As explained above, the rates of employment have evolved differently for males and females in the three sub-periods considered; that is to say, before, during and after the GR. Prior to the GR, the rate of growth of the rate of employment is positive for both, males and females. During the GR, this rate of growth turns to be negative also for both, females and males, being practically equal to zero (−0.03%) for females, and significantly negative for males, with the value being equal to −0.92%.

Data on the evolution of the rate of employment and the GEG for France, Germany, Italy, Spain and UK show a similar trend to that already described for the EU. The GEG decreases in all of them during the years considered, albeit with different intensities and rhythms. The initial situations, as well as the final ones, however, reveal some differential characteristics among the countries considered. In the two southern European or Mediterranean countries (Spain and Italy) during the years prior to the crisis, the male employment rate plateaued at 70% level or above. During the last three years of economic growth, the rate of employment for females was below 50% in Italy, being somewhat higher in Spain. In 2001 this gap was equal to 29.4 pp in Spain and 27.4 pp in Italy. However, in 2008 the GEG decreased to a value equal to 22.9 pp in Italy and 17.9 pp in Spain. This evolution, in both countries, was the result of an average growth rate of female rate of employment higher than that for males. In Italy, for the period 2001–2008 the average rate of growth for females was equal to 2.02%, compared to 0.33% for males. In Spain these values were, respectively, equal to 3.67 and 0.17%. The years of the GR contributed to correct the GEG in both countries, especially in Spain where it fell to 8.9 pp in 2013. The decline in Italy, although significant, was somewhat lower and remained, for the same year, at 18.2 pp. In both cases, this decrease was the result of a greater fall in the rate of employment of males compared to females. In the Spanish case, during the period 2009–2013, the average growth rate of the rate of employment for males was equal to −4.14%, while this same rate for women was equal to −1.91%. In Italy these values were, respectively, equal to −1.59 and −0.29% (see Table 1). In the three years of economic recovery, the GEG in Spain increased slightly with respect to the value registered during the GR due to the fact that the rate of employment grew faster for males than for females. However, the Spanish GEG in 2016 was located at 10.5 pp value, exactly equal to the average for the EU; while in Italy, this indicator remained practically constant at around the 18 pp level.

Among the countries, France showed the lowest GEG. In 2016, this indicator was equal to 6.6 pp; that is to say, 4 points lower than the EU's average and almost 12 pp lower than the value observed for Italy. During the 16 years studied, this indicator diminished by almost 8 points. Together with Spain, France is the country in which the reduction in the employment gap is most noticeable. Again, the pattern of behaviour of this indicator responds to the same characteristics already highlighted. In the years of economic growth a better performance of the average rate of growth for females than males is found. In the central years of the crisis, in this French case, we notice a negative rate of growth of employment for males and positive for females; while, during more recently, there is a somewhat higher growth for the rate of employment of females.

The UK and Germany have also some remarkable features. With regard to the first of these two countries, it should be noted that during the years prior to the crisis, the GEG maintained considerable stability, at least when compared with what was observed in other countries. In 2001, this indicator was equal to 13 pp and in 2008, it decreases to 11.7 pp. During the crisis, an inflection point is detected that leads the GEG up to 10 pp. This trend, however, has no continuity during the rest of the years which leaves this indicator in the UK at 9.5 pp in 2016. In short, the UK is the country with the less radical evolution of this indicator. In Germany, also, the GEG diminishes significantly during the whole period considered. The reduction almost halves, from a value equal to 14.1 pp in 2001 to 7.2 pp in 2016. However, the most remarkable fact in this country is that this reduction is accompanied at all times by an increase in the rate of employment for both genders, although, logically, the average growth rate of the rate of employment for females is always higher than the rate of employment for males. The years of the GR also marked a turning point, as in the rest of the countries, although in this case the characteristic is that the rate of growth of females' employment was positive and higher than that of males.

In short, on view of the GEG there was a positive evolution towards gender equality during the years of the GR. This finding is related to the fact that, the economic crisis seems to have affected negatively males' employment than females', leading to a general narrowing of the GEG in the EU. In fact, in the middle years of the GR it even reached its lowest historical values. However, the GEG indicator does not account for the type of employment that is destroyed nor, and this is the relevant argument, for the type of employment that is created and accessed by women. In subsequent sections, we discuss the evolution of the rates of unemployment and wages, which can give us evidence of the type of employment in which women performed better.

3.2 Gender Differences in Unemployment: The 'Gender Unemployment Gap' (GUG)

In this section, we show the evolution of the gender differences in unemployment. We proceed in a similar manner as in the previous section. In a first step, we explain the evolution of the general rate of unemployment, and analyse the evolution of gender differences both, in the EU in general and in the countries studied, in particular. We also split the period analysed into the same three sub-periods as above; that

Table 2 Rate of growth of the rate of unemployment (%)

	Pre GR	GR	Post GR
	2001–2007	2008–2013	2014–2016
All			
EU	−2.90	9.67	−7.59
Germany	−0.09	−6.59	−7.57
Spain	2.06	19.65	−9.08
France	−0.59	7.14	−0.64
Italy	−3.91	12.90	−1.01
UK	1.78	6.93	−13.74
Females			
EU	−3.17	7.92	−6.88
Germany	−0.03	−8.35	−8.11
Spain	−1.81	16.49	−7.09
France	0.47	5.39	−0.99
Italy	−4.70	9.35	−0.61
UK	2.26	7.30	−12.74
Males			
EU	−2.52	11.06	−8.03
Germany	0.02	−5.09	−6.43
Spain	6.32	22.86	−10.89
France	−1.63	8.74	−0.27
Italy	−2.91	16.35	−1.70
UK	1.69	6.69	−14.38

Averages for the periods
Source Authors' own estimates from Labour Force Survey (LFS)

is to say, the years prior to the crisis or pre-GR period (2002–2007); the years of the crisis or GR period (2008–2013) and the years of first signs of recovery, namely post-GR period (2014–2016). Table 2 contains the average rates of growth registered for each sub-period for the whole sample as well as for each gender.

Figure 2 shows the 'gender unemployment gap' (GUG) for the EU as well as for all the countries in our study (France, Germany, Italy, Spain and the UK). The GUG is defined as the difference between the rate of employment for females and the rate of unemployment for males as in Eq. 2.

$$\text{GUG}_{tr} = u^{f}_{tr} - u^{m}_{tr} \tag{2}$$

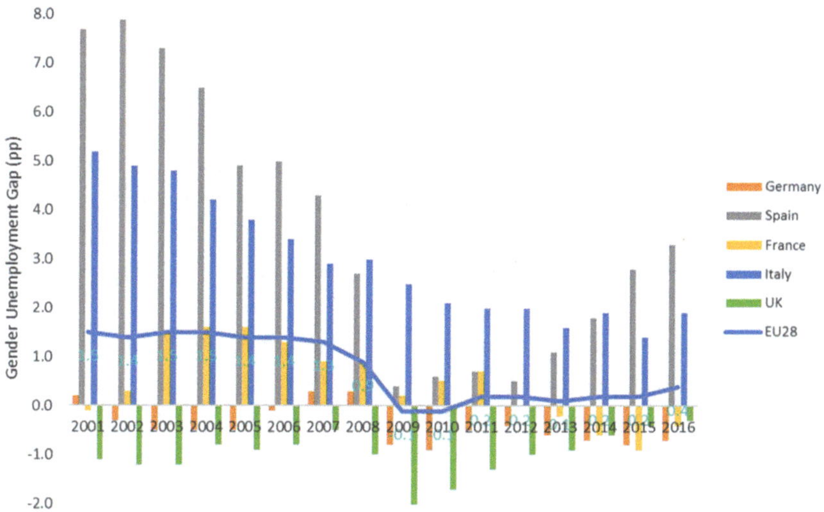

Fig. 2 Evolution of the 'gender unemployment gap' (GUG) in the EU and a selected group of countries. Period (2001–2016) (*Source* Authors' elaboration from LFS)

where u_{tr}^{f} represents the rate of unemployment for female of region r in year t and u_{tr}^{m} is the value of the rate of unemployment for males in region r in year t. Recall that, contrary to the case of employment in which the GEG is computed as the difference between the male and the female rates, the GUG is computed as the female rate minus the male rate.

As may be seen in Fig. 2, at the beginning of the period (2001) the rate of unemployment in the EU was equal to 8.7%. During the first years of the century, this rate grew slightly, to stand at 9.3% in 2004. However, once the effects of the cycle changed, associated with the technological crisis of the late 90s of the last century were overcome, the unemployment rate slowly decreased until reaching a value equal to 7% in the year 2008. In the central years of the crisis (2008–2013), it increased until reaching a maximum value of 10.9% in 2013; it then started a slow decline and stood at 8.6% of the active population in 2016.

The described evolution of the rate of unemployment hides very different situations in the different countries that constitute the EU. The most dramatic situation occurred in the Spanish economy, where the unemployment rate increased from 8.2% in 2007 to 26.1% in the third quarter of 2013. The average growth rate of the rate of unemployment during the years of the crisis was equal to 19.7%. From that moment on, it began to decrease, although at a significantly lower speed. In the years of recovery, the unemployment rate decreased at an average rate of 9.1%.[16]

Data for the cases of Italy and France are not as dramatic as for the case of Spain, although the years of recovery are not associated with a clear decrease in their respective unemployment rates. The values before the crisis have not yet been recovered. In the case of Italy, the unemployment rate practically doubled. In 2007 it was equal to 6.1% and in 2016, after a slight decrease, the value stabilised at 11.7%. The unemployment rate of the French economy increased by five points, from 6.7% in 2008 to 11.7% in 2016. The rate of unemployment in the UK best reflects a correlation with the economic cycle. During the years prior to the crisis, this rate was close to 5%, somewhat below its long-term equilibrium value. In 2011 it reached a peak (8.1%) while, at the end of the period considered, it returned to the value shown during the pre-crisis period. The German experience, as already mentioned in the previous section, is the most singular among the countries studied. After registering a value equal to 11.2% in 2005, the rate decreased to 4% value in 2016.

Observing the evolution of the rate of unemployment for the different genders allows identifying interesting patrols. At the beginning of the period, in 2001, the rate of unemployment for males in the EU was equal to 8.0%. At the end of the whole period (2016), the value was

[16]The unemployment rate in Spain has historically shown high records. The long-term average, an indicator that we could identify with the equilibrium rate of unemployment has been around 14% since the mid-1980s. The value then of the unemployment rate in 2016 would have to be compared with this equilibrium value and not so much with the unemployment rate before the crisis. In the medium term the recovery of the unemployment rate before the crisis would be very difficult to estimate.

equal to 8.4%. The rate increased until 2004; afterwards a decreasing trend emerged, which on average, amounted to 2.52% for the Pre-GR period. During the GR the rate of unemployment increased to an average rate of 11.06%; it again diminished at an average rate equal to 8.03% during the Post-recession period. Females showed a very similar trend. At the beginning of the period, the rate of unemployment for females was equal to 9.5%. Unemployment increased during the years 2002, 2003 and 2004 until it reached the peak 10.1%. From 2005 to 2008, a reduction in the rate of unemployment was observed, reaching a trough at 7.5% level. The GR exerts a negative impact on female's unemployment. The rate increased at an average rate equal to 7.92%, reaching the maximum value of 10.9% in the year 2013. The first years of recovery show a reduction in the rate of unemployment faced by females. The rate of increase (decrease) equalled to −6.9% on average; by the end of the period analysed the rate of unemployment for women amounted to 8.8%.

In light of Fig. 2, we observe that at the beginning of the period, the GUG reached a maximum value of 1.5 pp; that is to say, in the year 2001, the rate of unemployment for females was 1.5 pp, higher than the rate of unemployment of males. This difference plateaued for the whole Pre-GR period between 1.5 and 1.3 pp values. The year 2008 registered a clear decrease in the GUG, to the value 0.9. The historically minimum −0.1 pp was found in 2009, bringing females to be, for the first time, an advantage compared to males. Recall that GUG being negative implies that the rate of unemployment among males is higher than the rate of unemployment for females. This situation was repeated in the year 2010 to, again, become positive from 2011 onwards. As will be seen, these same tendencies are repeated for the rest of countries in our study; although with some singularities. A priori data seem to support a reduction in the GUG; that is to say, it seems that the crisis exerted a positive impact to diminish gender differences in unemployment. However, taking into account that the gap worsens again during the years of economic recovery, this improvement may be hiding not so much as an advance in gender equality, but an unequal behaviour of women and men in the labour market during the economic recession.

The trend described by the GUG in France responds to the aforementioned pattern. During the first years of the century, when European economies were emerging from a short recessive cycle, the gap increased to reach a value equal to 1.6 pp. With the first symptoms of the crisis, the rate of unemployment of females and males converged, leading to a reduction in the GUG; which, by the end of the crisis, is even negative. At the end of the period, however, a change in the trend is noted; although it is not yet possible to affirm whether it is a turning point or not.

The example provided by Germany has remarkable singularities. During the years before the GR, which, and as we have noted above, are years of strong recession in the German economy until 2005, when the behaviour of the GUG followed the pattern indicated. Between 2001 and 2005, it decreased until reaching a negative value equal to −0.5 pp at the end of the period. When recovery began, the gap increased to decrease again in 2009. Since then, and with small variations, it has remained negative. The same as for the German case, in the UK, the GUG takes negative values for all the years considered. It is the only country we are studying for which females' rate of unemployment is always lower than males'. In any case, the pattern of behaviour found for the rest of countries during the years of crisis and those of recovery is also observed. In the years prior to the GR, and as the effects of the crisis of the last century were overcome, the GUG decreased. In the year 2001, it was equal to −1.1 pp and in 2007 to 0.5 pp. From this moment on, and coinciding with the beginning of the GR, again the rate of unemployment for males grew more than for females and the GUG increased to −2.1 pp in 2009. By the end of the GR, an almost full convergence of the rates of unemployment between females and males is observed; the GUG being almost zero at the end of the period (in 2016, the GUG is equal to −0.3 pp).

The indicator that now occupies our attention (GUG) shows, at the beginning of the period (2001), the highest value of all those observed so far (7.7 pp). The rate of unemployment for females was unusually high in relation to that of men at that time. During the years of economic growth prior to the GR, however, and unlike what was observed in other countries, this indicator decreased uninterruptedly and with intensity. In 2008, the GUG was equal to 2.7. In seven years, therefore, the indicator decreased by five percentage points. In the years of crisis, and as concluded for other countries, also in Spain a different behaviour of females' and males' rates of unemployment emerged. Although unemployment for both (females and males) grew dramatically, to stand above 25% in 2013, the differential behaviour characteristic of the moments of expansion seems to fade. In 2012, the value of the GUG was equal to 0.5 pp, the lowest observed. However, when the economy began to recover, the different evolution of these two rates once again emerged. By the end of 2016, the GUG rose to 3.3 pp. In any case, what should be highlighted is that this gap has not yet returned to the values prior to the crisis.

Something similar could also have happened in the Italian job market. As we have just seen for the Spanish case, similarly in the case of Italy the period begins with a strong difference in the unemployment rates of men and women, which is reflected in a high value of the GUG. In 2001, the value of this indicator was equal to 5.2 pp, somewhat lower than in Spain but also well above the EU average. From that moment on, the rates of unemployment began to equalise and the gender gap closed, as seen in the decline in the value of the GUG to 1.6 pp in 2013. In Italy, the years of the crisis do not seem to exert such an intense effect as observed for other countries, including Spain. Although it is also true that during the years of economic recovery the gap remained very contained. In 2016, the value of the GUG was equal to 1.9 pp.

In short, the evolution shown by this indicator reveals some trends that may be highlighted as a conclusion. First, gender differences in this area are clearly decreasing. In countries such as Spain and Italy, which started from very high GUG values, it is clear that at the end of the period studied the differences in unemployment rates have narrowed significantly and, as a result, also the value of the GUG. In countries, such as Germany and the UK, spreads are clearly favourable to females; in the German case they were from the end of the last decade and in the UK from the beginning of the period. France also shows the same trend, as do all the EU countries. Second, it also seems evident that the rate of unemployment for females has a differential behaviour compared to the unemployment rate of males during the period of the crisis. This differential behaviour can respond to multiple causes on which we return later.

4 Gender Differences in Earnings: The 'Gender Pay Gap' (GPG)

In this section, we analyse the evolution of the gender differences in earnings in the EU and in the countries included in our analysis. As we have shown in the analysis performed to account for gender differences in employment and unemployment in the light of the GEG and GUG, our aim is to describe the evolution of earnings as well as the evolution of the 'gender pay gap' (GPG) in the period prior to the GR or Pre-GR (before 2008), the most detrimental years of the GR (2008–2013) and the first years of recovery or Post-GR (2014-onwards).

Before proceeding, it is important to highlight that data availability for the GPG depends on the structure of earnings survey (SES), which is not performed annually. Accordingly, we use the data provided by the Eurostat for the years 2006, 2010 and 2014, for which gross hourly earnings are available. Also the data on the GPG published for the period 2007–2015 are utilised in order to observe more closely the evolution of gender differences during the period of our investigation. Data from SES on earnings are available for all the countries as well as for the EU28; however, data on the GPG are only available at country level and they are missing in some cases. These limitations of data availability, however, do not prevent us from observing the evolution of gender differences before during and after the GR given that at least we have one point available for every sub-period and country in our study.

Table 3 provides the rate of growth of average hourly earnings from 2006 to 2010 and from 2010 to 2014. Figure 3 shows the evolution of the 'gender pay gap' (GPG) for the EU and for all the countries studied: France, Germany, Italy, Spain and the UK. The 'gender pay gap' (GPG) is defined as the difference between the earnings of males and females as a percentage of the earnings of males (see Eq. 3),[17] as follows:

$$\mathrm{GPG}_{tr} = \frac{w_{tr}^{m} - w_{tr}^{f}}{w_{tr}^{m}} 100 \tag{3}$$

[17]This is the method followed by the European Commission to compute the 'gender pay gap' (GPG).

Table 3 Rate of growth of average hourly earnings (%)

	Pre GR	Post GR
	2006–2010	2010–2014
All		
EU	5.15	3.62
Germany	2.92	7.95
Spain	9.79	5.07
France	3.35	11.60
Italy	7.28	5.87
UK	−6.84	−3.92
Females		
EU	5.69	4.11
Germany	3.40	8.64
Spain	12.39	6.23
France	3.46	11.92
Italy	6.69	5.39
UK	−6.45	−2.08
Males		
EU	5.12	3.51
Germany	2.91	8.72
Spain	10.08	4.62
France	3.72	11.72
Italy	7.74	6.35
UK	−7.48	−5.17

Averages for the periods
Source Authors' own estimates from Structure of Earnings Survey (SES)

where w^m_{tr} is the average gross hourly earnings of males in region or country r, at time t or, in our concrete case, year t, w^f_{tr} is the average gross hourly earnings for females in country r in year t.

Data for the EU as a whole reveal an increase in average earnings from 2006 to 2010 and from 2010 to 2014. While average hourly earnings in 2006 amounted to 13.41 monetary units (m.u.), the value reaches the 14.1 level in 2010 and the 14.61 level in 2014. This implies an increase equal to 5.2% from 2006 to 2010 and equal to 3.6% from 2010 to 2014, as may be seen in Table 3. Consequently, if we accept 2006 being representative of the period prior to the GR, 2010 as the representative of the GR and 2014 as an instrument to describe the post-GR period, we conclude that, during the GR the rate of growth of hourly earnings decreased by 1.53 pp.

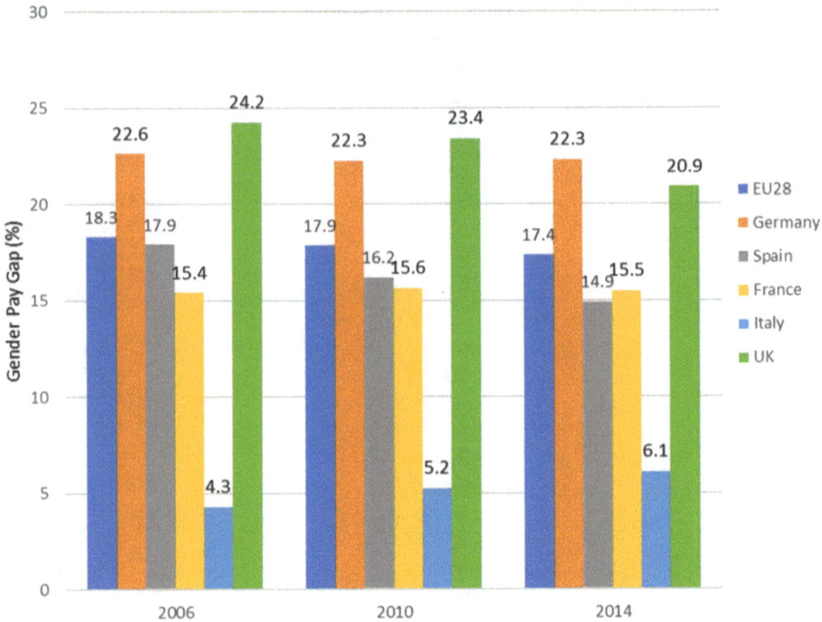

Fig. 3 Evolution of the 'gender pay gap' (GPG) in the EU and a selected group of countries. Years 2006, 2010 and 2014 (*Source* Authors' elaboration from LFS)

All the countries in our study, with the exception of the UK, show a similar behaviour: the earnings per hour worked increased. The rates of growth, however, differ. In the years prior to the crisis (see Table 3) the most intense increase occurred in Italy and Spain. These rates were moderated during the years of the recession, changing for Spain, from 9.79 to 5.07% and for Italy from 7.28 to 5.87%. The final result in both countries, however, is an increase in hourly earnings. In Spain, it increased from 11.13 m.u. to 12.84 m.u. and in Italy from 13.19 to 14.98. During the years of the GR, the greatest increases were recorded in France and Germany. In the former country, the increase was 11.6% and in the latter 8.0%. These two countries also had growth rates during the pre-crisis period. In absolute terms, this meant an increase in the hourly gain that happened, in France, from 14.01 m.u in 2006 to 16.16 m.u in 2014. In Germany these values were, respectively, 15.77

and 17.52. In the UK, as we have already mentioned, hourly income decreased in both periods. In 2006, the profits per hour were equal to 17.25 m.u and in 2014, they fell to 15.4 m.u.

The evolution of gender differences in earnings for the different countries as gathered by data on GPG in Fig. 3 allows grouping the countries in three different sets: (i) the countries for which gender differences in earnings have not increased; they either decreased significantly during the GR, which showed a stable GPG for the whole period (France and Germany); (ii) countries for which gender differences slightly increased during the GR as revealed by the GPG of Italy and, finally; (iii) countries for which gender differences in earnings diminished during the GR; that is to say, the countries showing a reduction in GPG (Spain and the UK).

For the two countries in the first group, that is to say, the cases of France and Germany, hourly earnings have increased from 2006 to 2014 for both, males and females. In France, the rate of growth of earnings is practically similar for both genders, approximately 3% in the period 2006–2010 and almost 12% in 2010–2014. However, females do always show a lower level of earnings, which supports the existence of a positive GPG for the whole period. In 2006, male earnings were 15.4% higher than female earnings. This difference, as revealed by the evolution of the GPG, slightly increased from 2006 to 2010 and to 2014; though the GPG plateaued at 15.5% average level in all the years analysed. In conclusion, the GPG in France has not significantly changed during the GR.

In the case of Germany, increases in earnings were practically identical for both genders (see Table 3) and also for the two periods of our study. However, while average hourly earnings in 2006 were equal to 17.5 m.u. for men, women only earned 13.54 m.u. This difference implies a value for the GPG equal to 22.6%. In 2010, being females' earnings equal to 14 compared to 18.01 of males, the GPG amounted to 22.3%. This difference between the earnings of both genders remained constant in the year 2014. According to this, we can conclude that, during the GR gender differences in earnings in this country almost remained constant.

The second group of countries, comprising Italy and Spain, register an increase in the average hourly earnings for both, females and males, from 2006 to 2010 and from 2010 to 2014. Initial earnings for Italian males were equal to 13.44 m.u. Those earnings increased by 7.74% from the period prior to the crisis and, at a rate equal to 6.35% from 2010 to 2014. In the case of the Italian females, initial earnings amounted to 12.86 m.u. The rate of growth of earnings from 2006 to 2010 was equal to 6.69% and from 2010 to 2014, at a rate of 5.39%. As a consequence of these growth rates, and taking into account the differential in earnings existing at the beginning of the period, it is easy to conclude that the GPG in Italy increased between 2006 and 2014. In the first year the value of this indicator was equal to 4.3%, while in 2014 it increased to 6.1%. In any case, it is convenient to notice that Italy is the country best performing in terms of the GPG, being the country where this indicator is historically lowest among the countries studied.

The Spanish GPG shows a decreasing trend. In 2006, the value of this indicator was equal to 17.9 and after decreasing to 16.2 four years later, in 2014 it was equal to 14.9. This trend is the result of a differential behaviour in the growth rates of hourly earnings. This statement is clear in view of Fig. 3. Between the years 2001 and 2007, this rate was equal to 12.39% for females and 10.08 for males. In the period 2014–2016 these values were, respectively, 6.23 and 4.62%.

Data for the UK reveal a similar trend to that described for Spain. In the year 2006, the GPG was equal to 24.2. In 2010, it decreased one pp to 23.4% value; the reduction continued until 2014, when it reached 20.9%. Unlike in Spain, in the UK, the relative convergence between the earnings of males and females occurred as a result of negative variations in the respective rates of growth of this variable (see Table 3). Between 2006 and 2010, the rate of growth of average hourly earnings for men decreased by 7.5% and for women by 6.5%. During the years of recovery (2010–2014) the rates remained negative, with values for men and women equal to 5.2 and 2.1%, respectively.

In short, the data that we have been commenting on the evolution of the GPG allows to confirm that, during the GR, gender differences, measured by wage differential in hourly earnings, remained constant

(Germany and France) or even decreased (Spain and UK). The only case in which a slight worsening may be detected is that of Italy. However, this country is the one showing the lowest GPG among all the countries studied.

5 Further Discussion of the Results

We have provided a picture of the evolution of labour market gender differences in the EU in the periods prior and posterior to the Great Recession (GR). Concretely, we have observed the evolution of the rate of employment, the rate of unemployment and the level of earnings during the period (2002–2016). In order to perform our study, we have computed the 'gender employment gap' (GEG) and the 'gender unemployment gap' (GUG) for the period (2002–2016) from the data published by The Eurostat from the Labour Force Survey (LFS). Additionally, we have used available data on 'gender pay gap' (GPG) from the Structure of Earnings Survey (SES) published also by The Eurostat for the period (2006–2015).

In a first step, we have analysed the evolution of these three dimensions of the labour market for the EU as a whole as well as for a set of particular countries: France, Germany, Italy, Spain and the United Kingdom (UK). In a second step, we have described the evolution of each variable separately for females and males and that of the corresponding gender gaps in employment, unemployment and earnings. This way of proceeding has allowed: (i) identifying the general impact of the GR on labour market outcomes; (ii) comparing the overall impact to that for each specific country separately for females and males; and, (iii) quantifying gender differences during the period analysed.

Data show that, during the GR gender differences have not significantly increased; moreover, the outcomes register signs of reduction for some of the countries studied. The positive evolution of the GEG provides evidence of the continued and increasing participation of females in the labour market from the beginning of the century. In the EU as a whole, this gap diminishes from 16.6 to 10.5% in 2016. What is more, the reduction registered is even greater for some countries. In Spain, the value of the GEG was equal to 29.4% in 2001, diminishing to 10.5% in 2016. In Italy, the respective values were equal to 27.4 and 18.4%. The gap in unemployment (GUG) points also to a more egalitarian behaviour of the rates of unemployment for women and men. However, this gap gives also evidence of a different behaviour between females and males during the crisis. The GUG significantly diminished during the crisis. In contrast, it increased during the years of recovery. Finally, the positive rhythm at which the earnings gap was narrowing prior to the GR slowed down during the GR. According to the data, during the years of the GR the GPG plateaued in France and Germany while in Spain and the UK it diminished. Italy is the only country for which the GPG increased during the crisis; though this is also the case with lowest GPG among all the cases analysed.

In light of this data, it would be straightforward to reach the conclusion that gender differences have diminished during the GR. However, a major question remains: what were the causes of the gender convergence in employment, unemployment and earnings during the GR? Obviously, gender convergence may appear for two main reasons. One desirable possibility is the improvement of female situation, which, *ceteris paribus*, would lead to women approaching men's labour market outcomes and, as a consequence, a narrowing of the gender employment, unemployment and earnings gaps. However, there is the chance for another reason to drive gender convergence: the non-desirable evolution of males' outcomes for the worse. That is to say, whenever we are dealing with outcomes measuring relative positions the individual position of all the parts in the set must be analysed before reaching any conclusion. This is precisely the case in our data. A very interesting piece of research by Brunet and Jeffers (2017), in which gender effects of the GR in 15 EU's countries are studied, the authors conclude that labour market gender gaps during the years of the crisis not always reflected an improvement of females' situation in the labour market. On the contrary, it is often the deterioration of males' condition the main reason for the narrowing of gender gaps.

In any case, the positive trend towards gender equality registered before the burst of the GR (Olivetti and Petrongolo 2016) also continued during the crisis. The indicator that most clearly reflects this positive evolution towards gender equality is the increase in females' rates of participation and employment. The increasing participation of females in the labour market responds to both demand and supply factors. From the demand side, the development of public and service sectors, especially health and education related vacancies, have proven to be major drivers for the increasing female participation in the labour market (Thévenon 2013; Anghel et al. 2011). Additionally, a typical contractual relationship, such as part-time contracts, fixed-term contracts or contingent workers, appear also to be positively correlated with the increase in female employment, perhaps for it matches the supply of female labour force. It is convenient to highlight that this patrol of occupational and sectoral segregation was not modified during the GR. These phenomena, as we mention below, also affect gender behaviour in unemployment and earnings.

The better employment performance observed during the GR for the different countries in the EU may also be related to a series of public interventions aimed to stimulate females' labour supply. Moreover, these policy measures may explain some of the differences observed in the light of the evolution of the GEG between the countries studied. As explained in the theoretical framework, the existence of international gender disparities may only be understood on the light of the different institutional frameworks governing in each country. We mainly refer to two types of frameworks. On the one hand, those regulating the labour market, such as union density or the existence and level of minimum wages, is one type. On the other hand, there is the important series of policies regulating family-labour relations, as is the case of parental leaving. Empirical evidence points at motherhood and childcare as the main barrier for females' labour market participation (Olivetti and Petrongolo 2017). In an attempt to solve this reality, there is a series of measures developed in the different EU countries oriented to help females with this regard of familiar responsibility. These policies have been oriented to constitute a work-life balance friendly institutional environment. Among the measures, there is the compulsory pre-primary education, the expansion of free childcare hours or the extension to fathers of the parental leaving. These measures may also help to raise full-term employment among females. The effect of these policies is, nevertheless, contingent of the interaction between the regulatory framework of labour relations as well as the degree of development of the remaining social policies (OECD 2017). Additionally, social behaviour patterns do also interact with these measures, driving to different results for the different countries. Existing differences between countries, then, may continue even if the same or very similar policies are implemented.

The evolution of the 'gender unemployment gap' may be influenced by several factors operating in opposite directions for each gender. It is convenient to highlight that, as shown in the present chapter, the GUG is relatively low for the EU in general. Before the GR the value of the gap was equal to 1.3%. The most remarkable finding, however, is not as much the value of the gap as the evolution it presents during the years of the crisis. A priori, we would expect higher values for the rates of unemployment of females in comparison to those registered of males. This hypothesis results from all the arguments developed in this chapter. In a very simple manner, a typical contract is more frequently used among females. In the context of recession, firms use initially these types of contractual relationships to adapt non-expected demand reductions without the necessity of affecting the level of wages. Accordingly, at the beginning of the period of recession we would expect employment to more intensely affect female workers and, thus, we would also expect to find a divergence between the rates of unemployment registered for females and the rates of unemployment registered by males during the years of recession. However, we observe that this has not been the case during the GR. The Spanish economy provides a convincing case study to understand this paradox. Between the years 2007 and 2013 3,440,900 job contracts were destroyed in Spain. In contrast, a total amount of 322,700 part-time contracts were created. If we decompose the number of job contracts destroyed by gender, we conclude that 75% of job destruction corresponds to males' job vacancies, being the remaining 25% job females' job destruction. Among the part-time new hiring, 62% correspond to males and 38% to females. Moreover, the relative presence of women in full-time jobs increased from 38.6% of total jobs in 2007 to 42.6% in 2013; while females' relative presence in part-time job diminished from 83 to 75% in the respective years 2007 and 2013. These flows of job creation and destruction allow hypothesising and explaining the convergence on the rates of unemployment of females and males during the GR; that is to say, the reduction in the GUG during the years of the crisis. Before advancing this hypothesis, it is convenient to go back to the research by Brunet and Jeffers (2017), where they point at a convergence process that could stem more from a relative worsening of male employment than from the improvement in females' labour market situation. Clearly, data for Spain are in line with this finding. Data show that female employment is less pro cyclical than male employment. Moreover, this stability is noticed for both, full-time and part-time female jobs.

However, we would like to focus attention on the first type of contracts; that is to say, full-time jobs. Women who have a relatively higher presence in public administration jobs, mainly in health and education (as is the case in Spain) act as an automatic stabiliser against gender discrimination; since employment in the public sector is generally more stable than in the private sector. In other words, employment phenomena are less pro-cyclical in the public sector, compared to the private sector. Stylised facts support this hypothesis: during the GR, the relative representation of women in public employment increased from 53% in 2008 at 56% in 2015. This 3 pp increase appears together with an increase in the participation rate of females equal to 2 pp (from 52 to 54%), giving evidence of the concentration on public sector of female workers.

This same hypothesis may also explain the evolution of the GUG during the years of recovery; when, as pointed above, a slight increase is registered. We can continue with the case study provided by the Spanish economy. From 2014, it is observed a quick recovery of the levels of full-time employment in the private sector, mainly concentrated among males. Between the last quarter of the year 2013, and the corresponding quarter of 2017, a total amount of 1173 jobs existed. From these, men covered 58%. The increase in the GUG may also be partially explained by the reduction in the rates of participation observed during the first years of the recovery period. In 2008, this rate was equal to 69% and, during the last quarter of the year 2017, it diminished to 64.5%.

The evolution of the 'gender pay gap' allows concluding the existence of a marked difference between the Mediterranean countries (Spain and

Italy) and our continental European examples (France and Germany); being the UK a particular case described showing the highest reduction in the GPG during the GR (see Coulter 2016). As shown along the chapter, Italy registers the lowest value for the GPG both, before and after the GR. However, for this country, a slight increase is detected; that is to say, gender differences in earnings increase during the GR. In fact, the value of the GPG is equal to 4.3% in 2006 and reaches 6.1% value in 2014. In contrast, in the case of Spain the value of the gap diminishes from 17.9% in 2006 to 14.9% in 2014; that is to say, 3 pp.

The value of the gap does not change for France and Germany, where these are around 15.5 and 22% respectively. As explained above, international gender differences in labour market outcomes are mainly caused by differences in labour market structures (labour supply and demand forces as well as different institutional frameworks). However, structural changes with this regard registered during the GR are not sufficiently significant in number, or in magnitude, to explain the changes (Mediterranean countries) or lack of changes (continental countries) registered. Moreover, it would be necessary to wait for a longer period of time in order to observe and judge their actual effect on labour market gender differences.

We are of the opinion that the trends observed during the GR are the clear response to some trends in the distribution of female and male employment. We refer to the following factors. First, these four countries show different distributions between sectors and occupations. More concretely, occupational segregation may differ among females before and during the GR. During the years of the GR, the bulk of employment destroyed was concentrated among non-qualified workers. A priori, this destruction may have similarly affected both, males and females. However, sectoral and occupational segregation tends to have a protective effect on females. Moreover, these female workers show a higher average qualification and, consequently, changes in gender differences may reflect not as much the proximity of wages between females and males but the gender differences in productivity caused by a different composition of the labour market. In Olivetti and Petrongolo (2014), data for different countries are provided. It is interesting to notice that the lowest gaps among highly qualified workers is found for the cases of Italy and Spain; which are obviously lower than the gaps found for the cases of France and Germany. Among the lowest qualified workers, France and Germany present a lower gap than that found for Spain although higher than the gap presented by Italy.

According to these findings, the different behaviour between Mediterranean and continental EU countries may respond to a change in the composition of female employment during the crisis or to a prevalence of a patrol well settled before the crisis (as would be the case of Italy). The lower presence of female employers in jobs of lower qualifications and, consequently, of lower remunerations, modifies the relative weight of qualified women on the overall wage for females. Moreover, if we also take into account that the GPG is higher among the less qualified workers, then the expected result is the reduction in the GPG as is observed for the case of Spain or a slight increase as observed in Italy. Our hypothesis could also explain the findings for France and Germany were the happenings developed similarly to those explained for the cases of Italy and Spain. However, it would be also necessary to assume for these two cases a more mixed distribution of females and males among the jobs of higher and lower qualification (Kunze 2017b).

Data in our analysis does not allow confirming that the years of the GR have strongly negatively affected gender equality. In fact, the historically narrowing of the gender gaps seems to have continued during the years of the crisis. Similarly, we cannot conclude that the evolution of the gender gaps have been singularly positive for the objective of gender equality, even though some indicators point to this direction. We have explained some of the hypothesis that could explain the paradoxes behind the unexpected evolutions; these, being sectoral and segregational occupations the major factors that allow supporting these hypotheses.

6 Concluding Remarks

We can conclude that gender disparities remain for the vast majority of the countries and years analysed. This fact gives evidence of the long path ahead for the challenge of gender equality (in the labour market, as here studied) to be reached. Moreover, the existence of theories and factors supporting the differential behaviour of the outcomes of females and males should not serve as an excuse to rest importance to the existing and illegal gender discrimination that the literature has shown. As pointed by Blau and Kahn (2017) policies and laws on gender equality in employment and measures to address the combination of familiar responsibilities and work as well as women's skills, can affect the degree of discrimination to reach gender equality. Moreover, fiscal policies affecting labour supply of females, increasing family benefits, subsidising child care and giving incentives for firms to hire females are paramount to reach gender equality (IMF 2017). Additionally, the "long-run impact of these policies on gender and labour market, as well as the division of labour within the family" (Blau and Kahn 2017, p. 850) are topics that still need further research.

References

Addabbo, T., Rodróguez-Modroño, P., & Gálvez, L. (2015). Gender Differences in Labor Force Participation Rates in Spain and Italy Under the Great Recession. *Revista de Economía Mundial, 41,* 21–42.

Agénor, P. R., & Canuto, O. (2015). Gender Equality and Economic Growth in Brazil: A Long-Run Analysis. *Journal of Macroeconomics, 43,* 155–172.

Anghel, B., De la Rica, S., & Dolado, J. (2011). *The Effect of Public Sector Employment on Women's Labour Market Outcomes* (IZA Discussion Paper No. 5825).

Babcock, L., & Lashever, S. (2003). *Women Don't Ask: Negotiation and the Gender Divide.* Princeton and Oxford: Princeton University Press.

Bausola, M., & Mussida, C. (2017). Regional and Gender Differentials in the Persistence of Unemployment in Europe. *International Review of Applied Economics, 31*(2), 173–190.

Becker, G. S. (1971). *The Economics of Discrimination* (2nd ed.). Chicago and London: University of Chicago Press.

Bentolila, S., Dolado, J. J., Cahuc, P., & Le Barbanchon, T. (2012). Two-Tier Labor Markets in the Great Recession: France vs. Spain. *The Economic Journal, 122,* 155–187.

Bertola, G., Blau, F. D., & Kahn, L. M. (2007). Labour Market Institutions and Demographic Employment Patterns. *Journal of Population Economics, 20*(4), 833–867.

Bertrand, M. (2011). New Perspectives on Gender. In O. Ashenfeltere & D. Card (Eds.), *Handbook of Labor Economics 4B* (pp. 1543–1590). Amsterdam and Boston: Elsevier.

Blau, F. D., & Kahn, L. M. (1992). The Gender Earnings Gap: Learning from International Comparisons. *American Economic Review, 82,* 533–538.

Blau, F. D., & Kahn, L. M. (1995). The Gender Earnings Gap: Some International Evidence. In R. Freeman & L. Katz (Eds.), *Differences and Changes in Wage Structures* (pp. 105–143). Chicago: University of Chicago Press.

Blau, F. D., & Kahn, L. M. (1996a). International Differences in Male Wage Inequality: Institutions versus Market Forces. *Journal of Political Economy, 104,* 791–837.

Blau, F. D., & Kahn, L. M. (1996b). Wage Structure and Gender Earnings Differentials: An International Comparison. *Economica, 63,* S29–62.

Blau, F. D., & Kahn, L. M. (2001). Understanding International Differences in the 'Gender Pay Gap'. *NBER* (Working Paper No. 8200).

Blau, F. D., & Kahn, L. M. (2007). Changes in the Labor Supply Bahaviour of Married Women: 1980–2000. *Journal of Labour Economics, 25*(3), 393–438.

Blau, F. D., & Kahn, L. M. (2013). Female Labor Supply: Why is the US falling Behind? *NBER* (Working Paper No. 18702).

Blau, F. D., & Kahn, L. M. (2017). The Gender Wage Gap: Extent, Trends, and Explanations. *Journal of Economic Literature, 55*(3), 789–865.

Blau, F. D., Ferber, M. A., & Winkler, A. E. (2014). *Economics of Women, Men and Work* (7th ed.). London: Pearson.

Boll, C., Rossen, A., & Wolf, A. (2016). *The EU Gender Earnings Gap: Job Segregation and Working Time as Driving Factors* (Hamburg Institute of International Economics (HWWI) RP176).

Boll, C., Leppin, J., Rossen, A., & Wolf, A. (2016). *Magnitude and Impact Factors of the 'Gender Pay Gap' in EU Countries*. European Commission. Luxembourg: Publication Office of the European Union.

Brunet, C., & Jeffers, E. (2017). Labor Market Gender Gaps and the GR: Evidence from European Union. Work in Progress.

Coulter, S. (2016). The UK Labour Market and the 'Great Recession'. In M. Mayant, S. Theodorophoulou, & A. Piasna (Eds.), *Unemployment*

International Devaluation and Labour Market Deregulation in Europe (pp. 197–227). Brussels, Belgium: European Trade Institute.
Croson, R., & Gneezy, U. (2009). Gender Differences in Preferences. *Journal of Economic Literature, 47*(2), 448–474.
De la Rica, S., & Rebollo-Sanz, Y. (2015). *Gender Differentials in Unemployment Ins and Outs during the Great Recession in Spain* (IZA Discussion Paper No. 9135).
Dreger, C., López-Bazo, E., Ramos, R., Royuela, V., & Suriñach, J. (2014). Wage and Income Inequality in the European Union. *Directorate General for Internal Policies*. Policy Department A: Economic and Scientific Policy. European Parliament.
EC. (2006). Communication from the Commission to the Council, the EP, the EESC and the CoR: A Roadmap for Equality Between Women and Men 2006–2010. *COM 92*.
EC. (2010). Strategy for Equality Between Women and Men 2010–2015. *COM 491*.
EC. (2015). The Strategic Engagement for Gender Equality 2016–2019. *SWD 278*.
EC. (2017). Report on Equality Between Women and Men in the EU. European Commission, Belgium.
EC. (2018). Tackling Discrimination at Work. *European Commission. Employment, Social Affairs and Inclusion*. Available at: http://ec.europa.eu/social/main.jsp?catId=158&langId=en. Accessed 5 Mar 2018.
Edin, P., & Richardson, K. (2002). Swimming with the Tide: Solidary Wage Policy and the Gender Earnings Gap. *The Scandinavian Journal of Economics, 104*(1), 49–67.
EIGE. (2017). *Economic Benefits of Gender Equality in the European Union*. European Institute for Gender Equality. Briefing Paper.
EIGE. (2018). *What is Gender Mainstreaming*. European Institute for Gender Equality. Available at: http://eige.europa.eu/gender-mainstreaming/what-is-gender-mainstreaming. Accessed 27 Jan 2018.
Elborgh-Woytek, K., Newiak, M., Kochhar, K., Fabrizio, S., Kpodar, K., Wingender, P., et al. (2013). *Women, Work and the Economy: Gains from Gender Equality*. IMF. SDN 13/10.
Garibaldi, P., & Taddei, F. (2013). *Italy: A Dual Labour Market in Transition. Country Case Study on Labour Market Segmentation* (Working Paper No. 144). *Geneva*: ILO.
Goldin, C., Lawrence, F. K., & Kuziemko, I. (2006). The Homecoming of American College Women: The Reversal of the College Gender Gap. *Journal of Economic Perspectives, 20*(4), 133–156.

Heckman, J. J. (1979). Sample Selection Bias as a Specification Error. *Econometrica, 47*(1), 153–161.
ILO. (2018). *Definition of Gender Mainstreaming*. International Labour Organization (ILO). Available at: http://www.ilo.org/public/english/bureau/gender/newsite2002/about/defin.htm. Accessed 27 Jan 2018.
IMF. (2017). *Gender Budgeting in G7 Countries*. International Monetary Fund.
Jaba, E., Pârtachi, I., Chistruga, B., & Balan, C. B. (2015). Gender Employment Gap in EU Before and After the Crisis. *Procedia Economics and Finance, 20,* 326–333.
Juhn, C., & Murphy, K. M. (1997). Wage Inequality and Family Labour Supply. *Journal of Labour Economics, 15*(I), 72–97.
Juhn, C., Murphy, K., & Pierce, B. (1991). Accounting for the Slowdown in Black-White Wage Convergence. In M. Kosters (Ed.), *Workers and Their Wages* (pp. 107–143). Washington, DC: AEI Press.
Kidd, M. P., & Shannon, M. (1996). The Gender Wage Gap: A Comparison of Australia and Canada. *Industrial and Labour Relations Review, 49,* 729–746.
Kunze, A. (2017a). *The Gender Wage Gap in Developed Countries*. CESifo (Working Paper No. 6529). Munich: Center for Economic Studies and Ifo Institute.
Kunze, A. (2017b). *The Gender Wage Gap in Developed Countries* (IZA Discussion Paper No. 10826).
Mueller, G., & Plug, E. (2006). Estimating the Effect of Personality on Male and Female Earnings. *ILR Review, 60*(1), 3–22.
Ngai, L. R., & Petrongolo, B. (2017). Gender Gaps and the Rise of the Service Economy. *American Economic Journal: Macroeconomics, 9*(4), 1–44.
OECD. (2017). *Report on the Implementation of the OECD Gender Recommendations. Some Progress on Gender Equality but Much Left to Do.* Paris: OECD.
Olivetti, C., & Petrongolo, B. (2008). Unequal Pay or Unequal Employment? A Cross-Country Analysis of Gender Gaps. *Journal of Labor Economics, 26*(4), 621–654.
Olivetti, C., & Petrongolo, B. (2014). Gender Gaps Across Countries and Skills: Demand, Supply, and the Industry Structure. *Review of Economic Dynamics, 17,* 842–859.
Olivetti, C., & Petrongolo, B. (2016). The Evolution of Gender Gaps in Industrialized Countries. *Annual Review of Economics, 8,* 405–434.
Olivetti, C., & Petrongolo, B. (2017). *The Economic Consequences of Family Policies: Lessons from a Century of Legislation in High-Income Countries.*

NBER (Working Paper No. 23051). Cambridge: National Bureau of Economic Research.

Piazzalunga, D., & Di Tomasso, M. L. (2015). The Increase of the Gender Wage Gap in Italy During the 2008–2012 Economic Crisis. *Society for the Study of Economic Inequality ECINEQ* (Working Paper 2015/381).

Rinne, U., & Zimmermann, K. F. (2012). Another Economic Miracle? The German Labor Market and the Great Recession. *IZA Journal of Labor Policy, 1*(1), 1–3.

Thévenon, O. (2013). *Drivers of Female Labour Force Participation in the OECD*. OECD Social, Employment and Migration (Working Papers No. 145). Paris: OECD Publishing.

UN. (2018). United Nations. Human Rights. Office of the High Commissioner. Available at: http://www.ohchr.org/EN/Issues/Pages/WhatareHumanRights.aspx. Accessed 25 Jan 2018.

Rich Become Richer and Poor Become Poorer: A Wealth Inequality Approach from Great Britain

Dimitra Kavarnou and Nikodem Szumilo

1 Introduction

We live in a world that has been growing increasingly unequal. It is a fact that, over the last century, the rich became richer and the poor became poorer. Over the last 30 years, the gap between rich and poor has reached its highest levels on record in most countries. In fact, 10% of the population worldwide earn almost 9.6 times more than the income of the bottom 10% (OECD 2015, p. 15). Back in 2011, this ratio was 9 times, something that shows the very fast pace in terms of the gap increase (OECD 2011). Similar results from a previous publication of OECD (2008) show that wealth was more unequally distributed than income, with some countries having low income inequality but high wealth inequality. Nowadays, according to the latest findings,

D. Kavarnou (✉)
University of Cambridge, Cambridge, UK
e-mail: dk545@cam.ac.uk

N. Szumilo
London School of Economics, University of London, London, UK

P. Arestis and M. Sawyer (eds.), *Inequality*, International Papers in Political Economy,
https://doi.org/10.1007/978-3-319-91298-1_7

wealth is more concentrated than income: on average, the top 10% share of the wealthiest households receive almost 25% of the income while they hold half of total wealth[1]; the next 50% of the households hold almost the other half, while the bottom 10% of households own about 3% of total wealth. This unprecedented level of wealth concentration towards the high end of the distribution has also been shown to have considerable economic effects including lower potential economic growth (OECD 2015).

As discussed in the literature, and as we will observe in this chapter, the increasing income and wealth inequality worldwide has increased economists' interest to investigate income and wealth distributions with a special focus on the recent growth at the top tails of both distributions (Piketty 2014; Benhabib et al. 2017).

Inequality (of both income and wealth) has become an increasing universal concern among economists, policymakers and citizens. The reasons behind this phenomenon have been under debate for a long time and it seems probable that it will continue to be an ongoing topic in future. This study aims to examine whether house price evolution in Great Britain over the last decade has played any role in changing household wealth distribution, contributing somehow to the increase in wealth inequality among households. Moreover, our scope also focuses on the geographical allocation of net aggregate and property wealth, in particular, across the several government office regions of GB in order to observe the wealth concentration patterns of the different household groups.

In the next sections, we build a theoretical framework drawing on the extensive international literature on wealth. In particular, we discuss, its constituents, the factors that affect wealth along with its effects on households, the well-documented term of 'wealth inequality' and the evolution of wealth inequality both globally and focusing on GB. For the purposes of our empirical analysis, data on household wealth for GB had been very limited. It is only after July 2006 that sufficient

[1]The way OECD measures wealth is discussed in their report Box 6.1. page 243 and in the appendix of the report from page 284 onwards (OECD 2015).

household wealth information has been effectively collected by the Office of National Statistics (ONS) through the Wealth and Assets Survey (WAS).[2] It is important to mention at this point that at the time our analysis was undertaken, data of wave 5 from latest WAS concerning the period July 2014–June 2016 were not yet released, while just before our submission, the report of the main findings of this wave was published. Therefore, most of our analysis is based on the earlier trends while some of our figures incorporate the most recent data and refer to the latest report released by ONS. Our empirical analysis includes data of the first four waves available covering data on household wealth from July 2006 to June 2014. After discussing the distribution of wealth across GB in Sect. 3, we provide some empirical evidence to show that house prices significantly affect wealth distribution in the country. Next, we present an extensive discussion of whether the changes in house prices have played any role to the increase in wealth inequality across the different government office regions of the country. Finally, we summarise and conclude.

Our results suggest that house ownership in most regions with the highest levels of productivity (such as London and South East) correlates to higher wealth but also shows a very strong relationship with how wealth is developing over time. House prices grew the fastest in regions where wealth was the highest to begin with. Notably these are also the most productive locations of the country and offer the highest per capita income. It is difficult to infer causality from these trends, thus our analysis should be treated as descriptive on this score. Nevertheless, we document that the trend for wealth to be increasingly concentrated amongst the richest is not only occurring for the overall distribution of households but also has very distinctive spatial patterns. The pattern appears to be dictated by house prices.

[2]According to ONS, it is a representative sample of the population following the sampling design process and how they have weighted the sample. There is no indication whether non-UK nationals were included: http://webarchive.nationalarchives.gov.uk/20160105235432/http://www.ons.gov.uk/ons/rel/was/wealth-in-great-britain-wave-3/2010-2012/index.html.

2 Literature Review

Our paper has been motivated by a pioneering work of Kuhn et al. (2017), which uses a dataset of Historical Survey of Consumer Finances (HSCF) with detailed household-level information across the US over seven decades (1949–2013) to observe income and wealth distributions. Their findings show, among others, that there is significant widening of income and wealth disparities in the US since World War II, identifying trends among different groups across the decades. The reason for these disparities is due to the heterogeneity of household portfolios across the wealth distribution. Interestingly, household portfolios systematically vary across the distribution. More specifically, stock and house price changes have differential effects on the top and the middle of the distribution. As highlighted, the portfolios of the wealthy households primarily include business equity and financial assets. On the other hand, the household portfolios of the typical middle class consist of highly concentrated and highly leveraged residential real assets. As a result of that, the increasing house prices cause significant wealth gains to the middle-class households. Finally, higher equity prices lead to substantial wealth increases in the richest households (Kuhn et al. 2017).

Roine and Waldenström (2015) in reviewing the long-run trends of income and wealth distributions found that inequality was at historically high levels almost everywhere towards the beginning of last century. During the first 80 years, wealth inequality decreased worldwide mainly because of the falling wealth concentration and the decreasing incomes of the top shares of the distribution. Since then, trends across countries for income and wealth distributions have been significantly differentiated, while, in periods of high growth, top shares also increase, whereas lower top shares are related to high marginal tax rates and even democracy.

As Campanella (2017, December 8) shows, there is a clear distinction between developing and developed economies. More specifically, in developing economies, over the past three decades of globalisation, we observed the creation of a booming socio-economic layer, the urban middle class, which further expanded the gap between cities and rural regions. However, in advanced economies, the combination of globalisation and technological progress has generated significant advantages to a small minority of highly qualified professionals, which adversely, squeezed the middle class. In these latter cases, the living standards for the middle and the bottom of the income scale have stagnated, due to the available cheaper labour abroad and the inadequate redistributive policies in home countries.

To begin with, it is essential to draw some distinctive lines between some significant concepts on this theme, such these of income, assets, debt and wealth (according to how they were defined by Kuhn et al. 2017).

- Income is regarded as the total sum of wages and salaries (including any professional practice, self-employment, rents, dividends, interests, transfer payments and business income).
- Assets consist of the following: liquid assets (checking accounts, savings, money market accounts and deposits), bonds, equity, cash value of life insurances, cars, business bonds, but also housing and other real estate.
- Debt is divided into housing (on owner-occupied houses and other property assets) and non-housing (car loans, education loans and loans on other consumer durables). Indebtedness is the other side of wealth. On average, almost half of the population of OECD countries is in debt (OECD 2011).
- Wealth constitutes the households' net worth, i.e. total assets minus total debt (Kuhn et al. 2017).

Wealth constitutes a significant component of household economic well-being since their access to resources can be affected by their stock of wealth. Nevertheless, due to scarcity of data on wealth and its distribution, studies often use data on households' income to track and monitor their economic well-being. In order to conceive the economic conditions and the households' well-being, it is important to investigate it "further than a simple measure of income" (ONS 2015a, p. 2) highlighting in this way the importance of the in-depth analysis of the household wealth distribution when examining national well-being.

As explained by ONS (2015a, p. 2), "the increase in home ownership, the move from traditional roles and working patterns, a higher proportion of the population now owning shares and contributing to investment schemes as well as the accumulation of wealth over the life cycle, particularly through pension participation, have all contributed to the changing composition of wealth".

Davies and Shorrocks (2000), when studying the distribution of personal wealth, specified that it refers to the material assets (in the form of real properties and financial claims) that can be purchased to the marketplace; however, some studies on wealth include pension rights. Therefore, they regard wealth as the 'net worth' of the non-human capital, that is assets minus debts. One of their major findings is that wealth is more unequal than income, while they have indicated an overall long-term decreasing trend in wealth inequality over the previous century. As discussed in their paper, possible reasons of wealth discrepancies constitute the lifecycle accumulation and the inheritance especially at the top-end share of the distribution.

As mentioned above, household's wealth is an important indicator of well-being and lifestyle. Households can maintain their living standards when income drops either unexpectedly due to unemployment or expectedly due to retirement or other causes, if there is enough wealth of an accessible form (or if there is access to borrowing). In addition to this, Crawford et al. (2016) pointed another aspect of wealth, which is that it can influence not only their owners' life style, but also their descendants' lives as wealth,[3] in contrast with income, could be bequeathed to the next generations.

Another pioneering study with interesting findings on the evolution of wealth and its trends on household level in the US comes from Wolff (2017), who examined the period between 1962 and 2016, focusing on the middle class. Wolff used mainly the Survey on Consumer Finances (SCF) and indicated that over the last decade asset prices in

[3]"Wealth holdings can also have implications for the descendants of those who currently hold wealth: when wealth is bequeathed from one generation to the next, it gives opportunities to recipients that might not be available to those who have not received inheritances" Crawford et al. (2016, p. 2).

the US sank between 2007 and 2010 while later they recovered. At the same time, median wealth dropped dramatically by 44%, while in terms of inequality of the net worth increased sharply. As discussed, the steep drop of the median wealth and the simultaneous increase in the overall net worth inequality is obviously arising from the high household leverage of the middle class and the very high share of houses as part of their wealth. Although mean wealth exceeded its previous highest during 2007, median wealth was persistently lower in 2016 by 34%. The author indicated that more than 100% of the rebound in both measurements was due to high capital gains on wealth.[4] However, this was counterbalanced by negative household savings. As for other liabilities, which kept on dropping for the middle households between 2010 and 2016, wealth inequality in the US increased (Wolff 2017).

Although income and wealth are two concepts closely linked, and therefore, the observed income inequality across many countries has direct effects on wealth inequality; the observation and the analysis of income and hence, of income inequality, is outside the scope of this chapter. However, the literature and the findings on income inequality are more extensive than those of wealth inequality; and this is due to data unavailability or at best a scarcity of data on wealth. On this relationship between income and wealth, Aiyagari (1994) and more recently Benhabib et al. (2017), among others, specify that in economies where concentration of wealth is mainly led by stochastic earnings,[5] there is a clear, positive relationship between income and wealth inequality. This is because higher earning risks would increase wealth concentration through precautionary savings, and therefore, under

[4]"More than 100 percent of the recovery in both from 2010 to 2016 was due to a high return on wealth but this factor was offset in both cases by negative savings" (Wolff 2017, p. 2).

[5]"The literature focusing on the factors determining skewed thick-tailed earnings distribution tended to disregard the properties of wealth accumulation. Motivated by the empirical fact that wealth generally tends to be much more skewed than earnings, an important question for the subsequent literature has been whether a stochastic process describing the accumulation of wealth could amplify the skewness of the earnings distribution. Alternatively, could skewed wealth distributions become skewed due to factors unrelated to skewed earnings distributions?" (Benhabib and Bisin 2017).

particular borrowing constraints this would end up to an increase in wealth inequality.

Another reason why wealth distribution is more difficult to be measured in comparison with income is that part of wealth is hidden by the so-called tax havens which makes the overall analysis of wealth with precision difficult. Alstadsaeter et al. (2017) in their paper estimated the household wealth owned by citizens of each country in offshore tax havens. From their findings, almost 10% of the global GDP is kept in tax havens around the world while for the UK in particular, citizens/residents have 16–17% of wealth hidden in tax havens. As the authors mention, "Offshore wealth has a larger effect on inequality in the UK" (Alstadsaeter et al. 2017, p. 3). Moreover, they discussed that in all countries, when accounting for the offshore wealth, inequality increased significantly compared to the tax data analyses observed. Therefore, from the above, the results on wealth inequality coming from studies that do not consider offshore wealth to tax heavens provide underestimation of the actual wealth inequality. Two fundamental outcomes of this paper are: (a) inequality significantly decreased in Western World during the first half of the previous century, and (b) it has sharply increased since 1980s especially in the US. The main driver behind the drop in inequality at the beginning of last century came from the interactions of multiple losses of wealth by the richest. As explained, both World Wars, the Great Depression of 1930s along with several policies against capital, such as imposing capital taxation, notably high rates of inheritance tax, nationalisations and rent controls, all decreased the significance of wealth and the accumulation of capital (Piketty and Zucman 2014). Later, over the last decades, the reason why wealth inequality has increased is due to the fast wealth concentration to the top income shares (Saez and Zucman 2016).

A number of studies have focused on documenting the evolution of income and wealth distributions. Piketty and Saez (2003) and later on Saez and Zucman (2016) used income tax data of the US to capture the income and wealth concentration over the previous century. The latter, based on the capitalisation approach, reached conclusions on wealth distribution replying on the observed income flows. This method is considered significant for the top-end households to which a big part of their wealth is held in assets, which further create taxable income flows. Regarding portfolios that do not generate taxable income such as owner-occupied housing, Saez and Zucman (2016) based their analysis on survey data.

As mentioned above, data on wealth internationally have always been very scarce. Davies and Shorrocks (2000) presented in detail the advantages and disadvantages of all the available sources of collecting empirical underpinnings on wealth distribution: (a) household surveys, (b) wealth tax data, (c) estate multiplier estimates and (d) the investment income method.

However, Crawford et al. (2016), when discussing the above methods and their application in the UK, argued that there was lack of any form of wealth taxation meaning that compared to other countries that use administrative data on wealth holdings for tax purposes, in the UK, this data is not significantly available.[6] Nevertheless, taxes on estates on death are available in various forms and therefore, the 'estate method' could estimate the wealth distribution by "multiplying the estate data by the reciprocal of the mortality rate" (pp. 36–37). As for the investment income method, it has also been used for over many years by using the income distribution and a rate of return multiplier. However, none of the last two methods provided any direct measurement of wealth distribution for the UK, nor informed details about the households below the top end. This is because not all properties in the country are liable for inheritance tax or generate income and in particular avoidance of estate/inheritance tax through passing on assets 7 years or more before death (Crawford et al. 2016).

Household surveys in the UK now play a rather significant role in collecting direct measures of the wealth distribution across the country. However, as discussed by Alvaredo et al. (2016), the weaknesses coming from the household surveys on wealth focusing mainly on the low response rate of the participants constitute notable defects in accurately capturing the wealth concentration towards the top tail of the distribution.

[6]Atkinson and Harrison (1978) provide some information of the estate duty.

Davies and Shorrocks (2000) emphasised that the studies on wealth after 1960s focused more on the causes of the disparities to individual or household wealth. This change in focus was led by the increasing importance of savings for retirement but also as a result of the increasing and improving micro-data sets that offer a plethora of individual and household characteristics that greatly contribute to accounting the differences in wealth.

What about the effect of income inequality on wealth inequality? Most studies find that increases in income inequality lead to simultaneous increases in wealth inequality. Dynan et al. (2004) when analysing whether households with higher incomes save a higher proportion of their income found that income inequality adds top wealth inequality since the higher income households save more.

Kuhn et al. (2017) used information on income and wealth from HSCF data in order to identify divergent trajectories of income and wealth inequality. Opposed to standard methods, which concluded that a rise in income inequality would lead to increased wealth inequality, the authors found that the opposite was the case during 1970s and 1980s in the US. In fact, during that period, wealth inequality decreased while income concentration at the top income households surged. According to their findings, wealth inequality started rising during the 1990s and it was only at the beginning of the financial crisis in 2007, that wealth concentration started being higher than before the 1970s. As for the period during the financial crisis, they identified that this was "the largest spike of wealth inequality in post-war America" (p. 5). Moreover, over the years that followed 2007–2008, wealth accumulation towards the top of the distribution, increased more than ever within the six previous decades, concluding that wealth distribution in the US nowadays, is more unequal than before (Kuhn et al. 2017).

Similarly, Davies and Shorrocks (2000), when examining the wealth distribution of several countries highlighted that wealth is distributed more unequally than labour income, consumption or total money income across a number of developed countries. As they argued, although Gini coefficient of income range between 0.3 and 0.4,[7] for wealth, it ranges from 0.5 and 0.9. Similarly, the estimated share of wealth for the top 1% of the households is in the range 15–35% of the total wealth, while their income is less than 10%. Moreover, similarly to Kuhn et al. (2017), they concluded that during the twentieth century, wealth inequality had a downward trend, however, it was characterised by several interruptions and reversals such as the one in the US in the mid-1970s.

According to the literature, consumption is also linked to wealth distribution. Although Muellbauer (2010), Carroll et al. (2011) and others examined the macroeconomic impacts of wealth on consumption, Arrondel et al. (2017), looked at the heterogeneity of the marginal propensity to consume wealth-based household surveys in France. They found that this heterogeneity is generated by disparities in wealth consumption and levels of wealth. One of their main findings is that there is a falling marginal propensity to consume wealth across the distribution for all net wealth components. More specifically, out of the financial wealth, the marginal propensity tends to be higher than the effect of housing assets, apart from the top of the wealth distribution. In fact, the marginal propensity to consume from housing wealth decreased from 1.3% at the bottom of the wealth distribution to 0.7% at the high end of the distribution. On the other hand, the marginal propensity to consume out of housing wealth rises with debt pressure and depends on the composition of debt. They found that the effect of wealth shocks on consumption inequality is limited. Nevertheless, they identified that if stock prices increase, there is a slight increase in consumption inequality, especially at the top of the distribution.[8]

---

[7]For developed countries in particular—"Wealth is distributed less equally than labour income, total money income or consumption expenditure. While Gini coefficients in developed countries typically range between about 0.3 and 0.4 for income, they vary from about 0.5 to 0.9 for wealth. Other indicators reveal a similar picture" (Davies and Shorrocks 2000, p. 3).

[8]"Overall, these simulation exercises show a limited effect of wealth shocks on consumption inequality. Increases in stock prices tend however to slightly increase consumption inequality" (Arrondel et al. 2017, p. 24).

Despite a long history of studies looking at the relationship between wealth and consumption, this question of the impact of housing wealth on consumption is still a subject of an academic debate. Buiter (2008) shows that housing wealth should not be the primary driver for non-housing consumption.[9] He empirically shows that higher housing wealth increases the cost of housing consumption; therefore, the impact on non-housing consumption should be small. In fact, in his model the only way in which the two could be related to each other is through relaxing the borrowing constraints. This is because housing collateral has a very strong impact on the ability of a household to borrow. Mishkin (2007) finds that increases in housing wealth have a larger effect on consumption than changes in the value of financial assets. Since he recognises that he cannot measure the effect precisely there is also a large body of literature that investigates this effect empirically. The work of Case et al. (2005) and Carroll et al. (2011) not only clearly link increases in housing wealth to consumption but also show that its impact is larger than the wealth effect of stocks. However, Buiter (2008) argues that housing wealth is not macroeconomic wealth as its changes are affecting homeowners and renters differently so that even if changes to house prices have an effect on individual households, the net aggregate effect should be zero.[10] Although micro studies support the claim that increasing house prices have a higher impact on homeowners there is little evidence that renters' consumption counteracts this phenomenon (Bostic et al. 2009). There is also research that accounts for the age of the household (Calomiris et al. 2012), and demographic changes that influence the housing wealth effect (Sinai and Souleles 2005); however, the conclusions remain unchanged. There is also evidence that changes in household wealth may not necessarily affect consumption solely

[9]"In a representative agent model and in the Yaari-Blanchard OLG model used in the paper, there is no pure wealth effect on consumption from a change in house prices if this represents a change in fundamental value. There is a pure wealth effect on consumption from a change in house prices if this reflects a change in the speculative bubble component of house prices" (Buiter 2008, p. 2).

[10]Changes in house prices are essentially (close to) zero sum game where positive changes are good for owners but bad for renters and future generations.

through relaxing borrowing constraints as households may also change their saving habits in response to exogenous shocks to the value of their homes. As housing is the major component of most households' investment portfolios, the impact of an exogenous shock to house values may affect precautionary saving rates and, therefore, affect consumption. Critically, this effect can occur without re-mortgaging thus would not be noticeable as an equity release. Christelis et al. (2015) showed that even when changes in housing wealth are decomposed into an expected and an unexceed component, both still have a significant positive influence on consumption. This shows that housing plays an important role in how households behave and has important implications not only for micro-level decision making but also for aggregate levels of consumption.

Furthermore, Davies and Shorrocks (2000) supported the view that wealth holdings are used for consumption smoothing when consumption is expected to increase or in cases that income is decreasing due to expected or anticipated shocks (e.g., due to unemployment or retirement). "This consumption smoothing role is particularly important when individuals face capital market imperfections or borrowing constraints" (Davies and Shorrocks 2000). Moreover, as described by the authors, the type of the economy and/or society is also defined by the patterns of wealth-holdings individuals and households are following and the way they hold wealth. Hence, several macroeconomic reasons such as the social status which is related to different types of assets can be used to study wealth.

To our knowledge, this is the first time that a study makes use of the latest data on wealth distribution available, that is the Wealth and Assets Survey (WAS) for Great Britain, and tries to relate the findings of this Survey on wealth in time and space, with the evolution of house prices in the country over the last decade. The findings of this analysis suggest that house ownership especially to the most productive regions of the country correlates to higher net worth. Moreover, this ownership seems to have a quite strong relationship with how wealth in these regions is developing over time. Residential prices increase rapidly in government office regions where wealth was already concentrated. This creates further thoughts about accessibility of all groups to these regions or their location decisions. These areas will constitute the most productive locations of the country and offer the highest income which will drive to additional wealth increase, and hence to the empowerment of inequality. Although we cannot infer causality from this trend, however, we notice that it is increasingly concentrated amongst the wealthiest households and it is not only occurring for the overall distribution of households but also, it seems to have very distinctive spatial patterns which are dictated by house prices.

3 Wealth and Assets Survey (WAS) in Great Britain

Focusing on the Great Britain over recent years, there are two sources that provide information and estimates on wealth: (a) the Wealth and Assets Survey (WAS), which as we will develop in more detail later on, it is "a longitudinal sample survey of private households which started in 2006", run and issued by the Office for National Statistics (ONS); and (b) the Personal Wealth Statistics (PWS)—which is "a long standing series based on administrative data"—generated by the HM Revenue & Customs (HMRC).[11]

Both of the above sources—WAS and PWS—use the term "wealth", but they differ substantially in terms of the methods applied for the calculation of wealth and the definitions used in their interpretation of how wealth is distributed across the country. For the purpose of our analysis, we are making use of the WAS. The main reasons against the selection of the PWS is it is not representative of the population. This argument is based on the ground that the statistics of PWS are applied on a sample of forms submitted to HMRC for administrative Inheritance Tax (IT) purposes, required by only estates that obtain a grant of representation (probate) and not a random representative sample of the population. Hence, although the WAS coverage refers to all individuals living in private households across Great Britain, PWS

[11]ONS (2012), The Quality of Data Sources on Household and Individual Wealth in the UK.

is limited to the sample of estates that need a grant of representation. As per ONS (2016), in 2010, this sample regarded approximately 31% of the individuals in the UK (which is not representative either). Moreover, in order to monitor the effect of house prices on wealth, it is essential the unit in use to be on a household and not on individual level. Since, PWS is presented at an individual level only, there is no direct link between the residence value and the individual wealth estimates, whereas WAS' estimates are on a household level. However, some of the disadvantages of WAS for the current study, constitute the following: (a) the fact that series commence in 2006, compared to the long existing series of data of PWS that go back in 1976; and (b) WAS self-reported wealth values are less accurate than tax returns.

WAS is funded by a consortium of government departments: Office of National Statistics (ONS), the Department for Works and Pensions, the HM Revenue & Customs (HMRC), the Scottish Government and the Financial Conduct Authority. "The WAS is a longitudinal survey, which aims to address gaps identified in data about the economic well-being of households by gathering information on level of assets, savings and debt; saving for retirement; how wealth is distributed among households or individuals; and factors that affect financial planning" (ONS 2015a, p. 2).

For a long time, household wealth data for Great Britain have been very limited with surveys only occasionally addressing only wealth questions.[12] It was only after July 2006 that WAS started addressing questions on wealth explicitly. Wave 1 consisted of interviews accomplished over 2 years (June 2008), referring to 30,595 households. The same households were interviewed for Wave 2 (July 2008–June 2010), where 20,170 households participated. Wave 3, lasted from July 2010 to June 2012 and lastly Wave 4 covered July 2012–June 2014 with 20,247 private households. The report of the main findings of the latest wave (5), concerning the period July 2014–June 2016, has just been released

[12]Housing wealth and liquidity wealth questions were included in the Household Panel Surveys over the years 1995, 2000 and 2005 (Crossley and O'Dea 2010); while particular questions on Pension Wealth were also included over the years 2001 and 2005 (Emmerson and Wakefield 2009).

including interviews addressed to 18,000 households between July 2014 and June 2016.

The samples included in the several waves of WAS covered private households in GB (excluding "people in residential institutions, such as retirement homes, nursing homes, prisons, barracks or university halls of residence, and homeless people").[13] WAS contains data at household and individual levels. However, for the purposes of this chapter, we are only making use of the household level.[14]

Due to the fact that a large amount of wealth is held by a relatively small number of households and individuals, WAS oversamples particular households on purpose by using income tax records, in order to address it to households with higher financial wealth. Vermeulen (2015) examined the significance of oversampling in order to generate efficient results for the high end of the distribution. As the author discussed, oversampling is not necessarily dealing with the biases because of the differential non-response and he considered that WAS was possibly underestimating the wealth concentration towards the upper tail. By using both WAS and the Forbes List, while assuming a Pareto distribution, Vermeulen (2015) identified that WAS actually underestimates the top 1% of wealth by 1–5%.

In the reports published by the ONS regarding the WAS, household wealth is divided into four components: property, physical, financial and private pension wealth. These four wealth components are defined as per below according to ONS (2015b, p. 2):

- *Property wealth*: considers "the value of any property privately owned in the UK or abroad (gross and net of liabilities on the properties)".
- *Physical wealth*: "includes the value of contents of the main residence and any other property of a household including collectables

[13]Subject to bias regarding wealth coming from the elder groups but rather unlikely to have any significant bias to the results of the younger groups (ONS 2009).

[14]For more information regarding the WAS questionnaires and the process of the Survey please read from the UK Data Service, https://discover.ukdataservice.ac.uk/catalogue/?sn=6709&type=Data%20 catalogue.

and valuables (e.g. antiques and artworks), vehicles and personalised number plates".

- *Financial wealth*: accounts for "the value of formal and informal financial assets held by adults and of children's assets".
- *Private Pension wealth*: considers "the value of all pensions that are not state basic retirement or state earning related". Moreover, "the value of private pension schemes in which individuals had retained rights in which they would or have received income".[15]

As argued by Crawford et al. (2016), physical wealth should be excluded from the sum of the total net wealth as the replacement value of goods is not an appropriate measurement for the value of the items people own. This bias is subject to underestimation/overestimation of the actual value of goods and therefore, should be excluded from the total net wealth.

Crawford et al. (2016) discussed the distribution, composition and changes of the household wealth in GB over the first three waves of the WAS, i.e. between 2006 and 2012. Drawing on the main conclusions of that paper, among other outcomes, the total wealth on average rose (real terms) during this period for the working-age households but decreased for the retirement-age households. Nevertheless, wealth held outside pensions dropped for all apart from the youngest households. Therefore, the conclusion reached was that the increased wealth is driven by increases in pension wealth for that particular period.

3.1 Discussion of the Most Recent WAS Waves 4 and 5 (2012–2014 and 2014–2016)—Wealth Distribution and Inequality Across Great Britain

Looking at the most recent report on the main findings out of the fifth wave of WAS, the aggregate total wealth of all households in GB was £12.8 trillion between July 2014 and June 2016, illustrating an increase

[15]ONS (2015b, quotations from Chapter 1, pp. 1–2).

in 1.7 trillion from the previous period (2012–2014). Median household total wealth also increased 15% from the previous period being at £259,400 from £225,100 of the last wave. At the same time, wealth inequality is in high levels in GB, as the total wealth held by the top 10% of households is around 5 times greater than the wealth of the bottom half during wave 5.[16]

To continue with the aggregate total private pension wealth of all households in GB over wave 5, it was £5.3 trillion increasing from £4.4 trillion the period before (wave 4). One of the striking findings though in relation to our study is that there was a great increase in the net property wealth for households in London compared with all other regions. More specifically, median net property wealth in London was £351,000 showing a 33% increase from the previous wave (4).

Comparing wave 5 with the previous waves, and more specifically with wave 4 over the period 2012–2014, in wave 4, the net property wealth in GB accounted for 35% of the aggregate total wealth during 2012–2014 (having dropped from 42% during the earliest period for which data are available—July 2006–June 2008). Physical wealth accounted for just 10% of the aggregate total wealth while financial wealth accounted for 14% of it during wave 4. Finally, the biggest share of wealth stands for private pensions i.e. 40% of the aggregate total wealth (having increased from 34% during the first wave in 2006–2008).[17]

Figure 1 presents some interesting findings of the distribution of wealth across households, the composition of wealth among the distribution with significant evidence of wealth inequality in GB. More specifically, Fig. 1a shows the comparison between the top 10% and the bottom 50% of the households across the four waves of the Survey. As can be seen from the graph, there are substantial differences between these two groups of households, but also the shares of wealth components of each group of households have substantially changed over the years. To begin with, during the first wave, we can observe that the

[16]ONS (2018).

[17]ONS (2015a).

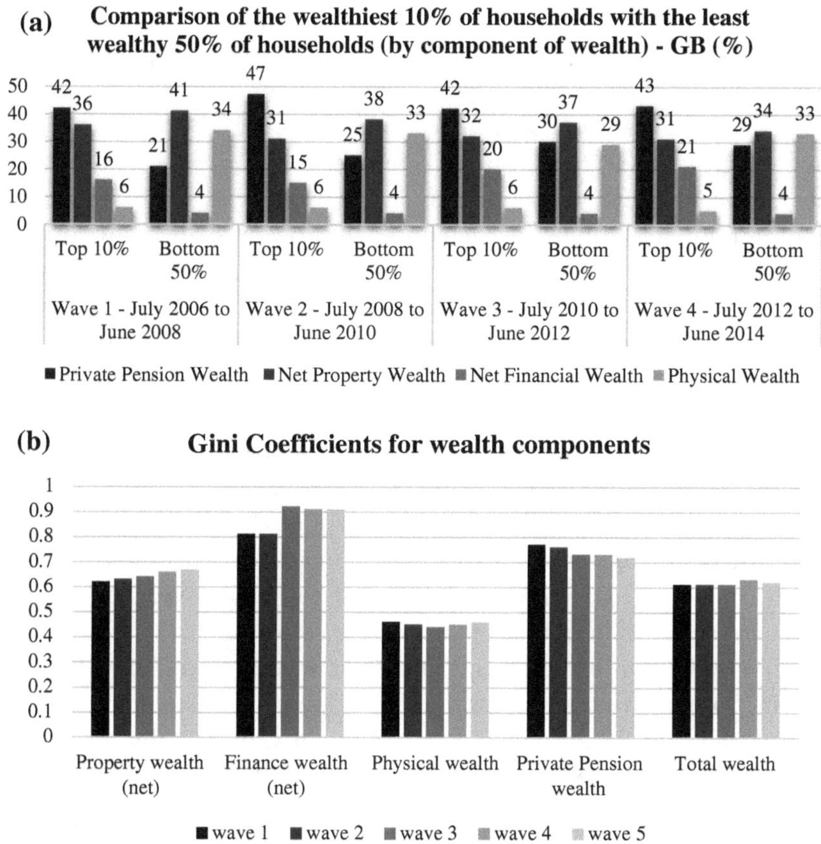

Fig. 1 **a** Comparison of wealthiest 10% of households with bottom 50% (by wealth component) during the four waves, GB; and **b** Gini coefficients of the aggregate total wealth in components (*Source* Wealth and Assets Survey (WAS)—Office of National Statistics)

wealth components significantly differ between the two groups where the biggest share for the top 10% is the private pensions (42%), followed by the net property wealth (36%), then the net financial wealth (16%) and lastly some physical wealth (6%). On the contrary, for the bottom 50% during wave 1, the biggest share of wealth accounted for net property wealth (41%), followed by physical wealth (34%), which is significantly higher than this of the top 10% group, then private pensions (21%) and lastly some very low financial wealth (4%). A similar pattern can be observed over waves 2 and 3 respectively, while in wave 4 which is the latest period of available data we can observe that: (a) private pension wealth has overall increased during the years for both groups, (b) net property wealth has decreased over the eight-year period for both groups, (c) financial wealth has increased for the 10% of households but has remained the lowest share of wealth for the bottom 50%, (d) physical wealth has remained the lowest share of wealth for the top 10% and has even decreased further during the years, while for the bottom 50% of households, physical wealth remains one of the biggest shares of their wealth and (e) possibly the most significant conclusion for our study is that the wealthiest households have a more diverged portfolio of wealth to which their wealth is dispersed between pension, property and financial wealth across all the waves of the Survey; while for the bottom 50% of households the main source of wealth is in properties (possibly their main residence) and physical wealth (including the value of contents of the main residence or vehicles)—an observation that is notable across all waves.

This Fig. 1a exhibits the components of wealth of the top 10% and bottom 50% of households until 2014. Some interesting findings on the inequality of wealth across households in GB over the latest wave (July 2014–June 2016) that have been included into the latest report released by ONS are related to the household total wealth distribution. As per these findings, the wealth ownership among the different groups of the population both the actual value (in £billion and percentage) some interesting outcomes are the following: (a) although the actual value of wealth of the bottom 50% increased from £962 billion in wave 4 to £1118 billion in wave 5, this group still holds just 9% of the total wealth, (b) the difference can mainly be viewed to the upper and middle wealth classes where, although the total wealth acquired by the top 10% has overall increased since the last wave from £4975 billion to £5595 billion their share has dropped by 1% in favour of the middle class who saw their aggregate wealth increasing from £5176 billion to £6066 billion, (c) another impressive outcome of the latest wave (5) is that the aggregate wealth held by the top 10% is almost 5 times more than that of the bottom 50% of the population (44% or £5595 billion by the top

10% compared to 9% or £1118 billion by the bottom 50%), a finding that highlights wealth inequality across GB.

The above conclusion about the wealth inequality has been very well documented by the literature over the years (e.g., by Atkinson and Harrison 1978; and more recently by Piketty 2014) and we can see that this inequality phenomenon continues being rather evident as wealth is mainly held by the wealthiest households.

Furthermore, by comparing the latest results with the previous waves (3 and 4) of WAS, the aggregate total wealth has increased over the years. More specifically, half of the households in GB hold just over £1 trillion, while the top 10% of households own almost half of the aggregate total wealth; these are figures that constitute evidence of very strong wealth inequality in the country. Some more interesting findings of the latest fifth wave concerning the period July 2014–June 2016, are that: (a) the bottom 10% of households have total wealth of £14,100 or less, (b) the median total household wealth is £260,400 while the top 10% of households have total wealth of £1,208,300 or more and (c) the top 1% of households hold the amount of £3,227,500 or more (ONS 2018).

Another interesting component of the ONS report about the wealth inequality in GB, is the calculation of the Gini coefficients of the aggregate total wealth as presented in Fig. 1b. Gini coefficient, which is the statistical measurement of the dispersion of wealth distribution, constitutes the most commonly used measure of wealth inequality and therefore, could not be disregarded.

We have added to this Fig. 1b the most recent outcomes of the fifth wave regarding the most recent period of the Survey. Gini coefficients take values between zero and one, with zero representing a perfectly equal distribution and one presenting a perfectly unequal distribution. As can be observed by the graph, Gini coefficients are consistently high across years and for all wealth components. Some significant outcomes that we could extract from Fig. 2, are: (a) physical wealth is the least unequal wealth component taking values between 0.44 and 0.46 across all waves—a figure that was expected as it constitutes the main wealth component of the bottom 50% of households. (b) The most unequally distributed wealth component is financial wealth with very high Gini

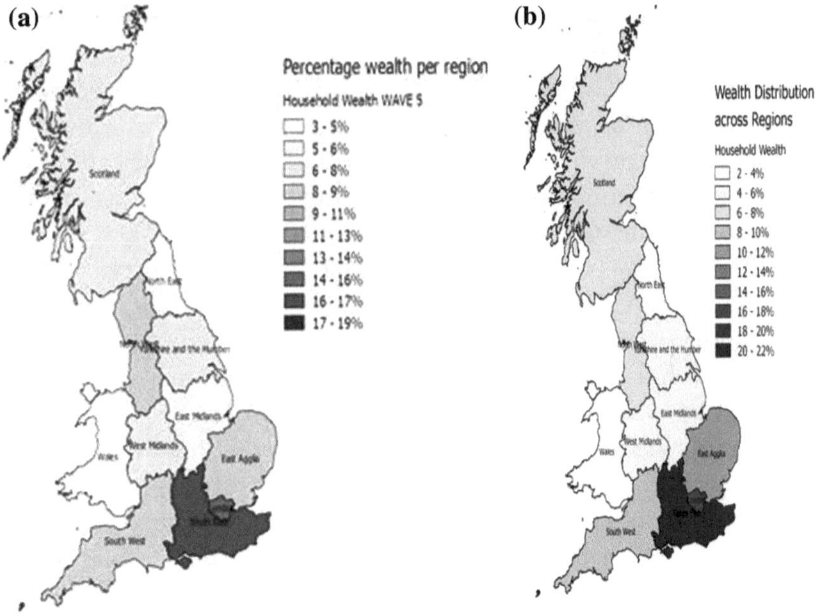

(c)

Region	Number of Households (2015)	Weath (%)	Actual Wealth (£billion)	Wealth per household (£)
North East	1,154,400	2	256	221,760
North West	3,057,900	8	1,024	334,870
Yorkshire and The Humber	2,280,700	6	768	336,739
East Midlands	1,945,900	6	768	394,676
West Midlands	2,383,900	6	768	322,161
East	2,538,700	11	1,408	554,615
London	3,253,000	18	2,304	708,269
South East	3,613,900	22	2,816	779,214
South West	2,355,200	10	1,280	543,478
Wales	1,325,100	4	512	386,386
Scotland	2,375,200	7	896	377,231
Total	**26,283,900**	**100**	**12,800**	
Average				**486,990**

Fig. 2 Percentage of aggregate wealth by region, **a** wave 5, July 2014–June 2016, **b** wave 4, July 2012–June 2014 and **c** Wealth per household by region (2015) (*Source* Own calculations using data from Wealth and Assets Survey (WAS)—Office of National Statistics [For the number of households by region (2015), data from ONS were used available from: https://www.ons.gov.uk/peoplepopulationandcommunity/birthsdeathsandmarriages/families/adhocs/005374totalnumberofhouseholdsbyregionandcountryoftheuk1996to2015])

coefficients from 0.81 over the first two waves to 0.91–0.92 over the three waves showing that financial wealth inequality has dramatically increased over the last 6–7 years. This finding is another evidence of high wealth inequality as financial wealth is the main component of the wealthiest households. As observed also by the Office of National Statistics, this increase in Gini coefficients of financial wealth over the last few years can be interpreted as difference in recovery of financial assets after the economic recession by those with higher levels of financial assets (i.e. the biggest losers were the lower wealth groups). (c) Private pension wealth is the only wealth component with decreasing Gini coefficients over the years. (d) Last, but not least, property wealth component has steadily increased over the years from 0.62 over wave 1 to 0.67 during the last wave. This shows a continuation in worsening of inequality in net property wealth between 2006 and 2016 (ONS 2018). This latest point constitutes a very strong evidence of the fact that the increase in house prices over the last years have misbalanced the net property wealth of the different groups of the wealth distribution in favour of the wealthiest households.

The next part of the discussion is looking at the distribution of wealth across the government office regions of GB (Fig. 2).

From this graph, it is obvious that wealth is unequally distributed not only across households but also across the regions of GB. More than 50% of the aggregate total wealth is concentrated towards the South of England (South West, South East and London) and especially the capital and the South East region. The rest of the country has a relatively more dispersed wealth distribution. It is interesting to note the difference in households' wealth by region. As can be seen from Table 2c, the average wealth held by households in Greater London region and South East is way above the country's average, in South West and East England moderately above average while to all the rest of the regions, the average household wealth is below average. In fact, in certain regions, it is even two or three times less than the household wealth of South East and London.

It is also very interesting to look at the findings of WAS regarding the Property wealth component in particular. As already mentioned, aggregate net property wealth in wave 5 accounted for 41% of the growth total wealth between waves 4 and 5, increasing by 17% i.e. from £3.9 trillion to £4.6 trillion over the period 2012–2016.[18]

To continue on the above findings on net property wealth, it is interesting to discuss the property ownership rates according to the location of the main residence of the household. ONS illustrates graphically the percentage change in the distribution of household net property wealth by region of residence where net property wealth includes the ownership of the main residence and any other property.[19] From this figure by ONS, the percentage change in median along with the 1st and 3rd quartiles of the distribution are presented where, during the period July 2012–June 2016, net property wealth across GB was unequally distributed and this inequality evolved further during these years. The post-crisis results show that apart from the North East region, all the rest of the regions of GB have a positive growth of net property wealth. The results highlight the striking increase in the net property wealth of London region. Since all quartiles of net property wealth of London region sharply increased within this short period of time, this gives a strong indicator of the house price increase particularly in London.

The question that has been generated out of the above figures is: How have house prices affected the evolution of this wealth inequality across the country? It is a fact from the above figures that wealth is unequally distributed across households and also unequally concentrated across the regions of GB. However, how the change in house prices over these years in the several regions of the UK have contributed further to wealth inequality has not been examined, or whether house prices have actually contributed in decreasing the disparity of wealth. The arguments behind the support of the first case, i.e. house prices have contributed to the increase in wealth inequality, would be based on the logical aspect that wealthy households would invest in the property sector and therefore, the increase in house prices would increase their wealth further. The supporting arguments of the opposite case, i.e. house prices have contributed to minimising the inequality of wealth,

[18]ONS (2018).

[19]ONS (2018, Fig. 24, p. 49).

lay with a different but logical argument too, that a great share of wealth held by the bottom and middle-class households is mainly consisted of property wealth (Fig. 1a); especially the value of their main residence and therefore, any change in house prices would drastically and positively increase their levels of wealth, hence, wealth inequality would decrease between the top and the middle/bottom part of the distribution. Kuhn et al. (2017), when investigating the US market, identified that "while incomes stagnated, the middle class enjoyed substantial gains in housing wealth from highly concentrated and leveraged portfolios, mitigating wealth concentration at the top" (p. 3).

However, one could say that there is a third case, i.e. both cases are true and the heterogeneity observed both in wealth distribution and in house prices across the different regions of the country create a third different combination of these two scenarios.

Davies and Shorrocks (2000) mentioned that when owner-occupied housing is the major component of the non-financial assets, then wealth is more equally distributed. Nevertheless, as these authors explicitly discussed, the opposite might be the case in countries where land values are especially important.

3.2 House Prices and Their Role on Wealth Distribution

Wolff (2017) in analysing the household wealth trends in the US between 1962 and 2016 highlighted the significance of the housing value cycle on wealth trends. As discussed by the author, one of the most notable effects on net worth leading to the Great Recession of 2007 was the house price explosion prior to it and the immediate collapse of the housing market. At the same time, the home ownership rate in the US significantly expanded over the last three decades and continued to increase but with a slower pace between 2001 and 2007. However, during the crisis of 2007–2009, the home ownership rate slightly decreased while after the crisis, although house prices recovered, home ownership rate continued to drop.

In the same paper, it was explained that the housing bubble in the years prior to the crisis, was largely due to the expansion of the credit availability for housing transactions and re-financing. This fact was because of: (a) the re-financing of the primary mortgages; (b) second mortgage and home equity loans or increased outstanding balances; and (c) softer credit requirements with either none or limited documentation—in turn, were so-called 'subprime' mortgages with excessively high interest rates and "balloon payments" at the expiration of the loans. For the above, the average mortgage debt per household hugely increased in real terms (more than 59%) between 2001 and 2007 while the outstanding mortgage loans as a share of the house values also increased (Wolff 2017).

House Prices in GB, followed a similar pattern to the US, in most of the regions during the last two decades. This pattern, however, affected in different magnitude each region of the country. House prices across the country sharply increased during the decade before the financial crisis, while towards the end of 2007 started collapsing until mid-2009 when house prices started recovering again in most of the regions. However, house prices in GB appear rather heterogeneous across the different regions of the country and is characterised by huge discrepancies among the different areas of the North, the middle and the South. House prices in the Greater London area and the South East have been rising faster than the other regions of the country.

Similar to the heterogeneity patterns across regions, house prices have also evolved differently over time and space/regions. Figure 3 illustrates the evolution of house prices in GB during and after the financial crisis. More specifically, it presents the percentage change of the median house price over the years 2007–2016. As can be seen, within this decade, since 2007 and especially after the end of the recession, house prices have sharply increased in most of the government office regions of GB. The median house price in London region has risen faster reaching a striking 68% increase over the last decade. East England and South East regions follow with 36 and 34% increase in the median house price of each region respectively. The South West and the Midlands (East and West) regions also present high growth rates (21, 17 and 16% respectively), while the north regions of England (East and West), Yorkshire and Humber, Scotland and Wales have reaching more modest house price growth rates (6–11%). As can be observed from Fig. 3, the market not only has completely recovered from the financial crisis, but instead house prices have outperformed in many regions of the country.

In particular, the South East has seen a much faster growth of house prices with double-digit annual rises persisting in London. While in most areas house prices declined during the financial crisis of 2008/2009, in some regions they have rebounded quicker than in others. In fact, in some places growth remained positive even during the economic downturn. The most expensive boroughs of London and the most unaffordable housing markets (as judged by ratio of house prices to earnings) outside of the capital (such as Cambridge and Oxford)

Region	%House Price Growth
North East	10
North West	11
Yorkshire &Humber	11
East Midlands	17
West Midlands	16
East England	36
London	68
South East	34
South West	21
Wales	6
Scotland	10

Fig. 3 House Price change 2007–2016 (*Source* Based on dataset from Land Registry)

continue to attract not only high house prices but also high income and wealth, including households that are able to invest in the property sector. This results in a high standard deviation of house prices as well as of their growth rates across GB.

As observed by Kuhn et al. (2017), the effect of house prices on households' wealth is substantially different along the distribution of wealth. This would mean that any changes in house prices would have a significant but differential effect on the several household groups as well as on the evolution of wealth inequality. In order to quantitatively identify this effect, the authors created a measure of house price exposure on wealth growth:

$$\frac{\Delta W_{t+1}}{W_t} = \frac{H_t}{W_t}\frac{\Delta p_{t+1}}{p_t} + g_t^R \tag{1}$$

where

$\frac{\Delta W_{t+1}}{W_t}$	stands for wealth growth,
$\frac{H_t}{W_t}\frac{\Delta p_{t+1}}{p_t}$	stands for the house price component, and
g_t^R	stands for the residual component which accounts for wealth growth caused by all other reasons but house prices

Therefore, any changes caused in house prices are reflected on $\frac{\Delta p_{t+1}}{p_t}$ which are adjusted by the house prices exposure $\frac{H_t}{W_t}$. This would mean that with house price increase, a bigger exposure on house prices, would cause further wealth growth. Any differences in saving rates of households or other sources of wealth would be included in the residual component (Kuhn et al. 2017).

3.3 Theoretical Framework

The theoretical framework presented so far from the literature, the presentation of the main findings of the WAS and the arguments on wealth distribution and wealth inequality in relation to house prices in time and space draw a picture of increasing wealth inequality, with strong concentrations towards the right tail of the distribution. Property wealth seems to be a significant wealth component for all household groups (top, middle class and some lower wealth households) and strongly involved in the evolution of their total wealth. House prices (especially considering the main residences of the middle and least wealth households) constitute the most significant asset components of property wealth and therefore, there are strong evidences that their evolution over time and space, i.e. over the last decade in focus and across the different government office regions of GB, dictate the patterns with which wealth is distributed over this period and across the regions.

But how does the house price evolution over the last decade correlate with the household wealth distribution of the different government office regions of the country? This is an interesting question that we try to approach. Although it is difficult to fully uncover the relation and patterns, but also to infer the actual causality of this relationship, to the following section, we have developed an empirical approach for GB.

4 Empirical Investigation

The method that we apply in this chapter for the identification of the effect of house prices on Wealth is the Inter-Quantile regression with bootstrapped standard errors.

The main aim of quantile regression is to estimate the conditional median or any other quantiles of the variable of interest. It constitutes the extension of a linear regression, as it is mainly used when linearity is not applicable. The reason why this method has been selected in particular is because it is the most suitable method when conditional quantile functions are of interest.

Moreover, a significant advantage of the quantile regression which is the main difference from the Ordinary Least Squares (OLS) is that its estimates are much more robust with the presence of outliers to the variables of interest. In addition to that, several measures of central tendency and dispersion offer a much more comprehensive analysis of the variables when using the quantile regression.

In particular, an Inter-Quantile Regression allows much easier interpretation of differences between different groups of the outcome variable distribution. In our case this is total wealth. As we have stipulated earlier, we assume that households with different levels of wealth will be exposed differently to changes in the dependent variables.

Therefore, the motivation for applying this empirical method is that we assume that the impact of different determinants of net wealth is conditional on total wealth. In this way, QR provides the capability to describe the relationship between a set of regressors and the variable of interest at different points in the conditional distribution of the dependent variable. Hence, by applying the Quantile Regression, we achieve our estimates being more robust against the outliers in our response measurements. This robustness to non-normal errors and outliers of QR provides a deeper understanding of the data, enabling us to account for the impact of a covariate on the distribution of y, and not solely its mean. In our study, taking into consideration that both wealth and house prices are measurements with great discrepancies among their observations including many outliers, the distribution of the values around their mean would create robustness issues.

The inter-quantile regression applied in this study is the regression of the difference in quantiles.

The model used is:

$$W_i = \alpha + \beta E_i + \gamma H_i + g_t^R \quad (2)$$

where

$W_{i,t}$ stands for the net aggregate wealth,
$E_{i,t}$ stands for the net financial wealth,
$H_{i,t}$ stands value of the main residence and reflects the impact of changing property values on wealth.
g_t^R stands for the residual component of Eq. 1 and in this regression takes the form an error term.

In this specification we capture the increase in the net financial wealth directly as although important to avoid the omitted variable bias in our estimates, we do not assume that it is of critical importance to our research question. Instead, we focus on property wealth, which we approximate with the value of the residence.[20] Together the two components[21] represent total wealth for the vast majority of the population and provide estimates that support the view that wealth growth depends on the price of the residence. For simplicity other components of wealth (pension and physical) are omitted. These are, of course, missing variables in this model but testing models that included them did not affect the results while it significantly increased computation time and the accuracy of the bootstrapped error estimates.

Since we have shown that house prices have been developing at different rates across the country we expect that the value of the main residence may be more important for different quintiles of the distribution. From this, we can point out that as house prices are increasing the households that own their homes are likely to slowly graduate to higher quintiles of the population while the households that do not benefit from the capital value appreciation of properties mainly rely on income and financial wealth. Note that this variable does not reflect the value of a property owned by the household but of their main residence only. This is a quite important distinction as it allows us to focus on the households that live in the locations where house prices are the highest and directly relate their household wealth with the value of their residence. It also enables us to link the location of the household wealth (to the respective government office region) with the location of the main residence of the household and not with their property wealth in general.

In contrast, the financial wealth is the component of household wealth that is not affected by the growth of house prices as there is no direct link between them. Its spatial distribution is more likely to

[20]As defined in Sect. 2 property wealth includes all properties held by the household. For the vast majority this will be the same as the value of the main residence.

[21]Pension wealth is left out to reduce computation time and increase the accuracy of point estimates. The estimates do not change when it is included but the (bootstrapped) standard errors increase.

stay constant over time and we expect it to be highly important for the richer households.

g_t^R stands for the residual component which accounts for wealth growth caused by everything else than house prices and financial wealth. Total wealth is measured as the sum of all wealth components listed in Sect. 2. We regress this value on the value of the main residence to test the hypothesis represented in Eq. 1. Including financial wealth into the regression controls for the omitted component of wealth that is likely to be correlated with the value of main residence. All other determinants of wealth are reflected in the residual term.

4.1 Data and Variables

As extensively discussed above, the data on Wealth distribution for GB are obtained from the WAS performed in four waves. The first wave consisted of interviews addressed to 30,595 households. Out of these households, 20,170 of them were interviewed again during the second wave. Finally, for the third and the fourth waves participated 20,247 private households (UK Data Service 2017). These datasets include information on the aggregate wealth of households along with some distinction to the several wealth components such as net financial wealth, value of the main residence and many others.

Regarding data that concerned the house prices of the different governmental office regions of the country, these have been collected from the Land Registry. This dataset includes all market transactions that occurred between 2007 and 2016. As shown in Fig. 3 and already extensively discussed, the average change in transaction prices was around 20%. However, this varied greatly across GB.

4.2 Empirical Results

The intuition behind using a quantile regression is supported by Fig. 4, which shows that for wave 4 different parts of the wealth distribution have vastly different mean estimates. Due to data unavailability for wave 5 (concerning the period between July 2014 and June 2016) at the

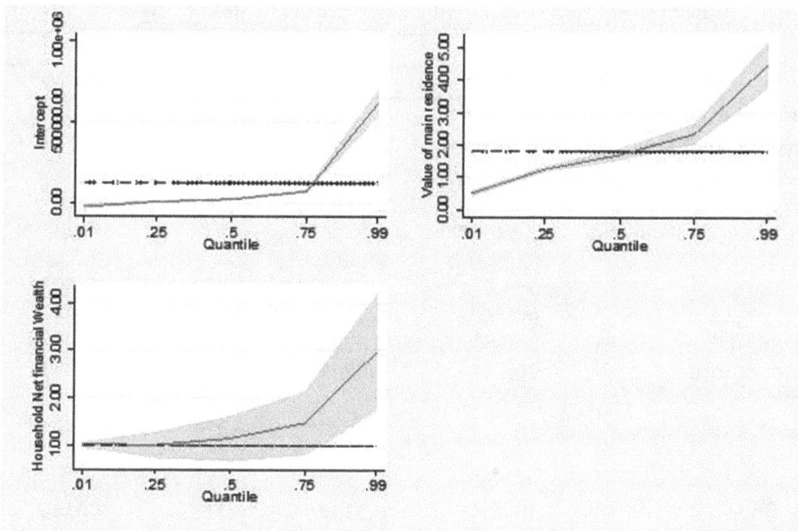

Fig. 4 Results of a quantile regression for wave 4 (*Source* Own calculation)

time of this analysis, wave 4 was the latest wave released (i.e. over the period July 2012–June 2014). It is clear from this figure that wealthier households benefit more from additional units of financial and property wealth but the most striking feature of the regression is the discontinuity between the 75th quintile and the full sample. This sharp increase right after the 75th quintile suggests that the wealthiest 25% households in GB react to changes in their wealth differently than the rest of the respondents.

Table 1 shows the results of a regression of total wealth on the value of main residence and net financial wealth from different percentiles in different time periods. The waves that have been used to this regression are the first four waves released by the ONS (i.e. referring to the time period July 2006 to June 2014) as at the time of the analysis these were the only waves available. The results are based on an inter-quintile regression, which allows us conditional means for different parts of the distribution. The estimates are presented for four categories of household wealth distribution selected so that the number of households in each group is equal.

Table 1 Inter quintile regression results. Dependent variable: Total wealth

Quintiles	(1)	(2)	(3)	(4)
	0.75–1	0.5–0.75	0.25–0.5	0–0.25
Wave 4 (2012–2014)				
Value of the main residence	2.103***	0.640***	0.475***	0.739***
	(0.27)	(0.0563)	(0.0551)	(0.0398)
Net financial wealth	1.495***	0.325***	0.139	–0.00808
	(0.263)	(0.0998)	(0.111)	(0.112)
Constant	544,671***	49,854***	16,845***	28,391***
	(49,935)	(2779)	(571.2)	(5124)
Pseudo R2	0.575	0.6376	0.6628	0.6927
Observations	20,241	20,241	20,241	20,241
Wave 3 (2010–2012)				
Value of the main residence	1.901***	0.588***	0.379***	0.748***
	(0.29)	(0.0397)	(0.0477)	(0.0394)
Net financial wealth	1.670***	0.311***	0.118	0.0145
	(0.518)	(0.0644)	(0.100)	(0.123)
Constant	459,572***	37,623***	16,440***	24,978***
	(34,061)	(2328)	(377.8)	(3961)
Pseudo R2	0.5513	0.6174	0.6412	0.6758
Observations	21,446	21,446	21,446	21,446
Wave 2 (2008–2010)				
Value of the main residence	2.044***	0.424***	0.264***	0.698***
	(0.379)	(0.0216)	(0.0102)	(0.0237)
Net financial wealth	7.022***	0.528***	0.371***	0.320***
	(1.705)	(0.0508)	(0.0427)	(0.0365)
Constant	432,725***	35,079***	14,009***	20,337***
	(48,185)	(1576)	(558.1)	(3698)
Pseudo R2	0.5522	0.6034	0.643	0.6854
Observations	20,165	20,165	20,165	20,165
Wave 1 (2006–2008)				
Value of the main residence	2.921***	0.410***	0.216***	0.674***
	(0.394)	(0.0174)	(0.0101)	(0.0328)
Net financial wealth	3.351***	0.447***	0.362***	0.215***
	(0.832)	(0.0446)	(0.0337)	(0.0350)
Constant	368,182***	25,672***	8,996***	20,854***
	(40,785)	(622.8)	(499)	(4580)
Pseudo R2	0.469	0.5644	0.6031	0.6455
Observations	30,587	30,587	30,587	30,587

Standard errors in parentheses
*** $p<0.01$, ** $p<0.05$, * $p<0.1$
Source Our own results

As can be seen from Table 1, one of the most striking changes when progressing from waves 1 (2006–2008) and 2 (2008–2010) to waves 3 (2010–2012) and finally to 4 (2012–2014), is that financial wealth becomes insignificant for poorest households (columns 3 and 4). While the impact of financial wealth on the bottom 25% households' wealth in the first two waves (2006–2010) is much smaller than for the wealthier respondents, all households increase their total wealth by holding financial assets. As can be seen, in waves 1 and 2 (2006–2010), net financial wealth appears significant across all quintiles of the distribution. However, in the latest waves—waves 3 and 4 (2010–2014)—this is not the case, as the results suggest that the poorest households (bottom 50% of the households) hold virtually no financial assets. Instead, their wealth is substantially and increasingly determined by the value of their main residence. This is illustrated by the fact that the coefficient of the value of the main residence for the bottom 50% of households increases steadily with time. This points to the conclusion that between the years 2006 and 2014, while financial assets became virtually irrelevant for the wealth of the poorest households, values of their main residence became the main source of their wealth.

However, the declining importance of financial wealth is not unique to households in the bottom half of the distribution. In fact, it appears that this occurs uniformly throughout the sample. In wave 4 (2012–2014), all households are less sensitive to financial assets and the wealth of the richest is interestingly two times less dependent on this type of wealth than it was in wave 1 (2006–2008). This difference shows how important changes in property wealth are for households in GB. With time, the impact of financial wealth decreases substantially which shows that the importance of the other component of total wealth must become more significant.

4.3 Discussion of the Empirical Results

In the following table, Table 2, we present the percentage changes of wealth to the different household quartiles across the government office regions of GB for the two latest released waves of WAS

Table 2 Household net property wealth, by region of residence: Great Britain, July 2006 to June 2016

	Percentage change between the 1st Quartile value in July 2012 to June 2016 (%)	Percentage change between the median value in July 2012 to June 2016 (%)	Percentage change between the 3rd Quartile value in July 2012 to June 2016 (%)	Percentage change between the median value in July 2006 to June 2016 (%)
All households				
England				
North East	–	23	0	−39
North West	–	8	10	−8
Yorkshire & the Humber	–	25	16	−9
East Midlands	–	1	13	−21
West Midlands	–	7	7	−16
East of England	–	8	8	−4
London	–	60	43	139
South East	–	13	13	15
South West	–	1	6	3
Wales	–	−5	6	−18
Scotland	–	8	7	5
Property Owners				
England				
North East	−9	−7	3	−11
North West	8	8	6	2
Yorkshire & the Humber	31	12	20	2
East Midlands	13	10	14	6
West Midlands	6	8	2	0
East of England	10	11	9	11

(continued)

Table 2 (continued)

	Percentage change between the 1st Quartile value in July 2012 to June 2016 (%)	Percentage change between the median value in July 2012 to June 2016 (%)	Percentage change between the 3rd Quartile value in July 2012 to June 2016 (%)	Percentage change between the median value in July 2006 to June 2016 (%)
London	40	33	42	60
South East	20	14	14	25
South West	1	10	9	11
Wales	0	5	13	4
Scotland	8	9	5	19

Source Calculated from Wealth and Assets Survey, Office for National Statistics (ONS) (i.e. 2012–2016). Although raw data for wave 5 have not been released by the time of this analysis and discussion, the recently released report on this fifth wave includes some very useful information.[22]

As can be seen from this table, between 2012 and 2016, the median of households' wealth increased by 60% in London, which is more than twice as much as for any other part of the country. Within the same period, Yorkshire and Humber median property wealth increased by one quarter, similarly to North East by 23%, while the North West, West Midlands, East England, the South East and Scotland had a moderate increase between 7 and 13%. Median household wealth in East Midlands and South West had a very slight increase of 1%, while the only government office region where the median household property wealth decreased was Wales by 5%. The figure is even more striking in the decade between 2006 and 2016, when median wealth increased dramatically in London, somewhat in the South East (15%), moderate to null increase in South West and Scotland, whereas median household wealth decreased in most other regions. The most outstanding decrease was in North East (39%) followed by East Midlands (21%), Wales (18%), West Midlands (16%) and moderate decrease to the rest of the regions.

The concentration pattern is evident for households that own their property as appreciation of house prices in London and the South East clearly allowed it to accumulate more wealth in these regions than the rest of the areas of the country. Interestingly, the most important difference between property owners and an average household is that the former group increased its median wealth in all regions apart from the North East. This suggests that wealth is increasingly owned by those who can afford to buy real properties while those who cannot see their wealth decreasing sharply.

The above results paint a dramatic picture of wealth concentration amongst the richest households that reside in the wealthiest regions of the country. As can be seen, there is also striking evidence of the fact that property ownership allows higher wealth accumulation. In fact, it

[22]ONS (2018).

appears that, on average, households that did not own any property or live in London or the South East were worse off while property owners in the capital saw their wealth increase dramatically.

More specifically, as can be seen from Table 2, looking at the median property wealth of the last two waves only, 2012–2016, property owners in London area have seen their wealth increasing by 33% within these four years. A substantial but more moderate increase can be observed in most other regions (5–12%) while the only region where property owners have seen their household wealth decreasing are in North East. Moreover, as for the decade between 2006 and 2016, these results confirm a more striking picture, considering also the effect of the financial crisis to the volatility of the median household wealth. As it can be observed, the median household wealth of the property owners in London region outperformed over this decade, where Londoners property owners have seen their wealth increasing by 60%. Other substantial increases in median property wealth can be observed in South East (25%) and Scotland (19%). Moderate increases in median household wealth can be seen in East of England and South West (11%), East Midlands and Wales (6 and 4% respectively). Slight to no change can be observed in North West, Yorkshire and Humber and West Midlands, while the only region where there is a negative growth to the median household wealth to the property owners of North East region.

Our results are also consistent with the expectation that the wealthiest households have much more varied sources of wealth than the poorest ones. Differences in income and asset allocation decisions may drive this disparity but it is difficult to establish the causal link from the available data on wealth from the WAS. Although in our analysis we attempt to show that geographical location plays a critical role in determining wealth and its growth over time, we acknowledge that there are several other factors that are not accounted for by the existing research. A concern for our results would be if the unidentified factors were correlated with house prices. For example, it may be that house prices in London increased because wealthier households have moved to the city. In our analysis this would present itself as an increase in wealth in the capital. In this sense, the results need to be interpreted as a high concentration of wealth in places where house prices are the highest. This however, does not mean that homeowners do not benefit from this trend. In fact, it appears that as the concentration of wealthy households in the South East regions grows the local homeowners are positively affected while renters see their living costs increase. This suggest an intersection between income and wealth inequality as those with either higher wealth or income appear to be crowding out those who do not own a property in the most desirable locations and cannot afford to either buy or rent it. The above can already be noticed to a number of cases in several posh or appealing neighbourhoods of the regions of the country, but especially London. This means that as the geographical concentration of wealth is growing, its benefits are accessible to an increasingly narrow group of households who either are already wealthy (through owning properties in the most desirable locations or otherwise) or have an income high enough to rent or support a mortgage in the most expensive locations. Higher house prices are correlated with higher wages but as the ratio of house prices to income in London and the South East has increased significantly more than in other parts of the country it is clear that accessibility of those locations to the poorest households has decreased. This has multiple implications, mainly for the distribution of wealth and income at the low end of the scale. While the lowest earners who own properties in London benefit from rising house prices and growing wages, those who are not homeowners see their net income decline. This means that the locations where wealth concentrates become increasingly exclusive, which has consequences for location decisions and contributes to the growing economic disparity between geographical locations. It appears that house prices play a crucial role in shaping wealth distribution but this house price growth happens not only through the increasing capital values but also through giving access to the highest income.

The unequal distribution of growth is quite likely to be endogenous to housing prices in the UK. The work of Hibler and Robert-Nicoud (2013) and Cheshire (1999) shows that housing supply is strongly related to land use regulations. As residents can influence local planning policy, they have an indirect effect on housing supply. In areas where houses are expensive the local population has a higher incentive to ensure that no new land is made available for construction. This is evidenced in the not-in-my-backyard attitude, which is especially prevalent in wealthy locations (Dear 1992). This suggests that political power shapes the supply of land for housing and determines the elasticity of prices to changes in demand. Consequently, the same change in demand would affect house prices more in wealthier locations where demand is less elastic. This means that the problem of increasing spatial disparities in income across the UK (documented by Martin et al. 2016) translate into actually magnifying the problem of wealth inequality. Although income growth is unequally distributed across UK locations, as presented above, a unit change in income will affect housing demand equally everywhere. However, with housing supply being more constrained in areas where more wealth is concentrated, the impact of a unit increase in demand would have a higher effect on house prices in places where homes have been already expensive. This is clearly consistent with Fig. 3, which shows that the house prices grew the quickest in locations where they were the most expensive to begin with. The correlation between income increases in places where house prices grow the most may not necessarily be unidirectional. While increasing incomes raise demand for housing there is also strong evidence that increasing house prices can affect local companies. A recent development in financial research shows that in locations where house prices increase entrepreneurship rates are also higher and the new firms are more successful (Corradin and Popov 2015). This shows that alleviating credit constraints allows higher economic growth and may lead to an increase in local income. In turn this may have an impact on housing demand.

This problem of income and wealth peaking or bottoming out in the same geographical areas is at the core of modern economic challenges in which income and wealth concentrate not only on people but also on space, identifying particular places and regions that are already at the top end of the distribution. The result is an increasing polarisation of economic resources in which the main winners are less correlated to productivity of individuals and more to their initial endowments. The key point is that changes in house prices are exogenous to renters (whose wealth does not benefit from increases in house prices) and households at the bottom end of the wealth distribution (who have little influence on where they live) while they may be at least partially endogenous to owners of the most expensive properties who have the highest income and are the only group that has a choice of where to live and whether to own a house or not.

All of the above results are consistent with our theoretical analysis and the hypothesis that house prices are a critical determinant of wealth not only because they are its significant component for homeowners but also because they affect other determinants of wealth. Importantly this applies not only to the level of this variable but also to its growth. Clearly, households that start from a higher base appear to accumulate wealth faster. However, the key contribution of our analysis is that we also show the correlation between the initial value of the residence and the growth rate in wealth. The causal process we suspect is driving this finding is not simply that higher wealth allows quicker accumulation of it, but also that location matters for wealth growth. Living in a location where house prices are high to start with gives the household an advantage in terms of access to finance and employment. These translate into better opportunities to grow and accumulate wealth over time. This is an additional component of wealth that has not been considered to date and is completely separate from the fact that house value appreciation increases household wealth.

5 Summary and Conclusions

The aim of this chapter is to identify the connection between the evolution of wealth and house prices as a significant share of household wealth in GB. Due to data availability on wealth in GB only between July 2006 and June 2014, our analysis was restricted in empirically looking within this short period of time only.

The theoretical framework of this study is built on the fundamental principles of wealth distribution and theoretical along with empirical evidence on wealth inequality around the world over time. The heterogeneity observed to household portfolios and their differentiated composition lead to a systematic variation of both wealth and income distributions that consequently drive to changes in wealth and income inequality across people.

Our focus is predominantly concentrated on the evolution of wealth distribution in GB over the last years and the links between this progression with the evolution of house prices. By using the main findings of the WAS, conducted in GB in waves over the last years, we examine the household distribution of wealth and its components across the government regions of the country. Moreover, we consider the evolution of house prices by looking at the percentage change in the median house prices of each region over this decade showing evidence of wealth concentration not only across the different income and wealth groups of the population but also across space.

In our empirical analysis, we confirm that the heterogeneity observed by the literature across the household portfolios is differentiated across the several quantiles of the wealth distribution and over time. Financial wealth becomes increasingly insignificant for poorest households (bottom 50%) over the last two waves of our analysis while the value of the main residence becomes increasingly more significant as it constitutes the main source of wealth for these households. As for the middle and upper class, findings are similar but with differentiated coefficients suggesting the different size of the effect. The upper-class households seem to have a more diverged portfolio being sensitive in financial assets. In addition, as observed both by our results and the related literature, differences in income and asset allocation decisions may constitute the main drivers of this disparity; however, given the available data from the WAS, we are unable to explain the causality of this disparity.

Moreover, a conclusion from a spatial point of view is that there is an intersection between income and wealth inequality, as households with either higher wealth or income appear to be crowding out the households that do not own a property in the most expensive locations and cannot afford to either buy or rent to these locations. Accessibility of those places to the poorest households will be highly deteriorated with multiple implications, mainly for the distribution of wealth and income at the low end. The above drives to considerable consequences for location decisions and contributes to the growing economic disparity between geographical locations and the further increase in wealth inequality observed among regions. It appears that house prices play a rather crucial role in shaping wealth distribution but this house price growth happens not only through the increasing capital values but also through giving access to the highest income.

Although in our study we attempt to give an outline of the links between the geographical allocation of aggregate and property wealth in GB along with the evolution of house prices across regions and time, it is significant for any future research to focus on several other factors that could not be accounted by the present research. To this direction, an extended dataset with detailed household information covering a longer period of time would establish an even better ground for our arguments.

References

Aiyagari, S. R. (1994, 1 August). Uninsured Idiosyncratic Risk and Aggregate Saving. *The Quarterly Journal of Economics, 109*(3), 659–684. https://doi.org/10.2307/2118417.

Alstadsaeter, A., Johannesen, N., & Zucman, G. (2017). *Who Owns the Wealth in Tax Havens? Macro Evidence and Implications for Global Inequality* (NBER Working Paper Series, Working Paper No. 23805).

Alvaredo, F., Atkinson, A. B., & Morelli, S. (2016). The Challenge of Measuring UK Wealth Inequality in the 2000s. *Fiscal Studies, 37*(1), 13–33.

Arrondel, L., Lamarche, P., & Savignac, F. (2017). *Does Inequality Matter for the Consumption-Wealth Channel: Empirical Evidence* (Cesifo Working Working Paper No. 6676).

Atkinson, A. B., & Harrison, A. J. (1978). *Distribution of Personal Wealth in Britain*. Cambridge: Cambridge University Press.

Benhabib, J., & Bisin, A. (2017). *Skewed Wealth Distribution: Theory and Empirics* (NBER Working Paper Series, Working Paper No. 21924).

Benhabib, J., Bisin, A., & Luo, M. (2017). Earnings Inequality and Other Determinants of Wealth Inequality. *American Economic Review: Papers & Proceedings, 107*(5), 593–597.

Bostic, R., Gabriel, S., & Painter, G. (2009). Housing Wealth, Financial Wealth, and Consumption: New Evidence from Micro Data. *Regional Science and Urban Economics, 39*(1), 79–89.

Buiter, W. H. (2008). *Housing Wealth Isn't Wealth. National Bureau of Economic Research* (NBER Working Paper Series, Working Paper No. 14204). http://www.nber.org/papers/w14204.

Calomiris, C. W., Longhofer, S. D., & Miles, W. (2012). *The housing wealth effect: The crucial roles of demographics, wealth distribution and wealth shares* (No. w17740). National Bureau of Economic Research.

Campanella, E. (2017, December 8). *Inequality and Coming Storm. Project Syndicate On Point.* https://www.project-syndicate.org/onpoint/inequality-and-the-coming-storm-by-edoardo-campanella-2017-12?barrier=accesspaylog.

Carroll, C. D., Otsuka, M., & Slacalek, J. (2011). How Large Are Housing and Financial Wealth Effects? A New Approach. *Journal of Money, Credit and Banking, 43*(1), 55–79.

Case, K., Quigley, J., & Shiller, R. (2005). Comparing Wealth Effects: The Stock Market Versus the Housing Market. *Advances in Macroeconomics, 5,* 1–34.

Cheshire, P. (1999). Cities in Competition: Articulating the Gains from Integration. *Urban Studies, 36*(5–6), 843–864.

Christelis, D., Georgarakos, D., & Jappelli, T. (2015). Wealth Shocks, Unemployment Shocks and Consumption in the Wake of the Great Recession. *Journal of Monetary Economics, 72,* 21–41.

Corradin, S., & Popov, A. (2015). House Prices, Home Equity Borrowing, and Entrepreneurship. *The Review of Financial Studies, 28*(8), 2399–2428.

Crawford, R., Innes, D., & O'Dea, C. (2016). Household Wealth in Great Britain: Distribution, Composition and Changes 2006–2012. *Fiscal Studies, 37*(1), 35–54.

Crossley, T. F., & O'Dea, C. (2010). *The Wealth and Saving of UK Families on the Eve of the Crisis* (Report R71). London Institute for Fiscal Studies. https://www.ifs.org.uk/comms/r71.pdf.

Davies, J. B., & Shorrocks, A. F. (2000). The Distribution of Wealth. In A. B. Atkinson & F. Bourguignon (Eds.), *Handbook of Income Distribution* (Vol. 1). Amsterdam: North Holland. https://ac.els-cdn.com/S1574005600800147/1-s2.0-S1574005600800147-main.pdf?_tid=f7fde0ea-d51b-11e7-b84e-00000aab0f6c&acdnat=1511970356_a9903741781b4fdbde5eb1fedd78824c.

Dear, M. (1992). Understanding and Overcoming the NIMBY Syndrome. *Journal of the American Planning Association, 58*(3), 288–300.

Dynan, K. E., Skinner, J., & Zeldes, S. P. (2004). Do the Rich Save More? *Journal of Political Economy, 112*(2), 397–444.

Emmerson, C., & Wakefield, M. (2009). *Amounts and Accounts: Reforming Private Pension Enrolment.* Institute for Fiscal Studies, IFS Commentary C110. https://www.ifs.org.uk/comms/comm110.pdf.

Hilber, C. A., & Robert-Nicoud, F. (2013). On the Origins of Land Use Regulations: Theory and Evidence from US Metro Areas. *Journal of Urban Economics, 75*, 29–43.
Kuhn, M., Schularick M., & Steins, U. I. (2017). *Income and Wealth Inequality in America, 1943–2013* (Cesifo Working Papers, Working Paper No. 6608). https://www.cesifo-group.de/DocDL/cesifo1_wp6608.pdf.
Martin, R., Pike, A., Tyler, P., & Gardiner, B. (2016). Spatially Rebalancing the UK Economy: Towards a New Policy Model? *Regional Studies, 50*(2), 342–357.
Mishkin, F. (2007). *Housing and the Monetary Transmission Mechanism* (Working Paper). Finance and Economic Discussion Series, Federal Reserve Board.
Muellbauer, J. (2010). *Household Decisions, Credit Markets and the Macroeconomy: Implications for the Design of Central Bank Models* (BIS Working Paper No. 306). Bank for International Settlements. https://www.bis.org/publ/work306.pdf.
OECD. (2008). *Growing Unequal? Income Distribution and Poverty in OECD Countries*. OECD Publishing. http://www.oecd.org/els/soc/growingunequal-incomedistributionandpovertyinoecdcountries.htm.
OECD. (2011). *Divided We Stand: Why Inequality Keeps Rising*. OECD Publishing. http://www.oecd.org/els/soc/dividedwestandwhyinequalitykeepsrising.htm.
OECD. (2015). *In It Together: Why Less Inequality Benefits All*. Paris: OECD Publishing. http://www.oecd.org/social/in-it-together-why-less-inequality-benefits-all-9789264235120-en.htm.
ONS (Office for National Statistics). (2009). *Wealth in Great Britain, Main Results from the Wealth and Assets Survey 2006/2008*. http://webarchive.nationalarchives.gov.uk/20160108204643/http://www.ons.gov.uk/ons/rel/was/wealth-in-great-britain/main-results-from-the-wealth-and-assets-survey-2006-2008/index.html.
ONS (Office for National Statistics). (2015a). *Main Results from the Wealth and Assets Survey: July 2012 to June 2014*. https://www.ons.gov.uk/peoplepopulationandcommunity/personalandhouseholdfinances/incomeandwealth/compendium/wealthingreatbritainwave4/2012to2014/\\mainresultsfromthewealthandassetssurveyjuly2012tojune2014.
ONS (Office for National Statistics). (2015b). *Chapter 1: Introduction and Demographics, July 2012 to June 2014*. https://www.ons.gov.uk/peoplepopulationandcommunity/personalandhouseholdfinances/

incomeandwealth/compendium/wealthingreatbritainwave4/2012to2014/chapter1introductionanddemographicsjuly2012tojune2014.
ONS (Office for National Statistics). (2016). *The Quality of Data Sources on Household and Individual Wealth in the UK*. https://www.ons.gov.uk/economy/nationalaccounts/uksectoraccounts/methodologies/wealthandassetssurveywas.
ONS (Office for National Statistics). (2018). *Wealth in Great Britain Wave 5: 2014–2016, Main Results from the Fifth Wave of the Wealth and Assets Survey Covering the Period July 2014 to June 2016*. https://www.ons.gov.uk/peoplepopulationandcommunity/personalandhouseholdfinances/incomeandwealth/bulletins/wealthingreatbritainwave5/2014to2016.
Piketty, T. (2014). *Capital in the 21st Century*. Cambridge, MA: Harvard University Press.
Piketty, T., & Saez, E. (2003). Income Inequality in the United States, 1913–1998. *The Quarterly Journal of Economics, 118*(1), 1–41.
Piketty, T., & Zucman, G. (2014). Capital Is Black: Wealth-Income Ratios in Rich Countries 1700–2010. *Quarterly Journal of Economics, 129*(3), 1255–1310.
Roine, J., & Waldenström, D. (2015). Chapter 7: Long-Run Trends in the Distribution of Income and Wealth. In *Handbook of Income Distribution* (Vol. A2). https://ac.els-cdn.com/B9780444594280000084/1-s2.0-B9780444594280000084-main.pdf?_tid=57c7d8ac-f478-11e7-a5df-00000aab0f27&acdnat=1515418516_ee56bd8a8bd26cc4220197a28f-b05fc9.
Saez, E., & Zucman, G. (2016). Wealth Inequality in the United States Since 2013: Evidence from Capitalized Income Tax Data. *The Quarterly Journal of Economics, 131*(2), 519–578.
Sinai, T., & Souleles, N. (2005). Owner-Occupied Housing as a Hedge Against Risk. *Quarterly Journal of Economics, 120*, 763–789.
Vermeulen, P. (2015). *How Fat Is the Top Tail of the Wealth Distribution* (Working Paper Series No. 1692). Household Finance and Consumption Centre, European Central Bank. https://www.ecb.europa.eu/pub/pdf/scpwps/ecbwp1692.pdf.
Wolff, E. N. (2017). *Household Wealth Trends in the United States, 1962 to 2016: Has Middle Class Wealth Recovered?* (NBER Working Paper Series, NBER Working Paper No. 24085). http://www.nber.org/papers/w24085.

Why Has Income Inequality Been Neglected in Economics and Public Policy?

Robert H. Wade and Michele Alacevich

> It is our job to glory in inequality and to see that talents and abilities are given vent and expression for the benefit of us all (Prime Minister Margaret Thatcher)

> If you end up going after those people who are the most wealthy in society, what you actually end up doing is in fact not even helping those at the bottom end (Prime Minister Tony Blair 2001, quoted in Lansley 2006, p. 24)

> I, like most of the American people, don't begrudge people's success or wealth. That is part of the free-market system (President Obama, Bloomberg)

> Poverty bothers me. Inequality does not. I just don't care (Willem Buiter, then Professor of economics, London School of Economics, *Financial Times*, 2007)

R. H. Wade (✉)
London School of Economics, London, UK
e-mail: R.Wade@lse.ac.uk

M. Alacevich
University of Bologna, Bologna, Italy
e-mail: michele.alacevich@unibo.it

P. Arestis and M. Sawyer (eds.), *Inequality*, International Papers in Political Economy,
https://doi.org/10.1007/978-3-319-91298-1_8

1 Introduction[1]

Like Gresham's Law, 'alternative facts' drive out facts.[2] If the economics profession and western public policy makers had not decided long ago that the trends of rising income and wealth inequality were *not* a problem, we might not have the angry, indignant mood infecting swathes of western electorates, and we might not have President Trump or Brexit or other manifestations of political polarization in western democracies.[3]

Most of the 63 million Trump voters (47% of those who voted) express anger and indignation at elites who have been shredding the bargain on which complex democracies rest. They see those elites as taking a share of income and wealth beyond any plausible measure of social value, squeezing the last cent out of their workers or customers and seeming to care little for the insecurities thrown up by technology and globalization. Of total employment growth in the US between 2005 and 2015, insecure employment in the categories of independent contractors, on-call workers and workers provided by contracting companies or temp agencies accounted for 94% (Katz and Krueger 2016). Outsourcing of employment plays a big role in what Weil (2014) describes as the 'fissuring' of the workplace—depressing wages, magnifying income and wealth inequality, and generating pervasive anger in those on the wrong end of the fissuring that the world is cheating them. In addition, many Trump voters resent that the

[1]This chapter draws on Wade's earlier essays, including (2004, 2006, 2009, 2011, 2014, 2016, and 2017); and on Alacevich and Soci (2018). We are grateful to Malcomb Sawyer, philip arestis and fanny alcocer for their comments.

[2]Thanks to Adrian Wood for this sentence.

[3]Trump also surfed on widespread perception that the political system is illegitimate. The latter perception is substantiated by surveys of thousands of election experts asked to assess the quality of hundreds of elections around the world, whose average put the US as 52nd among 153 countries on 'electoral integrity', as reported by the Electoral Integrity Project (Porter 2017). US voting turnout is one of the lowest in the developed world. In 2016, 232 million citizens were legally entitled to vote; only 132 million did so (57%).

government gives handouts to 'shirkers' and sticks them with the tax bill—the category of 'shirkers' being heavily coloured.[4]

They now see themselves as, finally, members of a winning team. They affirm their leader's strikes against pillars of the 'establishment' order (including the media and even the judiciary), and they forgive the administration's lies, 'alternative facts', authoritarianism, chauvinism, and billionaire composition at the top.[5]

One upside to the Trump phenomenon is that his insults and assaults have caused critics to ignite a wide debate about class, race, gender, and democracy. 'The president's many critics realize that long-festering social divisions must be confronted', say two commentators in *The New York Times* (Wertheim and Meaney 2018).

That observation raises the question of this paper. Why have these 'long-festering social divisions' not been 'confronted' long ago? More specifically, why have economists paid scant attention to the trends of rising income and wealth inequality over *the past three decades* or so in most of the western world, and espoused 'free trade' on grounds that it enhances overall economic growth; why have mainstream politicians ignored the plight of those on the losing side; and why have electorates acquiesced as inequality has widened? Why did the dog not bark?

We try to go beyond the obvious explanation for the low salience of rising inequality in economics and public policy—namely, that the rich have a vested interest in boosting issues for public policy attention which do not question their relative position and in obscuring those which might. We start with trends in the structure of modern

---

[4]Weinhold (2018) provides evidence on how the black share of population and black poverty rate affected the vote for Trump, at county and individual levels.

[5]On the billionaire composition, *The Financial Times* (2017) reported that Rex Tillerson, Donald Trump's first secretary of state, would be given a payout worth about $180m to sever all financial ties to Exxon Mobil, because before his selection, the Exxon chairman and chief executive was in line to receive about 2 million shares in the oil group, worth about $182m at then prices. Mr. Tillerson might consider himself hard done by compared to Stephen Schwarzman, the chief executive of Blackstone Group, the leveraged buyout firm, appointed by Mr. Trump to be head of the president's business council. Schwarzman was paid $799 million in 2015. On lies and 'alternative facts', Grassegger and Krogerus (2017) argue that they were not shoot-from-the-hip; they were carefully planned and micro-targeted on the basis of Big Data analysis of Facebook and other such data about individuals.

capitalism—especially rising concentration of capital ownership, rising debt to GDP, and rising inequality (especially income concentration). We argue that these structural changes tend to support—and be reinforced by—ideological changes, shifting what Gramsci called 'the philosophy of non-philosophers' to the right, and justifying the erosion of post-war social democracy and the rise of 'oligarchic democracy'. The shifts are reinforced by the proliferation of well-financed right-wing think tanks, while centre-left political parties have hardly dared to focus on inequality as a problem—instead directing attention to the (less-threatening) need to 'expand opportunities' and 'reduce poverty'. Finally, we argue that the conceptual apparatus of mainstream economics contains mostly implicit value premises which incline believers to think that rising inequality is not a problem, to the extent that they register inequality at all. Our brief history of the ersatz Nobel Prize in Economics, properly called the Bank of Sweden Prize in Economics, illustrates one mechanism by which neoliberal economics has been mainstreamed as 'the best and most scientific economics'.

2 Inequality Trends

There being abundant evidence of rising inequality, we offer just a few corroborating facts. In terms of the share of national income accruing to the top 1%, in the 1920s in both developed and developing countries (those few developing countries for which data are available), the figure was in the range of 15–20%. The share then fell steadily during and after World War II, reaching 5–10% by the late 1970s. Over the 1980s, coinciding with globalization, financialization, and the ascendance of neoliberal economic philosophy in Anglo-American and many developing economies, the share of the top 1% began to rise rapidly.

In the US, the share rose from around 11% in 1980 to 20% in 2013 (excluding capital gains); in the UK, from around 7 to 15%; in the three biggest European continental countries plus Japan, from around 7–8 to 10–13%. All of these six cases showed fairly steady increase in share of the top 1% (http://wid.world/February, 2013). The shares would be much higher with accrued (but not distributed) profits and tax evasion included.

In the US, during the four-year period of expansion during the Bush presidency (2002–2006) the richest 1% of Americans accrued 73% of the increase in national income (Palma 2011). This is not a misprint. As for wealth, the richest 1% owned about 35% of household and corporate wealth in 2006–2007, a figure which is certainly too low because of all the wealth hidden in tax havens; but even taken at face value it is a far bigger share than in most other developed countries.

In the UK, the average remuneration of FTSE100 chief executives rose by about 40% in FY2010—a year of close to zero GDP growth—to reach £4.2 million, or 145 times the median wage.

In the world as a whole the top one percent of the world's population own roughly the same resources as the remaining 99%. Since the Great Recession started in 2008, the number of high net worth individuals (HNWIs), with more than $1 million of liquid assets, has surged. In 2010 the number exceeded the previous peak in 2007, even as governments of developed countries implemented austerity budgets. Although most are concentrated in the US, Japan, and Germany (53% of the world total live in these countries), the fastest increase in HNWI numbers is in Asia-Pacific countries, whose total exceeded Europe's for the first time ever in 2010 (Treanor 2011). Billionaire net wealth on a world scale (number of billionaire times average net wealth) rose by 85% between 2007 and 2014. This too is not a misprint.

Hence the soaring demand for 'passion' purchases, from Ferraris to diamonds, art, and fine wines. Just a few years after the Great Recession of 2009 prices in the international art market were so sensational as to give Sotheby's and Christies their highest profits in years.[6] To this, we must add the educational arms race, as the wealthy compete to get their children into the most elite and expensive private schools; and the house arms race to buy the most expensive property in London and

[6]The Global Art Market Report (2018) says that 2017 saw premium-priced works hit unprecedented highs, with sales up in all major geographic markets; but growth was limited to the high end (Gerlis 2018).

hold it (empty) as an alternative form of international reserve currency. At the other end, the US stands out for having about the highest rate of mass incarceration per 100,000 in the world, while the UK has about the highest in Northwest Europe, which helps to keep the poor, minorities, and powerless walled off from the rich they might threaten.

3 The Response to Rising Inequality

To be sure, scholars have been analysing inequality trends for decades. The stream of publications, in the 1970s very small, has since increased considerably (see Table 1). But the group of scholars working on inequality issues has always been a tiny sliver of the economics profession, and mostly marginal to the mainstream. Anthony Atkinson, James Galbraith, Branko Milanovic, and Joseph Stiglitz, among others,

Table 1 Books with 'inequality', 'income inequality' in the title

	Inequality	Income Inequality
1946–50	14	0
1951–55	5	0
1956–60	14	1
1961–65	43	8
1966–70	66	6
1971–75	143	19
1976–80	199	22
1981–85	222	17
1986–90	251	31
1991–95	519	68
1996–00	725	118
2001–05	928	150
2006–10	1251	187
2011–15	1303	210

Source Own Construction

The table shows the number of books published, per five-year period, with 'inequality' and 'income inequality' in the title and held in the online catalogue of Harvard's Widener Library (title word, all languages, all locations, all formats), arguably the largest social science academic repository in the world. It is only a rough index of salience, in particular because words like 'inequality' can refer to phenomena far beyond income and wealth inequality. A similar measure for 'poverty' would pick up titles like *The Poverty of Historicism* have worked on the theme for decades. Piketty's *Capital in the Twenty-First Century* sold in huge numbers—around 1.5 million copies, hardback and e-copy, in the first year after the English language version in March 2014. The book by epidemiologists Richard Wilkinson and Kate Pickett, *The Spirit Level: Why More Equal Societies Almost Always Do Better*, sold 250–300,000 copies in 24 languages between publication in 2009 and mid 2014 (authors' personal communications). But these are recent exceptions, and their work has not triggered a lasting dialogue on possible policy shifts (Wade 2014; Alacevich and Soci 2018).

IMF researchers have published a few papers on the connection between inequality and growth, concluding that 'Inequality continues to be a robust and powerful determinant both of the pace of medium-term growth and of the duration of growth spells [the higher the inequality the worse the growth performance].... [T]here is surprisingly little evidence for the growth-destroying effects of fiscal redistribution at a macroeconomic level' (Ostry et al. 2014). But the research has had little impact on the operational thinking of the Fund (Wade interviews with Fund staff 2012; but see Grabel 2018 for a qualification).

The Occupy Movement, which erupted in North American and European cities in the summer of 2011, focused attention on inequality, framing the issue as the bottom 99% against the top 1%. This framing conveniently allowed the upper middle class (roughly the top 85–99 percentiles) to put themselves on the side of the angels. One of its constructive effects was to couple the pre-existing mass resentment against 'welfare scroungers' with the new rage against the (undeserving) rich, so that the focus was no longer entirely on the former (Table 2).

Pushed by budget pressures and the public sympathy evoked by the Occupy Movement, some politicians began to talk of the desirability of higher taxes on the rich. President Obama endorsed the 'Buffett rule' that millionaires should not pay a lower rate of tax than their assistants. The British Liberal Democratic Party proposed to introduce a 'mansion tax'—in the context of bringing *down* the top income tax rate; but its coalition party in government, the Conservative Party, did not support. The French Socialist president proposed a 75% tax rate on top incomes.

These proposals, then and now, everywhere run into fierce opposition. The Occupy Movement had little follow-on once the occupations

Table 2 Decile shares (%) of national income, US and average for 133 countries, 2009

	US	133 countries
D10	33	32
D5–9	55	52
D1–4	13	17

Source Palma (2011, Table 1)
D10 is the top decile of the population by income, D5–9 the middle 50%, D1–4 the bottom 40%

ended (the medium was the message). In the US, conservative organizations advocate lower taxes (especially on the wealthy), less public spending (except for military), free trade, and economic libertarianism. One such is the Club for Growth, which declared in early 2012, 'If we balance the budget tomorrow on spending cuts alone, it would be fantastic for the economy' (quoted in Krugman 2012b). It has long been accepted in policy circles and in the public at large that public action to reduce top-end inequality is (a) infeasible and (b) not legitimate.

The net result is that politicians have done little to curb income and wealth concentration. They and commentators have tended to steer public attention along the track of 'Does individual X deserve his £1.4 million bonus?', and 'Why should people [CEOs] be rewarded for failure?', which leaves intact the premise that 'whatever-corporate-boards-will-bear' should be given for 'success'. Once on this track, issues of the society-wide structure of income and demand-generation are conveniently by-passed.[7]

[7]The case of Leo Apotheker attracted condemnation. As newly appointed boss of Hewlett-Packard, he received remuneration of almost $10 million as a sign-on package, and just over $13 million on his termination 11 months later, or $23 million for 11 months of work. John Donohue, president of the American Law and Economics Association, commented, 'It's a shocking departure from capitalist incentives if you lavish riches on the losers'. He continued, 'Imagine if you were applying for a job, and you said, "I want to make it clear that if I do a terrible job, I want to walk away with a ton of money". Do you think you'd get hired? *Yet that's now standard practice in negotiating executive compensation*' (quoted in Stewart 2011, emphasis added). Another report says 'A hallmark of the gilded era of just a few short years ago, the eye-popping severance package, continues to thrive in spite of the measures established after the financial crisis to crack down on excessive pay'. The report quotes a director of governance for a labour-affiliated investment fund saying 'We repeatedly see companies' assets go out the door to reward failure. Investors are frustrated that boards haven't prevented such windfalls' (Dash 2011).

The obvious answer to our question as to why inequality has been kept on the side-lines of public policy and professional economics *even as it rose for decades* is that the rich have a vested interest in boosting issues for public policy attention which do not question their relative position, and in eclipsing those which do. As Upton Sinclair famously said, 'It is difficult to get a man to understand something, when his salary depends on his not understanding it'. Given that the rich have a vastly disproportionate influence in politics, civil service, and media, no surprise that the agenda of public policy does not draw attention to the need to change the distribution to make it less unequal—back to where it was in 1990, for example.

Guillaud's (2013) study of preferences for redistribution, across 33 democracies, shows how important are economic factors—income and occupational status—in the formation of people's policy preferences. This study uses preference data on responses to 'On the whole, do you think it should or should not be the government's responsibility to reduce income differences between the rich and the poor?' Possible answers: 'definitely should not be'; 'probably should not be'; 'probably should be'; 'definitely should be'. The strongest correlations across all the countries are between preferences and income and occupational status. 'The odds of a manager to oppose redistributive policies are increased by 40%, as compared to those of an office clerk, for instance' (Guillaud, op. cit., p. 57).

But Guillaud's is a simple exercise in correlation analysis of individual preferences. To go deeper into the neglect of rising inequality, we need to pull back from 'inequality' per se and start with the transformation of the structure and ideology of western capitalism during and after the 1980s.

4 Structure and Ideology of Western Capitalism

Conservative politicians and mainstream economists have celebrated the rise of 'market forces' since the neoliberal reforms of the 1980s. 'Neoliberal' refers to an economic and political philosophy whose economic axiom says that the market is the best institution for economic growth, and whose political axiom says that the market is the best institution for liberty. So 'the market' should be applied in all domains, everything should be financialized, homo economicus should be universalized. Deregulate (and maybe then differently re-regulate) markets, privatize public enterprises, fortify corporate control, lower personal and corporate taxes, relax capital controls, restrict the ability of trade unions to operate, give up full employment as a top macroeconomic goal, expand opportunities for profit in education and health, and above all, accelerate 'globalization'.

But the neoliberal champions overlooked what this process has fostered: a sharp increase in the concentration of capital ownership through successive waves of mergers and hostile takeovers, through the privatization of natural monopolies, and through the rising value of intangible assets (like patents, brands) relative to tangible assets (buildings, machinery) (Pagano 2014). *These trends in turn have caused entry barriers in many sectors to rise*—contrary to the ostensible aims of neoliberal philosophy. Firms facing less competitive pressure squeeze customers and their workers and pad up corporate profits and executive remuneration.

This amounts to a fundamental change of economic regime, from 'control of capital' to 'control by capital', guided by the principle of 'maximize shareholder value' (which is about value *extraction*, not value creation, the latter given little attention). It is not the way that most economists say market economies should work, nor the way that the standard economic models say market economies do work (Lazonick 2010).

The financial sector has led the way. In 1997, shortly before the start of the East Asian/Latin American/Russian/Long-Term Capital Management crisis, the value of financial transactions was about 15 times the world's annual gross product. By 2010, it reached almost 70 (but has since plateaued). Advanced economies have been particularly affected. In terms of the ratio of financial openness (foreign assets and liabilities to GDP) to trade openness (exports and imports to GDP), advanced and emerging economies were about the same in the mid-1980s. The ratio for advanced economies then shot up from 135% in the mid-1990s to 570% by 2016, while that for emerging economies rose from 100 to 180% (Canuto 2017). An analysis published in 2011 identified a supercluster of 147 mega firms accounting for a high share of the world's corporate revenues, which was dominated by finance: *all of the top 50 except one were financial firms* (Coghalan and MacKenzie 2011).

The distinction between finance and the rest of the economy is one component of a larger dual growth process involving a technologically dynamic sector (which includes FIRE [finance, insurance, real estate], manufacturing, information, and professional business services) and a stagnant and 'survivalist' sector (utilities, construction, education, health, private social services, and the 'Rest', made up of fast-food, arts and entertainment, recreational and other services). The dynamic sector is losing jobs (24% of the American work force worked in manufacturing in 1960, today, 8%), while the stagnant and survivalist sector acts as an employer of last resort (Storm 2017). As workers shift from the former to the latter, wage growth and productivity growth in the latter slow, and a growing part of the labour force becomes 'traumatized by job insecurity', in Alan Greenspan's words. Income inequality widens.

The other side of high income concentration is high debt, whether of households, corporate, or public entities. The debt component is necessary to support income and wealth concentration, because—at least when the economy is not growing super-fast—debt is necessary to sustain consumption demand (and also investment demand). The bizarre result (in the context of standard economic understanding) is that economic growth in the so-called advanced countries and in many middle-income countries has come to depend on sustained rises in debt—or on export surpluses, which imply rising debt elsewhere in the world. The outsized beneficiaries of this structure understandably believe it to be wonderful and have high confidence in it. They have little interest in exploring the contradictions that support it, and great interest in keeping 'inequality-as-problem' *off* the political agenda.

UNCTAD economists have been among the leaders in explaining how this type of monopoly capitalism works. They reintroduced an old character—the rentier—to describe the new predicament: 'What is new in this debate is not so much a preoccupation with "bad apples" or the use of potentially abusive practices by individual firms in isolation; rather, it is the concern that increasing market concentration in leading sectors of the global economy and the growing market and lobbying powers of dominant corporations are creating *a new form of global rentier capitalism* to the detriment of balanced and inclusive growth for the many' (UNCTAD 2017, p. 119, emphasis added). Bank of Sweden laureate Jean Tirole is another important contributor to our understanding of how giant enterprises influence both states and markets.

Crouch (2011) has explored how the familiar rhetoric of 'the market' obfuscates both the actual nature of neoliberal policies and the role of giant corporations in contemporary capitalism. He shows that the usual dyad of state vs. market conceals how giant corporations play a role which 'is more potent than either [state or market] and transforms the workings of both'. The result is 'a series of comfortable accommodations among all three' (Crouch, op. cit., pp. viii–ix).

These accommodations tend to weaken the achievement of political equality in western democracies, as measured by criteria of (1) effective participation, (2) voting equality, (3) enlightened understanding, (4) popular control of the political agenda, and (5) the inclusion of all adult individuals in the process of democratic deliberation (Dahl 1998, p. 38). For instance, media concentration reduces pluralism and limits possibilities for informed debate. An uninformed population cannot exercise political rights in full. Some states, notably the US, operate a system that makes it difficult for poor people or ethnic minorities to vote. And the drift towards broader responsibilities for isolated technocratic officials, notably in the European Union, condemns the less empowered segments of the population to irrelevance. Elections for the European parliament have regularly shown much lower voting rates than national elections (for an expanded discussion of the relationship between economic and political equality, see Alacevich and Soci 2018).

This skewed political landscape allows the blossoming not so much of 'market forces' as a synergy between giant firms and neoliberal economic truth, in which neoliberalism and 'free markets' provide a smokescreen behind which capital ownership grows more concentrated. As Crouch (2011) puts it, '*neoliberalism departs astonishingly from both the political and economic legacy of liberalism in not seeing any problem in a close relationship between firms and the state, provided the influence runs from firms to the state and not vice versa*' (p. 95, emphasis added; for a classic analysis of the threat posed to democratic institutions by the large corporation, see Lindblom 1977).

Britain's experience of privatization shows how neoliberal ideology—with its premise that capitalist business practice almost always beats soggy state inefficiency—has been used to obfuscate the reality. Prime Minister Margaret Thatcher wrote in her memoirs that the privatization of public services,

> was one of the central means of reversing the corrosive and corrupting effects of socialism. Just as nationalisation was at the heart of the collectivist programme by which Labour governments sought to remodel British society, so privatisation is at the centre of any programme of *reclaiming territory for freedom*. (quoted in Viviano 2018, emphasis added)

These sentiments fuelled a sell-off of just about every state-owned enterprise in the country during the 1980s and 1990s, and provided the gospel of privatization followed by leaders around the world. To be sure, there was a strong case for getting the British state out of many of the sectors it ran by the end of the 1970s, including railways, ports, coalmines, steelworks, and telecommunications, with frequent strikes and rates of return typically half that in the private sector.

But with minimal transparency and debate, many of the privatized enterprises passed not to the ownership of business-savvy British firms but to *foreign governments*. In the case of rail and bus lines, for example, most of them passed to member governments of the European Union and China. Of Britain's 23 major train operators, 18 are now foreign-owned, 16 by EU governments, 2 by China. Most of Britain's foreign state-owned rail and bus operations are reliably profitable, contradicting the neoliberal gospel of *inherent* state sloth and waste (Viviano 2018). These facts are virtually unknown in Britain.

Take woodlands. Britain has less woodland per acre than anywhere in western Europe. The Forestry Commission exists to maintain the woodlands. In 2010 the Conservative government announced plans to privatize the Forestry Commission, but was so shocked by the reaction that it backed off. Instead, it began to privatize in secret. A private company, created by the commission, has an agreement with the commission (which is a shareholder) to develop luxury chalets throughout Britain's woodlands (in effect, a scattered luxury hotel). Holding woodland leases of up to 125 years, it pays the commission a rent per chalet of an average £3000 per year, and rents out the chalets for up to £4000 per week. Since 2012, when the agreement went into force, the company has had the fourth highest profit growth of private companies in Britain. It has no competitors, no rival bidders, and no limit to its growth. The 2012 agreement stipulates that the commission is to ensure that 'the media and the public are not aware of new development site selection'. This is from a public body (Jenkins 2018).

5 Change in Ruling Class Coalition

To take this further, we need to pay attention to the changed nature of the ruling class coalition. In the post-war decades, politics in most western countries rested on a class coalition or pact between the skilled working class, professional middle class, and capitalists who were either entrepreneurs running their own companies or investors for the long term (Bresser-Pereira 2012). This coalition produced an 'establishment' governing elite, with a stewardship mentality concerned to foster the well-being of the whole society—in line with the momentum of national solidarity induced by the war and as a buttress to their own position. The focus on the well-being of the society at large meant keeping a cap on income inequality, so that the governing elite did not come to be seen as divorced from the rest of the society. International trade was small relative to GDP (compared to what came later), so capitalists (or their collective organizations), more dependent than later on the domestic market, understood wages to be not only a cost of production but also a source of demand. This understanding paved the way for the cross-class cooperation known as social democracy and the welfare state.

As globalization advanced from the 1980s, capitalists began to see wages only as a cost of production to be minimized, both by undermining trade unions at home and by offshoring production to cheap labour sites. The cross-class cooperation underpinning social democracy weakened as the former 'establishment' elite morphed into something closer to an 'oligarchic' elite. The dominant class coalition narrowed to financiers and rentiers, both dependent on income from the returns on capital, both operating on short-time horizons and 'winner take most' morality. Not that there was a visible change in political regime. Winters (2011) describes what happened as the emergence of a 'civil [not military] oligarchy'; a powerful oligarchic group coexisting with the pre-eminence of 'strong and impersonal systems of law' over oligarchs (p. 208). But this civil oligarchy was also what O'Donnell describes as an 'insidious oligarchy', which caused the 'slow strangulation of democracy' (cited in Karl 2000, p. 150). The new oligarchy used instruments of public policy to redistribute upwards, directly and indirectly, and to shrink the welfare state while turning much of what remains into a private profit centre. The implicit, sometimes explicit aim of this class is to keep its chalice of wealth and privilege full to the brim.

The United States is a dramatic example of the shift to oligarchy, all the more so because it has been the global hegemonic power since the World War II and the norms and practices dominant there tend to shape those in the rest of the world. The central policy goal of the Republican Party for at least the past 40 years has been upwards redistribution of income and wealth, through lower taxes on the wealthy and cuts in programmes that help the poor and middle classes (Krugman 2018). Its electoral successes have pulled the Democratic Party towards the same agenda, only less so.

Over the 2000s, high-income households have been paying their lowest share of federal taxes in decades, and corporations frequently avoid paying any tax. In 2008, the 400 highest-income individual tax filers paid only 18% of their income in federal income taxes; in 2007, just 17%; and they pay little by way of payroll taxes or state and local taxes, which are major burdens on middle-income families. They pay so little because most of their income is classed as capital gains, three quarters of which go to the top 1%. The rate on capital gains is the lowest since the days of President Hoover. President George W. Bush rammed the tax cut on capital gains and another on dividends through Congress in 2003 on the wave of euphoria over the 'victory' in Iraq (Krugman

2012a). The Clinton administration, by contrast, was positively socialistic; during the first term the top 400 taxpayers paid close to 30% of their income in federal taxes.

Yet during the Bush decade of frenzied tax cutting for the rich the Republican Party also happened to lower some tax rates for the poor (and earlier, the Reagan administration instituted the earned income tax credit, which became a remarkably effective antipoverty program by giving working families thousands of dollars a year in tax refunds). Since the Bush decade Republican leaders have sought to correct such oversights and raise taxes on the poor and working class, in the interests of 'fairness' and 'eliminating welfare scroungers' (*New York Times* 2011).

Moreover, pressure has been building for several years up to 2018 to water down the Dodd-Frank reforms that Congress passed after the near-disintegration of the US financial system in 2008. The financial services lobby says that it wants lower capital ratios, more scope for risky trading with taxpayer-backed funds, and less consumer protection. It says that these steps will help economic growth—but the real motive is to raise bank profitability and with it, executive bonuses. As O'Conner (2018) remarks, 'The desire of a small number of very wealthy people to become still richer should not drive public policy'.

In Britain the Labour Party government over the 2000s deliberately refused to stand up to people who through technically legal but morally reprehensible ruses end up paying a minuscule amount of tax on their copious wealth. Labour Chancellor Alistair Darling boasted that he wanted London to be a welcoming home for Russians, Chinese, and Saudis, which meant low taxation and 'light-touch regulation' (Kampfner 2011).

Iceland experienced much the same. Over the 2000s, the conservative, market-liberalizing, bank-privatizing Independence Party government shifted the tax burden onto the bottom half of the income distribution, by almost eliminating the tax on capital gains and by lowering the threshold at which families start paying taxes. The ostensible aim was to boost incentives for entrepreneurship. Instead it boosted the incentives for bankers to lend recklessly, eventually driving the economy over a cliff (Wade and Sigurgeirsdottir 2011).

6 Interests of the Middle Classes

If it is unsurprising that the already-rich defend inequality and try to translate their riches into political power with which to limit downwards redistribution, it is surprising that the middle classes have acquiesced. To understand middle-class acquiescence, we have to look more closely at trends in income distribution.

Consider Fig. 1 (Palma 2011). It shows the national income shares of population deciles in the US from 1947 to 2006. We see, first, the sharp rise in the share of the top decile, D10, starting around 1980, the time of the Reagan/Thatcher neoliberal reforms, and continuing till the end of the series in 2006. We see, second, something more surprising: the share of the middle 50% of the population (D5–9) remained fairly constant at a bit more than 50% through the whole period from 1947 to 2006, falling a little in the 1980s but then stabilizing (not shown in the figure, the trends for both D7–9 and D5–6 are roughly constant). Third, we see that the share of the bottom 40% (D1–4) fell steadily after 1980, meaning that *the rising share of D10 was at the expense of the bottom 40%, not the middle 50%.*

This pattern—the middle half of the income distribution has managed to defend a share of national income roughly in line with its share of population, while the top 10% increased its share after 1980 at the expense of the bottom—is also found in many other middle- and high-income countries (Table 1).[8]

What are the political effects, in terms of support for or opposition to politicians who urge measures of downwards redistribution (e.g. higher taxes on the wealthy, higher minimum wage, larger supply of public services)? You would think that as the very rich soar ahead, leaving behind not just manual workers but also the middle class masses (including doctors, academics, civil servants, CEOs of smallish companies), the middle classes would mobilize politically to champion less concentration at the top. They do not. Why not?

---

[8]See Hazledine (2014) for qualifications to Palma's argument.

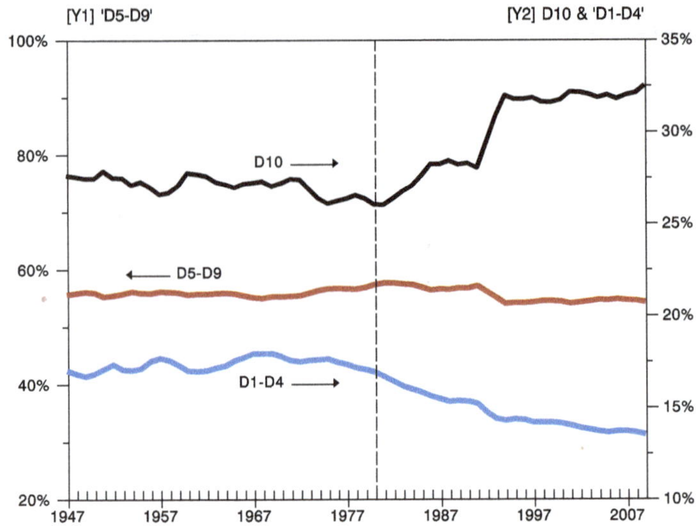

Fig. 1 Share of US income deciles, 1947–2009 (*Source* Palma 2011)

- The middle classes have not been squeezed as the rich got a larger share, so rising inequality at the top is not so threatening to them. The squeeze has come on the bottom 40%, which in most countries is politically emasculated. How the middle classes have managed to sustain a share roughly in line with share of population is unclear. But part of the answer may be that many middle-class professions, especially in the public sector, have relatively strong unions or professional associations, as compared to the working class.
- Middle and upper middle classes have been able to increase their consumption faster than their (slowly increasing) incomes by borrowing—from the financial resources available as wealth holders at the top seek to multiple their wealth by buying sophisticated financial assets, at the other end of which are retail loans. Over the 2000s, the rise in household debt to household income in the US and other Anglo-American economies allowed aggregate demand to grow at the rate required to sustain the process of capital accumulation, despite stagnant wages; in effect, the capitalist elite operated a 'part-pay/part-lend' strategy rather than pay the required level of wages.

- Some components of the economic conservative package are very appealing to the middle and upper middle classes. In particular, the promise of lower taxes is a sure vote winner, even if the tax cuts benefit the rich most of all. When the British Labour Party's Tony Blair stepped down as prime minister in 2007 and was replaced by Gordon Brown, Brown at first did so well in the opinion polls that he was tempted to call an early election. When the Conservative Party's Shadow Chancellor Osborne promised to abolish inheritance taxes the political balance changed so much that Brown called off the early election. In Italy, centre-left Prime Minister Matteo Renzi opened the national electoral campaign in 2017 with (unspecified) promises of tax cuts. When many commentators remarked that this promise smelt of (right-wing) Silvio Berlusconi, Renzi tried to reassure his political base that 'cutting taxes is a leftist policy'.
- The current generation of the middle classes has internalized the Reagan/Thatcher values of individualistic aspiration: 'winners should take most', 'let failures fail' (Lakoff 2002). It expects to rely on its own efforts to get ahead—or at least, this is its self-image, which is to the reality what self-importance is to importance. Its members reject the idea of a symbiosis between rich and poor. They might be prepared to acknowledge that the prosperity of the free class of ancient Romans depended on a substructure of slaves; but not that their own prosperity depends on the existence of a lower wage class.
- The middle classes invest their surpluses in replicating their advantages, and fear loss of these advantages more than they value the prospect of gain. Talk of 'reducing inequality' prompts middle class anxiety that the government may try to raise those *below* them in the income hierarchy, which worries them more than those above them rising even further away. Better to let the rich keep their income than have tax-financed transfers used to boost those below them—all the more so when (as now) many in the middle classes see themselves on the edge of the abyss, loaded up with debt, and worried about unemployment and the prospects of their children. After all, their roughly constant share of national income means that they have been roaring ahead of the bottom 40%, whose share of national income has dramatically declined, and this is a measure of *their success*.

- The middle class holds a negative stereotype of the working class (bottom 40%), which legitimizes resistance to redistribution, which might benefit the latter. This stereotype corresponds roughly to the second breakpoint in the income hierarchy (after the one at roughly the 99th percentile), between those with a college degree and those without. Over the past several decades, the economic benefit of college education has steadily risen. In the US, the average college graduate made 38% more than the average high school graduate in 1979, but 75% more today. Moreover, college graduates are much better at passing their advantages on to their children, who are more likely to get married and stay married, much less likely to have children out of marriage, less likely to smoke, more likely to read to their children, and have wider friendship networks. The bottom 40 to 50%, in contrast, have more disorganized families and more disorganized social networks (Brooks 2011). With them as the reference group, the college educated have a ready narrative at hand which justifies pulling up the drawbridge and opposing 'redistribution'.

Discussion of class preferences needs to be qualified by country effects. Guillaud's (2013) study of preferences for redistribution in 33 (mostly OECD) countries finds that in 10 of them, more than 30% of respondents said it 'definitely' or 'probably should not be the government's responsibility to reduce income differences between the rich and the poor'. The US and New Zealand lead the way, with more than 45% opposed to redistribution; Australia and Canada are also well above 30%. The UK is just over 30%. The Anglo sphere stands out for the high portion of the population hostile to income redistribution.

Still, what is most striking about country effects is that everywhere a *majority* of respondents think that it 'probably' or 'definitely' is the government's responsibility to reduce income differences between the rich and the poor; and in most of the 33 countries, a large majority. And yet ....

7 Conservative Ideology

Political ideologies and cognitive beliefs which justify the existing distribution of material conditions of living are *widely believed*, including by people who accept that they have little prospect of becoming rich but agree that those who are or become rich should be able to keep what they have.

Ideologies are not like holy water sprinkled onto interests; they do not simply justify whatever interests want. Rather, they have a causal role akin to 'switchmen' who determine the tracks along which human attention and behaviour travel, to borrow a metaphor from Max Weber. Interests are then analogous to the engines which pull or push the attention and behaviour.

The ideational explanation for the neglect of inequality is that large parts of western electorates—not just the rich and middle classes—have accepted a conservative worldview which pulls the switches in favour of *a vision of a moral society* in which the role of government is to encourage largely free, private markets, protect property rights, and *accept the income distribution which results from those markets and the existing distribution of property rights* (provided the government does not rig the markets in favour of its cronies).

In this conservative worldview, the welfare state, and government policies to reduce income inequality, weakens the *moral* fibre of society by eroding self-reliance, family solidarity, and the scope for private charities (Lakoff 2002). Lakoff estimated that, as of the late 1990s, about 40% of the American electorate believed the whole package of this worldview, and another 20% believed major parts of it.

Philosophers have provided a raft of arguments to justify inequality and to reject John Rawls' partial defence of redistribution. For example, Nozick (1974), in *Anarchy, State and Utopia*, argued that as long as exchanges between persons are voluntary, whatever distribution of rewards produced by those exchanges is legitimate. The book remains highly prized in conservative circles.

The normal popular response to hard economic times is to demand more regulation and social insurance. But the hard times since 2008 saw the conservative worldview surge in popular support. Friedrich von Hayek's polemic *The Road to Serfdom*, published in 1944, rose to 240 on the Amazon Best Seller's List in 2010. Hayek argued that Beveridge's 1942 proposals for a welfare state in Britain (including a National Health Service) would curb economic freedoms and then by inevitable slippery slope, curb political freedoms too (hence 'serfdom'). The book's sales were propelled upwards by conservative talk-show hosts prescribing it as a guide to the nefarious intentions of the Obama's administration (Farrant and McPhail 2010). Ayn Rand's *Atlas Shrugged*, with its celebration of the captains of industry whom the government was always trying to tear down, has enjoyed a similar surge of favourable attention, including from many who fail to see that it is not only anti-government but also anti-democratic. The libertarian economist Ludwig von Mises expressed the novel's key message succinctly when he wrote to congratulate Rand on the book's publication in 1957, saying:

> You have the courage to tell the masses what no politician told them: [that] you are inferior and all the improvements in your conditions which you simply take for granted you owe to the efforts of men who are better than you. (Frank 2011, p. 147)

The fuel for the historically unprecedented surge of popular support for the conservative, free market, cut-the-welfare-state ideology in *hard times* is fear of—terror of—'big government' and 'elites'. The Tea Party movement in the US had its genesis in 2009 in the battle over bank bailouts, and went on to highlight the unholy alliance of big business and big government as the defining issue of public policy, holding up the 'free market' as the moral alternative. Get government intervention out of the way, it says, and all deserving people can climb the bean stalk, scramble through the hole in the sky, and arrive in the land of freedom, peace, and prosperity.

In an extreme case of 'false consciousness' Tea Party supporters overlooked their movement's financing largely by millionaires and billionaires grown rich from big business, not by the entrepreneurs of small and medium enterprises whom they celebrated. They—and anti-government conservatives more generally—overlook the extent to which private firms in many sectors depend on government contracts; which in sectors like health, education, and prisons is at the cost of public provision of the same.

But visceral anti-government sentiment in the US now goes far beyond conservative circles. 'You can trust the government to do the right thing most of the time' elicited agreement from about three quarters of American respondents in the mid 1950s, and only about 10% today (Rashbrooke 2013).[9]

8 Right-Wing Think Tanks

Ideas, ideologies, worldviews do not just float upon the air. To be influential they must be carried by organizations and embedded in institutions. Intellectual work to justify inequality and broadcast the rationale was going on long before the Reagan/Thatcher policy shifts. An active right-wing movement created well-endowed think tanks, such as the Hoover Foundation (1919), the American Enterprise Institute (1943), the Mont Pelerin Society (1947), the Institute of Economic Affairs (founded in London in 1955), the Cato Institute, the Heritage Foundation and the Manhattan Institute (all founded in the 1970s), the Mises Institute (1982), to name some of the early ones. The movement also financed advocates in other organizations, including political parties and university departments (Phillips-Fein 2009; Roemer 2011). As inequality began to rise in the late 1970s, these organizations were ready to squash critics with arguments like 'you are just practicing the politics of envy' and to advocate 'the market' as both an efficient mechanism for coordination and incentives, backed by ersatz Nobelists in economics.

Most of the thousands of groups which call themselves free-market or conservative think tanks refuse to disclose their sources of funding. But enough is known to reveal that they typically act as sophisticated corporate lobbying groups, cooperating to promote the views of the people

[9]Kaplan et al. (2016) find that people's *political* beliefs are more resistant to challenging argument and evidence than their *non-political* beliefs. They exposed 40 self-identified strong liberals (in the US) to counterarguments to statements they previously indicated strong agreement with; measured their brain responses (with functional MRI); and then asked them their post-challenge belief strength. They found that their non-political belief strength declined substantially more than their political belief strength. And that the challenge to political beliefs correlated more strongly with higher activity in the systems of the brain that process emotion—in particular, identity and *internally-focused* cognition (as in searching memory for counter-arguments to the counter-arguments).

who fund them. One expert explained why such think tanks are more effective than other public relations agencies:

They are 'the source of many of the ideas and facts that appear in countless editorials, news articles, and syndicated columns'. They have 'considerable influence and close personal relationships with elected officials'. They 'support and encourage one another, echo and amplify their messages, and can pull together…coalitions on the most important public policy issues'. Crucially, they are 'virtually immune to retribution…the identity of donors to think tanks is protected from involuntary disclosure' (Jeff Judson, quoted in Monbiot 2011a).

A *transnational network* of neoliberal think tanks has been active in spreading the neoliberal faith around the world for the past several decades. One node is the Atlas Economic Research Foundation, renamed Atlas Network in 2011. It was created in 1981 by the man who was an early member of the Mt Pelerin Society and had created the Institute of Economic Affairs in London in 1955. Its purpose is to foster neoliberal think tanks everywhere, on a fairly standard blueprint, which appear to their publics to be fully national and independent, and help them converge in their thinking (produce editorials and comment columns which can then be adapted to local contexts, for example). It explicitly follows Hayek's strategy for effecting an intellectual and then policy revolution laid out in his essay 'Intellectuals and socialism', 1949: first, shape 'public opinion' to favour the neoliberal worldview; second, shape policy agendas of governments in line with this public opinion (Djelic and Mousavi 2019).

The left has developed few equivalents to the well-endowed right-wing think tanks. The centre-of-the-road Brookings Institution in Washington, DC is regarded as the US's most prominent 'centre-left' think tank.[10]

Media ownership and media bias also matter. The bias is overwhelmingly in favour of the conservative worldview. The British newspaper reading public, for example, is exposed to a foghorn of right-wing

[10]The Economic Policy Institute is active on the political left and widely respected; but it is tiny and receives less attention than Brookings.

opinion. Over the 2000s the right-wing national newspapers accounted for about 75% of sales (including *Sun, Daily Mail, Telegraph, Times*), the non-right-wing ones, 25% (including *The Financial Times*).

The right-wing bias in the idea-generating and idea-promulgating organizations, coupled with the marginalization of trade unions, leaves the bulk of the population more exposed to anti-tax, anti-state, anti-solidarity ideology than in the post-war decades. So with the track-switches in the hands of those providing intellectual justification for inequality, 'interests' of the rich pull public policies and institutions in the direction of income and wealth concentration at the top.

9 Centre-Left Political Tactics

Given the prevailing configuration of interests, organizations, and ideologies, centre-left parties made a tactical choice.[11] In the words of Liddle (2007), one of the principal ideologues of the British New Labour Party, 'In the mid-1990s, the leaders of New Labour made a fundamental policy choice. In government [they had been out of government since 1979] they would not explicitly prioritise a lessening of inequalities between top and bottom. Instead their social justice priorities would be to tackle poverty, worklessness and economic and social exclusion.

Several reasons were clearly important in Labour making this choice.... [First, a sense] that intellectually Thatcherite neoliberalism was triumphant, and that the post-war welfare state consensus had irretrievable broken down and could only be rebuilt on a basis that incentivised (and did not penalise) hard work at all levels of society.

[Second], New Labour ... seized on the discourse of globalisation to provide a deeper intellectual rationale.... New Labour portrayed globalisation as an inexorable force of nature beyond political control—making irrelevant old egalitarian and interventionist social democratic responses and requiring a thorough rethink of the means of achieving social justice, if not a redefinition of its goals' (p. 2).

---

[11]We thank Carlos Fortin for emphasising this point.

But it was not just a matter of tactics. Leading centre-left figures really did believe in a vision of a moral society close to that of neoliberal conservatives: one in which, to quote two British theorists of the 'Third Way', 'the key to justice as fairness can be seen in terms of the procedural securing of *opportunities* rather than a substantive commitment to patterned relative outcomes' (Buckler and Dolowitz 2000, emphasis added; see the echo in the epigraph from Tony Blair).

Another leading intellectual on the British centre-left, Will Hutton, likewise defines 'fairness' as rewarding individuals in proportion to the amount of discretionary effort they deploy to achieve socially useful results, provided they actually achieve them. The aim of a centre-left government should be to make access to riches dependent on 'talent, effort and virtue', as distinct from making outcomes more equal (Hutton 2010). This is neoliberalism lite.

We saw earlier that in most of Guillaud's 33 countries a sizable majority favour a government role in narrowing the income gap between rich and poor, and presumably favour a protective welfare state against untamed globalization, precarious jobs, and inequality. Centre-left parties in power have conspicuously failed to deliver on these preferences—on the contrary, they have tolerated the worst excesses of financial capitalism and colluded with the centre-right to put the cost on the less well-off. This helps to explain the fall of social democratic parties across the developed world.

10 Economists' Neglect or Defence of Inequality

If any profession could have raised the salience of inequality, it is economists. On the contrary, generations of economists have provided intellectual justification for neglecting inequality and even for opposing efforts to rein it in. Their modal stance has been close to the one enunciated in *The Financial Times* by Buiter (2007), while professor of economics at the London School of Economics, 'Poverty bothers me.

Inequality does not. I just don't care' (2007).[12] Economist Deirdre McCloskey recently claimed that redistributive issues are a misleading preoccupation. '[T]he absolute condition of the poor has been raised overwhelmingly more by the Great Enrichment [that is, economic growth spurred by the Industrial Revolution] than by … redistribution'. The average per capita income from before the Neolithic Revolution to the present has taken the shape of an ice-hockey stick, horizontal for more than ten thousand years, then abruptly surging after 1800, concomitant with the spread of the Industrial Revolution and economic growth. In this context, inequality is irrelevant for McCloskey: 'The share of the bottom 10 percent is irrelevant to the noble and ethically relevant and actually attainable purpose of raising the poor to a condition of dignity' (2016, pp. 46–47).

Columbia University economist Jagdish Bhagwati declares that the work of inequality scholars is 'ludicrous', 'irrelevant data mongering', 'lunacy'. The philosopher Harry Frankfurt describes it as 'drily formalistic', 'fetishistic', 'alienating' (Bhagwati 2007, p. 67; Frankfurt 1987, p. 23, and pp. 41–42). Further examples could easily be given (see, for example, Alacevich and Soci 2018).

In general, economists have defended inequality with two instrumental (not explicitly moral) arguments. The first stems from the conception of the market as a *coordination* mechanism, allocating scarce resources to competing ends (Roemer 2011). Equilibrium prices in a competitive market (assuming no externalities or public goods) produce a Pareto-efficient allocation of resources. In particular, a competitive labour market produces the optimal functional income distribution, such that each factor of production earns the value of its marginal productivity. The relative remuneration of banker, bishop, and bin man

[12]Wade later asked his then LSE colleague Buiter whether he really had no concerns about the economic, social, and health effects of inequality. 'Of course not, why should I care what David Beckham earns?' Wade asked a celebrated economist, also at LSE, why he thought that economists had neglected inequality. 'That's not true', he said with the air of a baseball player hitting the ball out of the stadium. 'What about Tony Atkinson and Branko Milanovic?' He inadvertently made Wade's point. For an anecdote about the art of neoliberal paradigm maintenance as practiced inside the World Bank, see Milanovic (2018).

must be fair, provided markets are competitive. This is comforting for the banker and the bishop.[13]

Extending this proposition from the model to the real world, mainstream economists tend to presume that (1) any 'political' interference with the market-determined income distribution has efficiency costs, just like any other interference with the price system (managed exchange rates, tariffs, credit subsidies, industrial policy) and (2) that the efficiency costs of political interference in market-determined income distribution are typically large. The premise is that 'markets may be imperfect, but governments are even more imperfect'. A senior advisor at the British Treasury remarked, critically, that when any policy proposal under discussion prompted the words 'price distortion', it was more or less dead in the water (personal communication 2011).

To people not steeped in neoliberal economics, this argument has some way to go before it can even be called simplistic; but it has commanded wide *emotional* agreement among economists, because it fits so well with mathematically tractable models of competitive markets as the core institution of a *moral and prosperous* society.[14]

[13]A Fellow of the Institute of Development Studies, Sussex University, sat next to the senior-most civil servant at the Department of International Development at a dinner. The Fellow told the Permanent Secretary that he could immediately double his salary by going to work for a specified firm. The Secretary assured him: 'You must do it! You would double your contribution to society' (personal communication).

[14]The saga of the UNDP publication, *Making Global Trade Rules Work for People* (2003), illustrates the hardball inter-state political forces that can be brought to bear against institutionally based challenges to key ideas of the mainstream. The book argues that the rules for trade are set by and for the interests of rich countries, producing inequitable and inefficient outcomes for developing countries; and presents an agenda for reform. The director of UNDP tried to dissociate UNDP from it by removing the UNDP logo from the cover (though the whole project was organized and largely written by UNDP staff). He wanted the cover to show only the logos of the foundations which had provided financial support. However, at the same time, pressure came on the foundations from some governments to dissociate themselves from it by removing their logos, presumably in the hope that this would help to block publication. All refused except the Ford Foundation, which ironically had provided the most finance. In the end, the UNDP logo stayed on, despite (alleged) threats to its budget and to personnel appointments if UNDP remained associated with the book. The UNDP person in charge of the book project contracted with a commercial publisher, Earthscan, to publish it, so as to by-pass a potential UN veto and get wider readership. After printing had started, WTO lodged a strong protest, and the head of the project ordered printing to stop while most references to WTO were replaced with phrases like 'the multilateral trading system'. The book was not allowed to be launched on UN premises in New York. Instead, the launch took place at the Rockefeller Center, attended by a packed

Economists' second instrumental justification for inequality is based on the conception of the market as a mechanism of *incentives* for the development of skills and innovation—a mechanism for resource creation as distinct from resource allocation. Only by allowing individuals to keep most of the market value they (claim to) help create will they be diligent and creative. The assumption is that individuals choose neither their occupations nor their balance between 'work' and 'leisure' on the basis of intrinsic satisfactions, but only on the basis of *extrinsic* material rewards. If they are allowed to retain a large fraction of the value-added they help to produce, they will choose occupations which add more value to society and will choose more work and less leisure. Then, as Tony Blair avowed in the second epigraph, their hard work and creativity will rebound to the benefit of the rest of the society, including the poor, through 'trickle-down'.

These arguments for not worrying about inequality are underpinned by several others that constitute the syndrome of mainstream economics. One is what Albert Hirschman described as the typically reactionary rhetoric of the 'jeopardy thesis', that is, the idea that curbing inequality would endanger market efficiency and ultimately growth (Hirschman 1991). In McCloskey's (2016) perspective, curbing a minor preoccupation (inequality) would imperil the actual source of widespread well-being (growth of GDP).

A second is that, in the longer run, demand does not matter for productivity and economic growth. What matters are supply-side factors such as labour market regulation, business taxes, personal income taxes, skills of the labour force, and the state of competition. Demand, real wages, inequality, drop out of the neoliberal story (Storm 2017).

A third argument, at a more fundamental level, is that the capitalist economy is composed of a private and a public sector, in which the private sector and production for the market is the domain of the

gathering of ambassadors and Permanent Representatives. The director of UNDP said in his speech, 'This book has given me sleepless nights'. See also Wade (2013) on the art of inter-state power maintenance.

'economic' (and 'natural') and the public sector and production of public goods is the domain of the 'non-economic' (and 'artificial'). We saw earlier why the postulate of state and market as the basic dyad of the economy does not stand. The large corporation is a fundamental element of the picture. Neither state nor market agent, the giant corporation invalidates market mechanisms and state sovereignty at the same time.

A fourth component is that the economy and society consists of people and entities on a continuous scale of incomes and occupations, without classes and relations of production—just as, in the international economy, there is no structure of core and periphery, rather a continuous scale of incomes and production structures, analogous to the runners in a marathon race whose position is determined by each runner's internal capabilities and tactics. This mirrors the worldview of the rich and middle classes noted earlier, that they have achieved their position thanks to their own efforts and are none too happy for their taxes to be used to lift up the less diligent and enterprising people below them.

A fifth element in the syndrome is expressed in the definition of economics as the study of choices under scarcity; as Lionel Robbins famously put it, 'Economics is a social science which studies human behaviour as a relationship between ends and scare means which have alternative uses' (Robbins was a professor of economics at the London School of Economics for several decades after 1929, building it up as a bastion of anti-Keynesian and anti-Marshallian economics). The corresponding idea of society is a set of rationally self-maximizing individuals competing with each other for scarce resources and cooperating, up to a point, to create a government. Altruism, community, cooperation, solidarity feature only as means to obtain scarce resources, a very masculine idea.

Sixth, and even more fundamental for understanding economists' neglect or justification of inequality, economists have a continuing faith in Lionel Robbins' assertion that interpersonal comparisons of utility implicitly involve ethical claims and should be excluded from the science of economics. Their faith in the 'value neutrality' doctrine is bolstered by its tight connection to the core of the discipline, namely general equilibrium theory and Pareto judgements. For our purposes here, the key point is that the faith justifies economists in refusing to consider whether low-income individuals gain more from additional income than high-income individuals lose from reduced income, saying all such questions are beyond economics.

Ironically, philosophers and other social scientists rejected the positive-normative or fact-ethical values distinction half a century ago, as what Davis (2016) describes as 'a naïve vestige of pre-war logical positivism'; but the positive-normative distinction remains fundamental to the identity of economists as economists. So the discipline remains an ethics-free zone (beyond some recent and limited codes of conduct to protect honesty in research), in a way not true of other disciplines which also have far-reaching impacts on populations and biosphere, including engineers, doctors, lawyers, and anthropologists (Colander 2016).

Finally, also at the DNA level, the mainstream discipline grows out of concepts from Newtonian physics, concepts of equilibrium, balance, harmony, and future time as a predictable extrapolation of the past, except for random shocks called 'risks'—concepts which prompted Newton to describe the universe as 'running like clockwork' and to joyfully exclaim, 'O God, I think Thy thoughts after Thee'. The discipline which sees the core institution of society—the market—in these terms is unlikely to find problems with income distribution, provided no 'market imperfections'.

Economics education, especially in Anglo-American universities (among which are the world's top ranked economics departments), inculcates these fundamental ideas. Teaching of the history of economic thought and comparative economic systems, which might expose students to other conceptions of economics, largely disappeared from university syllabi as the Cold War wound down.[15] Strangely, the economics

[15]Asked what attainments contribute to success in the profession, only 3% of 212 graduate students in American economics departments said that 'having a thorough knowledge of the economy' was 'very important', and 68% said it was 'unimportant' (Colander and Klamer 1987). The argument of Frey and Eichenberger (1993) leads one to expect that continental European graduate students would rate knowledge of the economy more highly. However, the economics taught in the most prestigious European economics departments tends to be hard-line neoclassical/American economics. Racko (2011) found that Latvian students being educated at the Swedish

profession hardly ever discusses 'capitalism', instead referring to 'the market system', which makes it easier to avoid discussing what the economic system is for and in whose interests it is working.

The history of the ersatz Nobel Prize in Economics captures the deep entanglement of a particular inequality-sanctioning politics at the peak of the discipline. The prize was created in 1968 in order to send the message to Sweden and the world that *economics has an intellectual stature commensurate with medicine, physics, and chemistry, and that neoliberal economics is the best economics.* The prestige attached to the Nobel name—the prize is regularly cited as the ultimate act of recognition of worth, even genius—helped to make neoliberal economics into the 'common sense' of the post-1980s era, till today (Mirowski 2015).

The Bank of Sweden was to celebrate its 300th anniversary in 1968. Earlier, the governor came up with the idea of creating a Nobel Prize in Economics so as to hit three birds with one stone: first, mark the anniversary; second, promote the case for the central bank to be made independent of government, unencumbered by political accountability, run for the public good by economists who were every bit as objective scientists as doctors, physicists, and chemists; third, use the prize to promote the neoliberal regime of truth, for he and several economist colleagues were passionately opposed to social democracy, to the Social Democratic Party then governing Sweden, and to the whole Swedish model with its incentive- and morality-sapping welfare state. He would finance the prize out of central bank revenues, and steer the composition of the awarding committee to ensure that the prize went disproportionately to neoliberal economists.

Economics School in Riga, known for its hard-line neoclassical/American approach, acquired over two years much stronger beliefs in free markets and associated norms than a matched pool of students being educated at Latvian universities—including the belief that their beliefs had a strictly scientific foundation. For a fascinating and shocking account of the three-decade-long battle at the University of Sydney to allow courses in political economy in the Economics syllabus, where proponents were opposed by successive heads of department and heads of the university but supported by a student movement, see Butler et al. (2009), whose title, *Political Economy Now!*, comes from a banner that students draped around the top of the university tower for all to see.

He approached the Nobel family and the Nobel Foundation, who both said that Nobel's will stated explicitly that there should be five prizes, no more. The Parliament was also opposed. He then suggested 'The Bank of Sweden Award in Economic Sciences in Honor of Alfred Nobel', knowing that it would be abbreviated to Nobel Prize in Economics and that he could ensure the award ceremony was held at the same time and place as the other Nobels. The Nobel Foundation remained opposed, but relented when the governor used his regulatory leverage to allow the foundation to invest in a wider range of securities. The head of the Nobel family agreed, but on explicit condition that the prize should not be referred to as the Nobel Prize in Economics; and unconfirmed reports say that government officials used her tax problems to make her an offer she could not refuse. At more or less the same time, the bank announced the creation of the prize, even though negotiations were still continuing. Fait accompli. Much later, the successor head of the Nobel family described the prize as an unparalleled example of successful trademark infringement.

From the first awards in 1969 till today, full-on subscribers to the neoliberal political economy canon have been far over-represented relative to their numbers in the economics profession. They have remained at roughly 38–40% of the cumulative stock of winners since 1993. Virtually all the winners have been American or spent large parts of their career in America. Only one of the 79 laureates is a woman, and she (Elinor Ostrom) was a political scientist. This is the result, apparently, of the committee's objective valuation of the truth in economics.[16] It remains a deeply masculine discipline, in line with the conservative worldview and the spirit of Lionel Robbins.

---

[16]Compare the laureates of the Leontief Prize for Advancing the Frontiers of Economic Thought. The prize was established in 2000 in honour of Wassily Leontief, professor of economics at Harvard and Tufts and pioneer of input-output analysis (Nobel, in contrast, made his money by inventing dynamite and owning a company which manufactured weapons of war). The 34 Leontief laureates (to 2018) come from a much wider range of perspectives and nationalities, and seven are women.

11 Ready Diversionary Tactics

E.E. Schattschneider (1960) famously said, 'The definition of the alternatives is the supreme instrument of power'. The final element in our account of why inequality has long been neglected is that there are easy ways to define inequality in ways that do not touch the rich or even to sanction it with the language of egalitarianism. One of the favourites is to define 'reducing inequality' as 'reducing poverty', which all political parties and religions can sanction (provided the poor are 'deserving'). Another is to conflate 'reducing inequality' with 'increasing social mobility', which also commands wide legitimacy (though in fact largely unrelated to reducing inequality). Still another, mentioned earlier, is to conflate 'reducing inequality' with 'curbing bonuses for undeserving bosses'. Always to hand are justifications based on 'freedom' as the ultimate value, and on the trickle-down theory, which both miraculously allow the dizzying concentration of income and wealth to be justified in the language of egalitarianism. See Margaret Thatcher's and Tony Blair's epigraphs.

There are also broader ways to divert attention from rising inequality and from political party agendas which favour upwards redistribution. Fostering racial, cultural, and religious enmity is a familiar route. So is blaming foreign enemies for national problems, and here 'the Soviet Union' and more recently 'Putin-Russia' have proved useful for denying or minimizing national realities. J. Edgar Hoover's G-men were convinced that Communist subversives were the root cause of civil rights unrest and protest. Today we see the hysteria again in the belief that Russian trolls somehow managed to shift the crucial 78,000 votes that officially determined the election's Electoral College outcome—as distinct from the all-too-American causes of American derangement.[17]

[17]Paranoia as a technique of rule—for achieving cooperation and acquiescence—was taken to a high pitch in the Cold War. When 21 out of 7000 American POWs during the Korean War refused repatriation to the US after the armistice in 1953, American political leaders and commentators started a panic about communist 'brainwashing' as a tool of internal subversion via mental manipulation. The vagueness of the concept and its racist undertones served to heighten the hysteria. The New York Times editorialized that the 'non-repatriates' offered 'living proof that Communist brainwashing does work on some persons'. The paper and other commentators

12 Summary and Conclusions

The sharp increase in concentration at the top of national income distributions over the past two to three decades should have prompted a large body of social science research and public debate around the question, 'When are the rich too rich?'. Instead, the response has been muted, both in the academy and in politics (except with reference to particular bosses seen to have failed at their job who nevertheless receive golden handshakes). When protest did emerge its political consequences were in line with Horace's dictum of 2000 years ago: 'What will this boaster [a poet who promises to write wonderful verses but cannot keep his bombastic promises] produce in keeping of such mouthing? / The mountains will labour, to birth a laughter-rousing mouse!' (Horace 1942, 19 BCE, p. 463).[18]

Inequality is kept in the background because of the wide acceptance of the idea that whatever distribution results from 'free markets' must be better than what results from 'government intervention' (beyond limited welfare transfers and tax exemptions for 'deserving poor'). It is a reflex of the same forces which have eroded the welfare state, curbing its scope and turning more parts of it into private profit centres.

In this chapter, we have asked the more specific question of why electorates have acquiesced as income concentration increased. Of the several factors discussed here, we recap just three. First, economists—who constitute the most influential profession in shaping norms of public policy—are trained to presume that inequality is an *inevitable* outcome of the market as a coordinating mechanism, and a *necessary* outcome for the market to function as an incentive mechanism, a presumption which inclines them to be relaxed about the existence of the 'filthy rich' and not ask questions like 'when are the rich too rich?'

ignored the fact that some 22,000 North Koran and Chinese POWs refused repatriation to their countries (Carruthers 2018). Today, 'election hacking' is used to explain Trump's victory and turn attention away from domestic causes, including precarious employment and soaring inequality.

[18]Horace's original is tighter: 'Quid dignum tanto feret hic promissor hiatu? / Parturient montes, nascetur ridiculus mus'.

Second, middle and upper middle classes have managed to protect their share of national income in many countries even as the share of the top few percentiles rises at the expense of the politically marginal bottom 40%. This helps to diffuse middle class anger at the rise of the super-rich. The upper middle classes, enjoying rising shares, increasingly resort to 'gated community' politics, opting out from public health and public education, which erodes the quality of the public system, heightens the stigma against it, and justifies the need for high inequality. Also, neoliberal fiscal policy packages normally include tax cuts from which they benefit, and they hear 'redistribution' as meaning that the working class would come closer to them, which threatens their status and causes more anxiety and resentment than the rich soaring away from them. Better to pull up the drawbridge.

For these and other reasons the middle classes have not been responsive to centre-left parties trying to build a new cross-class consensus for a more equal society—not just in terms of opportunities but also in terms of outcomes. And so even centre-left leaders not sympathetic to neoliberalism lite have hardly tried to do so.

Third, there are multiple, head-nodding ways to shift attention from functional and personal income distribution onto safer, more consensual grounds that do not challenge the existing distribution. 'Reduce inequality' can be equated with 'reduce poverty' or 'increase social mobility' or 'curb the bonuses of undeserving CEOs'. Higher inequality can even be celebrated as the way to get more income to the poor. Or it can be presented as the unavoidable by-product of achieving the highest value, freedom.

Analysts on the centre-left can help to build a cross-class consensus for a more equal society by providing a sound intellectual basis for advocating more equal outcomes than exist in the Anglo-American economies, and for showing that top-level income concentration at present levels is neither inevitable nor necessary for efficiency and creativity.

There is no mystery about 'solutions'. The familiar list includes: progressive taxes and transfers that raise government tax revenues and social spending, thereby positively affecting aggregate demand and employment; policies to reduce the size and leverage of the financial sector; capital controls, when required.

A less familiar list includes 'predistribution' institutions to enable a large part of national populations to receive income from the returns on capital, rather than, as today, only a small part—so that many rather than few can accrue income while they sleep. The institutions could take the form of a sovereign wealth fund paying out, eventually, a universal basic income; or the form of ownership-broadening trusts which borrow on capital markets to buy shares in companies and return dividends to members of the trust (employees, customers, neighbours), who could buy membership out of their returns rather than out of current income or savings (Ashford et al. 2012). The disadvantage of the latter is that it bolsters labour support for the principle of 'maximize shareholder value' as the main aim of corporations. The more equal distribution of capital income should be complemented by the expansion of bank-based financial systems, especially networks of decentralized, non-profit, or low-profit financial organizations to lend to typically neglected sectors, including certain types of infrastructure, multi-family housing for low- and middle-income households, also small and medium enterprises (including social enterprises). The latter tend to be by-passed by stock-market systems, yet their growth should be a high priority for those concerned to counter the trend towards ever more monopoly capitalism. Something like the New Deal era Reconstruction Finance Corporation (RFC) deserves to make a come-back in the US and elsewhere, as a pilot agency for far-reaching reforms in the present financial system (Block and Hockett 2018).

And we need a 'digital New Deal'. As companies shed workers in preference for AI the same companies should redeploy those workers—encouraged by tax incentives—into work not subject to AI, such as customer services, data analytics, and more, or into cross-company work forces to provide public goods, such as extending rural broadband (Foroohar 2018).

But the question remains of how to persuade political leaders and opinion-makers like the World Bank and the IMF to focus on inequality as a problem, separate from poverty, social mobility, and CEO bonuses. The short answer is that until radical changes are made in how political parties and candidates fund themselves—or until several more multi-country crashes have roiled the world economy, or until a mass revolt against oligarchic rule—inequality will remain on the margins of public policy even as corporate power and top-end income share remain at current levels of concentration or go even higher.

The British historian Tony Judt can have the last word: 'Sadly, contemporary intellectuals have shown remarkably little informed interest in the nitty-gritty of public policy, preferring to intervene or protest on ethically-defined topics where the choices seem clearer. This has left debates on the way we ought to govern ourselves to policy specialists and "think tanks", where unconventional opinion rarely finds a place and the public are largely excluded' (2010, pp. 158–159).

References

Alacevich, M., & Soci, A. (2018). *A Short History of Inequality*. Newcastle upon Tyne: Agenda Publishing.

Ashford, R., Hall, R., & Ashford, N. (2012). Broadening Capital Acquisition with the Earnings of Capita as a Means of Sustainable Growth and Environmental Stability. *European Financial Review* (October–November), 70–74.

Bhagwati, J. (2007). *In Defense of Globalization*. New York: Oxford University Press.

Block, F., & Hockett, R. (2018, July 9–12). *Democratising Finance*. Democratising Finance Conference, Madison, Wisconsin.

Bresser-Pereira, L. C. (2012, September 11). Personal Communication.

Brooks, D. (2011, November 2). The Wrong Inequality. *International Herald Tribune*.

Buckler, S., & Dolowitz, D. (2000). Theorizing the Third Way. *Journal of Political Ideologies, 5*(3), 309.

Buiter, W. (2007, February 14). Economists Forum. *Financial Times*.

Butler, G., Jones, E., & Stilwell, F. (2009). *Political Economy Now!: The Struggle for Alternative Economics at the University of Sydney*. Sydney: Darlington Press.

Canuto, O. (2017, September 13). The Metamorphosis of Financial Globalization. *HuffPost*.

Carruthers, S. (2018, January 20–21). When the U.S. Feared Brainwashing. *New York Times (International).*
Coghalan, A., & MacKenzie, D. (2011, October 19). Revealed—The Capitalist Network that Runs the World. *New Scientist.*
Colander, D. (2016). Creating Humble Economists: A Code of Ethics for Economists. In G. DeMartino & D. McCloskey (Eds.), *The Oxford Handbook of Professional Economic Ethics* (Chapter 36). New York, NY: Oxford University Press.
Colander, D., & Klamer, A. (1987). The Making of an Economist. *Journal of Economic Perspectives, 1*(Fall), 100.
Crouch, C. (2011). *The Strange Non-death of Neoliberalism.* London: Polity Press.
Dahl, R. A. (1998). *On Democracy.* New Haven: Yale University Press.
Dash, E. (2011, October 1–2). Way Out the Door Still Paved in Gold for Some U.S. Executives. *International Herald Tribune.*
Davis, J. B. (2016). Economists' Odd Stand on the Positive-Normative Distinction: A Behavioural Economics View. In G. DeMartino & D. McCloskey (Eds.), *The Oxford Handbook of Professional Economic Ethics* (Chapter 11). New York, NY: Oxford University Press.
Djelic, M.-L., & Mousavi, R. (2019). How the Neoliberal Think Tank Went Global: The Atlas Network, 1981 to Present. In Q. Slobodian, D. Plehwe, & P. Mirowski (Eds.), *Nine Lives of Neoliberalism.* New York and London: Verso Books.
Farrant, A., & McPhail, E. (2010, July–August). Does F. A. Hayek's *Road to Serfdom* Deserve to Make a Comeback? *Challenge Magazine, 53*(4), 96–120.
Financial Times. (2017, January 5). Tillerson in Line for $180m if Confirmed, 4.
Foroohar, R. (2018, March 18). Why Workers Need a 'Digital New Deal' to Protect Against AI. *Financial Times.*
Frank, T. (2011). *Pity the Billionaire.* London: Harvill Secker.
Frankfurt, H. (1987). Equality as a Moral Idea. *Ethics, 98*(1), 21–43.
Frey, B., & Eichenberger, R. (1993). American and European Economics and Economists. *Journal of Economic Perspectives, 7*(4), 185–193.
Gerlis, M. (2018, March 14). Big Picture Reveals Art Market's Wealth Gap. *Financial Times.*
Grabel, I. (2018). *When Things Don't Fall Apart: Global Financial Governance and Developmental Finance in an Age of Productive Incoherence.* Cambridge, MA and London: MIT Press.

Grassegger, G., & Krogerus, M. (2017, January 28). The Data that Turned the World Upside Down. *Motherboard*. Available at: https://motherboard.vice.com/en_us/article/how-our-likes-helped-trump-win.

Guillaud, E. (2013). Preferences for Redistribution: An Empirical Analysis Over 33 Countries. *Journal of Economic Inequality, 11*(1), 57–78.

Hazledine, T. (2014). Does the Centre Hold? Testing Palma's Proposition. *Development and Change, 45*(6), 1409–1415.

Hirschman, A. O. (1991). *The Rhetoric of Reaction: Perversity, Futility, Jeopardy*, Cambridge, MA: Belknap Press of Harvard University Press.

Horace. (1942). *Satires, Epistles, and Ars Poetica* (with an English Translation by H. Rushton Fairclough). London: William Heinemann, and Cambridge, MA: Harvard University Press.

Hutton, W. (2010). *Them and Us: Changing Britain—Why We Need a Fair Society*. London: Little Brown.

Jenkins. S. (2018, April 27). Beware: There Is Something Very Rotten in Britain's Forests. *Guardian*.

Judt, T. (2010). *Ill Fares the Land*. New York: Penguin.

Kampfner, J. (2011, August 26). The Wealth Should Pay More Tax. Why Has It Taken So Long? *The Independent*.

Kaplan. J., Gimbel, S., & Harris, S. (2016, December). Neural Correlates of Maintaining One's Political Beliefs in the Face of Counterevidence. *Science Reports, 6*(39589).

Karl, T. L. (2000, January). Economic Inequality and Democratic Instability. *Journal of Democracy, 11*(1), 149–156.

Katz, L., & Krueger, A. (2016, March 29). *The Rise and Nature of Alternative Work Arrangements in the US, 1995–2015*. Available at: https://onlabor.org/wp-content/uploads/2017/05/katz_krueger_cws_-_march_29_20165.pdf.

Krugman, P. (2012a, January 21–22). Superlow Taxes at the Top. *International Herald Tribune*.

Krugman, P. (2012b, February 18–19). Moochers Against Welfare. *International Herald Tribune*, 9.

Krugman, P. (2018, March 17–18). U.S. Voters May Be Wising Up. *New York Times (International)*.

Lakoff, G. (2002). *Moral Politics: How Liberals and Conservatives Think* (2nd ed.). Chicago: University of Chicago Press.

Lansley, S. (2011, October 5). Tinkering on the Brink. *Guardian*.

Lazonick, W. (2010). Innovative Business Models and Varieties of Capitalism: Financialization of the US Corporation. *Business History Review, 84*(4), 675–702.

Liddle, R. (2007, December). *Creating a Culture of Fairness. A Progressive Response to Income Inequality in Britain*. London: Policy Network.
Lindblom, C. E. (1977). *Politics and Markets*. New York: Basic Books.
McCloskey, D. N. (2016). *Bourgeois Equality: How Ideas, Not Capital or Institutions, Enriched the World*. Chicago: University of Chicago Press.
Milanovic, B. (2018). *Global Inequality* at: http://glineq.blogspot.co.uk/2018/02/how-is-world-ruled.html.
Mirowski, P. (2015, December). *The Neoliberal Ersatz Nobel Prize*. Manuscript.
Monbiot, G. (2011a, September 13). Who Drives the So-Called Think Tanks Crushing Democracy for Corporations? *The Guardian*.
Monbiot, G. (2011b, November 8). The 1% Are the Very Best Destroyers of Wealth the World Has Ever Seen. *The Guardian*.
New York Times. (2011, August 31). The New Resentment of the Poor. Editorial. *Times Digest*.
O'Connor, S. (2018, March 20). Cities Only Work if They Accommodate Rich and Poor. *Financial Times*.
Ostry, J., Berg, A., & Tsangarides, C. (2014). Redistribution, Inequality and Growth. *IMF Discussion Note*, SDN/14/02.
Pagano, U. (2014). The Crisis of Intellectual Monopoly Capitalism. *Cambridge Journal of Economics, 38*(6), 1409–1429.
Palma, J. G. (2011, January). Homogeneous Middles vs. Heterogeneous Tails, and the End of the 'Inverted-U'. *Development and Change, 42*(1), 87–153.
Phillips-Fein, K. (2009). *Invisible Hands: The Making of the Conservative Movement from the New Deal to Reagan*. New York: Norton.
Piketty, T. (2014). *Capital in the Twenty-First Century*. Cambridge, MA: Harvard University Press.
Porter, E. (2017, January 5). Dysfunction in U.S. Democracy. *New York Times (International)*.
Racko, G. (2011, December). On the Normative Consequences of Economic Rationality: A Case Study of a Swedish Economics School in Latvia. *European Sociological Review, 27*(6), 772–789.
Rashbrooke, M. (2013). *Inequality: A New Zealand Crisis* (p. 53). Wellington: Brigit Williams Books.
Roemer, J. (2011). Ideological and Political Roots of American Inequality. *Challenge, 54*(5), 76–98.
Schattschneider, E. (1960). *The Semi-sovereign People*. New York: Holt Reinhart and Winston.
Stewart, J. (2011, October 1–2). Failure in Business Should Be a Risk of Capitalism, Not a Chance for Reward. *International Herald Tribune*, 14.

Storm, S. (2017). *The New Normal: Demand, Secular Stagnation and the Vanishing Middle-Class* (INET Working Paper).
Treanor, J. (2011, June 22). World's Wealthiest People Now Richer than Before the Credit Crunch: World Wealth Report Reveals Soaring Numbers of Rich Individuals in Asia Pacific Region—But Slower Growth in Britain. *The Guardian*.
UNCTAD. (2012). *Trade and Development Report 2012*. Geneva: United Nations.
UNCTAD. (2017). *Trade and Development Report 2017. Beyond Austerity: Towards a Global New Deal*. Geneva: United Nations.
UNDP. (2003). *Making Global Trade Work for People*. London and Sterling: Earthscan.
Viviano, F. (2018, February 16). Who Keeps Britain's Rail Lines Afloat? *New York Times (International)*.
Wade, R. H. (2004, June). On the Causes of Increasing Poverty and Inequality, Or Why the Matthew Effect Prevails. *New Political Economy, 9*(2), 163–188.
Wade, R. H. (2006). Should We Worry About Income Inequality? In D. Held & A. Kaya (Eds.), *Global Inequality: Patterns and Explanations* (pp. 104–131). Cambridge: Polity Press.
Wade, R. H. (2009, July). From Global Imbalances to Global Reorganizations. *Cambridge Journal of Economics, 33*(4), 539–562.
Wade, R. H. (2011, September–October). Global Trends in Income Inequality: What Is Happening and Should We Worry? *Challenge Magazine, 54*(5), 54–75.
Wade, R. H. (2013). The Art of Power Maintenance: How Western States Keep the Lead in Global Organizations. *Challenge Magazine, 56*(1), 5–39.
Wade, R. H. (2014, October). The Piketty Phenomenon and the Future of Inequality [Special Issue on Piketty's *Capital*]. *Real-World Economics Review, 69*(7), 2–17.
Wade, R. H. (2016). Economists' Ethics in the Build-up to the Great Recession. In G. DeMartino & D. McCloskey (Eds.), *Oxford Handbook of Professional Economics Ethics* (Chapter 15). Oxford: Oxford University Press.
Wade, R. H. (2017). Globalization, Growth, Inequality, Poverty: The Globalization Argument and the 'Political' Science of Economics. In J. Ravenhill (Ed.), *Global Political Economy* (5th ed., Chapter 12). Oxford: Oxford University Press.

Wade, R. H., & Sigurgeirsdottir, S. (2011, January). Iceland's Rise, Fall, Stabilisation and Beyond. *Cambridge Journal of Economics, 36*(1), 127–144.
Weil, D. (2014). *The Fissured Workplace: Why Work Became So Bad For So Many and What Can Be Done To Improve It.* Cambridge, MA: Harvard University Press.
Weinhold, D. (2018, March). *Class and Cultural Conflict in America Today: Lessons from the 2016 Presidential Election* (Working Paper). Department of International Development, LSE.
Wertheim, S., & Meaney, T. (2018, March 13). The Epitome of the Ugly American. *New York Times (International).*
Wilkinson, R., & Pickett, K. (2009). *The Spirit Level.* London: Allen Lane.
Winters, J. A. (2011). *Oligarchy.* New York: Cambridge University Press.

Index

P. Arestis and M. Sawyer (eds.), *Inequality*, International Papers in Political Economy,
https://doi.org/10.1007/978-3-319-91298-1

FSC
www.fsc.org
MIX
Papier | Fördert
gute Waldnutzung
FSC® C083411

Kolibri 360 GmbH
Ferdinand-Jühlke-Straße 7
99095 Erfurt, Deutschland
produktsicherheit@kolibri360.de